Communicate
with Confidence!

Other Business Titles by Dianna Booher

CLEAN UP YOUR ACT

SEND ME A MEMO: A HANDBOOK OF MODEL MEMOS

CUTTING PAPERWORK IN THE CORPORATE CULTURE

GOOD GRIEF, GOOD GRAMMAR

THE NEW SECRETARY: HOW TO HANDLE PEOPLE AS WELL AS YOU HANDLE PAPER

TO THE LETTER: A HANDBOOK OF MODEL LETTERS FOR THE BUSY EXECUTIVE

WRITING FOR TECHNICAL PROFESSIONALS

THE CONFIDENT COMMUNICATOR

FIRST THING MONDAY MORNING

EXECUTIVE'S PORTFOLIO OF MODEL SPEECHES FOR ALL OCCASIONS

THE COMPLETE LETTERWRITER'S ALMANAC

WRITE TO THE POINT (AUDIO SERIES)

BASIC STEPS FOR BETTER BUSINESS WRITING (VIDEO SERIES)

BUSINESS WRITING: QUICK, CLEAR, CONCISE (VIDEO)

CLOSING THE GAP: GENDER COMMUNICATION SKILLS (VIDEO)

CUTTING PAPERWORK: MANAGEMENT STRATEGIES (VIDEO)

CUTTING PAPERWORK: SUPPORT STAFF STRATEGIES (VIDEO)

PEOPLE POWER! (AUDIO SERIES)

GET YOUR BOOK PUBLISHED (AUDIO SERIES)

Communicate with Confidence!

How to Say It Right the First Time and Every Time

Dianna Booher

McGraw-Hill, Inc.

New York   San Francisco   Washington, D.C.   Auckland   Bogotá
Caracas   Lisbon   London   Madrid   Mexico City   Milan
Montreal   New Delhi   San Juan   Singapore
Sydney   Tokyo   Toronto

Library of Congress Cataloging-in-Publication Data

Booher, Dianna Daniels.
    Communicate with Confidence! : how to say it right the first time
and every time / Dianna Booher.
      p.   cm.
    Includes bibliographical references and index.
    ISBN 0-07-006455-5 — ISBN 0-07-006606-X (pbk.)
    1. Business communication.   2. Oral communication.
3. Interpersonal communication.   I. Title.
HF5718.B654   1994
651.7'3—dc20   94-13665
                                             CIP

        7 8 9 0 DOC/DOC 0 5 4 3 2 1   (HC)
      14 15 16 17 18 19 20DOC/DOC 0 5 4 3 2 1 (PBK)

ISBN 0-07-006455-5
ISBN 0-07-006606-X (pbk.)

*The sponsoring editor for this book was Betsy N. Brown, the editing supervisor was
Christine H. Furry, and the production supervisor was Pamela A. Pelton. It was set
in Baskerville by North Market Street Graphics.*

Printed and bound by R. R. Donnelley & Sons Company.

 This book is printed on recycled, acid-free paper containing a
minimum of 50% recycled de-inked fiber.

*To my husband, Vernon Rae, for the emotional support,
freedom, and encouragement to write "just one more book"*

Contents

Introduction

What's in It for You?

The little girl sat in her patio swing, shivering. She wore a big parka, with the hood up, her legs covered with a blanket. Her head was buried in a library book. Her mother stuck her head out the back door and called to her, "Honey, what are you doing, sitting outside reading where it's so cold?"

The little girl looked up. "Well, my teacher told us that if we wanted to be good students we should do a lot of outside reading."

That's been the story most places all too often. Miscommunication between managers and employers. Between customers and suppliers. Between Sales and Service. Between politicians and taxpayers. Between husbands and wives. Between parents and children. We're just not communicating all that well.

In corporate offices, in lawyers' suites, in bedrooms and boardrooms around the world, "miscommunication" surfaces as a cause—the cause of poor job performance or a lost sale, the cause of a lawsuit, the cause of a broken relationship. Communication more than any other skill determines success in sales, marriage, or management.

Communication is the soul of management: analysis and solid decisions translated into clear messages that influence people to act and feel good about their performance.

In survey after survey—from senior executives reminiscing about their career success to recruiters hiring college graduates—communication always tops the list of skills for success. Whether a valid or invalid measure, the lack of communication skills tags people as being less competent, less attractive, and less qualified as leaders.

Where communication is concerned, some people think they've got it made because they have an extroverted personality. But that's not necessarily the case. An outgoing, life-of-the-party personality doesn't necessarily equate to sensitivity to others, which is the core of goodwill. Both introverts and extroverts need specific skills.

That's not to say, of course, that either personality type doesn't know how to communicate. We all communicate up to a point—up to the point where our habits set in. Until someone makes an insensitive remark. Until someone asks us for our advice and then argues against it. Until someone ignores our ideas in a meeting. Until we're tongue-tied with a group of complainers. Until we're defensive about how we are handling the current project. Until someone calls us arrogant. Until we fail to persuade our team or customer to take action. Until a friend tells us we need to learn to negotiate rather than dictate. Until someone won't accept "no" for an answer. Until a spouse wants out of the marriage.

When we find ourselves in any of these situations, we need to change the way we're communicating—to increase our skills with a specific technique that jump-starts us past habit and on to progress. We need to stop hoping we "get through" and ensure that we do.

That's the "why" of this book.

Communication Is a Life-or-Death Matter

That's not an overstatement. Ask lawyers, engineers, system analysts, or secretaries which creates the most frustration and failure—the technical part of their job or dealing with people—and they'll agree on the latter. Samson of biblical fame killed 10,000 Philistines with the jawbone of an ass. Similar destruction occurs on a daily basis with the same weapon.

Consider these benefits of communicating well. You'll—

- Get the correct information quicker.
- Build credibility with customers and colleagues.
- Develop more intimate relationships.
- Build loyalty in a supportive climate.
- Unleash creativity within yourself and others by building on each other's ideas.
- Improve teamwork.
- Facilitate problem solving.
- Build consensus for decisions.
- Motivate others to work more effectively.

- Conduct and participate in more effective meetings.
- Save time and energy, reduce rework, and increase productivity with clear instructions and discussions.
- Avoid needless arguments.
- Reduce hurt feelings—yours and those of others.
- Overcome paralyzing anger, fear, or shyness.
- Respond to feedback and criticism appropriately.
- Give more constructive criticism.
- Solicit helpful advice.
- Give the kind of advice others can really use.
- Negotiate for what you want without diminishing the other person.
- Win more cooperation when others' response is voluntary.
- Stand firm on your opinions without giving offense.
- Give and accept appropriate praise and compliments.
- Manage your own conflicts without escalating them.
- Mediate others' conflicts without getting burned yourself.
- Exercise more power over decisions affecting you.
- Influence and motivate others without strong-arm tactics.
- Find ways to "work around" difficult personalities.
- Generate enthusiasm for your ideas and proposals.
- Receive more invitations to accept leadership roles on committees.
- Receive more invitations to speak publicly to influence others.
- Increase your own and others' job satisfaction.
- "Pick other people's brains" profitably: ideas, experiences, habits, attitudes, and hard-core facts.
- Broaden your network of friends.
- Build your self-esteem by learning to be assertive.
- Defend your rights without manipulating or offending others.
- Handle insults, sarcasm, or other verbal abuse with style.
- Reduce your fear of vulnerability and decrease feelings of loneliness.
- Listen better so that others feel understood and valued.
- Generate meaningful or entertaining conversations.
- Reduce cross-gender conflicts because of style differences.
- Understand meanings from those of other cultures.

- Improve your physical health by reducing stress caused by misunder-standings.

- Improve your mental health by growing as a person and developing more supportive relationships.

- Lead others to mutual benefits and goals.

In 1978, Daniel Yankelovich published his famous findings from research about changing workplace attitudes. With the diminishing impact of rewards to increase motivation of employees, job satisfaction now comes primarily from other sources: being recognized for individual contribu-tions and working with people one likes in a pleasant environment. Both of these "rewards" are a result of superior communication—either from one's supervisors or from peers or customers.

How to Use This Book

Here are some suggestions to improve your communication skills in general:

- *Listen to the conversation of others.* Be an eavesdropper. Not only will you hear hilarious stories and arguments that make you want to take sides even when you don't know the players, but also you'll learn how tone affects others' reactions and how ambiguous words create confusion. You'll notice what works and what doesn't work for other people. Then compare your observations with the tips given in this book.

- *Consider your options and alternatives for saying things before you speak.* Try to become aware of the various responses open to you when someone accuses you, angers you, praises you, or motivates you. Simply being aware of your options and ways to express those options will expand your communication horizons. No single comment is always appropriate. You want to develop flexibility in responding to different people on different occasions. Notice the various options outlined here.

- *Identify at which level most of your relationships exist.* For example, do you merely recognize or acknowledge others as mere acquaintants, with a perfunctory comment such as "Nice day, isn't it?"; "How are you doing this morning?"; or "How are things going?" Are you a step closer as casual friends in that you know each other well enough to gossip about people or to discuss upcoming events or facts of common interest? Are you close friends who share opinions, beliefs, and values? Or has your relationship progressed to the intimate-friendship stage that permits you to share feel-ings and thoughts about yourself and others and pass on judgments. In other words, have you as friends granted each other the freedom to say things that will improve each of you as a person? With awareness of the levels of intimacy, you'll develop your sense of what's better said and left unsaid in spur-of-the-moment situations.

■ *Read widely.* You'll build your vocabulary, you'll pick up nuances of meanings, and you'll even learn to differentiate between the "tones" of various authors (sarcastic, condescending, motivational, straightforward).

■ *Select tips to follow and practice.* If people don't seem to give you appropriate advice, for example, memorize the associated tips in this book and then try them out on your next perplexing situation. The more you practice these guidelines, the more confident you will be and the less mechanical the techniques will become.

■ *Use the book as a refresher.* If you're attending an upcoming convention or cocktail party where you fear you'll be ill at ease in chitchatting, reread the tips associated with small talk, such as topics of conversation and exit lines for leaving a small huddle to join another.

How do you know if you're successful at communicating? The response you get. Are you having the desired effect on people? In other words, are you making them think, feel, or do something you want? What seems to be their impression of you? Do others try to dominate you, control you, ignore you, abuse you? Can you work effectively in groups? Does your team accomplish its goals with a minimum of clashes? Do you weigh others' words and understand and evaluate their messages appropriately? Effective communication involves the messages you send as well as those you receive—what you say, what you hear, what each of you *thinks* the other said and heard.

Failure to communicate is the frustration of modern management. All human relationships depend on communication. Personally or professionally, it's a life-or-death issue.

Dianna Booher

Acknowledgments

The principles of communication have been of interest since the Greek philosophers Aristotle and Socrates wrote; graduate students, management consultants, and Gallup pollsters still find the subject worth covering. I'm indebted to all these philosophers, researchers, and writers who have published their findings and thoughts in this broad field, and encourage you to examine the bibliography for an extensive list of their works.

Specifically, I want to thank my clients for their help in conducting research in their organizations. To the many individuals in my workshop or speech audiences, I'm also grateful. When they single me out after a presentation to share their own experiences of success or failure in communication, they always reconfirm my central theme: communication skills can make or break a relationship or career. They keep me on target by asking for practical, usable tips and continually provide me with new anecdotes on the fundamentals. Thanks to each of you who've passed on your experiences to me.

Finally, I'd like to thank those on staff who worked with me specifically to prepare this manuscript and to those who will help "launch" it: Polly Haase, Cinda Benton, Janet Houston-Spore, Nancy Koenig, and Bill Strong. These teammates are the most competent, positive, productive, and encouraging supporters that an author could have.

Dianna Booher

Communication is the soul of management: analysis and solid decisions translated into clear messages that influence people to act and feel good about their performance.

—DIANNA BOOHER

Language is a wonderful thing. It can be used to express thoughts, to conceal our thoughts, or to replace thinking.
—KELLY FORDYCE

Words are what hold society together.
—STUART CHASE

Men govern with words.
—BENJAMIN DISRAELI

Language is the dress of thought.
—SAMUEL JOHNSON

The greatest problem in communication is the illusion that it has been accomplished.
—GEORGE BERNARD SHAW

Talk is by far the most accessible of pleasures. It costs nothing in money, it is all profit, and it completes our education, found and fosters our friendship, and can be enjoyed at any age and in almost any state of health.
—ROBERT LOUIS STEVENSON

The ability to deal with people is as purchasable a commodity as sugar and coffee. And I pay more for that ability than for any other under the sun.
—JOHN DAVISON ROCKEFELLER

1

Establishing a Track Record for Truth

When gamblers go to the race track, they consider the prior winners when placing their bets. When investors buy stocks, they look at the past performance of the mutual fund or the corporation. When voters go to the polls, they consider the voting record of the candidate before casting their ballot for or against. Yes, hunches and name recognition play a part in all these situations, but over the long haul performance profoundly affects our decisions about whom we believe. The same is true in leading, learning, or loving: credibility counts.

TIP 1: Find Commonalities.

People like people who are like them. And people believe and trust people they like. Try to discover attitudes, likes, dislikes, family backgrounds, experiences, personality virtues or quirks, careers, goals, or values that you have in common with others; then emphasize those commonalities. People reason that if you're like them in some ways, you're probably like them in other ways. Therefore, they begin to transfer trust as friend to friend.

TIP 2: Show Concern and Compassion.

People tend to trust people who show concern for them. When they bleed, they want to know others bleed with them. Even companies have to show concern over self-interest in times of crisis. During the Pepsi needle-syringe-tampering reports, you may recall the criticism some expressed in the company's handling of that crisis. When the public asked about the possibility of recalls, Pepsi officials embraced logic: the cans were bottled at different plants in different parts of the country; there was no logical pattern for the alleged tampering incidents. No recalls: logical decision. But Pepsi received criticism not for what they said, but for what they didn't say. The absence of what some believed to be concern about public safety. The same is true on an individual level. People have to feel your concern before they hear your words.

TIP 3: Demonstrate Cooperation with Good Intentions.

To be credible, you must demonstrate that you are acting in good faith to the best of your knowledge and ability. People must believe that you want to cooperate to help them achieve their personal and career goals. People will forgive you for poor judgment, but rarely for poor intentions.

TIP 4: Be Consistent.

We communicate by actions as well as words. We communicate by what we say and what we don't say; by which policies we enforce and which policies we don't enforce; by what we allow work time for and what we don't allow work time for; by what we fund and what we don't fund; by behavior we reward and behavior we punish; by what we do and what we criticize others for doing; by what we ask for and what we're willing to give in return. To be credible, our words have to match our policies, performance, and plans.

TIP 5: Demonstrate Competence.

People flock to experts, star performers, wise decision makers, and winners. People don't intentionally invest their money in poorly performing stock;

neither do they want to invest trust in people they doubt can achieve what they claim. To be led, either by words or actions, followers need to have faith in your competence to perform. They want to know you can win the game. They want to know you can finish the project successfully. They want to know you can turn the company around.

So how do leaders inspire confidence in their abilities while seeming modest and likable as people? They as leaders have to acknowledge accomplishments but avoid arrogance. Difficult, but not impossible. How? The attitude behind the talk turns the tables.

TIP 6: Be Correct.

Few people set out to be incorrect; it's just that when they have missing information, they make assumptions or reason wrongly. Instead of informing, they misinform unintentionally. Whether or not people routinely ask for the source of your information or conclusions, be ready to provide it. If they ask for sources, rather than be offended, welcome such testing questions as credibility checkers.

Why would people want sources for relatively insignificant information? Because we test validity on *all* important matters by considering the source. How do we test the source of important information? By checking the credibility of *all* information coming from that same source. Credibility is circular. Credibility in the insignificant breeds credibility for the significant. Once you're caught in an error, credibility creeps back ever so slowly.

TIP 7: Admit What You Don't Know.

When people smell blood, they dig. Here's a conversation that illustrates the fervor generated by the smell of bluff:

"How much does your company contribute each year to charity?"

"Hundreds of thousands of dollars."

"Most of it to United Way or to individual causes?"

"Both."

"What amount goes to United Way?"

"I think our goal was $240,000."

"Did you meet it?"

"I'm sure we did."

"Many companies don't meet their goals, you know. They just tout the goal as PR and never come through with the money."

"Ours does."

"Were you on the United Way committee?"

"Not exactly."

"What do you mean 'not exactly'?"

"Not this year, I wasn't. But I have served in prior years."

"So you're really not sure of the exact figures this year?"

"Not exactly."

"So you don't know the exact figure donated to United Way this current year?"

"No."

"So can you tell me the other specific organizations you contribute to regularly?"

"Not without checking."

"So you're guessing at the total amount given to charity each year, right?"

People push when they smell bluff and guff. It's a simple principle, easy to remember, easy to accomplish, but difficult for some people to swallow: Nothing makes people believe what you do know like admitting what you don't know.

TIP 8: Be Complete.

Are you telling all you know? Recognize the difference between lies, half-truths, omissions, and cover-ups. True, but incomplete, statements can lead to false conclusions; literal truth, when offered without complete explanations, can lead to literal lies. Knowing smiles accompanied by long silences can elicit wrong conclusions. Lying happens in numerous ways. Intentions stand center stage here. Ultimately, questionable intentions cast doubt about character.

TIP 9: Be Current.

Give up outdated data, opinions, and stereotypes. With information overload, data more than two or three years old can't support your decisions. Correct, but outdated, statistics soon become incorrect. Recollect.

TIP 10: Be Clear.

Sometimes the better we understand something the worse job we do of explaining it; our familiarity makes us careless in describing it. It's difficult to remember when we didn't know something that has become second nature. Ambiguity creeps in when we least expect it. Meanings depend on context, tone, timing, personal experience, and reference points.

Back in the days when copier equipment was said to "burn copies," an Army colonel hand-carried an important document to his new assistant and asked her to burn a copy. When the paper did not resurface on his desk in a few days, he discovered that the assistant had recently transferred from a high-security division. She had had the document incinerated. Are you clear? Are you sure? The best test of clarity is the result you see.

TIP 11: Avoid Doublespeak.

The previous tip referred to unintentional ambiguity due to carelessness or incompetence. With this tip, I'm referring to intentional gobbledygook—explanations meant to obscure rather than enlighten, convoluted details and irrelevant facts simmered together to make mush for the ear.

A financial consultant related this situation to me about his firm: "We have two boilerplate formats for our reports to clients. When we go into banks and find several ways we can help them, we use the first format. That report gives our findings and list of recommendations right up front. But if we go into banks and can't find much wrong—we don't have many recommendations for improvements and have charged them a big fee for the audit—then we use the second boilerplate. We begin the report with background on our company, the credentials of our auditors, the various audit procedures used, and then we finally get around to the findings and recommendations." He ended with "But I don't think we fool anybody." He's right. Purposeful gobbledygook only brings into question one's intentions.

TIP 12: Avoid Exaggeration.

Was the score 50 to zip or 30 to 10? Did you have to wait half an hour or half a minute? Did the caller slam down the phone or hesitate to talk? Did the supplier raise the prices on your raw materials 10 percent or 2 percent? Exaggeration makes great humor but destroys credibility.

TIP 13: Evaluate Criticisms and Objections.

If you reject or refute criticisms and objections out of hand, without hearing them out and giving yourself time to consider them fully, you lose credibility. People identify you as a reactor rather than a reflective, credible thinker. The more thorough your consideration of contradictory information the more credible your final opinion or decision.

TIP 14: Accept Responsibility for Decisions, Actions, and Results Where You Have/Had Some Control.

Watch comments such as the following, unless they are absolutely true: "We had no control over that project in our department." "Upper management made those decisions." "Competitors forced us into those arrangements." "Those policies are set by the government." "If it were my decision, I'd handle it differently." "I wasn't given a say in the matter." Shirkers suffer credibility gaps.

TIP 15: Keep Confidences.

When people know you share personal, confidential matters about others with them, they'll fear you'll do the same thing where they're concerned. Keeping confidences when "nobody would know you told" speaks volumes about character. Those who observe your discretion in deciding to keep quiet about hurtful or personal information involving others bridge to other favorable conclusions about your credibility in times of stress.

TIP 16: Avoid Lying "Offstage."

When you lie to a third person in front of a second person and that second person knows you're lying—for whatever reason—you lose credibility with the second person. Once observers have recognized your willingness to lie to others, they will doubt your truth-telling to them in a tight spot.

TIP 17: Be Sincere and Genuine.

Sincerity is easy to fake and hard to make. That is, people who pretend to be sincere can pitch an earnest plea, look at you with pleading eyes and straight face, and promise plums that dance in your head. But genuineness comes from character and is therefore harder to make. You either are or you aren't. What you experience is what you share. What you value is what you give. What you say is what you believe.

TIP 18: Be Vulnerable.

Believing people requires risk on the part of others. If others risk trust, they want to know that you share their risk: the risk of being honest; the risk of exposing your own weaknesses and foibles; the risk of telling things that might hurt you if used against you; the risk of stepping up to the plate and giving it all you've got when you swing. Taking risk in being transparent inspires others to risk taking you at face value.

TIP 19: Make Your Appearance Work for You.

Picture yourself lying on the operating table in a hospital emergency room. A guy in sweats and Nikes jogs toward your bedside and says, "I'm Kelly, the brain surgeon. I'll be ready to operate in a moment. Just let me give you this shot first." Would you have a few second thoughts? Appearance counts. Physical appearance, dress, grooming, posture, presence, and poise either underscore credibility or damage it. Look the part you want to play so others will believe and applaud your lines.

2

Conversing One on One

The vacuum created by a failure to communicate will quickly be filled with rumor, misrepresentations, drivel, and poison.
—C. NORTHCOTE PARKINSON

Think as wise men do, but speak as the common people do. —ARISTOTLE

Blessed is the man who, having nothing to say, abstains from giving in words evidence of the fact. —GEORGE ELIOT

The more you say, the less people remember.
—ANATOLE FRANCE

It's a tossup as to which are finally the most exasperating—the dull people who never talk, or the bright people who never listen.
—SYDNEY HARRIS

When ideas fail, words come in very handy.
—JOHANN WOLFGANG VON GOETHE

Sometimes you have to be silent to be heard.
—STANISLAW J. LEE

One great use of words is to hide our thoughts.
—VOLTAIRE

It is a sad thing when men have neither the wit
to speak well, nor judgment to hold their
tongues.   —JEAN DE LA BRUYERE

There are no facts, only interpretations.
                              —FRIEDRICH NIETZSCHE

He knew the precise psychological moment when
to say nothing.   —OSCAR WILDE

Tact is something that if it is there, nobody
notices it. But if it not there, everybody
notices it.   —no attribution

It would not be so bad to let one's mind go
blank—if one always remembered to turn off
the sound.   —no attribution

The meaning of your communication is the
response you get.
                              —JOHN BANDLER AND RICHARD GRINDER

Rare is it that a day goes by without our having to communicate. We even have a special term for people who choose not to participate: the hermit. Communication skills in our day-to-day life and relationships create the difference between misery and defeat or success and satisfaction. The following guidelines will help you communicate what you intend in those everyday situations such as lunch with a customer, a committee meeting on a team decision, a hallway briefing on the state of a project, an explanation of your expense account charges, a conversation with a colleague on the trade-show floor, or a dinner with your boss and spouse.

TIP 20: Recognize That Those in Less Powerful Positions Want to Win Your Goodwill; Interpret Their Words and Behavior Accordingly.

If you're the boss, you're going to get more attention to your preferences, quicker response to your requests, and overt approval of your ideas. Don't, however, jump to the conclusion that all this happens because you're necessarily an excellent communicator, that your requests have more merit than others, that your ideas are necessarily better. If you want honest feedback in your position of power, you'll have to work hard for it.

TIP 21: If As a Powerful Person You Want to Build Rapport with Others, Remove the Status Symbols and Power Barriers.

Be aware of the kind of power you have with different groups. You have *reward* power if you can somehow positively influence what will happen to another person. You have *coercive* power if you can negatively influence another's future. You have *positional* power if by your position as boss or director or police officer or flight attendant you can force your will upon another. You have *expert* power over someone if you have knowledge they need. You have *referent* power over people if you can influence through your personality. Being aware of these power pockets forces you to take your interactions with certain people more seriously. They will.

If you want to minimize this power and relate to others on equal footing—if you want an honest opinion from them that they may be reluctant to give—you have to remove the status reminders. You may want to sit beside them, not across the desk from them. You may want to arrive at the cocktail party in your own car, not in a limo. You may want to take off your name badge and introduce yourself by name and forget the title. You may want to join them in the lounge rather than invite them to the country club.

Rapport-building hinges on such small steps.

TIP 22: Assess Others' Knowledge and Experiences Exactly.

If you assume your listeners are more knowledgeable than they are, they may misunderstand your message, give up on trying to understand your explanations, or become frustrated or angry because they think you're "putting on airs."

A VP at a large oil company attended a session where he'd asked the controller to explain to the first-line supervisors and managers how to complete a specific form justifying their annual budget requests. During the opening session, the controller illustrated the budget form using a figure of several million dollars for purchase of equipment. At the break, the vice president wisely took the controller aside and asked her to lower the dollar amounts so as not to make the supervisors feel small because their responsibilities did not involve such large expenditures. That vice president picked up on an important subtlety.

On the other hand, you can err in the opposite direction. If you assume your listeners know less than they actually do, you may insult their intelligence, bore them, or waste their time on already-known information. You want to meet them exactly at their knowledge and interest level. To do that, ask yourself five questions: What's their primary interest in this situation/event/issue? How much do they already know and from what likely source and perspective have they received information? How will they use this information for themselves? Why would they want to know this? What reaction will they have to the subject—skepticism and doubt, loss of face, defensiveness, support? These answers will help you reach them appropriately eye to eye.

TIP 23: Set a Level Playing Field.

Before you speak, make sure what you're about to say doesn't contain words or phrases that imply your superiority to the other person. Example: "I want you to meet Jana Jones, who works *for* me" versus "I want you to meet Jana Jones, who works *with* me." Example: "Haven't I told you about bothering me with those kinds of details?" versus "I'd prefer that you handle those kinds of details without involving me." Example: "I try to spend as much time abroad as possible when my job allows" versus "I like to travel when I have the time."

TIP 24: Avoid Coming Across As a One-Directional Communicator.

That is, you don't want to get a reputation as a "teller." Several months ago I was standing in a trade-show booth when a man walked up, stuck out his hand to shake mine, and began: "My name's _____. I notice we're competitors here at the show. We've got a booth over the way, booth number 399. You probably remember that Ford RFP that came out about four months ago. Well, if you're wondering about it, we've got it sewed up. I understand you people bid on it. That was really a formality, because one of the VPs there had already made contact with us and wanted us in. That was an easy sale for us. You know what I mean? Don't you wish all of them were that easy? It's going to be a big contract. Three hundred thousand before they're through. Well, nice to meet you. Just wanted to stop by and say hello."

All of this came out without his ever taking a breath and without my ever having an opportunity (or inclination) to cut in and respond. Don't be a hit-and-run speaker.

TIP 25: Avoid a Reputation As a Manipulator.

People with strong personalities at times take advantage of less able communicators—or those with no goal for a particular conversation or meeting. They manipulate others before they realize what's happening to them. They outsmart people by seducing them with flirting. They deceive them with misused facts. They pretend to feel something they don't. They shame others into acting against their best interests. They dominate others through sheer tone. They play martyr when it suits them. They tempt others with unkept promises and false power. Over time, such tactics work against the people who use them.

TIP 26: Be Interested, Not Just Interesting.

The heart of the principle involves putting aside self-interests long enough to devote attention to someone else. Yes, we are attracted to life-of-the-party people because they amuse us. But interested people win us. They make us want to stick to them like glue. Nothing is so flattering as to have someone show personal interest in our job, our background, our experience, or our views.

TIP 27: To Express Interest in Someone, Soften Whatever It Is You're Doing.

Soften you voice, soften your tone, soften your smile, soften your posture, soften your touch, soften your eye contact, soften your nod. Softening communicates openness.

TIP 28: Use Radical Language to Be a Leader.

You have to shake people out of complacency to lead them in a new direction. You have to be clearly focused to inspire followership. You have to intrigue others to tempt them to make a change with you.

TIP 29: Have a Sense of the Dramatic When You Talk.

Would you rather have someone tell you about a movie or see it for yourself? So would I. We like action—in the voice, in the face, in the body, in the scene. Add a funny twist to the story. Use description to set the scene. Add gestures to give a story a sense of place. The only benefit you as a conversationalist have over a manual or memo is animation. Use it.

TIP 30: Learn to Self-Disclose.

People feel loyal to you only when you are willing to let them get to know you. They can't like someone they don't know.

If you consider the closest, most meaningful relationships you have in the workplace, they are based most often on self-disclosure. Those initial conversations and invitations are often overt: "Let's spend some time together after work—I'd like to get to you know you better." Or: "Well, I've told you my life story. Tell me about yourself. You have family? . . ."

Practice disclosure by sharing facts about yourself—where you work, projects you handle, hobbies you enjoy, trips you've taken, sales you've lost. The subject doesn't matter as much as the fact that you're willing to share information about yourself. Over time and with practice, you'll gradually feel at ease when sharing values, opinions, and goals. The relationship will develop accordingly.

That, of course, doesn't mean in every conversation you're going to have the energy to unload. If a friend self-discloses and you fail to do so, that friend may feel suddenly you're no longer interested. He or she feels imbalance in the conversation. Therefore, when you're too tired or preoccupied to share mutually, at least let the friend know it's a lack of time or energy rather than unconcern.

And don't think the self-disclosing necessarily makes you more vulnerable to attack and hurt. Just the opposite is true. Self-disclosure can bring you the protection of friendship and loyalty from those who come to understand and appreciate your values, ideas, and intentions. Emotional distance creates mental illness. To disclose improves your mental health.

TIP 31: Confess Your Weaknesses.

If you want to be approachable, you have to present yourself as human. You have to be willing to let others see your weaknesses and your blunders. If you admit a weakness, you demonstrate to the other person that you trust that person to keep your secret. That friend, in turn, will feel he or she can trust you with personal confidences. Under this principle, I've heard people owning up to eating a whole pie, losing a deal because of arriving too late for a meeting, and not liking their moody teenagers. Rather than pounce on such secrets, most people will take a peak at your deficiencies and then help you hide them you so you'll not be embarrassed. Your willingness to appear openly before others allows them to identify with you as a kindred human being.

TIP 32: Keep in Mind That Being Logical May Be Ineffective.

Communication involves the emotions as well as the intellect. Emotional arguments have proved very successful where logic has failed to move people. An appeal to someone's self-interest may ensure more buy-in than a logical explanation of fairness to all concerned.

TIP 33: Visualize the End, and Then Construct the Means.

Decide what reaction you want from your audience, then decide how to structure your message to get that reaction. Do you want your audience to be emotional about the decision? Then choose anecdotes and stories to bring them to commitment and action. Do you want them to come to a rational conclusion? Then choose facts and logic to develop your idea. Do you want them to get involved personally in implementing your plan? Then apply your ideas to the work in their own departments. Picture the goal line and then decide how to develop your idea to get people there.

TIP 34: Pay Attention to the Meta-Message.

Gerard Nierenberg coined the term "meta-message" to describe those messages that come through between the lines; they come from the context, the relationship, the timing, the purpose, and the person speaking. For example, Susan calls her colleague Jack for the third time in one day. She says, "Hi, it's me again." He responds: "I'm working on the Caliver report; it's due in half an hour." His message is not intended as an update on the progress. His words and tone mean: "Why are you bothering me again? I don't have time to talk now."

Another example: A husband comes home with a new sports car. The wife asks: "Why did you buy that car?" He responds: "The gas mileage is as good as anything else on the road." Her tone and words didn't ask for his reasons for the purchase. Given their earlier conversation about his being selfish and never considering her opinions, she meant, "Why do you disregard me and not include me in your decisions?"

If you've ever wondered why someone responds negatively to "positive" words, consider the meta-message. A senior executive walks into a meeting and says, "Sorry to keep you waiting. A call came through from London that I simply had to take." Another executive in the corner may greet the late-arriver's apology with a scowl; to him, the meaning was: "I outrank you and have the power to keep you waiting."

A boss says to a subordinate: "I simply can't approve that transfer for you. It's not in your best interest in the long run." The subordinate may reject the seemingly "caring" statement and instead get the meta-message that he is a child in need of protection for his own good.

We deal with some meta-messages every day and recognize them as such: You say to a good friend who tosses out a ridiculous idea: "You idiot—that's off the wall." With your big smile and strong relationship, he knows you really mean, "Thanks for the laugh." We understand such. With other meta-messages, we walk away from a conversation feeling disappointed or "zapped" but don't understand why.

With any meta-message, a response to only the words is insufficient. If an argument or discussion follows, it will most certainly be off the subject. Listen and respond to the meta-message; that's where the action is.

TIP 35: Don't Hide Behind Your Words to Avoid Hearing the Message.

Because meaning comes from relationships, timing, circumstances, and intentions, words play only a small part—but they serve as an excuse if you want to pretend not to understand the message.

> HUSBAND: (*To wife at convention.*) When are you coming home?
>
> WIFE: Probably sometime Saturday. (*Pretending not to understand his tone that says, "I think you're staying longer than necessary," she simply answers the question.*)

You can't often get away with hiding behind the words. Conversational meaning is bigger than the words we say.

TIP 36: Match Your Tone to Your Intentions.

Different linguists and psychologists have provided a variety of labels to describe habitual styles/tones of communicating:

Accusing/blaming. "It's your fault we missed that deadline." "Don't ask me why we didn't hire more people to start with—I knew better." "Well, I was only reacting to what you said earlier about not having sufficient budget."

Appeasing/placating. "Please, let's just forget it. It doesn't really matter." "Would you please consider changing the deadline?" "Just tell me what you want me to do now and I'll get on it."

Computing/disassociating. "The deadline is August 1." "Two people cannot get the job done." (There are no personal references, no feelings, no emotion.)

Analyzing/diagnosing. "The contract did not really call for an August 1 deadline. You, as manager, selected that date. Was your intention to test our commitment? To force us to abandon our quality procedures?" "Why are you saying that to me?" "You know, the reason you're feeling that way is that you're insecure within yourself."

Dogmatic. "We will lose the business if we miss that first deadline." "It can't be done that way." "You're wrong." "It has to be blue."

Dramatic/effusive. "We kill ourselves and you're still not pleased." "This is the stupidest plan we've ever used—there's not a company on earth that could meet that deadline." "Either give me an answer today, or I quit." "I wouldn't transfer her out of here for a million dollars; she knows all there is about inventory management."

Straightforward/leveling. "I'm disappointed that we missed the deadline. I had two people helping and thought that would be sufficient, but evidently it wasn't. We need to hire more help."

Do you recognize any of the above as a habitual style of yours? If so, is that the way you intend to come across?

TIP 37: Avoid a Patronizing Tone.

Patronizing people sound as though they're doing you a favor to enlighten you on the subject. Whether such a person knows anything on the subject or not, he or she always expresses an opinion—and makes those with more expertise feel stupid for bothering to have such expertise. People get a strong urge to argue with this individual, even if they don't disagree, because of that person's superior, haughty manner.

TIP 38: Don't Talk Down to People—Even Kids.

Instructional manuals that contain statements such as these make users think they were written for an idiot. If so, the idiot certainly wouldn't be reading the manual! "Plug the appliance into the electrical socket." Or: "Accidents frequently happen."

TIP 39: Avoid Moralizing.

We like "lessons," but generally not when they come from someone who adopts a mother-superior tone. Employee: "We found four widgets that had the threads stripped." Manager: "Every time you skip the inspection, you have things like that happen. Your people are careless."

A habitual, moralizing response grates against people's sensitivities, particularly if the message comes from peers.

TIP 40: Hear Silence As It's Intended.

There's the old adage, "Silence is consent." People who believe that are in for a big disappointment. When you make a statement that's met with silence, it can have several meanings:

1. The person is reflecting on what you said and considering your opinion.
2. The person is in complete agreement and thinks no response is necessary.
3. The person thinks he or she understands (and is unaware of not understanding) what you said.
4. The person agrees and intends to act immediately.
5. The person agrees but has no intention of acting.
6. The person is too angry to speak.
7. The person is reflecting on what you said and rejecting your opinion.
8. The person is too overcome with revulsion to speak.
9. The person is giving you an immediate rebuke.
10. The person wasn't listening and is nodding with his or her mind in neutral.
11. The person hears you, is confused, but doesn't want to appear ignorant by asking you to elaborate further on something you think is perfectly clear.
12. The person is so confused that he or she doesn't know how to ask for clarification.
13. The person is in a state of shock.
14. The person is depressed.
15. The person is stalling.
16. The person feels too powerless to respond.

If you want to confirm what the other person's silence means, stick around long enough to read further body language or hear further comments to get confirmation.

Making a statement in a staff meeting that is greeted with silence can mean total opposition or total agreement. Better to find out which than to have the project, policy, or procedure sabotaged later. It's up to you, the talker, to probe for meaning of the silence.

TIP 41: Recognize the Implications of What's Not Said.

"You really did a superb job this time" can bring questions about what was wrong with the job completed last month. When you congratulate people for accomplishments, consider who in the meeting didn't receive congratulations. A male office manager insists that he no longer comments on new hairdos because he once supervised 44 female employees where he made the mistake of offering a compliment to one in the presence of another.

TIP 42: Use Silence to Your Advantage.

If you don't want to commit yourself with an oral response, you can use silence to mask your own opinions or emotions. With practice, you can *gain* attention with silence (by a long pause before you respond—one that builds suspense and adds weight to what follows), or you can *avoid* attention with silence (by accepting, as if you've "moved on" mentally). Silence can build intimacy. Only when people don't know each other well are they uncomfortable with silence between their exchanges. People who feel intimate with each other understand silence as a "communion of thought."

Comfortable silence gives you time to reflect on what has been said, to make a decision, to change the subject, to create psychological distance with the past and get ready to move on mentally. Silence is a very versatile conversational tool.

TIP 43: Eliminate Contradictory Body
Language and Words.

Your customer asks you if you can expedite the order "this one time," and you grimace while saying yes. Your colleague asks if you've got time to lend an ear about a problem that person is having closing a sale. You say, "Okay, yeah, sure" while glancing at your watch and fidgeting with the papers on your desk. Your boss asks if you're sure you can have the report finished by 5 o'clock. You say it'll be no problem while sighing heavily, running your fingers through your hair, and then beginning to massage your temples as if you've got a splitting headache. Either say what you mean, or act out what you mean. But don't make the messages contradictory.

TIP 44: Check for the Hidden Agenda Before You Bite
Hook, Line, and Sinker.

Does the other person's body language support or contradict the words? If so, why would he or she want to conceal the truth? Does this person's message contradict common sense—contradict what the person has said or done in the past? Does this person seem to be beating around the bush with a small stick rather than landing it in the middle? Do you have a "gut feeling"—racing heart, sweaty palms, knots in the stomach, dry mouth, tense shoulders, a pounding headache? If so, your body is telling you to look behind the words.

TIP 45: Believe Body Language over Words.

Others' body language can cancel their words, but their words can never override their body language. Unless they're superb actors, the body language gives the true picture.

TIP 46: Don't Polarize People.

Some people seem to get great joy out of driving a wedge between people rather than bringing them together. They bring up controversial issues in cocktail-party circles. They play devil's advocate in every meeting and recruit associate demons to side with them. They pass on thoughtless comments that one group or person said to the group spoken about—"just to make them aware." This person's mission in life is to cause division; as a result, he or she usually gets knee-jerk reactions and decisions based on emotion rather than on solid thinking.

TIP 47: Voice Your Disagreement After, Not Before, Asking the Other Person's Reasons for His or Her Opinion.

If someone expresses an opinion and you immediately express an opposing view, you both lose. Why? Because the person who first expressed an opinion will often consider your contradiction rude or the beginning of an argument. A typical response will be for the person to refer to the earlier statement and begin delineating reasons as support.

You both win, however, if you hear an opinion with which you disagree and then ask immediately for that person to elaborate on the reasons behind that opinion. Then, if you feel comfortable with the situation, you can state that you hold a different opinion, giving your reasons. At the end of the conversation both of you will have learned something about the other side and neither will feel as though you've had an argument/disagreement.

Quite possibly, if you had stated your disagreement early on, the other person would have simply kept quiet, preventing a valuable exchange of ideas.

TIP 48: Bring Up a "Touchy" Subject Only with a Warning.

Prepare people with some lead-in like, "I know this isn't a popular topic and some of you don't want to make a commitment one way or the other, but . . ." or "I know most of us hate prejudice in all its forms and it's not my intention to pinpoint . . ." or "Some people definitely do not share my concerns about X, but I want to express them anyway. . . ."

Otherwise, with such an abrupt change of subjects—a touchy one at that—others may "pop off" and embarrass themselves or "can" you in the process.

TIP 49: Use Indirectness to Test the Waters Before Diving In.

Toss out a comment indirectly, get the other person's reaction, and then go ahead with the comment or claim that you were unclear about your meaning. It's a face-saving ploy to get the other person to commit attitude, feelings, or opinions first.

TIP 50: Avoid Dogmatic Pronouncements.

"That's not the way it happened at all." "You're being ridiculous." "You can't do that." "Are you crazy?" "Everybody knows that . . ." "That'll do no good at all." "You're wrong." "That's not true." "You misunderstood." Such statements make enemies of friends or followers.

TIP 51: Consider "I" Messages to Make Others Less Defensive.

If I say to you, "*You're* wrong about that contract!" you'd likely be taken aback and feel defensive. If, on the other hand, I say, "*I* disagree with your interpretation of that contract," you're likely to respond: "Oh, where?" or "Well, you're entitled to your opinion and I'm entitled to mine."

If the store owner says to the customer, "You must sign this agreement before we will process the order," the customer may respond, "Oh, yeah? I don't have to do anything with your paperwork. I can walk out of here." But if the store owner says, "I need to have this paperwork signed so that our processors can set up the delivery date," the typical customer will respond internally, "Okay, I need to sign it if I want to get delivery without a hassle."

The difference between an "I" message and a "you" message sounds enormous.

TIP 52: Substitute *And* Statements for *But* Statements.

The "but" statement negates the first part of your sentence. The hearer ignores the first part and focuses on what comes after the "but."

But statement: "I respect your work, but I don't agree with this new idea."

And statement: "I respect your work. And I have reservations about this new idea."

But statement: "I hear what you're saying, but I don't agree."

And statement: "I hear what you're saying. And I have a different view."

But statement: "I understand your point, but you're missing mine."

And statement: "I understand your point, and I'd like you to understand mine."

But statement: "You're dependable, but you're impulsive."

And statement: "You're dependable. And you're also impulsive."

TIP 53: Respond Rather Than React.

Reacting to comments or a situation implies a knee-jerk, uncontrolled response without thought to the implications or results. Responding to someone's comments or a specific situation means a deliberate, thoughtful response that leads to the result you intend.

TIP 54: Distinguish Between Defending Ideas and Being Defensive.

Defending ideas shows commitment and analytical forethought. Defending your position to others in such a way as to convince them to come around to your view is almost always appropriate, as long as you are straightforward in your words and even-tempered in your tone.

Being defensive, on the other hand, puts people in a negative light. The defensive person steps into the arena of emotion, responding with excuses and fears. Moving away from logic, a defensive person moves away from credibility with listeners.

TIP 55: Don't Make Arguing an "Ego Trip."

When you attach ego to disagreement, you typically stop listening and start planning your counterattack. You often miss what the other person is really saying; "winning the argument" becomes your mission rather than hearing an opposing view and honestly deciding whether you might agree with some of it or whether you are even more convinced you're right. In other words, don't go after a win as if you're playing tennis. Look at the difference as an opportunity either to confirm your own thinking or to change it.

TIP 56: Dig for the Bigger Problem Beneath Arguments About Trivialities.

A buyer says to the sales rep, "I thought you told me you'd call Wednesday morning?"

"Yes, I did. But the management meeting lasted all the way to noon. I hope the hour's delay didn't inconvenience you."

"Yes, it did. I've already placed my order with another firm."

You can be sure the problem was bigger than this one hour's delay.

A secretary says to the boss, "Do you or do you not want coffee inside the conference room?"

"Just put it outside the door so we can get to it at breaks."

"Well, last time you wanted it inside the room."

"Yes, but we've got a different purpose and group for this meeting."

"I've got sugar, not Sweet-n-Low."

"Please buy artificial sweetener, like I told you."

"I'll have to go to the store myself; the cafeteria here is out."

"Then go to the store."

You can be sure the difficulty is over something larger than the coffee details for the meeting.

The person who seems to be "unreasonable" or "difficult" is usually hurt on a deeper level. The trivial argument is just a symptom.

TIP 57: Be Firm, but Not Inflexible.

You want to be firm enough that people don't consider you wishy-washy in your opinions and goals. You want to state opinions convincingly and forcefully so that you can influence others if that happens to be your goal. But you don't want to be so goal-driven that you seem to disregard what others say or feel. Your topic, your timing, and your temperament all indicate the appropriate firmness and flexibility to display in any given situation.

TIP 58: Adopt a Problem-Solving Orientation When Presenting a Problem.

Before going to a customer with a problem . . . or to a boss with a mistake . . . or to a spouse or friend with a disappointment, spend some time working on a solution. You don't want to hide the problem, of course, if delay will only compound the problem. But rather than focusing on how a mistake, problem, or disappointment occurred, focus your conversation on resolving, improving, or altering the outcome.

TIP 59: Define Things in Terms of Cooperation Rather Than Competition.

Look for ways to cooperate on projects, decisions, or goals rather than focusing on differences. "Well, it's clear we both want to keep the customer happy. You think it's by price and I think it's by better service. Let's weight both of those." With such a statement, you focus on cooperating to win, not competing to see who's "right" and "wrong."

TIP 60: Recognize Unanswerable Questions.

Ever since we sat in fourth grade and Ms. Witherspoon asked us the capital of Louisiana, we've felt compelled to answer questions. And if we are in a place of leadership or authority, we feel the urge even more strongly. But some questions defy answers. Identify which they are and save yourself the frustration.

TIP 61: Don't Rain on People's Parades.

Some people go through life focused on telling people what won't work for them, what they should or should not have done, and what will create trouble for them. When people share a dream, they most often want support, not caution. Think twice before becoming the naysayer about people's ideas, plans, and dreams.

TIP 62: Frame the Positive Angle.

How can you position what you want to say so that people accept the message in a positive light? A manager at a large computer company had as his mission to put together an online database that would make life easier for all his telephone support people, but he could get no cooperation from them. Here was the situation.

As part of a licensing agreement and fee, users received telephone support by calling an 800 number. The problem was that when a call came in on a complex question, the reps would spend hours researching the answer; but there was no record of that call or answer. Therefore, there was a lot of duplication of research effort, a big backlog of customer calls, and numerous complaints about delays. The manager's goal was to have the reps record their answers and send him a copy so he could put the answers into an online database. But, despite the explanation of help, he got absolutely no cooperation from the reps.

After reading his memo to solicit their written answers, I understood why. The memo began: "As you know, we are legally obligated to provide a four-hour response on all customer calls. Currently, we are backlogged with customer calls and making little or no progress; complaints continue to grow. . . ." A negative approach.

I suggested a rewording of the memo: "How would you like to get through your stack of backlogged customer calls quickly? How would you like to have all the researched answers to customer calls at the tip of your fingers? Help is on the way. For the next 30 days, I'm asking you simply to record and forward to me a copy of . . ." This positive approach generated a much better response.

The positive framing means to say what you're for, not what you're against; what you're going to do, not what you're not going to do; what you can do, not what you can't do.

The positive angle takes a little thought, but the results are well worth the effort.

TIP 63: Use Positive Rather Than Negative Words.

Clinical psychologists say that we hear and remember positive wording better than negative wording—particularly instructions. When someone reads a sign that says DO NOT DUMP TRASH HERE, that person has to switch tracks. "Hmmm. I can't dump trash here. Then where? Oh, I can dump trash over there." However, if the sign reads DUMP TRASH IN THE BIN NEAR THE BACK DOOR, the person can avoid the switching technique.

Not: "I wasn't able to reach him on the phone."

But: "We never spoke to him by phone."

Not: "I don't know whether I should make that purchase."

But: "I question the wisdom of that purchase."

Not: "I don't know many people here."

But: "I know none of the people here."

Not: "I can't have this ready until Friday."

But: "I can have this ready for you on Friday."

Not: "They can't correct that problem until they redesign the motor."

But: "When they redesign the motor, they're going to correct that problem."

Not: "Our managers don't communicate with each other."

But: "Our managers should find ways to communicate about cross-departmental projects on a regular basis."

Not: "We'll have to go into debt."

But: "We will issue bonds."

The positive message or instruction sinks in easier, further, faster.

TIP 64: Place Positive Statements Before Neutral Ones.

A husband and wife sit down to the dinner table for a bowl of soup. She tastes the soup and says, "Did you put oregano in this soup?" He responds, "Yes, I certainly did. But not enough for you to taste it—you're so particular. You're going to know the next time I volunteer to cook dinner." She would have gotten a much better response with a positive lead-in: "This soup tastes different somehow. I like it. Did you put oregano in it?"

When people hear a neutral statement, they may be tempted to "read into it" past conversations or react defensively for any number of reasons. Better to use the positive statement first so the person knows how to interpret what follows.

TIP 65: Express Your Opinions As Opinions Rather Than Irrefutable Facts.

The difference is usually one of tone and word choice:

Fact: "The contract will turn on delivery date. We'll lose them."

Opinion: "I think the contract will turn on delivery date. I'm afraid we'll lose them."

Fact: "Gary will resign if we don't give him this raise."

Opinion: "Gary has been interviewing with other firms. I think he'll resign if we don't come through with this raise."

Others will be less defensive with such wording, and you'll save face if you're wrong.

TIP 66: Express Your Opinions As Statements, Not Questions.

"Don't you think that restaurant is too expensive?" will likely get a response such as, "No, not really." The other person will continue with his or her plans, and you'll feel as though your opinion was ignored. Instead respond to the statement of plans with, "I think that restaurant is too expensive." Then other people can agree or disagree, but at least they'll understand you were stating an opinion to be considered.

TIP 67: Identify Your Own Feelings, Needs, and Opinions So You Can Permit Others to Do the Same.

If you're in the habit of suppressing what you really want to say, denying yourself the opportunity to stand up for your rights, squashing your opinions for the sake of harmony, then gradually you'll lose your ability to read other people's verbal cues. You'll lose your sense of listening between the lines. Claim your rights and need to express yourself so you can feel comfortable when others claim those same rights with you.

TIP 68: Own Your Statements.

Put yourself into your wording. State opinions as if you own them:

Not: "This food isn't good."

But: "This butter tastes rancid to me."

Not: "You get so hyper about money."

But: "I think you get supercritical about how I spend money."

Not: "That office next door is too loud."

But: "I find it hard to concentrate with that hammering going on next door."

Not: "Just drop the subject, please."

But: "I don't think we're getting anywhere with this discussion. What do you say if we just table this discussion for another week?"

Not: "Relax, there's no problem."

But: "I think you should relax until next week when you know for sure if there's a problem."

When you stake a claim to an opinion, people pay respect.

TIP 69: Say What's on Your Mind Without Shifting to a Hostile Tone.

When anger threatens to overcome you, breathe deeply, slow down, and lower rather than raise your voice. Your words and opinions will sound firm and factual, not emotional and irrational.

TIP 70: Don't Switch from "You" to "Me" Back to "They" When You Want a Response About Your Own Situation.

A colleague met me in the hall after a speech about productivity with this comment: "You know what you ought to do when you start to work here? You ought to tell them you have to have your own PC at home because otherwise they won't let you switch to flexible hours. I've told them I set personal goals like you advocate in your speech and can be very productive working alone at home. But my boss is old-school; they just don't see how they can manage an at-home employee. You have to be someone they want to hire badly and then use that as a bargaining chip before you look for a job these days."

Meaning? When he started off talking about me, I thought he was commenting on the possibility that I might want employment with his company. Then I gathered that he might be talking about his own personal frustration with not getting approval for at-home work. Finally, I concluded that he was expressing a general opinion about how to bargain for at-home work—an opinion that perhaps I should share in my next speech. The principle involves ownership. Better to talk *to* me, *about you*, or *about others* with the proper pronouns—I, me, you, they, we.

TIP 71: Don't Tell Others How to Think or Feel.

People resent those who presume to read their minds—even if those presumptions are correct. Example: "We know you'll like the carpet we're shipping equally as well" generates an "Oh, yeah?" Example: "Certainly you can appreciate the situation you've put us in" generates "No, I can't." Example: "As I'm sure you're aware" triggers "No, I wasn't." Example: "We know you'll find the trip exciting and profitable for all your staff" elicits "I'll be the judge of that."

TIP 72: Encourage Others to Vent Emotions So They Can Clear Their Minds to Hear You.

When people "charge" you with angry words, you'll do better to let them have their say than to try to stop the flow in midstream. When they get cut off, they can't listen to the other side of the story or your explanation for wanting you to hear how they feel. Think twice before making these comments: "Please take a few moments to compose yourself, and then we'll talk" or "Just wait a minute, now" or "Stop yelling at me." Instead, encourage others to flush themselves of emotion. They'll be drained of the anger or excitement and better able to hear your response.

TIP 73: Seek Out the Causes of Behavior; They'll Be More Worthwhile and Revealing Than the Behavior Itself.

When there's a dispute or problem that leads you to question somebody about what was said, to whom, about what, in what circumstance, the tendency is to dwell on the chronological sequence. To resolve the issue quicker and more effectively, try to focus on the "why." Use such probes as "Why do you think Belva said that to you?" "Why did you think I wanted the calendars today?" "What did you think would happen if you told Jerry about the delay?" "Why did you think replacing the machine would be a better solution than repairing it?" The "whys" are a preventative measure; they tell you how to work around future misunderstandings.

TIP 74: Express an Opposing Viewpoint to Build Credibility, to Entertain, or to Do Someone a Favor.

Most people get bored with people who always agree with them. Can you imagine trying to read a novel without all the amusing repartee between hero and heroine? Differences of opinion stoke the fire. That same holds true even in a live social setting. My college-age son, contemplating dumping his current girlfriend for a new one, recently remarked: "You know I can talk to Patty even better than Carole. Carole just says what she thinks I want to hear. Patty really tells me what she thinks."

It's not an opposing opinion that upsets most people; they react negatively only when that opinion is conveyed with a haughty, hostile, or negative attitude.

TIP 75: Be Tactful, Not Offensive or Insensitive.

To be more specific: When you're brief, be polite. If you're aggressive, smile when you say it. If you're emphatic, be pleasant with the command or opinion. If you're negative, be diplomatic with your word choice. If you're right, don't rub it in.

Tact calls for two essentials: You have to be alert enough to know when tact is necessary—to be sensitive to people's self-esteem. And you have to be quick-witted enough to come up with graceful wording.

TIP 76: Don't Ask Others to Cover Up for Your Insensitivity.

Administrative assistants and secretaries will have a special place in heaven for their role in softening the blow to others' self-esteem caused by insensitive bosses who "can't be bothered about feelings when there's work to be done."

TIP 77: Consider the Price of "Nice."

When you, for whatever reason, decide to be "nice" as a way of life, you may be doing yourself and the other person serious harm. If you make a habit of not speaking up to disagree, not stating your feelings, not making waves about the action that involves you, you often grow resentful. And that resentment frequently leaks out in other ways—by sabotaging projects, by withdrawing emotionally from the person, by doing less than your best, by exploding over minor issues.

As a result, when you later respond with anger, you seem emotional, and your behavior is labeled "inappropriate." Worse, feelings on both sides of the relationship grow cold. No one can always identify with the truly submissive, withdrawn, angry person—the relationship withers.

TIP 78: Verify Assumptions—Your Own and Those of Others.

A manufacturer's rep was puzzled by the client who refused to accept a "line through" on his quotation for furniture. When the customer changed his mind about the color of a product, the rep told him simply to ink through the change and return the contract, thinking the customer would value the speed in getting his furniture ordered and delivered. On the contrary, the customer delayed placing his order for another three days while the rep sent a clean contract with the one-item change. Why neatness over speed? The purchasing agent's boss valued neat paperwork and considered inked changes "sloppy work." So much for assumptions about what customers value.

We make similar invalid assumptions almost daily. As a newlywed, I stumbled to the kitchen at 4:00 a.m. to cook my college-student husband a full breakfast before he went off to his roofing job. About two months into the routine, I left the kitchen a moment and then returned to see my husband scraping his scrambled eggs into the disposal. "What's the matter? They weren't done right?" I asked.

"Sure, they're fine."

"Then why didn't you eat them?"

"Honey, I'm sorry. I just have trouble eating eggs and toast at 4:00 a.m."

"But I thought you said you liked a big breakfast? That your mom always cooked you a big breakfast?"

"I did. But that wasn't at 4:00 a.m."

No more early mornings for me in the kitchen.

Of course, we don't become aware of assumptions until something happens to let us know those assumptions are not shared. It's impossible to verify all assumptions before taking action or responding and impossible to trace assumptions back to what exactly led us to make them. The goal is to be alert to the pitfalls.

Example: "I noticed you didn't turn in any referrals for prospects on the new accounts. Does that mean you're upset about the compensation program?" Such a probe gives the other person responsibility to deny or verify such feelings.

If someone winks and says to you, "I heard the pilot had a difficult time landing the plane because of a 'temporary physical condition,'" what would you think? That the pilot was intoxicated? Or would you consider pregnancy? Did you consider that the pilot might be female?

We typically assume everybody sees things as we do, values the same things we do, wants the same things we do. Assumptions blind us, limit our thinking, and bring us to wrong conclusions.

TIP 79: Check Out Inferences.

We hear words; we draw conclusions from those words. That can be a critical communication gaffe. Make a habit of checking out what you think the words, tone of voice, body language, and context mean. You could be right; you could be wrong.

Manager: "I still have not seen your report." (The statement could be an observation, yet it contains the word "still" as if the manager might be exasperated.)

Employee: "I'm sorry. We had three people out this week. Are you wondering if the project is going to be finished on time?" (The employee checks out the manager's real concern.)

TIP 80: Read Others' Cues and Clues to Determine the "So What?"

When people make statements about "they" or "other people" when presenting a sorry state of affairs, you may be puzzled as to the significance. Why are they telling you? To determine the answer, use "so what?" probes: "What does all this mean to you and your job?" or "So how does this policy affect you personally?" or "So, are you concerned personally about the results?" With your probing question, you're giving them "permission" to be open with you and get personal about their feelings or concerns. Then you can personalize your response and be appropriately empathetic.

TIP 81: Check Out Hunches When Someone Denies Intentions.

People often reveal things they don't intend to reveal. Then, when you question them directly about whether they feel this way or that way, they become vulnerable, cautious, and guarded. If you tip your hand with a comment such as, "Are you saying you think Bill was wrong in firing that consultant?" the other person often becomes suddenly aware that the feeling he or she intended to hide has become transparent. People will deny such sentiments if you push them. Before you tip your hand, check out hunches by asking less direct questions to verify the person's true intentions with the original statement.

TIP 82: Challenge Generalizations.

"The marketing people never consider the credit risks involved when they make those offers." "Management doesn't give a whit about the long-term effects on our families." "Customers won't pay extra for a feature like that." Always dig for the basis in reality. Collect the specifics as evidence before you accept the generalization as truth.

TIP 83: Test Old Axioms.

Conventional wisdom can be dangerous to your future if you accept these axioms at face value. Besides, they're often contradictory: "He who hesitates is lost" versus "Fools rush in where angels fear to tread." "In the counsel of many is wisdom" versus "You can never please everybody." "Don't make waves" versus "Be a risk taker." Don't accept truisms out of hand simply because they've been around a long time. Any truth has its exception.

Rather than pass off some glib cliché as your own opinion, reconsider its truth in light of each new situation.

TIP 84: When You're Listening, Have a Penchant for Details; When Speaking, Take Your Cue from the Listener and Your Purpose.

If you're the listener, consider yourself the leader. After hearing the big-picture message, sift through the detail to see if it really supports the conclusion you just heard. Look for nuances of meanings, gaps in logic, and further application in other tasks or situations. On the other hand, if you're the speaker, let the listener lead. Give as much or as little detail as the listener's interest and your purpose dictate. No more and no less.

TIP 85: Differentiate Between Showing Deference and Being Patronizing.

The difference is one of attitude and choice. People show deference when they consciously choose not to embarrass someone, when they keep quiet so as not to offend someone, or when they respond with respect because of someone's position or age. The attitude that others hear through the words shows respect, acceptance, and graciousness.

A patronizing attitude, on the other hand, comes through in facial expressions, sighs, knowing winks, or direct comments that "excuse" the other person: "Of course, operators, we don't expect you to be able to understand the inner workings of these machines. We'll worry about a failure should that occur." The attitude that shows through the words or gesture is patient tolerance and superiority.

TIP 86: Avoid False Courtesy.

"Do you mind if I speak up?" "May I say something?" "If you'll allow me to state an opinion . . ." "If you're open to suggestions, I think . . ." "Not that my opinion is worth much to you, but . . ." Such phrasing has nothing to do with courtesy; it's thinly masked hostility.

TIP 87: Get People's Attention First if You Really Want Them to Hear You.

Conversation is common. If you want people really to pay attention to what you're saying, you have to rise above the norm. Here are four options:

Make a sudden move. If you're sitting in the doctor's waiting room reading a magazine and somebody beside you stands up, you automatically look up—even if you know who that person is and why he or she is standing up. Movement attracts attention. If you want someone who seems preoccupied to listen to you, stand up and move across the room to speak. Lean forward at the table to present your ideas. If you're standing in the hallway, ask the person to follow you to a seat. Just move.

Repeat. If you're puzzled by a road sign, you reread it—maybe several times. People sometimes need more than one hearing before things sink in. Repetition is the backbone of commercials. Repeat several times in several ways what you want to be heard.

Be novel. People have short attention spans. If you want to extend their attention beyond the typical 20 seconds, you have to get your point across in a unique way. Be flippant, make a joke, startle them with an aggressive statement, make a gross overstatement or understatement, use a unique analogy, or carry on two sides of a dialogue. Just be novel to expand their attention to your idea.

Be emotional. What people let slide when spoken softly they'll hear when underscored with a little emotion. Raise your volume, soften your volume, plead, cry, or laugh. Emotion attracts attention to straightforward statements.

TIP 88: When Constantly Interrupted, Stop Talking Immediately and Abruptly to Make the Interrupter Aware of What He or She Is Doing.

You can also use courtesy and lightly call attention to someone's habit of cutting you off with statements like: "Pardon me, I'm not finished." "May I finish this thought?" I didn't get to finish what I was saying." "I need another few seconds to explain why I feel that way." "I didn't get to elaborate a moment ago about my reasons." Making people aware that they're crowding you makes a dramatic impact on them without sounding rude.

TIP 89: Don't Step on Others' Sentences.

Sometimes we're so closely identifying with or confirming what the other person is saying that we want to jump right in while they're expressing themselves. That rapport-building identification should not concern you. But you want to watch habitually crowding others when they speak: not giving them an opportunity to respond, interrupting them when they're clearly not finished, talking over them with an intent to dominate.

Once it becomes a habit to step on others' statements, it's hard to help yourself. And some people are not so gracious as to let you get away with it. If you catch yourself frequently interrupting people, get someone to help you with the annoying habit. Ask that person to signal you with a raised hand or the sliced-throat gesture to make you aware when you cut them or other people off.

TIP 90: Signal the Other Person When You Receive a Message.

On occasion, the most hurtful response is no response—particularly when the other person has shared deep feelings. At home, probably more often than at work, we are tempted to "sit tight" on a message and not acknowledge that we heard.

> WIFE: I think we should take a four-day weekend soon.
>
> HUSBAND: (*Silence.*)
>
> WIFE: It has been six months since we've been away together.
>
> HUSBAND: (*Silence.*)
>
> WIFE: What do you think?
>
> HUSBAND: Okay, okay, okay. I'll check my calendar tomorrow. What do you expect me to do about it tonight?

The husband doesn't realize that he escalated the conversation simply because he gave no acknowledgment that he heard the first comment. Acknowledge another person's comment to you and you'll be surprised how the "nagging" from a boss or spouse stops.

TIP 91: Avoid Playing Tour Guide Through Your Own Conversation.

This habit surfaces after each statement: "Am I not right?" "Correct?" "You follow me?" "You understand?" "Okay?" "With me?" "Clear to this point?" Such hand-holding comments lend an air of false patience with a slow learner.

TIP 92: Give Glib Reassurance Sparingly.

"Don't worry, it'll turn around for you." "You win some, you lose some." "Aw, they'll come around—give it a week or two." In effect, a comment such as "We'll work it out later" often means "I don't want to get into that discussion, so let's change the subject" or "I've got problems of my own right now and don't have time for yours." Such comments cut people off from feeling understood.

If they felt it necessary to pass on the problem or concern, they'd like the chance to go into the details. It's not that they're necessarily looking for a solution; they may simply want to feel that someone appreciates the difficulties they're facing. They may need moral support that doesn't come through thoughtless clichés. Such support comes from having someone understand the circumstances.

TIP 93: Develop Your Memory. Those Who Forget What Others Tell Them Make People Angry.

Yes, you can blame some forgetfulness on age. As we grow older, we need more memory cues; but most of us forget because we don't make an effort to remember. We tell ourselves things like, "I'm not good at remembering names" or "I'm a little fuzzy on the details, but I never forget a face." These attitudes are nothing more than permission to ourselves to forget.

Practice remembering things by forcing yourself to note details and then recalling them later, just for the heck of it. Memorize axioms, quotations, number sequences, or instructions to exercise your memory muscles. Use mnemonic devices such as repetition, rhymes, acronyms, acrostics, or chain-linking as an aid. I make up sentences out of such cues and recite the sentence until I manage to find a scrap of paper on which to dump the information. My best ideas come when I'm listening to self-help audios while exercising.

Why do we remember some things and not others? Because of the relative value we attach to the information. For example, if someone throws you a "lead" (someone you should call who might be interested in buying your product), you'll remember the name—dollar signs are attached. When you receive certain information, you immediately have to attach some importance to it so that you advance that data to long-term memory. Otherwise, you'll throw it out with the rest of the memory trash in a matter of moments. Simply be more conscious about what you want to retain as you take it into your head.

Do, however, continue to dump your memory trash daily. There's no use cluttering your memory with things you can record somewhere and retrieve at will from paper or the computer. And once you get to paper, record things; people who have good memories never trust them. But because they've attached a value, forced the information into long-term memory, and have taken the extra step to write something down, their memories take over and they rarely have to refer to the written record again.

TIP 94: Don't Tell Others What They Already Know.

Yes, you can repeat for emphasis, but don't state the obvious. Examples: "I see you've already called a taxi." "You're limping." "The cord has to be plugged in before it will work." "Statistics can be misleading." "We're experiencing a lot of change during this downsizing."

TIP 95: Don't Overload Yourself with Information to the Point of Distortion.

Yes, your brain is a complex computer, but even computers run out of storage space. If you've attended a meeting or listened to a tape where information floods you, stop long enough to digest what you've heard before you lose everything.

TIP 96: Don't Overload Your Listener with Data That Has to Be Processed Before Being Usable.

Raw computer printouts of numbers are of little use to the senior executive unfamiliar to reading such data in that format. Most people find themselves in similar situations. To be usable, information has to be interpreted. Don't tell me that most of the salespeople in your territory sell an annual volume of $700,000. Is that high? Low? Typical of the industry? An incredibly successful job? Cause for alarm? Interpret.

TIP 97: Relate the Unknown to the Known.

It's difficult for most of us to understand the national debt. However, a newspaper reporter used the following analogy to bring the debt into perspective: If Ross Perot were a corporation, he'd rank as number 223 on *Fortune*'s list. If he were financing the national debt, he'd be penniless in three days. Now that's understandable.

Talk about health care in terms of football injuries if you're addressing high school students. Relate the inner workings of a spacecraft to that of a car for people at General Motors. If you're talking to dietitians, put the quality movement in terms of meatloaf.

TIP 98: Make Information Easy to Access.

When my son finished his college degree in business analysis with computers, he was anxious to show me what those tuition checks produced. He volunteered to set up a more functional inventory system at our company. When finished, he handed me a binder with a copy of all reports the system could produce, along with a written description. Exasperated that I seemed to have difficulty remembering what data each report showed, he decided to set up the report menu with questions: "What is the price for each video?" "Which titles need to be reordered when?" "How many copies have we sold of audio X in the last two years?" Finally, we were speaking the same language.

That's what I mean by making information easy and accessible. In any given situation, that may mean the labels you attach, the language you use, or the method (spoken, E-mail, written, satellite, or manual) you choose.

TIP 99: Reduce the Number of Interpreters.

Consider how often instructions get distorted when they pass through several people on the way to the user. Recently, I asked an assistant to check on prices and procedures for some photography: sitting fees for portraits, number of poses, makeup and wardrobe staff, product shots, and mass duplication for both color and black-and-whites of both portraits and products. My assistant had to talk to the photographer's receptionist, who talked to the photographer, who talked to the studio manager, who talked to corporate headquarters, who talked to their freelancers, who talked to the mass-duplication vendor—who then relayed all the answers back down the line. Needless to say, the answers we finally got did not match the questions.

TIP 100: Interpret Facts and Statistics Rather Than Serving Them Raw.

In a recent meeting with a speaking bureau, I overheard someone discussing a meeting planner's $80,000 budget for an upcoming convention. One account executive commented, "Speaker Smith charges $5000 for a keynote speech." (Meaning: *Maybe we should recommend him to the meeting planner, who will be delighted to get such a good speaker at such a low cost.*) The second account executive commented, "Yeah, you're right; the client will think the guy's no good unless his fee is at least $10,000. Maybe we should recommend Speaker Jones."

Statistics get jumbled even easier than facts. Our survey indicates employees want more control over discretionary vacation days and more time off during the 8-to-5 day. Twenty-nine percent said they wanted "More control" and half said "more time off." Is that half of the total displeased employees? Or half of 29 percent? Or are 79 percent displeased about vacation and time off? How displeased? How many vacation weeks did the typical displeased respondent have this year? What were the other survey questions and answers?

Statistics and facts do not speak for themselves. They need interpretation.

TIP 101: Get Acronyms and Abbreviations Right.

Some people pepper their conversation with acronyms and other technical jargon to let their audience know they're one of the "in group" and to sound knowledgeable. That's good—if they're accurate. But nothing makes an individual look more foolish than to be throwing around an acronym like an insider when they've got the letters reversed.

TIP 102: Don't Use Jargon As Snobbery.

For some, jargon is an attempt to show superiority, to exclude others, or to confuse others. Take it as a sign of insecurity and a cover-up for not being able to communicate at the appropriate level with a larger, lay group of people. In today's workplace, we're all technical—only on different subjects. Not knowing how to step over the boundaries of one's own jargon-filled job to express an idea so others understand is an inadequacy to be overcome, not a sign of superior intelligence or know-how.

TIP 103: Avoid "As You Are Aware" Statements Intended As Put-Downs.

People sometimes use such a phrase, knowing that the listener is not aware. The phrase often implies superiority and directs attention to their difference in knowledge of the subject. Anytime you purposely make another person feel unknowledgeable, he or she will be looking for an opportunity to return the dig.

TIP 104: Use the Simple Word When the Simple Word Will Do.

Why do otherwise intelligent people use the biggest word possible to express a simple idea? Take your choice: They're trying to show off their education; they're trying to impress someone they think is more educated than they are; they are trying to obscure rather than clarify; they feel it's their responsibility to enlarge everyone else's vocabulary; they're trying to build their own vocabulary by practicing a new word. Mark Twain said, "I never write 'metropolis' when I can get the same price for 'city.' " Good writers and orators have known for centuries the value of using the simple word. In Lincoln's Gettysburg address, of the total 268 words, 190 have only one syllable.

TIP 105: Substitute New Words Permanently for Those You Can't Pronounce.

When I was taping an audio series for Nightingale-Conant, I discovered—after about 10 tries with the producer over my shoulder—that I can't pronounce the word *error.* So I've learned to live happily ever after; I say *mistake.*

An acquaintance of mine misspeaks *relevant;* instead she says "revelant" and seems unaware of the mispronunciation. Ask a trusted friend to point out such mispronunciations in your own conversations so you can make a permanent correction or substitution.

TIP 106: Select Powerful Verbs.

Verbs carry the weight of your thought. Don't bury them or string them out.

Lackluster: I don't know if the test results are conclusive.

Powerful: I doubt the validity of the test.

Lackluster: This is an exciting product line for our customers.

Powerful: These products will excite our customers.

Lackluster: We should offer a higher level of service even if we have to charge customers more for that service.

Powerful: I recommend better service at a higher cost.

TIP 107: Cut Adjective and Adverb Clutter.

"Haste makes waste." These are words of fact, or at least they sound like fact. Nouns and verbs bear the weight of your message. "Too much speed in carrying out tasks results in extra time being spent to redo things that were done inefficiently to begin with." These are words of opinion, adjectives and adverbs. "You should carefully consider a variety of alternatives" sounds stronger this way: "Consider your alternatives."

Unless you intend to hedge, develop the habit of speaking with nouns and verbs, omitting descriptive words when possible. They weaken your words—just like pouring water into tea.

TIP 108: Avoid "et cetera" and Other Substitutes for Lazy Thinking.

When you cite a list of things, objects, procedures, or activities, don't use a catchall phrase such as "et cetera," and then add on phrases such as "any way, shape, or form," "by any means whatsoever," "by any manner or means," "other similar situations, or "other considerations too numerous to mention." *Et cetera* has a precise meaning: in the same manner. Correct use: "10, 20, 30, 40, et cetera." The et cetera means "continue numbering as in this pattern." It doesn't mean, "and-what-have-you stuff I don't want to take the time to say." Question yourself as to whether you're throwing in a phrase as a substitute for thinking long enough to be precise.

TIP 109: Rid Yourself of Junk Words.

"Sort of," "a lot," "okay," "right," "type of," "more or less," "you know what I mean," and "you get the picture" add fat and sugar to the communication menu. They lead to a vocabulary deficiency in conversation.

TIP 110: Be Specific.

Tasks go uncompleted, questions fail to get answered, and promises are broken often because people are not mind readers. Nonspecificity causes more customer-service problems than defective products ever could.

Other examples of mind-reading exercises: "I'd like you to do research into this problem and propose solution by the end of the month." Does this boss want a lengthy questionnaire distributed to all employees? Want to hire a market research firm for an industry survey? Want to telephone a few key supervisors involved with the problem?

"You did a great job!" What was great? The analysis? The fact that I kept it under budget? The customer's reaction?

"Give me some feedback on the seminar." Bluntly? Diplomatically? Did it help me personally? Do I think others from the department should attend? Did I think it was worth the cost? How helpful or entertaining were the speakers?

Such requests and statements grope in the darkness of abstraction. Notice improvement in the following:

Nonspecific: When you talk so rudely to me, . . .

Specific: When you tell me I'm fat, . . .

Nonspecific: When you don't talk to me, . . .

Specific: When you don't talk to me about your work projects, . . .

Nonspecific: You don't seem to care about your work anymore.

Specific: You have missed four deadlines this month.

Nonspecific: Do you know why you can't get along with people?

Specific: We've had three people ask to be removed from your team. Do you know why?

TIP 111: Push Other People to Be Specific.

Don't overlook the most straightforward approach to get people to be specific so you can understand what they mean. Use some of the following probes: "Could you be more specific?" "Please fill me in on the details." "Do you have a particular situation in mind?" "Can you give me a specific example of what happens?" "For instance?" "Such as X or Y?" "How many are you talking about?" "To what extent is that the case in your department?" "Can you put a percent to it?" "Can you give me a specific number to work with?" "When does that happen?" "Where is that happening?" "How is that happening?" "Why is that happening?" "Who exactly is involved?" "So what's your assessment of the situation?" "So what exactly do you want me to do?"

You'll be surprised at the gulf between first mention and the answer to these probing specifics.

TIP 112: Choose Precise Words.

We demand precision in most professional situations. A doctor uses the exact scalpel size to perform an appendectomy. A pharmacist fills a prescription to the exact gram. A machinist runs the lathe to the one-hundredth of an inch. Even a Sunday driver has to stop behind the white line at the intersection. Yet we often accept communication as an "art," an imprecise activity that can't possibly be error-proofed. Reexamine the idea that just any word will do. Choose the most precise words and you may be surprised how little rework is required.

TIP 113: Use Concrete Words Rather Than Abstract Ones.

Concrete words describe those activities, objects, or people you can visualize: *car, house, pocketbook, teenager.* Abstract words can be used in so many contexts that their meanings becomes muddled: *Meaningful results, on-the-job crises, employee freedom, management support*—each of these phrases will have different meanings to different people in different situations. Many people find themselves in arguments when their words are so vague they don't realize they actually agree.

A husband says to his new bride, "Honey, I really want a large family."

She looks a little apprehensive. "Uhhh, I was thinking small."

He says, "But large families have more fun. Kids help each other out. They learn to give and take. And sacrifice for each other. And holidays are so much fun with a houseful."

She says, "Yeah, but small families are nice, too. The relationships are closer, more intimate. And the kids have to get along—there's nobody else to run to. And you can afford to give them a better education. All the advantages."

He says, "I'm disappointed that you feel that way."

"Me, too. I . . . didn't know you felt that strongly. I guess we should have discussed how many kids we wanted before we got married."

The next day on the golf course he complains that his wife won't agree to three kids. She calls her mother to confide that two kids is all she can handle. Two? Three? One extra toothbrush between a large family and a small one? Large and small are relative terms.

Prefer concrete words to abstract ones.

TIP 114: Beware of Misleading with Connotation and Denotation.

Is a "feisty" woman powerful or amusing? Is a "hulk of a man" intimidating, forceful, or just big? Is an "adequate performance" worth a raise or does it need improvement? The denotation of a word is the dictionary definition. The connotation of a word is the associated meaning given in context and with culture.

Between denotative and connotative definitions, there's a world of misinterpretation and swayed opinion. Of great concern to social scientists is that the use or misuse of a single word can change the entire results of an opinion poll. If you intend to lead others to your way of thinking subtly, select your words carefully. If you prefer a neutral opinion, select the denotative word or phrase.

Denotation	*Connotation*
house	home, hovel
price	investment, fee
agreement	opportunity, contract
low cost	a real value, cheap
temporary	alternative, makeshift
strong	tenacious, obstinate
initial	pioneering, primitive
odorous	fragrant, foul-smelling
change	stimulate, agitate

firm	confident, opinionated
satisfactory	ample, adequate
end	finish, abort

TIP 115: Make Semantics a Big Concern.

People often use a disclaimer such as "well, that's just semantics" to downplay the importance of their word choice. Don't you get a completely different message from each of the following versions?

"Robert is meeting with the lawyers this afternoon."

"The lawyers are meeting with Robert this afternoon."

"The lawyers and Robert have scheduled a meeting this afternoon."

"Both Robert and the lawyers are getting together on this issue this afternoon."

Who initiated the meeting? Is it formal or informal? Will the decision be official or not? Is Robert in trouble? Much of the interpretation comes from the word choice—semantics.

"How was the seminar?" Answer: "Not bad." Isn't "not bad" a different message than "quite good"?

Entire businesses have renamed their employee titles because of the crucial importance of semantics to convey new management philosophy: from "salespeople" to "consultants" to "associates." Semantics is no small matter.

TIP 116: Remember That Personal Experience Affects Interpretation.

I grew up on a cotton farm in the south, where we defoliated for boll weevils and other vermin regularly. As a preteen driving across country with my family on vacation, someone pointed out the car window to a "flea market." I glanced at the warehouse-looking structure, expecting to see a breeding lot for fleas.

When I use the word "storage facilities" in Houston writing workshops, people interpret "oil tanks." In Silicon Valley, they think disk space.

TIP 117: Remember That Meaning Comes from Context.

When a patient in the mental hospital says to you "I want to go home," you don't necessarily take it seriously or try to help get the paperwork and permissions completed. However, when a college student is talking about "going home" for the holidays, you feel supportive and offer encouragement. When a manager wants to "go home" after a long day of work, you know the trip is short and that he or she will be back the following day. When a psychologist talks about "going home" mentally to heal childhood wounds, you may begin a new thought process that lasts for years. Meaning doesn't come from words. Meaning depends on who says the words to whom, when, and for what purpose. The more common the word, the more meanings it likely has.

TIP 118: Don't Attach Too Much Significance to a Less Than Well-Chosen Word Used Carelessly.

Have you ever caught yourself stewing over one little word in a bigger context? Turning that one word over and over in your mind and chewing it up for all the misery it provides? Let's say your spouse says, "We've got briefcases and paperwork all over the house. This fit you've been in over that Delco project is wrecking your entire schedule. You're bringing more and more work home lately."

Response? "Fit, huh? So he thinks it's a fit, huh? I'd like to see him keep his cool if he were in my shoes!" The word "fit" sets you off. A better-chosen word might have been "dither" or "predicament." You've got a choice—take the comment for its full context and message or play off the one poorly chosen word that brings up an entirely different message and emotion.

When pinched with the poor word, don't blow the comment out of proportion. Consider the entire context.

TIP 119: Use Honest Words.

Have you ever read a tourist brochure enticing you to a vacation getaway that disappointed you? Once there, you understand that "sun-drenched" meant "hot," that "tucked away in the valley" meant "inaccessible except by donkey," that "relaxed atmosphere" meant "no room service," that "surrounded by water activities" meant "two lakes with a paddle boat," that "moderately priced" meant "creaky furniture and no maid service."

Be as honest with your words as with your pocketbook.

TIP 120: Never Say *Never, None, All, Everything, Totally, Constantly.*

When you use one of these words, the other person will typically focus on the exception rather than the general rule you meant to discuss.

Assessment: "You never come home in time for dinner with the rest of the family."

Response: "I don't know what you mean. Last Thursday I was home in the middle of the afternoon."

Assessment: "You always complain about where we eat lunch, Harry."

Response: "No, I don't. Yesterday we ate seafood. I hate it but didn't say a thing."

Assessment: "You're constantly late with your status reports."

Response: "I don't know what you're talking about. I turned it in a week early in June."

You'll be focused on the exception rather than the real issue that needs attention.

TIP 121: Minimize Times When You Have to Use *Should, Must, Will, Ought* Statements.

All four words sound abrupt, intimidating, even condescending in situations where you might be perceived as "telling people what to do." Even if you intend your comment only as friendly advice, the words make listeners feel inadequate or stupid somehow, as if they should have known better or acted wiser. These "hot" words make people say "Oh, yeah? Who are you to tell me what I should/must/will/ought to do?" Even if you do have to tell someone what to do, why not wear a velvet glove rather than a boxing glove?

TIP 122: Recognize Weasel Words As Escape Hatches.

Zero in on the little words that slip into sentences: *maybe, possibly, could, sometimes, wish, may possibly cause, could attribute to, seems to, appears to be, might be a consideration.* The most frequent customer-service problems involve what the customer considers "unkept promises." When there's a problem, customer-service reps insist they never made the promise that customers thought they heard. Service reps focus on the "may," "might," or "sometimes," and customers overlook such hedge words.

When you're on the receiving end of promises, question people about the escape words they use. When you're on the giving end, state as much as you can verify or promise—no more and no less. Of course, you can't state absolutes that aren't absolutes. But realize that such words and phrases drain the power from your claims; predictably, people pounce on them.

TIP 123: Don't Destroy Your Position with Disclaimers.

A consulting firm that inspects property in distant cities for potential investors and then sends them a report on the condition of the property asked me to review some of their reports for format, organization, and persuasive appeal. After reading the first few, my reaction was, "Why would I hire this firm for an opinion?" The boilerplate reports included an appendix full of disclaimers saying in effect, "We make no judgments about the investment value of this property." The numerous disclaimers invalidated the contents and value of the rest of the report!

We often do the same thing in conversation: "You're not going to agree with what I'm about to say . . ." Therefore, we set up the conversation so that what follows sounds invalid and full of holes.

TIP 124: Avoid Ending Every Statement with a Question.

"I thought the speaker was boring, didn't you?" "The lounge should be renovated also, don't you think?" "The customer knew of the price increase, right?" "Let's hold the meeting outside the city, what do you think?" Tag questions at the end of statements make people sound tentative and unsure of their opinions or facts.

TIP 125: Recognize the Royal "We" As an Epithet.

When someone doesn't want to own up to decisions, he or she can always hide behind a committee decision. "We have decided this benefit is an unnecessary expense." "I have decided . . ." takes more courage. Leaders use it to own their decisions; managers frequently shun it to avoid accountability and repercussions of their decisions. Others notice the distinction.

TIP 126: Pay Attention to the Stress on Words.

Notice how the meaning of this sentence varies as I change the stressed (italicized) word(s).

Rosita said Sonya heard the committee arguing about the decision.

Rosita said Sonya heard the committee arguing about the decision.

Rosita *said* Sonya heard the committee arguing about the decision.

Rosita said *Sonya* heard the committee arguing about the decision.

Rosita said Sonya *heard* the committee arguing about the decision.

Rosita said Sonya heard *the committee* arguing about the decision.

Rosita said Sonya heard the committee *arguing* about the decision.

Rosita said Sonya heard the committee arguing *about the decision.*

Inflection may carry the message. Learn to recognize the stress in your words and those spoken by others.

TIP 127: Eliminate Redundancies.

Here's a list to start your thinking. Choose one or the other, but not both: fitting and proper, workable and feasible, absolutely and positively, accurate and correct, beneficial and helpful, hazardous and unsafe, the sick and unhealthy, the disadvantaged and underprivileged, the powerful and elite, serious crisis, important essentials, desirable benefits, basic fundamentals, final outcome, separate and distinct, alternate choices, past history, joint partnership, advance warning. And the list goes on with each nightly news broadcast.

TIP 128: Grapple with Grammar.

Here are the common mistakes and a shortcut or simple rule to help you avoid each:

Correct misused verbs.   Gone-went, do-don't-doesn't, lie-lay, sit-set, affect-effect, was-were.

Use "-ly" on adverbs.   The boss writes quickly. They decided promptly. The committee meets regularly.

Differentiate between good and well.   *Good* describes an object, place, idea, person, thing. *Well* describes how something performs: Fido is a good dog. Fido eats well.

Drop unnecessary prepositions on the end of sentences.   *Not:* "Where's the paper at?" *But:* "Where's the paper?" *Not:* "These are the designs I worked on." *But:* "I worked on these designs." *Not:* "Which team is Harry on?" *But:* "Harry is on which team?" *Not:* "Where did the contract go to?" *But:* "Where did the contract go?" Some prepositions sound fine at the end of sentences; others sound limp. Let clarity be your guide.

Eliminate double negatives.   The following words mean no/not/negative; use only one of them in any sentence: *no, not, never, none, no one, nowhere.*

Choose correct pronouns. When you come to a confusing sentence using *who* or *whom,* here's a trick: Substitute *he* or *she* for *who* and *him* or *her* for *whom* and you'll make the right choice. When the choice involves a list of other people, leave out the other names and you'll choose *me/I, he/him, she/her, us/we* correctly. Example: "Give the order to Jim, Joanne, or me." Leave out Jim and Joanne: "Give the order to me." It's a fail-safe system for choosing correctly.

TIP 129: Use Poor Grammar Only for an Intended Effect.

Ain't can mean "I'm just one of you people—forget I'm the regional VP." Don't use it when you're not sure if your audience knows that you know better. Make a conscious choice for an intended effect. Then think about it twice more.

TIP 130: Use Up-to-Date Slang.

Nothing makes a 40-year-old manager look more foolish than using teenage slang. And the problem with picking up slang from your kids is that as soon as you've learned it, they've changed it. Either stay "with it" or give up the effort and speak plain English.

TIP 131: Overcome Sloppy Diction.

Watch dropping the ends of words, running words together, and otherwise making it difficult for people to understand you. If you've ever dialed a company and had a receptionist respond as unintelligibly as a robot on fast-forward you understand the irritation.

TIP 132: Avoid Being So Overly Precise That You Sound Like a Stuffed Shirt.

We shall? We will? He proceeded to tell me? He continued? Is it I? Is it me? Let clarity versus awkwardness be your guide. Of course, proper grammar is important, but remember that grammar rules are not static. Usages become archaic. And some things people remember as "rules" never to be broken have never been rules at all; they are matters of style. Such word choices and phrasing may make your conversation or your writing seem awkward and stiff. Be precise in meaning and proper in grammar where clarity is concerned, but less formal in matters of style.

TIP 133: Use Your Speaking Voice, Not Your Writing Voice.

As a rule, talkers *include* the people; writers *remove* the people. After conducting business and technical writing courses for the past 14 years for corporate clients, I've discovered that people have two voices: a writing voice and a talking voice. They'll say to you, "I suggest that we terminate the project." You say, "Why don't you put that in a memo for me." A week later you receive the memo, which says, "It is recommended that this project be terminated." Who suggested it?

Another difference: writers also use a stiffer vocabulary than talkers. A salesperson will say on the telephone, "I'll check to see if we have that rocker in stock and call you back next week," then write, "Your preference for item #AG349 has been received. After verification of the availability of that merchandise, you will be notified no later than September 12 as to whether your order can be processed immediately." You'll notice that the salesperson used the coldest, longest, vaguest word possible for each concept.

If you want a helpful technique for testing the proper voice, read your own documents aloud. If they sound stilted to your own ear, they will sound the same way to someone else's. If you want to know if your talking voice sounds stilted at a cocktail party, see if people "tighten up" around you. Do they check their own slang, colloquialisms, and lively banter and slink off as if they'd been chastened?

TIP 134: Speak with the Appropriate Formality or Informality.

After some introductions, "Hello, how are you?" is appropriate. Others call for a "Hi. Nice to meet you folks." Colloquialisms like "we've been fightin' this tooth and nail" are in order in some groups, not so with other groups. To be unduly stiff in your word choice can be as inappropriate as showing up at McDonald's in a tux or arriving at the symphony in cutoffs.

TIP 135: Take Cues About First-Name/Last-Name Preference from How the Other Person Answers the Telephone.

Assuming that everyone welcomes being called by first name is arrogance to the powerful and a put-down to the lower-level employee. Using their last names may set up a formal, impersonal tone to some people. Far more women are called by their first names than men, particularly comparing those with titles such as "Dr." It is generally up to the people of higher status/position to give permission to lower-status individuals to use their first names. They are announcing equality, an act that by its very nature underscores their power and status.

To know others' preferences, listen to how they answer their own telephones: First name only? Last name only? Both first and last? If still unsure, ask them politely what they prefer. Err on the side of formality.

TIP 136: Recognize Name-Dropping As an Attempt to Gain Status.

Dropping names of the great, the near-great, the powerful and the near-powerful sends a message to listeners that the speaker is making a stab at gaining admiration and increasing his or her own stature by association. It's really a self-belittling move.

TIP 137: Avoid Sexist Language.

Eliminate nouns that are gender-specific and metaphors understood primarily by only one gender: for example, football analogies to women or ballet analogies to men. Use police officer rather than policeman, flight attendant rather than stewardess, chair rather than chairman. All colonels are not male, and all secretaries are not female.

Suggestions: (1) Prefer speaking or writing the plural rather than to omit half the human race. *Not:* "An employee will need *his* badge to get into the building." *But:* "Employees will need *their* badges to get into the building." (2) Alternate references between the genders. (3) Omit the pronouns altogether: "An employee will need a badge to get into the building."

TIP 138: Know the Value of Understatement.

When you overstate the case, others start digging for the gaps. If you don't believe it, notice your reaction the next time someone says to you, "The most bizarre thing just happened. Hilarious. You won't believe it. This person walks in and . . ." The typical reaction after such a lead-in is a letdown. A that-wasn't-so-funny/bizarre reaction. We're set up for disappointment.

As a speaker, I'd much rather the introducer understate the benefits he or she expects my audience to gain than to overstate them. Otherwise, I'm traveling uphill.

TIP 139: Don't Exaggerate.

Did you get 22 calls or 6 on the ad? Did you have a "fabulous" job offer, or was it adequate enough to make you consider a move? Was the warehouse barrel "smoldering," or did it go up in flames and destroy valuable merchandise? Exaggeration for a good story is acceptable; people understand "creating the mood" to generate a good laugh.

But when people exaggerate routinely, over time they destroy their credibility. Others will not accept "problems" as problems. They'll not greet "successes" as successes. They'll not use "facts" as facts.

TIP 140: Fight the Urge to Top Off the Tank.

Just as though topping off the gas tank before heading cross-country, some people feel as though they have to "top off" everybody else's point. They always have a "can-you-top-this?" story after everyone else's. A funnier joke. A worse problem. A heavier workload. Fight the urge to always top what anybody says.

TIP 141: Avoid Overqualifying.

Have you ever walked into a lawyer's office and asked his or her opinion about whether you should go to court on a particular issue? And after an hour, you walk away still not knowing the lawyer's expert opinion? That's because some lawyers fear making an outright statement or judgment that may come back to haunt them. They fear being taken out of context. They fear being misquoted. They fear that the consequences will be more severe than they predicted. Some people walk that same legal tightrope on every issue. Nothing is a yes-or-no question. It all depends. . . .

TIP 142: Cut Long Prefaces to Your Points.

Ever since we learned the oral book report in the school system, we have tended to start at the beginning. We catch a colleague in the hallway: "Hey, I've got a great idea; you're going to love it. First, let me give you a little background." Wrong approach. Your colleague will never understand your background until he or she has the point. Prefaces confuse and lose people.

TIP 143: Avoid "Speaking with Footnotes."

Don't let yourself get sidetracked on minor issues. My grandfather's stories rambled on in this fashion: "The other day—I guess it was Wednesday—no it must have been Tuesday because that's the day I went by to feed the horses—one of Harold's boys came over, or maybe it was his cousin. Name's Christopher. About six years old. And Harold had told him not to cross the street by himself. Of course, he plays out in the front all the time, but there's usually somebody at home to watch him. Well, they weren't bidding much on my horses that day. . . ." You get the picture. When you know a great deal about your subject, it's tempting to continue to toss in tidbits, but remember that people follow a straight path easier than a circuitous one. Where do you want to lead them? Go straight there. If they want an excursion later, they'll ask.

TIP 144: Self-Edit Your "Thinking" Details.

Some people talk through details to analyze a situation and by the time they come to the end of their discussion, they know what they think. The problem with that process is that others may not want to follow the same thinking route. They typically prefer that you cut to the chase.

Maybe the habit of dumping the details comes from being graded on the curve in the school system. The more students recite or write, the greater the evidence they've read the assignment and the better the resulting grade. Not so in conversation.

TIP 145: Unwind Motormouths.

When people who have a reputation for long-windedness ask, "Do you have a minute?" agree with their phrasing: "Yes, I do have about three minutes before I have to make a call/attend a meeting/get back to my project." You've put them on notice that your time is not unlimited while saying "yes" to them.

A second technique involves continually bringing them back to their point. "So what was it you wanted to tell me about the insurance form?" "I'm not following what this has to do with the issue of X." "So, can you help me on the Y problem?"

Finally, you can always interrupt their monologue with a brief question that elicits a one-word answer from them. Then when they interrupt themselves to answer your question, you have regained the floor.

TIP 146: Use the One-Minute Gag Rule.

If you speak for longer than one minute at a turn without giving the other person a chance to respond, chances are great that you're becoming long-winded and that you're going to lose the other's attention. Make it a habit to relinquish the floor every 60 seconds until someone invites you to continue.

TIP 147: Distinguish Succinctness from Bluntness.

The difference is tone. Yes, you want to be succinct with the details, to choose words well. But a one-word answer often sounds blunt, curt, insolent, surly, discourteous. At best, it can be misinterpreted or unclear. Add a sentence elaboration just for the sake of tone, if not clarity.

> CALLER 1: Do these staplers come in black?
> CALLER 2: No. (*Sufficient, but blunt.*)

> CALLER 1: Do these staplers come in black?
> CALLER 2: No. They come only in gray and brown. (*Succinct.*)

> CALLER 1: What did you think of his report?
> CALLER 2: Boring. Long. (*Sufficient, but blunt.*)

> CALLER 1: What did you think of his report?
> CALLER 2: It contained little of value to me personally but others found useful information in it. (*Succinct.*)

TIP 148: Challenge the Expert When the Expert Is Obnoxious.

Try a little splash of irreverence. Instead of holding court with the rest of the admirers, confront an obnoxious expert with the confusion created: "I'm sorry, but you lost me." "Can you explain this so that someone outside your field can understand it?" "I'm afraid I couldn't agree to something I don't understand. I need to have an explanation without the jargon, the abbreviations, and the footnotes." If such directness doesn't persuade the know-it-all to be clearer, question him or her until you get the answers you need. After enough interruptions like, "What does that mean?" "So what does that refer to?" "So why is that number significant?" most will usually come down off their lofty perch and speak plain English.

TIP 149: Judge People's Content, Not Their Delivery.

We've all heard stories about the shabbily dressed "guest" who turns out to be the owner of the entire hotel chain. We know that physical appearances can be deceiving—whether athletic ability, political clout, or riches are concerned. However, we fail to remind ourselves of the same principle in conversation. The shop supervisor who suggests a new assembly process may pepper his or her speech with poor grammar, stammering sentences, and repetitious details but come up with many money-saving ideas. Try to pay attention to content without being distracted by delivery.

TIP 150: Don't Reject Out of Hand What Someone Is Saying Solely Because the Words They Use Seem Technically Incorrect.

Many people know what they mean—they just can't say it well. For example, a prospective client called me one day to ask if I spoke on negotiation. Just before I started to tell him no and refer him to a colleague better known for "negotiation" programs, I decided to probe further. After he began to elaborate his objectives for the meeting he was planning, it became clear that he really wanted a talk on *persuasion* for his salespeople in the audience. They needed to be able to use both logic and emotion to consult with their own customers about their needs and then persuade them that their company was the best provider of the product or the service. Big difference. But I almost missed a profitable engagement by simply taking his term "negotiation" at first blush without investigating.

TIP 151: Resist the Urge to Nitpick.

"I read in the paper this morning that something like 16 banks have gone under in Texas alone this year." Response: "Yeah, I saw that. Actually, it was 18."

"I heard Janie resigned to go back into advertising—Chicago firm, I think." Response: "She's been wanting to get back in the ad biz for years. The job was in Pittsburgh, she said."

The correction may be subtle or overt. The effect is the same. People feel "corrected." Well they may be, but they won't necessarily appreciate it. Avoid the temptation to nitpick about facts that don't matter.

TIP 152: Avoid One-Up Phrases.

These one-ups are common put-downs: "Oh, didn't you already know that—I guess I should have told you." "It may be of interest to you that . . ." "I guess you had no way of knowing, but . . ." "As you'll soon discover . . ."

TIP 153: If You Must Correct Someone, Do So Gently.

If you think you must correct someone's statistics or "facts"—that they would be glad to know the exact, correct number, name, or location—then do so with tact. Try these tactful turns: "The actual figure is X; however, your conclusions are exactly right" or "You've interpreted very closely; only one minor correction; the location was Y" or "It was my understanding that X is the exact figure, but you're so right about Y" or "I read an updated report on that today; the final story is that . . ."

TIP 154: Don't Make Judging Other People a Hobby.

People-watching can be an amusing pastime—how they walk, how they talk, how they dress, how they eat, how they work. But passing on judgments can cast the commentator in a bad light: "Look at her jacket. Browns and taupes have been out of style for at least three years" or "Look at the way he cocks his head to the left when he talks to people. He always comes across as such a know-it-all" or "Her desk looks like a cyclone hits it every weekend. No wonder she's always asking for an extension on her deadlines. She's just plain disorganized."

Yes, we all make personal observations about people, but voicing them to others can be habit-forming.

TIP 155: Avoid Doormat Statements.

Common routines: "Nothing is wrong, and I don't want to talk about it." (Meaning: "Something is wrong, but I want you to have to wait to know what it is.") "Don't bother about me—I'll be okay." (Meaning: "Please consider me.") "I guess I'll have to live with it." (Meaning: "I don't intend to live with it.") Such attempts aim to put the other person in a bind to act; the words say "There's no problem, take no further action," but the tone means "You'd better take some action." So, should listeners keep probing or drop the issue? Either way, they usually lose and resent it.

TIP 156: Avoid Sour-Grapes Lines.

Do these have a familiar ring? "I don't think I'd accept such an award." "I'm glad it's not me." "I'm glad I wasn't put in that position to say no." "I don't have time for that sort of thing." "Honestly, I'm relieved to have lost that contract." If lying to yourself eases the pain, go ahead. But others will probably smell jealousy.

TIP 157: Watch Diversionary Tactics.

People can create a distraction and sabotage a project in three ways: (1) Make light of a serious request, situation, or concern. (2) Simply stall by changing the subject. (3) Steal someone's thunder by delivering the punchline for their presentation before they get to it. Any of these tactics create a lasting, unfavorable impression with the speaker and with the observers.

TIP 158: Don't Bark Orders.

Adding courteous words helps: "please" and "I'd appreciate it if you would. . ." Adding an explanation to the order makes it even more palatable: "Do not use this entrance. The inside roof is under construction." "Do not use this copier; it is out of toner."

TIP 159: Never Issue an Order You Can't Enforce.

Words come easily; enforcement does not. And once you've put your commitment in words for the world to read or hear, you have to be committed to follow through. Without that commitment and resources, credibility goes out the window.

TIP 160: Squelch Automatic Put-Down Responses When Somebody Presents a New Idea.

"So what's your complaint with the way it's done now?" "So what's your gripe?" "Come again?" "You're way off base." "Where did you get that idea?" "I think you've misunderstood something along the way." These "welcoming" comments sound as though they come from a person on a hot wire fence. The person may appear to be receptive, but the reaction feels like an electrical jolt.

TIP 161: Make Only Promises You Intend to Keep.

Once retailers have people on their "hot check" list, it's difficult for that person to pass another check in that store. Likewise, people who promise action they don't intend to take get labeled. If you don't mean the following statements, don't use them: "I'll see what I can do." "I'll try to find time." "I'll check the files to see if we've got something on that company."

"I'll keep the information handy in case we have a need." "I'll help you if I can." "Maybe sometime we can get together." "Let's chat about that later."

Once people learn you have no intention of doing what you say, it will be a major construction effort to rebuild credibility.

TIP 162: Make Invitations Specific.

"Why don't we get together for lunch sometime?" comes across as "I might possibly want to spend some time with you, but I'm not sure. Why don't you call me with a specific time and I'll see if I've still got the urge?" If you really do want to spend time with someone, be specific: "Why don't we have lunch next week? How about Wednesday at Reno's Deli about 1 o'clock?" Or, if you honestly don't know your schedule or think the other person doesn't know his or hers, try, "Let's have breakfast together next week. I'll check my calendar this afternoon and call your office to see if you're available next Thursday or Friday." Only a specific invitation sounds sincere.

TIP 163: Make Invitations Vague if You Think You Should Spend Time with the Other Person but Don't Really Want to Badly Enough to Make a Commitment.

I've had an acquaintance who has been saying to me for two years when we meet at parties, "Call me for lunch sometime." After about five such invitations, I took him seriously and phoned with an invitation to breakfast or lunch any day of the week for the next 10 days. Seems that he was "behind, rushed, overextended" for an indefinite period of time. Had he really wanted to get together, he would have responded, "Gee, I'm really behind with several projects for the next two weeks. But what if I phone you Monday the 22nd, and let's see if we can set a date by then."

If you don't want to make a commitment of time, be vague. People will get the message—all of it.

TIP 164: Avoid Challenges to Someone's Integrity.

A sure way to make enemies in a meeting is to challenge someone's integrity with statements or questions like these: "What is your agenda for getting this done so fast?" "Who asked you to do this?" "What's in this for you?" "What are you not telling us?" "Who should we ask for the other side of the story?"

TIP 165: Judge Others on Their Intentions As Well As Their Actions.

Have you ever known a satisfied customer to give a "testimonial" to another prospective customer that lost, rather than won, the sale? Have you known someone who planned a going-away party to show appreciation that fizzled? Or have you seen someone take up a collection for a gift when the small amount embarrassed the recipient? Have you ever heard an emcee introduce a speaker, minimizing rather than maximizing the speaker's credentials? Well-intentioned words sometimes fall flat.

Give people credit for a big heart even if they don't have the knowledge or skills to perform like they intend. Particularly, this rule applies when others make mistakes while "helping" you—mistakes that cost more to correct in time and effort than if you had done the task yourself. The tendency is to judge others on their results and ourselves on our intentions. Give people the benefit of the doubt when they talk.

TIP 166: Make Your Own Intentions Known, Even if Your Action Doesn't Hit the Bull's-Eye.

If what you do flubs, people are left on their own to interpret your intentions by the results. If somehow the award ceremony left the person feeling put down rather than praised, be sure to explain your intentions behind your words. Help people give you the benefit of the doubt.

TIP 167: Beware of People Who Swear They're Telling the Truth.

Watch for people who insist: "Trust me—we're not the kind of vendor who gouges in a crisis." "You can trust us to give you an honest opinion, no matter what the fees involved." "I swear he said it." "Can I be frank with you?" "We don't make this information readily available to all our customers, but I want to be up front with you." "Let me be honest with you on this." Such lines indicate other than the truth.

Those who always tell the truth never think to call attention to the fact that they're telling it.

TIP 168: Show Total Belief to Ferret Out Liars.

When someone starts a whopper and you show obvious disbelief (with a raised eyebrow or a questioning tone), they'll grow cautious and often tone down their story. On the other hand, if you doubt that someone is telling the truth, show no signs of skepticism. Your demeanor and accepting attitude will entice him or her to continue until the statements become so outlandish as to be obviously a lie.

TIP 169: Don't Hide Behind "They Didn't Ask Me Not To."

Shared confidences are trusts. When people don't have the good sense to know that something should be held in confidence even when they were not specifically asked to do so, others question their judgment. Good judgment about such issues generally reflects good character.

TIP 170: Be Authoritative if You Want Control.

Your manner, appearance, speech, writing—all should work in tandem. Don't tell us what you're going to try to do, do it. Don't stand to the side looking contemplative; command space. Be sure; act the part.

The most famous experimental studies on the subject of obedience to authority were those conducted by Stanley Milgram, who used a "shock generator" with a panel of 30 switches supposedly controlling electrical shocks from 15 to 450 volts. The volunteers were taken into a room and told they were part of an experiment on teaching learners. Each time a learner, strapped in a chair in the next room, gave a wrong answer, the volunteer was supposed to administer a shock. With each "learner error," the volunteer was supposed to increase the voltage. No matter the screaming and the pleading of the "learners" next door, the volunteer was asked to continue the shocks. The idea was to see how long these volunteers would continue to administer what they thought were painful shocks when told to do so by the authority figure—a doctor in lab coat in charge of "scientific research."

The results? Although physically free to leave the room and quit the experiment, fully 65 percent of the volunteers were obedient to the end, giving screaming "learners" the maximum of 450 volts. Such is the power of our ingrained social pressure to obey authority.

If you act like an authority figure, people generally comply.

TIP 171: Sound Logical if You Want to Deliver Powerful Messages.

Make sure your message includes analytical statements, that your points are organized, that you use transitions from point to point, that you have a goal for meaningful conversation. When your words sound like you know where you're going, people often make room for you and even follow you to your logical destination.

TIP 172: Feel Free to Be Illogical.

To an engineer, the charge, "that's illogical" may be the kiss of death. The rest of the world doesn't necessarily cower under the weight of that accusation. "Thou shalt be logical" is not one of the Ten Commandments. The trick to minimizing the frustration of defending yourself is to acknowledge openly and quickly that your decision or behavior was not based on logic. You're off the hook. People can accept that all decisions, conclusions, or actions do not rest on logic. Feelings are fine.

TIP 173: Be Ready to Justify Any Decision You Make.

Although feelings are fine, people may work better and cooperate better when they have reasons. Although someone may hold a powerful position to command, real leadership calls for motivation. Rather than feeling annoyed at having to justify decisions, leaders accept such challenges to inspire and motivate others to follow.

TIP 174: To Be Quotable—Speak in Bumper Stickers.

Have you noticed that the media quotes some celebrities or authorities more often than others? Or that two doctors may share the same credentials and knowledge about laser surgery, but one will be interviewed in six magazines or journals while the other will never be asked for an opinion at all? If you want to be remembered by others, if you want to be quoted by your friends to their friends, if you want to be mentioned from the lectern as a leader, try to pepper your speech with pizzazz. Learn to turn a phrase so it's witty, amusing, provocative—not just adequate to cover the subject. Can you visualize your opinion as a bumper sticker?

TIP 175: Don't Assume the Other Person Has Power to Control Your Destiny.

Do you remember the age when you thought your parents could fix whatever happened in the world? We sometimes assume those in positions of authority have that kind of all-encompassing power to make or break us. As a result, we get angry at "what they don't do and could if they would." Respect the power that such people have, but don't attribute to them powers to control events or circumstances out of their realm of influence. You'll wear a grudge in your manner and voice.

TIP 176: Don't Create Obligations Among Others to Enhance Your Sense of Power.

Have you ever bought someone lunch when it was raining and nasty outside so they'd "owe you one" in a meeting later that day? The President buys congressional votes on the current legislation by offering to play golf with senators.

Large or small, the problem with such arrangements is that they build resentment in those who feel obligated. It's like being a tax cheat and worrying when you're going to find the IRS on your doorstep to collect.

TIP 177: Credit Your Source for New Ideas.

It's not a matter of split-the-appreciation pie. Others may get credit for the idea, but you get credit for knowing when, where, why, how, and if to use the idea in any given circumstances.

It's much safer to make your source known up front than to take credit and have others discover the truth later and point out the idea's true origin. Preachers, playwrights, and politicians through the years could have headed off charges of plagiarism had they taken this tip to heart. Those who can push their ideas through to the top via another individual and still get credit continue to flood ideas on those who shower them with praise in return.

TIP 178: Ask for Others' Opinions.

Asking for an opinion from someone doesn't obligate you to act on that opinion. But the fact that you have asked others to contribute to decisions has value to both you and the other person. The President's multiple advisers for every decision feel honored to offer their views whether or not he acts on them. Consider the pride with which citizens tell about being asked to testify before Congress about a personal experience or career expertise. Simply having someone ask for an opinion is a compliment.

TIP 179: Respond to What's Right with Suggestions Even if You Can't Use Them.

Consider it a sign of interest and helpfulness when others offer you suggestions. Respond in kind: "Thanks for mentioning that. You've got a good idea. We'll mull that over when we get together again" or "You may be right. It's a little different way of looking at things. Maybe we should give it serious thought" or "Your idea has real merit—we tried something similar last year but could never make it completely workable" or "You have a sound point. My concern with that would be X. However, maybe there's a way to work around that" or simply "Thanks. I need all the ideas I can get. Surely something will click."

TIP 180: Tell People How Much You Need Them.

People need to feel needed. Your staff won't stay with you nearly as long when they need you as when you need them—and they feel it. Put that sentiment in words often: "You're very good with numbers. It's a good thing we have you" or "I don't know what I'd do without you to keep me organized" or "I need your help—again. I'm always calling on you, aren't I?"

TIP 181: Give People All the Glory They're Due When They Know the Inside Scoop.

What good is shaking hands with a celebrity if you can't tell anybody? What good is a commendation if nobody hears or sees it? What good's a secret if nobody knows you know? Enjoyment comes in the telling. So, if you want to know what somebody else knows, you have to pay your dues. Tell them they must be special to have such an inside track, to be trusted with such information. Then watch them let those confidential details slip right out their lips; they have to give you information to verify that they really do know something important. Your strokes for their knowing simply bait them. When you ooh and aah over what they know, they'll just keep right on telling you what you want to know.

TIP 182: Show Pleasure in the Success of Others.

Jealousy and envy can be displayed prominently in silence. When someone tells of their good fortune or another person brings that achievement up in your presence, join in with your commendation. "It sounds like things are going well for you" or "That's terrific. You should have told us sooner" or "Wow. I can say I knew you when . . ." or "So come on, tell us. What kind of hoops did you have to jump through to pull that off?" or "Say, that's difficult to accomplish. I've tried it myself with very little success. Tell me how you did it." While lifting others into the limelight, you'll also raise yourself in the process. That's called class.

TIP 183: Let Another Person Know He or She Is Superior to You in Some Skill.

My husband, who has mastered this principle, always has more advice and help than he can use on home repairs and fishing. He simply lets someone with those skills know that he respects their expertise, and they're glad to show him how much they *really* know. For hours. At personal cost. People enjoy being helpful when they know the admiration is genuine.

Examples: "I just don't have the mechanical aptitude." "What's your solution? Nothing comes to my mind." "Could you help me out of this mess I've created for myself?" "You have far more experience in these situations than I do. What would you suggest?" "I know this seems simple to you, but it's complex to me." "Thanks for making me look good with this. You did a fine job." All such expressions give credit where it's due and make people feel good about themselves.

TIP 184: Let Others Impress You if You Want to Make a Good Impression Yourself.

Dale Carnegie introduced this principle decades ago—we win friends by making others feel important. People like to talk about themselves, so encourage them to do so. Then let them know you admire or respect them for some insight, talent, skill, philosophy, or attitude. We like those who like us.

On the other hand, we don't appreciate those who say by word, tone, or expression, "So what? I'm underwhelmed."

TIP 185: Think About the Imposition and the Options Before You Ask for a Favor.

Ask yourself the following questions before giving yourself permission to ask a favor: Is the favor a real imposition? Are you asking the other person to spend time, effort, or money that you wouldn't be willing to spend yourself on the project? Will the other person say "yes" out of guilt? Are you giving the other person an option to say "no" without their feeling guilty? Only if you can answer "yes" to the last one should you ask the favor.

TIP 186: Don't Presume on a Friend; Ask for Permission.

Friends will love you even more for the courtesy you've shown when you don't impose on their good nature. Use the following when the occasion calls for it: "Do you agree that we should do X?" "Will it be an inconvenience if I run back by my office for a moment?" "Don't let me speak for you—do you agree?" "Do you have a problem with my doing X? I can certainly wait if you think that's best."

TIP 187: Use the Ben Franklin Technique to Win a Friend.

Ben Franklin grew frustrated with a rival printer who seemed always to oppose him on any issue he favored in legislative gatherings. But Franklin determined to make a friend of him. Books in those days were hard-to-come-by treasures. So Ben Franklin knocked on his rival's door and explained that he did not own a copy of a particular book and asked the enemy if he'd be so kind as to lend his copy. Quite shocked at the humility and request, the enemy loaned him the book. Franklin took the book home, kept it for a week, and then returned it with his thanks. The rival became his friend, proving Franklin right on an effective way to win people over.

Asking for favors takes humility. Showing humility allows the other person to feel benevolent and/or powerful. With those ego strokes, much of the hostility in a relationship melts. An additional reminder: Be sure the favor is one that requires little time, money, or effort.

TIP 188: Take the Pressure off Others When They Make an Unintended Gaffe.

Someone says to you, "Did you see that new brochure they came out with? It looks like something out of a 1950 Sears catalog—fine print, no color." When they discover that you designed the brochure, they'll feel as though somebody punched them in the stomach. And the pain of embarrassment will be associated with you—even though the words came from *their* mouth. In such cases, be magnanimous. Laugh it off. Use a light retort, such as "Yeah, it only won honorable mention at home as well."

If the gaffe is serious enough, share your own blunders to let him or her know you identify with the embarrassment. The offender will be grateful for a long, long time. To any other observers, you'll look like a class act.

TIP 189: Select the Setting That Suits Your Purpose.

A conversation in the hallway around the watercooler takes on a more ominous tone in the boss's office. A telephone complaint doesn't sound as serious as a written one. A challenge from the lectern packs more punch than one behind a gold club on the green.

TIP 190: Change Your Physical Environment to Promote the Interaction You Want.

Notice the difference in how you interact with a doctor as you get shuffled around his or her office, from bed to X-ray lab to the comfy desk-and-chair conference room. Notice the difference in speaking manner and audience reaction to a speaker behind a lectern as opposed to the same speaker in the aisles. Buyers and sellers take on different postures and purposes, depending on whether they're sitting across a desk or sitting on a sofa in the lobby.

Use this environment-body-mind link to promote the interaction you want: As boss, if you want to decrease your status to be "one of the gang," sit down rather than stand up to speak. If you want to encourage interaction among the office staff, change the traffic patterns in your large open space. Literally build the interaction you want.

TIP 191: Measure Your Relationship with Others by the Kind of Conversation They Share with You.

On the shallowest level, people share clichés: "The project's going a little slowly. I've seen better days." "Hang in there." "There's always the weekend."

On the next level, people care enough to share meaningful facts: "We have to keep the project under 500 dollars." "Jim said he was going to hire three engineers before fourth quarter if we won the Hyatt contract."

On a more intimate level, people begin to feel free to share opinions and judgments: "If Jim hires those three engineers, I still don't think it will mean we can finish the project on time—I think we're in trouble on this contract" or "I think you're going about this in the most expensive way. I think you have a short-term view of the whole issue and that it's going to make Lucille angry. That's dangerous."

On the most intimate level, people share feelings: "I'm discouraged with trying to set up a health-care plan that suits everybody. Frankly, I wish I'd never accepted this leadership position. All I'm getting from peers is animosity, and all I'm getting from my family is anger about my weekend work."

If you want to gauge the progress of a relationship from the other person's point of view, listen to what he or she is willing to tell you: clichés and perfunctory remarks? facts? opinions and judgments? personal feelings?

As the relationship grows, you'll notice these verbal cues along the way: You'll begin to use "I," "you," "we," and "us" more often. You'll develop a verbal shorthand between you—inside jokes and references to your history together. You'll notice you've been collecting commonalities: shared assumptions, expectations, values. You begin to "interpret" for each other. "So what you're really saying is you wanna dump the project?" If you want the relationship to grow, all these verbal clues become welcome signs.

TIP 192: Recognize That Intimacy Breeds Distance.

> When you don't know someone well, you feel freer to state your opinion; you're not so concerned about hurting the relationship if you disagree. The possible consequence or loss doesn't threaten you. But as you spend more time together and intimacy develops, you discover "sore spots"—things you can't talk about. Why? Because you've come to value the relationship and you fear if you open your mouth to disagree and offend that person, you'll damage the relationship. Intimacy means you have more to lose. That's why the pendulum continually swings from intimacy to distance back to intimacy. Expect and accept that cycle.

TIP 193: Select the Implicit or Explicit
Channel with Care.

> Have you ever heard anybody say, usually with pride, "I'm just the kind of person who says what's on my mind." Get out of the way. Yes, that person may be honest, but brutally honest, leaving wounded people in his or her path. A leader this person will never become. What is proper and acceptable, we say explicitly. What might offend, we imply. Why? Because we're civilized. People matter.

3
Making Small Talk
a Big Deal

A bore is someone who has no small talk.
— MICHAEL KORDA

*Inject a few raisins of conversations into the
tasteless dough of existence.* — O. HENRY

*The minute a man is convinced that he
is interesting, he isn't.* — STEPHEN LEACOCK

*There are few wild beasts more to be dreaded
than a talking man having nothing to say.*
— JONATHAN SWIFT

*One of the troubles of small talk is that it
usually comes in large doses.*
— no attribution

Wit is the salt of conversation, not the food.
— WILLIAM HAZLITT

*Talk to anyone about himself and he will
listen without interrupting.*
— HERBERT V. PROCHNOW

Small talk means having a little loose change in your pocket. Like quarters
at a pay phone, nickels at a gum dispenser, or dollars at a toll booth, it'll

come in handy when you least expect it. When it comes to small talk, know when to jiggle it, spend it, or save it.

TIP 194: Work at Building Rapport.

All small talk is not the same. With some people, you walk away having killed a few moments. With others, you feel a real connection and a desire to get to know them better. What's the difference? The effort one or both of you have made at rapport-building. What helps make the connection? Calling the other person by name several times during the conversation, mentioning other things you have in common—mutual acquaintances, places you've lived or visited, experiences you've shared, career or personal goals, showing interest in that person's views or pastimes, matching the other person's delivery style, voice volume and tone, emotion, and body language as you talk.

Basically, people like and feel a kinship with others who like them, appreciate them, enjoy the same things they do, and are helpful to them. Time and attention make the connection that lasts.

TIP 195: Know When Small Talk Is Appropriate.

When you're thinking of lapsing into small talk, be sensitive to the other person's mood and circumstances. On an airplane, when your seatmate is obviously preoccupied, leave him or her alone. Neither would you try to engage someone in small talk when the person is dashing down the hallway to make a meeting. On other occasions, small talk is inappropriate because of the person involved. If the CEO has unexpectedly called you in for "a little chat," this is not the time to take the lead. Let him or her dictate the topic and pace with which you get down to business. The same is true with customers. Develop a sixth sense about those who appreciate small talk and those who don't.

TIP 196: Accept the Fact That Some People Don't Want to Make Contact at All.

Some people fear contact with others, even in a brief way. They see small talk not as an opportunity for rapport-building but as an infringement and inconvenience. A salesman waiting for other registrants at a seminar asked an older guest nearby if he knew of a good Italian restaurant. The older guest turned away without answering. The salesman repeated the question louder, and the older guest again turned back to the conversation with his wife.

After the salesman gave up and stepped onto the elevator, the wife turned to her husband and asked, "Why didn't you answer him?" The husband mumbled, "If I'd have named a restaurant, he'd have wanted to know how to get there. If I'd have told him how to get there, he wouldn't have understood and I'd have had to go with him. And if I'd have had to go with him, you would have been left here alone. And if you'd been left alone, you would have griped and complained. And you know how I hate a griping, nagging wife. We'd have been in divorce court before you know it, and I couldn't bear the thought of you on the street being picked up by the likes of that salesman."

Reading the signals from those people isn't difficult; simply respect their wishes.

TIP 197: Think Twice About Using Small Talk on the Telephone.

Your timing for small talk is more, not less, crucial when you phone someone. When you're face to face, the other person can signal you with closed body language that he or she is busy, distracted, or involved in an intense conversation with someone else and prefers not to be disturbed. Not so with the telephone. If you've placed the call, you're in control and you may be intruding. Therefore, don't assume that people expect, or welcome, a little chitchat before you get down to business.

Picture yourself in your office: Your assistant brings in express mail from a customer who has rejected your latest contract. A meeting that you're leading starts in five minutes and you're still working on the agenda. A colleague has just placed a note in your in-basket requesting to talk to you about Geraldine who's resigning at the end of the day. Your phone rings and a colleague says, "So, Larry, how's it going? The team didn't look so good last weekend. What do you think happened?"

Remember you have a one-up position when placing a call, and the other person can't make a quick getaway. The timing can be devastating to your reputation. Know where you're going with the call and be prepared to get there. If the other person sends you a cue that small talk's in order, you can always change course and accommodate the lighter mood.

TIP 198: Risk Being the First to Say Hello.

You can narrow your odds of being snubbed if you look for someone with open body language and a timid expression, somebody "in between" conversations, or somebody who makes eye contact and returns your smile. Somebody has to risk rejection and it might as well be you as the next person.

TIP 199: Introduce Yourself in a Way That Allows
People to Respond or Connect.

> "Hello. I'm Ty Wycosky, one of the team in from San Francisco." Or, "I'm Maria Garcia. Bill Thomas is one of my customers." Just add one other phrase in addition to your name that gives people a clue about what you might have in common so they can ask about or comment on it.

TIP 200: Help People Remember Your Name.

> When others look panic-stricken about not being able to remember your name, take the pressure off: "I'm George Stallings—we met last week in the bank lobby when the lady in front of us brought in 16 jars of pennies." They'll be grateful, and you'll feel less embarrassed.

TIP 201: Remember Others' Names.

> Listen to a name the first time you hear it. Repeat it aloud and ask the owner to verify that you have it correct. Use it immediately in the conversation over the next three minutes. Study the face. Take a mental snapshot. When people aren't looking at you, note tiny details that make them memorable. Fix their face, body structure, hairstyle, mannerisms in your mind just as though you were studying a mug shot to identify the person who robbed your house. It's the detail that makes people easy to latch to a name.
>
> The next step is to associate the name with a visual picture—of that person or a concrete item the name conjures up. Like a cartoonist, pick out one outstanding feature and exaggerate it in your mind. The next time you see that person that feature will "jump out" at you and trigger the name. A big, lumbering guy named Jack might trigger the association of a lumberjack because of his size and manner. Associate "look-alikes" with celebrity names, features with animals, mannerisms with occupations, and so forth. Write the name down if necessary as soon as you can do so without being obvious about what you're writing.
>
> Names are important—listen to them, repeat them, attach them, and fix them in your mind for later recall.

TIP 202: Personalize Greetings.

> Instead of the typical, perfunctory comments when meeting people, make them feel special by adding their names and mentioning specifics that apply only to them. *Not:* "How's it going?" *But:* "Tina, how's it going with your latest project?" *Not:* "Good morning." *But:* "Good morning, Rita. Looks like you and I are stuck in a rut with these same cafeteria muffins

every morning." *Not:* "How's the world treating you?" *But:* "Jack, how're those engineers treating you?"

TIP 203: Gain Partial Credit by Recalling the Meeting if Not the Other Person's Name.

When someone approaches you and you recall the face but not the name, at least prove that you haven't forgotten the person totally. "It's nice to see you again. I believe we met at the BBA convention in Anaheim. You had just changed jobs at Kellogg. Help me with the name again."

You can often get people to help you by introducing them to others in your group; they'll supply the name before you have to. Bingo, you've got the name.

Be honest if you draw a complete blank on the name, and they offer no help. They'll know the truth, and you'll gain another strike by lying about it. Try humor: "Your name again? I have trouble remembering my own sometimes. The aging process, you know" or "I'm sorry but I'm terrible with names—I even run through my kids' names like a laundry list before I get to the one I want."

TIP 204: Recall to the Person Your Topic of Conversation the Last Time You Were Together.

Others will be flattered that you remembered, and your comment serves as proof that you did indeed pay attention and consider them important. "John, you gave me so many tips about mutual-fund investing last week. I enjoyed our talk very much."

TIP 205: Position Yourself in the Flow of Traffic.

If you have trouble entering groups and breaking into a conversation, stand near the food, the doorway, the band, the dance floor, or the water fountain. People will surround you, and you'll have many opportunities to start conversations. When you find someone you want to spend longer than two or three minutes with, you can always move to the side and continue on a less superficial level than "opening lines."

TIP 206: To Relax Yourself, Strike Up a Conversation with Someone Who Looks Shy and Uncomfortable.

That person will be grateful for someone to talk with and will respond to almost any topic you toss out. As you and the other person build up your confidence, you can part ways or bring others into your circle.

TIP 207: Play Host Rather Than Guest.

Friends of mine, Bob and Jane, always seem to know everybody at every party, circulate well, and seem busy and hurried to get to the next group. Finally, I discovered their secret to being in the middle of every huddle. They simply took it upon themselves to play hosts rather than guests. They join a quiet group, introduce themselves to the person beside them, and then turn to another person on the right or left or passing by and say, "Mike, have you met Sam? He's with Allied. A chemical engineer." Bob listens to them talk a few moments and then is off to make the next introduction, to freshen someone's drink, to show someone to the coat room, or to beg someone to sing the latest hit.

Those who consider themselves guests, on the other hand, take a passive role and often feel either trapped by a bore or neglected by the most entertaining group.

Don't wait for others to introduce you, offer you food, suggest that you tell a story, or lead you to meet the new manager. Instead, play host yourself and look for things to do: CDs to play, food to replenish, people to introduce, traffic to monitor, entertainment to encourage or praise, name badges to make, people to hug.

TIP 208: Bring Along Your Own PR Person.

If you feel immodest singing your own praises and your purpose is to get attention from the "right" people, consider making the rounds with a friend who can make the offhanded comments you can't. "Hey, guys, I've got someone you should meet. Marguerite. She's leading the new development team for the StarFish package. That's the project that's going to fund all our retirement condos in Hawaii!" or "Al, have you met Rosalinda? She's just sold over a quarter million worth of widgets her first four months. Pretty impressive, huh? I'm standing close so it'll rub off on me."

TIP 209: Don't Intrude.

Be aware of groups who seem to be involved in an intense, confidential conversation. They'll be standing nose to nose and toes to toes, and glare at anyone who approaches. If you enter such a conversation by accident, you can excuse yourself with, "I'm sorry. I didn't know you were involved in a confidential conversation" and move on.

TIP 210: Choose a Topic Appropriate to the Group, the Atmosphere, the Relationship, and Your Purpose.

Begin with one of the three options open to you: Ask a question. State a fact. Voice an opinion. Generally, you're safe in discussing the other person's area of expertise or your own, the current affair you're attending, or the day's news.

General topics

- Vacations
- Jobs—most interesting, least interesting, most rewarding
- Career goals for the next 10 years
- Company culture
- Promotions/awards—who's getting them
- Hobbies
- Sports
- Current projects
- A specialty or unique skill
- Happenings embarrassing/amusing/meaningful to you
- Your/their hopes for the future about an issue/problem/fear
- Community activities, causes, problems
- Current newspaper headlines
- Current court cases
- The arts—movies, plays, books
- The latest exploits of your favorite cartoon strip
- A funny thing that happened to someone you know
- New restaurants/amusement parks
- Their hometowns (new features, likes, dislikes, leading industries, sources of shame or pride)
- Game-playing

  "If you could change occupations without any retraining, what would you like to do?"

  If you could have dinner with anyone in the world, who would you choose?"

  "If you had a million dollars to donate to charity, where would it go?"

  "What do you like/dislike most about your job/hours/this city/this state?"

  "Who was the most influential person in your life/your work?"

  "Who was your favorite boss/teacher?"

  "What's your most embarrassing moment?"

  "What's the funniest, clean joke you know?"

  "So whom do you admire the most?"

■ Poll taking

"So how does each of you think the ruling should go?"

"So how high/low do you think taxes/interest rates will go?"

"So how many people are you guessing will accept the retirement package?")

Talking with a child

School subjects liked/hated

One new thing they've learned during the week

Culture of the school—what's fun there

Their parents' work

Favorite teacher

What they do after school

Their best friends and what they like about them

Favorite TV programs

Talking with a VIP

"Do you dread being away from your family?

Does changing time zones so frequently bother you?

How do you manage to keep your schedule straight?

When do you find time to shop?")

"To what do you attribute your success?"

"To whom do you attribute much of your success?"

"What's the most rewarding thing about your career?"

"What would you advise someone just starting out in your field?"

"Would you do things differently if you had to start over?"

"Who gave you your first break/job?"

"What was the best career decision you ever made?"

"Do you try to keep your personal life and business life separate or do they mesh well?"

"Does your spouse appreciate your success?"

"What does your family think about your success?"

Talking with the ill or bereaved

"I imagine she had such a wonderful/full/interesting life."

"So tell me about the happy times with her."

"So tell me what kind of person he was."

"John has told me so much about your mother. He said she was . . ."

"So, are others involved in his care?"

TIP 211: Use Opening Lines That Lead Someplace.

Try a few of these as staples:

"What's this economy doing to your business/industry?"

"What do you think about the party?"

"Did you read the paper today?"

"How do you fit into the picture they're discussing?"

"What's your role in this project/group/crowd?"

"What experience have you had in this arena?"

"I'm not familiar with your industry/group. Will you give me a little background?"

"How's life treating you this month/this week/today?"

"Am I interrupting a personal conversation?"

"So tell me who won today—you or the lions?"

"Someone told me you were the one to ask about X? I need advice."

"Jim told me to be sure to come talk to you."

"Sherry wanted me to say hello for her."

"It's certainly pretty/noisy/cold/fun in here, isn't it?"

"The atmosphere here reminds me of my junior prom/our last sales convention/our board meetings."

"Doesn't Ginny look gorgeous/happy/excited/pleased/proud tonight?"

"Isn't this food delicious? Do you know what's in it?"

"I don't know a soul here, so I'm going to barge right in and eavesdrop."

"What do all these people here have in common?"

"How was the traffic/parking/weather on the way in?"

"How do you know the host/group/boss/couple?"

"People seem to be enjoying themselves, don't you think?"

"So what do you do for a living?"

"So what do you do when you're not working?"

"Are you enjoying the cruise/party/project/seminar?"

"Your clothes are fascinating/classy/so colorful."

"Where do you call home?"

"So, have you spent your entire career in this industry?"

"Do you come here often?"

"Do you know many of these people?"

"This group sounds like the one having the most fun. May I join? I could use a laugh."

"You people look like movers and shakers. May I join you?"

"This group looks so intense. I'm wondering what the topic is?"

"I've just been standing here listening, but you've touched a passionate chord in me. I think . . ."

"I've got a question. Do you know if . . . ?"

"I need help. Can you tell me where I could find . . . ?"

"I've always been interested in X, but know very little about it. Can you tell me more about it?"

"I've always wished I knew more about starting a business or managing people? What's the most difficult thing you face?"

"I'm always interested in unusual names. Tell me the origin of yours."

"So what's going on in your life now?"

"We haven't talked in awhile. Give me an update on X."

"You know, I see you often, but I don't think we've met. My name's Barbara."

TIP 212: To Stir Quiet People to Expression, Select a Topic About Which They Can Feel Passionate.

Such conversational options as patriotism, gratitude, respect, generosity, hatred, or morality tug at the shy person's heart to speak up and offer feelings and opinions.

TIP 213: Know Which Topics to Avoid.

Religion. Politics. Race. Ethnic groups. Family. Economics. Frightening probabilities. Criticisms of others. Personal tidbits about others. Personal problems such as your ex-spouse's shenanigans or your daughter's drug problem.

Avoid any subject that equates to a rut—don't be known as the person with the one-channel chat. Of course, any of these topics may be appropriate with the right person, purpose, and timing. But they're pitfalls waiting to trap you. Proceed with caution.

TIP 214: Play the Part of the "Stranger in Town" with Class.

If you seem to be the only one in a group who doesn't know the others or much about the event or purpose, ask questions about the city, group, features, history, accomplishments, or future plans. People love to talk about themselves, and their city or professional or social group is an extension of themselves. Never comment negatively on the person's city or group affiliation. Negatives earn the same response as pointing out egg stains on someone's clothing.

TIP 215: Develop Your Timing Instinct Before Bringing Up an Appropriate Subject.

Check to see who's entering or leaving your group. How long do you have before you'll be interrupted to move into the serving line or hear the entertainment? If people seem bored with small talk, they're ready to get down to the main purpose of your discussion. If they seem stiff and ill at ease, you probably need to dwell a little longer with chitchat before getting into hard-core discussions.

TIP 216: Read the Other Person's Mindset by Examining His or Her Opening Comment.

If you ask "How are you?" and the other person responds with, "I'm hanging in there," you can assume that person wants to talk about a current difficulty or problem. If the person answers, "Great, how about you?" in an excited tone, he or she is in an exuberant mood. The same "Great, how about you?" wrapped in a flat tone says the person wants to avoid the discussion altogether—it's business as usual.

TIP 217: Relax Your Body Language if You Want a Relaxed Conversation.

When people stand erect, tense, and "on guard," those talking to them unconsciously begin to mirror that posture. As a result, the entire conversation becomes uneasy, stiff, formal. If you want to be light and amusing, relax your body and the tone of the conversation will follow.

TIP 218: Recognize That the Response You Get Will Often Reflect Your Own Tone and Delivery.

If you toss out an opener with an amused smile and light tone, people will usually respond in kind. If, on the other hand, you have a furrowed brow and look depressed when you asked their opinions on the economy, they may think you expect a serious dissertation on the subject. Rather than tackling the topic, they'll often give an offhanded comment and move on.

TIP 219: Ask Easy Questions First to Relax People.

People have a fear of being sucked into conversations over their heads and left to drown. When introducing a new topic, toss out a question that requires an easy response, not an essay. As the other person relaxes in your presence, you or others can develop the topic with more specific questions and leads.

TIP 220: Ask for Opinions Rather than Information.

When you ask others for information, "What is the latest news on the XYZ case?" either they can tell you or they can't. If they tell you, it's no big ego stroke for them simply to share common information. If they can't come up with the information, they'll feel uninformed or ignorant.

When you ask for an opinion, however, people feel complimented. No matter whether they're informed or up to date, people always feel free to express opinions, and flattered that you ask for them. They'll talk longer and more eloquently if your question touches issues about which they feel passionate. The more interest you show in that opinion, the more complimented they feel.

TIP 221: Don't Ask Questions Too Broad to Answer.

"What do you think we need to do to get a handle on poverty?" "What do we need to do about TV violence?" "What's wrong with the youth of today?" Such questions sound too global for anyone to be interested in tackling them. Narrow the focus to one aspect of these issues, and you'll find more people have opinions to share.

TIP 222: Tickle People's Creative Fancy.

> If you know someone has special expertise in your topic or your topic is of general interest, toss out a project/problem that you "might" do/solve some-day: "I'm thinking of re-covering all the windows in my house. Got any ideas?" or "I'm toying with the idea of writing a book for my grandchildren—sort of a legacy. What kinds of things do you think I should include?" or "I'm planning a roast for an upcoming retirement luncheon. Got any gags or appropriate one-liners?" Asking for their input can compliment them and give them an enjoyable creative workout.

TIP 223: Pique Others' Curiosity
with an Incomplete Comment.

> Choose a subject that people will have some interest in, even though they may lack knowledge about it, and toss out a half-baked but intriguing observation. Try something like: "I'm planning to sell everything I own within six months" or "Kids are smarter than their years these days" or "I just saw Kim racing up 14 flights of stairs." "Give me a moment to calm down. I'm considering murder at the moment." "Teenagers—I've come to the conclusion that they're not real people." Such will spur them to ask you to elaborate, and you're into a new topic. If it doesn't work and they show no interest or miss the cue, shake your head as if still intrigued by a past conversation and then move on to something else.

TIP 224: Avoid Questions That Lead People On
When You Have No Interest in Their Answers.

> I call this the you-talk-while-I-look-around-and-see-what-else-is-happening ploy. "Tell me what you think about the state of communism today?" "You read a lot, don't you? Tell me about some of the books you like to read." That kind of question puts the other person on the spot to take the conversational ball while knowing you're going to tune out. This dishonest baiting question makes the other person feel downright foolish.

TIP 225: Don't State the Obvious.

> When you toss out a question/observation/comment such as "Times have changed, haven't they?" you'll probably get no response at all. It's not that the subject is too complex, but just the opposite. The topic is too mundane or monotonous to elicit a response.

TIP 226: Jump Over the Ho-Hum Screen.

> Give people the "so what" up front. Tell them why they should care before they tune you out. Everybody needs an enticement to listen—even for fun.

TIP 227: Add Fresh Information or Observations
Rather Than Echoing What's Been Said.

> When somebody makes an observation, even if you agree with it exactly, don't just nod or comment with a phrase like "So true." Instead, add a fresh idea, a new fact, or an illustrative anecdote. Take your turn at dribbling the ball, even if you're standing still on the court.

TIP 228: Ask to Be Enlightened When
the Conversation Is Over Your Head.

> Everybody is ignorant, only on different subjects according to Will Rogers. Your lack of knowledge will not necessarily be a hindrance to small talk; on the contrary, the more knowledgeable person will enjoy the solo attention his or her expertise brings. Just don't try to fake it by throwing in tidbits that will sound awkward to others. Instead, invite others to educate you: "I'm afraid I know so very little about the publishing industry. Tell me more about it." "I've had my head buried in six feet of paperwork for the past week and haven't the slightest idea what you're referring to. Give me a quick update, please."

TIP 229: Keep Your Mouth Shut if the Conversation
Is *Way* Over Your Head.

> On the other hand, if someone is talking about the latest developments in nuclear fission, you can't expect that person to give you a college course in 10 minutes. Either just listen to others involved in the discussion and learn what you can, or excuse yourself. Don't make an entire group play catch-up while someone educates you with details that you don't really care to know.

TIP 230: Take No More and No Less Time
Than a Subject Is Worth.

> The difference between stimulating and dull comes down to pacing. Don't keep racing the engine when the conversation sputters. Simply echoing

what another person has said grinds on people's nerves. Either add something new to the topic, ask a question to get the other person to elaborate, or move on out to the open road on another topic. The idea is to keep a steady pace for as long as possible with both of you sharing driving duties. Unless you're discussing something that seems to be vitally important to the other person, change the subject every five minutes.

TIP 231: To Share the Topic, Change the Pace.

To introduce surprise or arouse curiosity, change the pace of the discussion in one of three ways: louder or softer volume, faster or slower speech, more or less emotion. If the group is leisurely winding down on a topic, rush in with a fast line that shows upset at what happened to you the day before. If the group is moving along at a good clip, overlapping each other's lines, and running away with wit, take a deep breath and make a drawn-out, slow-paced, intense, provocative statement. If they are intensely serious, toss out a one-liner to generate a laugh. Any change of delivery gets attention.

TIP 232: Add Description as Elaboration.

Consider facts the skeleton of your conversation. Put flesh on the bones with elaboration. Set the scene. Paint pictures. Explain why. Don't just say, "Stephen is a funny character." Why is he interesting? When? Doing what? Saying what? Deciding what? Let us see Stephen in motion and come to our own conclusion. Don't just say, "The project is going to open new doors for us." Where? When? Why? How? With whom?

TIP 233: Make Your Aim to Entertain.

By entertain, I don't necessarily mean a song-and-dance routine or even amusing stories or witty one-liners. Entertaining has a broader meaning— making people enjoy themselves. Entertainment includes enlightening them on a subject of interest, letting them enlighten you on a subject, giving new information, exchanging different views on an issue, or meeting new people with unusual experiences and opinions. Entertainment rarely includes a lecture or debate; both tend to make people increasingly uncomfortable.

TIP 234: Work on Witty Remarks.

To be effective, witty lines must be prompt and clever. You can have a stock of ready-made ones for various occasions, or you can develop them on the spot. The trouble with those developed on the spot is that they lose their effect if not prompt. And if they are prompt, you don't have time to screen them. The downside of a witty remark at someone else's expense can mean long-lasting, devastating results. When you do come up with originals spontaneously, save them for a repeat performance.

TIP 235: Tell Good Stories.

Stories can make a point more clearly, emphasize a point you've already made, give evidence of anyone else's point, translate fuzzy thoughts into clear ones, keep interest, build or change the culture around your workplace, or just relax and entertain people. Your story doesn't have to be funny; it can arouse empathy, create surprise or shock, inspire pride, or anger people so that they take action.

Even a story that has a weak point, if well told, serves to entertain. Embellish as you like as long as the primary outline of what happened and why is true. Know when to add detail and when to omit it. Know when to use a preface with your story and when such filler is irrelevant. Know when to pause and when to interrupt yourself. Know when to slow down or speed up. Know when to throw in a bumper-sticker line before moving on to the end. Create suspense just before the punch line or conclusion. In short, dramatize your delivery.

TIP 236: Try to Relate Your Stories to the Subject at Hand.

Although not always necessary, the story has a bigger bang if it illuminates or further illustrates the point of the current conversation. Look for at least a narrow bridge from a key word in what has been said so that the story seems to fit. "Carl, your comment on your daughter's attitude about her grades reminds me of a friend back in college. This guy walks into my dorm room . . ." Because this is not a speech or a sermon, the whole gist of the story doesn't have to be "on the point," but there should be some trigger word or thought that generates it.

Of course, if you're looking for a new subject, let your story be the lead-in. Build a bridge after the story and hand the subject to someone else: "So somebody tell me I'm not alone in feeling that X. Anybody been in a similar situation?" The idea is not to tell a story that leaves people with the reaction, "So what?"

TIP 237: Make Other People the Hero or Heroine of Your Anecdotes.

When you toss out anecdotes of recent incidents, you don't always have to be the hero or heroine. Tell something amusing/enlightening/strange that happened to a friend, coworker, family member, acquaintance, or neighbor. People will enjoy your conversation without getting the feeling that you're self-centered.

TIP 238: Respond With a "Saver" if Your Remarks Breed Silence.

My husband has a flippant line when his comment gets a ho-hum response. After the silence, he picks up the slack with, "Not of grave importance, but it killed a minute," which always brings a chuckle or smile. Try others: "Not a front-page news story, but interesting nevertheless" or "May not be something that will pull you out of a national crisis, but could save the cat" or "So I can tell you are big X fans here" or "Funny, my mother loved the story."

If the flippant comeback seems inappropriate, you can pretend you were serious and intended the remark as a conclusion to the subject under discussion. Allow a brief pause and then take up a new topic.

TIP 239: Do a Reality Check Frequently to See if People Are Really Interested in What You Have to Say.

To test for a follow-on story, toss out a come-on and see if the other person invites you to elaborate: "The same thing happened to me on vacation last year" or "That sounds like my boss—always getting into such scrapes."

Or ask an unexpected question. If they can't answer, take that as a good indication that they're bored. Either change the subject, relinquish the floor, or move on.

TIP 240: Give Your Listener a Chance to Leave if Bored.

On occasion, you and another person may find yourself like two fish washed up on a dry beach. You can't get back into the conversational swim and you're not sure how motivated the other person is to flop toward the water. Try "Well, I know you have several people you want to say hello to, so I'll let you go" or "I won't keep you—there are so many people here that it's hard to find time to chat with everyone."

TIP 241: When You're Caught Not Listening,
Give a Keep-Talking Nudge.

If you let your mind wander and the other person discovers you're not listening, you will offend. When you suddenly notice the other person has
stopped talking and is waiting for your response, give the person a nudge
until you can get reoriented: "So then . . . ?" or "I'm not too knowledgeable
on that, as I said earlier . . ." or "So you mean that . . . ?" or "Could you
repeat that?" or "I'm sorry—I didn't understand what you were asking." or
"Would you say it another way?" or "I missed your point, I'm sorry." Often
people will continue talking and give you a clue where they were.

   If that doesn't work, try the straightforward approach. "I'm sorry, I
missed your last comment" or "It's so noisy in here I'm having a hard time
hearing you" or "I'm sorry, you lost me. I'm still thinking about what you
said a minute ago when you mentioned . . ." or "I'm lost; something you
said a moment ago made me think of . . ."

TIP 242: Avoid Current Stock Fillers.

Watch peppering your talk with stock fillers such as "That's incredible."
"Awesome." "All right!" "Thumbs up." "No kidding." "You don't say."
"Follow what I'm saying?" "You with me?"

TIP 243: Unwind a Nonstop Speaker with a Popquiz.

When you want to stop someone's monologue, break in with two or three
short-answer questions. You don't seem rude because you're asking the
speaker to keep talking with questions that signal interest. But the idea is to
take control. When the person stops the monologue to give one- or two-word
answers to your specific questions on the subject, you have an opportunity to
regain the floor and redirect the conversation or end it.

TIP 244: Encourage People to Continue What They
Were Saying Before Being Interrupted.

They'll love you for saying, "Please continue what you were telling me."
"Please finish your story; you had me intrigued." "So back to what you
were saying . . ." "Don't stop now; I'm just starting to understand your
point." Such encouragement is an invitation few can resist and most
remember forever.

TIP 245: When Someone "Pulls Your Leg," Release It.

Granted, I'm more gullible than the average person. When somebody with a quick wit or a penchant for gags takes me for a ride in conversation, I go right along unaware to the very end. Living in Okinawa at the worldly age of 19, I often talked about my home state of Texas. One day my boss strolled into the office late, with this explanation: "We had to have the pest control people out to my house this morning. Last night I kept hearing this noise in the next room, like shoes scuffling across the floor. Sure enough, when I checked it out this morning, it was a big roach—the size they have in Texas—pushing my shoes around in the closet."

"Really? That's scary."

He became hysterical. And he repeated the story to everyone who would listen for the rest of the day.

When someone obviously puts one over on you, let it go. To get angry or "explain it away" ruins the moment. Just accept the fact that you're going to be the butt of the joke on occasion and enjoy the "fame" along with everybody else.

TIP 246: Cover Your Own and Others' Faux Pas with Past Ones.

That's right. If you've just stuck your foot in your mouth with your last comment, you can take the pressure off by making your own history an amusing anecdote. Say something like, "I've got a history here. Charm school I did not attend. In fact, last month . . ." Relate the past blunder along with your embarrassment, and the group will begin to empathize with you. Your "entertainment value" will displace the awkward humiliation of your latest blunder. People are gracious with those who admit their mistakes.

With another person's gaffe, use the same maneuver: "Hey, don't worry about it. I've done worse. Did I tell you about the time when . . ." The others in the group will admire your graciousness and "sacrifice" in lessening someone else's embarrassment. And the person you're covering for will love you forever.

TIP 247: Tactfully Reject Questions That Are Too Personal.

Often people seem to feel as put on the spot as they did in second grade when their teacher asked them what their dad did for a living. We grow up thinking we must answer all questions asked of us, or at least we feel uncomfortable not doing so. Instead, develop some gracious or witty deflectors: "I don't like to discuss that sort of thing on Tuesday evenings. Or Wednesday mornings. Or Saturday nights." "The only people I give that information to are my doctor and my analyst." "Even my hairdresser doesn't know for sure." Or be straightforward enough to suggest they withdraw the question: "Why would you ask that?" or "Why do you need that information?" or "I'm sorry, but that's personal with me."

TIP 248: Signal Before You're Offended.

If you have strong feelings about a particular subject, let the group know before they offend you and embarrass themselves. For example: "I've gotta warn you—I've got some pretty radical opinions about that. We'd better steer clear of that issue" or "I'm getting a little uneasy with this topic. I'm on that project team, you know." Others will appreciate the warning.

TIP 249: Consider Your Options When Listening to a Person with "Fixed" Ideas.

You can always remain silent to avoid a debate. If, however, you're bursting at the seams to have someone hear the opposing viewpoint, walk across a neutral zone before you try to speak. Don't begin with "yes, but's . . . , which sets up a debating tone for what is to follow. Instead try "You've made some very good points. I have a different view for other reasons. From my perspective . . ." or "I don't think I've ever heard anyone express that view exactly. My own thoughts on the subject are quite different. I feel that . . ." "I think I understand what you're saying. I feel differently. I believe . . ."

TIP 250: Be Noncommittal if You Want to Avoid Debate.

After someone voices an opposing view, after someone makes a slur you don't want to be associated with, or after the topic moves to one you'd rather not discuss, try the most appropriate of these comments: "Other people, I'm sure, feel just as you do." "The workplace keeps you on your toes—that's for sure." "Life's full of surprises." "You've got a point." "You think so?" "Yes, I've heard people say that." "Hmmm." "Well, . . . we've about exhausted that subject." "Mind if I change the subject for a moment. I've been wanting to ask you about . . ."

TIP 251: Avoid Editorializing.

On controversial topics, avoid stating a dogmatic opinion if you don't know the other person well. Dousing someone's emotions on their pet peeve or cause is a good way to get burned.

TIP 252: Accept Specific Compliments with Sincerity.

If you're like most people, you feel a little uncomfortable with a compliment. It's not that you don't appreciate the compliment; it's that you feel "on the spot" in front of others. There's elegance in a straightforward response: "Thank you very much. It's nice of you to call attention to that" or "Thanks. I'm glad you noticed" or "I appreciate your saying so" or "Wow. You made my day." "Thanks for commenting on that. I try very hard to X."

TIP 253: Prepare Self-Effacing Comebacks for Frequent, Vague, or Insincere Compliments.

Some compliments are immediately recognizable as "lines," or even as insincere flattery. Responding to them with sincerity makes you feel duped—as if you didn't know the difference.

A more comfortable response is a light, even self-effacing comeback. An acquaintance asked me one day: "Are you an ardent feminist? If not, then may I tell you you're gorgeous." Response: "Thanks. I write comments like that down in my journal every night. Then when I get angry at my husband, I just pull 'em out and consider my other options."

TIP 254: Gossip at Your Own Great Risk.

How to define gossip? People who say they don't gossip will admit talking about others' lives. Rare is the person who never passes on a fact or commendation about another's achievements, work, family, attitude, or character.

Why are people fascinated by gossip? It's a way of cutting others down to size, of showing up hypocrisy in those in places of fame or great fortune. On the beneficial side, it's a way of sharing common values and affirming with the listener that we feel the same way about a situation. Gossip also keeps us up to date and protects us. What we don't know about a pending merger may hurt us. Others gossip just to fill the conversational lull or to gain attention for having the "inside scoop."

What makes gossip negative is intention and tone. Talking *about* versus talking *against*. Negative information—or negative intentions with neutral information. Avoid passing on hurtful information, information that you would not want passed on if you were in the other person's shoes. And remember that all people may not be as "open" as you are. Even if the gossip is "good" gossip, be sure it's truth, not rumor.

TIP 255: Stop Gossip Without Offending the Spreader.

The reply that cuts gossips short is, "Oh, I didn't know that. He always speaks so highly of you." How's a person to continue after that line? It's effective in stopping almost any negative comment, but it feels like a slap in the face to the person talking. Try a gentler approach like the following. *Gossip:* "I hear Bill Barnes really gave you guys in Audit a mouthful today." *Response:* "He was upset, yes. But we worked through it. So, what's new with you?" *Gossip:* "Did you hear that Tseuko didn't get the promotion?" *Response:* "No, I didn't. I guess I'll have to ask her the reasons myself. You know how rumors go." *Gossip:* "I hear their company is about to go under." *Response:* "Rumors run rampant, don't they? I guess we'll hear the real truth sooner or later."

TIP 256: Squelch Complaints.

Even if others happen to agree with you, they'll notice your poor taste in complaining about the room, the food, the guests, the entertainment, the lack of planning, or anything else about the circumstances or events. You'll appear to be ungrateful for being included.

TIP 257: Don't Hard-Sell When the Purpose Is Chitchat.

Don't take advantage of people who have come to relax and get to know others on a personal level by turning your time with them into a sales call. Yes, a brief overview as a teaser of what you do, maybe. But don't put them on the spot for a further commitment unless they open the door and very overtly invite you in.

TIP 258: When You Meet Two VIPs at Once, Don't Focus on One and Ignore the Other.

Although one will be flattered at your obvious attention, he or she will have to be the one to bring the buddy into the conversation and will feel awkward in doing so. If you ignore either, both will feel uncomfortable.

TIP 259: Make a Graceful Exit.

When you're ready to end a conversation, wait until after *you've* just finished talking, not immediately after the other person has introduced a new topic or pauses midcourse. Use a closing comment such as "Excuse me. It's been nice to talk with you." "Well, so much for my views on X. I think I'll get something else to drink." "Excuse me. I want to catch Bob before he leaves." "Excuse me for monopolizing your time. I'll let you visit with someone else now."

TIP 260: Recognize the Importance of Small Talk.

If you're on the other end of the conversation when someone initiates small talk, recognize its value to them, if not to you personally. Conversation isn't simply for passing on useful information or getting a job done. More and more in our high-tech, impersonal workplace, people want emotional involvement and connection with others. Talking—about anything—helps establish, maintain, and adjust relationships to keep them in good order.

4

Winning People Over to Your Way of Thinking: Being Persuasive

*People are usually more convinced by reasons
they discovered themselves than by those found
out by others.* —BLAISE PASCAL

*One of the best ways to persuade others is by
listening to them.* —DEAN RUSK

*I would rather try to persuade a man to go
along, because once I have persuaded him, he
will stick. If I scare him, he will stay just as long
as he is scared, and then he is gone.*
—DWIGHT EISENHOWER

*If I had eight hours to chop down a tree I'd
spend six sharpening my axe.*
—ABRAHAM LINCOLN

Statistics are no substitute for judgment.
—HENRY CLAY

*I'll not listen to reason. Reason always means
what someone else has got to say.*
—ELIZABETH GASKELL

People never outgrow their need to be persuasive. Salespeople have to persuade customers to buy. Customers have to persuade salespeople that their time invested in servicing their account will pay off over the years. The entry-level employee hopes to convince the manager to approve a raise. The manager wants to be persuasive with new ideas and proposals to the CEO. The CEO has to persuade employees to be loyal, customers to buy, and the public to invest.

The challenge of persuasion faces all of us. These guidelines will take you beyond the typical "hoping for the best" attitude to awareness of what works best and how to prepare for your biggest opportunities.

TIP 261: Establish Credibility.

People believe people they like, people who are similar to them, people who are trustworthy, and people who have demonstrated expertise. Work on one or all of these to build your credibility with any given group. (Use Chapter 1 in this book as your bible.) The higher your credibility, the greater impact your message will have. Aristotle summed it up this way: "Persuasion is achieved by the speaker's personal character when the speech is so spoken as to make us think him credible. We believe good men more fully and more readily than others; this is true generally whatever the question is, and absolutely true where exact certainty is impossible and opinions are divided."

TIP 262: Understand the Three Dynamics of Persuasion: Logic, Character, Emotion.

Back to Aristotle. He says there are three means of being persuasive: ". . . (1) to reason logically, (2) to understand human character and goodness in their various forms, and (3) to understand the emotions—that is, to name and describe them, to know their causes and the way in which they are excited."

In short, after your boss thinks you're trustworthy, you must make him or her angry at the unfairness of "the system" so as to change it. And then you'll have to give proof of that unfairness.

You'll have to excite the customer about the status he or she will enjoy with the new product, and then you'll have to convince that customer it's the best of its kind on the market. Finally, the buyer will need to believe you're an honest salesperson who tells the complete truth.

You'll have to make donors feel compassion for the homeless, show them exactly where and how their money will help, and then demonstrate your own integrity and concern in the process of your fund-raising.

Most of us in the business world hate being labeled "emotional"; instead we want to be known as rational, logical thinkers. But emotions do underlie our decisions even at work. In any persuasive transaction, stir in all three ingredients: logic, emotion, character.

TIP 263: Identify the Appropriate Emotion of the Moment.

Which emotions do you need to tickle most frequently in the workplace? Anger, pride, envy, love, peace, comfort, belonging, surprise—the same ones felt whenever humans come together.

The idea of rewarding an employee with a gold watch for 25 years of service has this principle as its foundation. The ceremony surrounding the presentation elicits the emotion of high school or college graduation, a scouting award, or a junior achievement badge. It's the symbol and the emotion of the thing that counts.

When you want to persuade a manager to keep you in the job, appeal to the feelings of rejection encountered by that person when he or she was kicked off the starting line-up for one lousy foul. When you want to persuade parents to buy a bicycle, remind them of the day their grandfather taught them to ride and the thrill of independence riding to the store for bread. When you want to persuade a CEO to spend extra money on a glitzy annual report, remind him or her of the pride in bringing home a straight-A report card.

Even in business situations, specific, identifiable emotions may carry as much or more weight than logic. Decide which emotional appeal to make depending on your task and your decision maker.

TIP 264: Talk About Rewards and Incentives to Those People Who Think in Terms of Payoffs.

Some people wake up every morning looking for ways to make their life better: how to save time, how to save money, how to move ahead in their careers, how to be better managers, how to get their coworkers to like them, how to win the lottery, how to complete a crossword puzzle. If these people are the group you have to win over, highlight the personal and corporate benefits of acting on your ideas.

TIP 265: Talk About Facts and Statistics to Those Who Think Analytically.

These people don't buy cereal without figuring out the cost per ounce. Even if they are persuaded by emotion, they'll ask for the supporting evidence so as not to be embarrassed should anyone ask the reason for their breakfast choices. They don't believe in "soft dollars," "soft skills," or "soft data." Quantify everything.

TIP 266: Talk About the "Bandwagon" to Those Who Like to Jump On It.

Whether to save the effort of thinking for themselves or to meet their needs of belonging, these people pay a great deal of attention to what everyone else is doing. Passwords here include: "The trends show . . ." "Experts in the field seem to think . . ." "The leading-edge companies have implemented . . ." With these people, you need to provide testimonials of what others think of your ideas.

TIP 267: Talk About Obstacles to Be Overcome to Those Who Welcome Challenge and Change.

Some people wake up each morning ready to climb mountains. Tell them they can't do something and they start circulating petitions. Routine bores them. Tell them the system doesn't work, tell them you can't afford something, tell them it's too late or too early for a change—and that's when they'll start to work. Motivate them to act on your ideas by presenting them as obstacles to be overcome. Negative circumstances merely challenge them to climb mountains of opportunity.

TIP 268: Sell What People Want to Buy.

Don't limit your thinking to product and services here. I'm also talking about ideas, policies, concepts, and feelings. Think along two channels: what people *want* and what they *want to avoid*. Align your pitch with one of these benefits:

Want to have

Money	Opportunity
Prestige/status	Good reputation
Fun	Time
Possessions	

Want to be

Successful	Healthy
Unique	Smart

Liked   Rich

Loved   Stylish

Want to feel

Happy   In control

Successful   Important

Comfortable   Competent

Safe   Free

Guilt-free   Dignified

Committed   Respected/admired

Sexy

Want to avoid

Wasting effort   Being criticized

Losing time   Feeling stupid

Being forgotten   Being in danger

Losing possessions/money   Worrying

Losing reputation

TIP 269: Appeal to Self-Interest.

Yes, people do make decisions for the good of motherhood, apple pie, and country. But they feel an even stronger tug when the decision has something in it for them personally. So, don't just tell the manager that the new computer network will save the company over $400,000 in maintenance support during the next five years. Show how it will speed up preparation of the department's audit report and help get the paperwork off the manager's own desk. The more personal the benefits, the stronger the tug.

TIP 270: Create Immediacy.

A father may read in the newspaper that insurance companies are going bust right and left, and he'll shake his head with regret and turn the page. But let his college-age son interview for his first job with an insurance company and the father will clip that news story to send to his son, along with a note to "check this out before you accept that job."

IBM or General Motors may announce pending layoffs of 20,000 people in the next quarter, and you'll empathize with those families affected. But if you're an employee there, you'll start preparing your résumé and talking to friends about job possibilities.

Don't tell employees that if XYZ legislation passes, their health-care costs will rise. Tell them that their deductible will slide from $200 to $1000 and you'll have their attention.

To spark interest and action, the situation has to touch people's daily lives. The closer the interest or the pressure, the more attention people pay. Talk personally. Make problems hit home.

TIP 271: Use Associations from the Past.

Why does the President speak from the Oval Office when he needs extraordinary credibility for a difficult decision? Because the camera frames Old Glory standing in the background. That symbol subtly evokes patriotic moments in our history when the President took a stand in a major crisis and pulled the nation together in victory. To be persuasive, try to evoke associations with other people, other groups, and other successes to lead people to transfer that past confidence to the present situation.

This principle is at work when you have a decorated military general speak for the tax increase: Voting yes is the patriotic thing to do. The principle is at work when you see a toddler in an insurance commercial: Buying insurance will give your kids the same security of your own childhood.

This principle is at work when you see a stay-at-home mom buttoning the jacket of her 6-year-old before the child leaves for school: Buying brand X cough syrup is what your own loving mother would do.

How do you know your employees will enjoy a 1960s party at their annual convention? Remind them of the success of their senior prom. Will this negotiating ploy work with the new customer? Remind your boss of past contract negotiations where you came out a winner. Will the bond campaign for the community convention center win support? Most likely, if you can remind the voting crowd of the bond-funded theater they currently enjoy.

TIP 272: Ride with the Flow As Far As You Can Go.

We tend to continue to do things "because we've always done it that way." People resist change. Many voters still hold the political beliefs learned at their parent's knee. They watch TV ads for things they've already bought. They read cartoon series they've followed for 10 years and watch TV reruns for a lifetime.

For you, that means it's easier to ride the flow of opinion as far as you can. Find out what people feel comfortable with currently, and then present your idea as "a slight modification" rather than a "new" idea altogether. Think how much easier it would sound to you if someone asks you to "revise your report to include X" versus "rewrite your report." To "alter" sounds easier than to "rewrite" from scratch.

To avoid resistance to a "new" policy or procedure, just "alter" the old one.

TIP 273: Use the Lesser-of-Two-Evils Approach.

If the decision you want from your listener is not particularly pleasant or desirable, consider creating fear about the other alternatives. Outline what happens if they stay with the status quo, what happens if they do X, what happens if their competitors or customers do Y. Your purpose is to get the listener to decide *against* the other options rather than necessarily deciding *for* your option.

The American public makes a similar choice every year at election time.

TIP 274: Provide a Better and Best Option.

Should your decision maker not go for your best option, don't let the entire plan or idea fall flat. Determine a second, lesser objective that you can present as a "second best" option.

TIP 275: Use the Jelly Principle.

When I was sick as a child, my mother used to put cough syrup in a spoon of jelly to camouflage the taste. The same principle comes in handy with bitter messages. You may have to wrap them in more pleasing ideas or get them across in more subtle ways.

TIP 276: Try the Tom Sawyer Approach.

Twain's Tom Sawyer let Huck Finn whitewash his fence for a little of nothing—just because they happened to be friends. The furniture salesperson sets up the same situation. The shopper: "I guess I like the blue chair better than the green one." Salesperson: "I'm not sure if we have it in stock. I may have just sold the last one. That has been our most popular chair. People practically grab that off the floor at that price. Better give me a moment to check the computer before you get your hopes up." What happens? All of the sudden the shopper has a definite preference for the blue chair.

What happens in the furniture store unfolds around the conference table. You can create momentum for your idea if you let people understand that nothing is a sure thing, that the time is now (maybe not later), that the money is available now (maybe not later), that the XYZ department is willing to cooperate now (maybe not later), that the customer is ready to sign the deal now (maybe not later). You get the picture.

Put the pressure on the other foot. Create high demand and low supply. Your listener must act now or miss the supply of opportunities.

TIP 277: Let the Decision Maker Hear from the Converted.

Second-hand testimonials are not nearly as effective as the words straight from the mouth of those already converted to your way of thinking. If possible, bring these satisfied users/buyers/believers/beneficiaries to the discussion with you—in person or by letter, video, or satellite. Unscripted and in their own unique way, let them speak to the effectiveness or truth of what you say.

TIP 278: Play on the Power of Your Expertise.

We rarely question our CPA, our neurologist, our air-conditioner repair person when they tell us the causes of our difficulties and recommend solutions. Why? There's power in the perception of specialized expertise. If you establish credentials early in a certain field, people seldom question them. They'll give you the benefit of the doubt on your facts and conclusions more often than not.

TIP 279: Roll with Realities Rather Than Hope for Martyrs.

In a perfect world, perfectly good ideas would be implemented. You have to understand political realities of the workplace—pressures from colleagues, customers, and coworkers that may force others to veto your ideas and plans. Find ways to help people handle those realities rather than expect them to become martyrs for your sake.

TIP 280: Choose Your Timing.

The time to sell roofs is right after a tornado. The time to sell investment expertise is after the stock market takes a drastic upturn or downturn. The time to sell a quality process in your organization is after you've been removed from the bidder's list because of the rising percentage of defects in your deliveries. Timing is crucial. Ask any politician.

TIP 281: Create a Favorable Atmosphere.

Meeting planners claim that registrants rate educational seminars higher when they're held in resort locations. Job applicants prefer jobs where they are interviewed in plush surroundings. Shoppers shop longer where music plays in the background. Diners linger longer over meals served in comfortable restaurants. So it stands to reason that the principle can work for you.

TIP 282: Stand Up for People to Take You Seriously.

If your office culture is generally laid-back, with people walking in and out to see the boss without appointments, with no-agenda meetings, with "your office or mine" casualness, you may want to get attention to the seriousness or urgency of a problem by changing the atmosphere drastically. Be formal. Do the out-of-the-ordinary. Use a flipchart or overhead. Make it official. A stand-up presentation adds to your authority. Put people on notice that your idea deserves unusual attention.

TIP 283: Present Your Idea to Several Small Groups Rather Than One Large Group.

Groups take on a personality all their own. Any large group presents the problem of getting to know individual members. Their experience, attitudes, uses for what you have to say, biases and needs, and personal agendas vary so that you're at a great disadvantage to make your ideas relevant and clear to all concerned.

In smaller groups, you can select the details of most concern to the fewer individuals and relate your facts to their experiences, fears, and hopes. A less formal presentation to a smaller group will usually generate more participation and questions that give you important feedback and allow you to rechart your course. And, of course, you can build rapport quicker and easier because you seem more "approachable" to them.

Aside from the extra time involved, smaller is better.

TIP 284: When There's a Parade, Take the Last Spot.

If you're one of several people trying to persuade your audience to choose among you, ask for the last time slot. By the time the others finish with all their statistics, charts, and promises, the buyers will have grown weary and forgetful. Your presentation will be the last on their mind.

TIP 285: Know the Criteria Before Pushing the Solution.

Gain agreement on a group's or boss's criteria and then work backward: What does the decision maker consider the most important issue? A selling price under $5000? A maintenance agreement with a 4-hour response for problems? Delivery within 60 days? A vendor with a TQM program in place? Unless your criteria matches theirs, you'll look like a solution waiting for a problem to happen.

TIP 286: Limit Your Objectives.

Rome wasn't built while they were working on Sicily. You can't accomplish everything at once. Determine your primary objective in presenting your case, and focus your efforts on accomplishing that one goal. If your chief concern is getting your boss to hire three extra people in your department, leave discussions about rearranging the workstations and lobby until another day.

TIP 287: Make a Conscious Decision About Whether to Present All Sides of an Issue or Only Yours.

If you expect a hostile audience, one biased against your plan from the beginning, present all sides—all options and the pros and cons of each. When chances are great that the group will hear other options and arguments before the decision is made, you'll create the extra credibility of being thorough, open, and objective about all the facts and alternatives.

If the audience is either positive or neutral, present only your alternative—an overview or message, the action you want, and the detail to take the action. Then do a quick test before you conclude. "Are you ready to decide, or would you like to hear other alternatives and why I'm suggesting we reject those alternatives?" If they want more options, you can provide them with thorough analysis. If they don't want to hear other options and trust your judgment based on criteria they agreed with, then you'll not waste their time on the "also rans."

TIP 288: Organize Your Ideas for Greatest Impact.

The simple approach calls for these steps:

1. Get attention.

2. Overview the conclusion/action/decision you want and the key benefits.

3. Build your case in detail:

- Create or confirm a need.
- Show how your idea, plan, service, or product will meet that need.
- Elaborate on the benefits overviewed earlier.
- Discuss how your ideas, plan, product, or service will be implemented (the practical day-to-day how-tos).

4. Call for a specific action/decision.

In developing item 3, you have a plethora of arrangements for specific points: Move from problem to solution, point out the cause and the effect, move backward from the effect to the cause, compare and/or contrast two options, or compare options to the criteria. Just get a plan and stay with it.

A clearly organized presentation represents clear thinking and leads to a fast, favorable decision.

TIP 289: Use the Bad-News-First Approach.

You disarm people when you give them the downside of your proposal first. They're disappointed. Then you present the upside and things seem brighter. By the time you finish with your presentation, they've gained enough momentum to feel that the bad news wasn't such a handicap as they first thought. Keep the momentum moving upward rather than downward.

TIP 290: Calculate the Minimum Gain You Would Need to Justify Investing Time or Money in Your Idea.

Many ideas languish on the table of indecision because we can't calculate "the hard dollars." If we invest in training our salespeople to write better proposals at a cost of $X, what will be the payoff? Do we keep track of how many more deals they close after the proposal-writing course? But what if the price of the product they're selling rises or a competitor changes the marketplace drastically? How do they pinpoint with certainty that better proposals alone will make the difference in their sales volume? We face such issues daily.

When it's difficult to quantify savings or gain in time or money on a new idea, consider what the minimum time or dollar savings would need to be to make the idea worthwhile. What if the training resulted in our improved proposal that won the $12 million contract with Universal, Inc.?

Getting people to agree on a minimum is easier than getting them to agree on a valid, "real" number.

TIP 291: Point Out What You Know for a Fact
and "What Seems to Make Sense."

> Always separate facts from subjective opinion. We are constantly taking in
> information about what happens around us and drawing conclusions based
> on that information. The problem is that information is rarely complete so
> we "fill in the blanks" and then forget which part we filled in. Then when
> we're questioned on a particular piece of information that was an inference
> rather than fact, we lose credibility for our factual information as well.
> Head off such situations by pointing out what you know for certain and
> what you have inferred from those facts.

TIP 292: Credit Other People for Their
Sound Reasoning.

> Position yourself as an ally of anyone who thinks clearly. When people bring
> up opposing views, question them about the basis of the views. Understand
> their reasoning and let them know you understand that reasoning. Only
> with "we're in this together" positioning will you overcome the feeling of
> "us" against "them."

TIP 293: Recognize That People Support What
They Help Create.

> Rally support for your ideas in a subtle way by asking people to contribute
> to them. Tell them what you're about, what your goal is; then set about ask-
> ing for their thinking on the subject before you put together your formal
> presentation of the idea to the entire group. What figures, resources, or
> anecdotes can they supply for you? If this plan meets with opposition, what
> do they think the focus of that disagreement likely will be? If others react
> negatively, what would they suggest you try as second best?
>
> The White House uses this strategy in building support for major legisla-
> tion in Congress. They seek out the facts, the opposing views, and the sup-
> porting views *before* the vote, not during.

TIP 294: Encourage Others to State Their Own Needs
or Problems to Be Solved.

> People believe what they do and say themselves. What's better than your
> overviewing a need that your idea, product, or service can meet? Let your
> listeners voice those need themselves. Walk to a flipchart and ask the group
> to help you list problems they're having on the job relative to X. Or grab a

napkin at the lunch table and ask your boss to help you identify things that need improving "by whatever solution we come up with." Encourage others to speak up, stand up, question, conform, counter—just get them talking and moving. Then, rather than your having to convince others of a need, they will believe what they have just told you in their own words.

TIP 295: Invite Others to Try On Your Idea.

How many times have you heard the lament, "If I could just get the boss to try it, she'd like it." That's why we get toothpaste, cereal, and soap in the mail. A parent says, "If I could just get Johnny to go to the party, I know he'd have a good time." The professor says, "If I could just get the students to read poetry, I know they'd like it." The car salesperson says, "If I could just get people to come in for a test drive, I know they'd be sold."

The same is true with ideas. People can't try new ideas on over old ones. Have you ever tried a new suit of clothes on while wearing the old one? You have to persuade people to throw away the old policy, procedure, machine—at least for a time—for them to give the new policy, procedure, equipment a fair trial. To persuade others to try on the new idea, you have let them play with the idea first—discuss what-ifs, who-withs, where-necessarys, whys, and how-tos. Only then will they really put on the idea and wear it awhile.

TIP 296: Be Careful About Opening with a Broad Question.

Wrong approach: "So tell me a little about your operations now—what's automated and what's not?" First of all, the other person will be reluctant to answer because he or she doesn't know where the question is leading. Second, much of the answer would probably be irrelevant to the discussion at hand. Even with the consultative approach, people want to know where you're trying to lead them. If you start with a question, focus it and give the benefits or the point of knowing the answer.

TIP 297: Ask a Question That Showcases a Benefit.

"What are you spending now on dry cleaning the uniforms?" Follow up: "This new fabric doesn't need to be dry-cleaned at all."

Raise a question: "How much time do your engineers spend in preparing these charts each month?" Follow up: "This software package can generate such a chart with fewer than six keystrokes." Raise a question: "Do your managers look forward to performance appraisal conferences?" Give a response: "Our external consultants can identify performance problems objectively with this survey before these problems lead to termination."

TIP 298: State Quantifiable Facts Rather Than Opinions.

Studies do show that people give credence to people who take the time to back up what they're saying with hard facts and data. Yes, initial impressions count, but hard evidence counts most of all. For things you find difficult to measure and quantify, come up with an estimation. But don't pick a number out of the air. Be prepared to share your logic behind the number. Be straightforward that your numbers are estimates and share your rationale behind them.

Notice the difference in impact and authority in these statements: "We spent $82,000 from February to October on temporary staff in the Operations and Accounting departments" versus "We've spent a lot of money on temporary staff this year" or "Hyong completed his project three months earlier than his deadline and $50,000 under budget. The customer gave him the highest satisfaction rating we've received in our six years work with that company" versus "Hyong deserves a raise—he's dependable and customers respect his work."

TIP 299: Cite Your Sources and Ask for Those of Others.

"They" have probably become the most vocal group in our society. "They say" this and "they say" that. When you have credible sources to support your information, cite them. When the other person tosses out objections based on "they says," ask specifically where those ideas, statistics, policies, or preventatives originated. Then, when given a credible source, ask how current the information is.

TIP 300: Turn Information, Facts, and Features into Benefits.

As you prepare, with every point you plan to make picture your listener asking, "So what is that supposed to mean to me, my department, my company?"

Feature: "This printer prints X characters a minute."

Benefit: "This printer can turn out one of your 200-page proposals in X minutes. If your clerk prints out only 10 per day for these engineers, she'll be saving Y minutes."

Feature: "Our shelter provides 100 adult beds and 50 children's beds for the needy."

Benefit: "Your donation will provide temporary housing for 100 women who don't want to return to abusive husbands."

Feature: "Your corporate sponsorship of the seminar will pay for the keynote speaker's travel and lodging."

Benefit: "Your corporate sponsorship of the seminar will allow your site manager a five-minute introduction at the beginning of the program to overview your services."

Big difference.

TIP 301: Vary Your Intensity.

If you intend to build to a passionate appeal, you can't start out screaming. Consider how the singer begins with a timid croon, builds with up-and-down variations, and finally crescendos to a rousing finale. Do the same with your own delivery.

TIP 302: Increase Your Pace to Increase Comprehension—Up to a Point.

The typical listener thinks about six times faster than the average person speaks. When you want to keep others' attention, you have to increase your speaking rate. Otherwise, they take a mental recess. You don't, of course, want to speak so quickly that you don't articulate. Variety is the key. Slow down for complex technical information (if you can't skip it altogether) and speed up for the remainder of your persuasive points.

TIP 303: Personify Abstract Concepts or Inanimate Objects.

People have a difficult time dealing in abstractions. Because they are emotional beings, people respond to things they can touch, feel, and understand. Give human characteristics to abstractions to arouse the listener's emotions.

Examples: "This machine is temperamental; you have to make love to it before it responds to what you want." "This company is like an octopus; it has so many arms reaching out in the marketplace that one arm can get cut off without severe pain to the rest of the body." "This organization is sick; it's underfed; its energy is drained. We've simply got to find operating capital."

TIP 304: Speak Metaphorically.

Metaphors create powerful pictures. One metaphor can convey a lifetime of experience or a head full of logic. In one of my client workshops, a sales rep presented an analogy of data files to socks. Black dress socks worn every day to the office represent data files needed daily; dress socks go in the top drawer for easy access just like data files you retrieve often must be easy to access. White athletic socks worn for exercising only on the weekends represent data files that you need only monthly or quarterly; these white socks are stored in the middle bureau drawer for limited access just like data files you don't need to get to often. The rep's green plaid socks, worn only when Aunt Martha comes to visit, represent the data files needed only once a year. Those plaid socks are stored in the bottom bureau drawer for infrequent access just like files you may never need again. His audience immediately understood his explanation about quick access to disk storage space.

We occasionally explain the various fee arrangements of our licensing of training programs to customers with this analogy: "As you determine which is the best fee arrangement for your organization, consider it a mortgage." You can pay for a house all cash up front, or you can pay for it over time with interest. With our licensing fee, you can pay for the entire course and all master copies up front, or you can pay participant by participant. The last arrangement will cost you more over time, but you have your money free to use for other things as you go along. Customers understand the concept: they can make an outright purchase or they could take out a mortgage.

Metaphors clarify what would take hours to explain in detail.

TIP 305: Use Anecdotes and Stories to Make Your Points.

Aesop did. Jesus Christ did. Norman Lear does. People can digest only so much factual information. Anecdotes tie it all together—logic and emotion. Don't tell us what kinds of problems users can have if the system crashes. Tell us what happened to Joe Smithers when his hard disk crashed in the middle of his budget preparation. Don't tell companies that they should have a disaster recovery plan in place. Tell them what happened to customer data within companies in Florida when the last hurricane hit. Don't tell people how the typical salesperson responds to incentive awards. Tell the sales manager that Gerry Wainwright won a trip to Hawaii and has tripled her sales as a result of the contest. Stories hit the heart and head.

TIP 306: Use Humor to Raise Receptivity.

Humor acts as a pleasant distracter, lessening tension so people feel more comfortable examining the pros and cons of an idea. A humorous approach—we're not talking slapstick, just witty or light—keeps attention and drives away boredom. Laughter lowers defenses and raises receptivity.

TIP 307: Package Ideas Like Products.

People are lazy thinkers if you permit them to be. Make your concept understandable by its packaging. Politicians, policies, and plays are packaged like soaps and telephone services. For example, insurance rates, employee compensation, unemployment, and tax incentives can all be packaged as "health-care" issues in Washington. Think beginning, middle, and end (idea, action, implementation) and tie them all together in one packaged concept.

TIP 308: Create Slogans.

Politicians package their ideas in soundbites. Charities create a poster goal. Conventions display a theme banner. If you can summarize your point in a short, witty slogan, do so. Make it catchy and current.

TIP 309: Triple Things—Use Triads and Alliteration.

One of the first lessons in speech writing is the use of triads (groupings of three). If you can add alliteration (repetition of the sound from word to word), so much the better. Our ears love the sound of:

Government of the people, by the people, for the people.

Blood, sweat, and tears.

Clearly, quickly, concisely.

Motivate, renovate, captivate.

Pray, prepare, preach.

They want jobs, they want justice, they want respect.

Change the rhythm or omit one word or phrase in any of the above groupings and you lose the impact.

TIP 310: Don't Be Too Cute.

At least weekly, I receive a direct-mail piece that catches my attention: a funny cartoon, a glitzy color, a sly slogan, a provocative question. My problem is determining what is being sold. I don't know exactly what the letter-writer is asking me to buy, decide, or do. If you have to work for it, the point is not persuasive.

TIP 311: Select Selling Words.

Get people's attention with words like these: new, updated, exciting, fashionable, fast-acting, cost-effective, low-cost, no-risk, easy to use, successful, prestigious, opportune time, select few.

TIP 312: Prefer Powerful Phrasing.

"I would suggest . . ." sounds like you're not quite sure, that if you were in a position to make a suggestion and if it didn't fluster anyone, you might suggest that maybe . . ." Use instead: "I suggest." Rid your language of such weak phrases.

Not: "I think we should attempt to get approval on this before it's too late."

But: "Let's get immediate approval on this."

Not: "It seems to me that . . ."

But: "I believe . . ."

Not: "I've been thinking lately that maybe someone could . . ."

But: "After careful thought over the past two months, I've decided that . . ."

Not: "This plan could work if we really push it."

But: "With our support, this plan will work."

Can you hear the ring of positive thinking and authority?

TIP 313: Use Both Rounded and Exact Numbers.

Exact numbers sound more credible: "The number of employees dissatisfied with their paychecks was 51.4 percent" sounds exact, therefore accurate. Rounded numbers, on the other hand, give the appearance of estimations. Yet "slightly over half" is easier to remember than 51.4 percent of the employees surveyed. So which to use if you want the numbers to be both credible and memorable? Use the exact number first, and then round it off with later references.

TIP 314: Make Statistics Experiential.

People digest numbers with great difficulty. Yes, pie charts and bar graphs help. But if you can go beyond that, do so. Try to make statistics both visual and experiential. For example, randomly survey your audience by asking them to raise their hands; then equate those findings to the random survey you did previously. Or do as one manager did when he dramatically ripped a dollar in two to illustrate what the administration had done to his budget for the upcoming year. Yes, supporting statistics lend credibility to what you say. But do all you can to help your audience digest them.

TIP 315: Never Let Facts Speak for Themselves.

Facts need interpretation. According to Mark Twain, "There are three kinds of lies: lies, damned lies, and statistics." If you don't believe it, tune in to the next political campaign. People can make facts and numbers mean almost anything. Interpret yours.

TIP 316: Consider the Legitimacy of the Printed Word.

To some people, putting something on paper means it's official. For this reason, even small-business owners print all their fee schedules, prices, and terms and conditions on "official" letterhead. To quote them orally makes them subject to negotiation. When traveling in unfamiliar countries, you can determine which street vendors dicker and which don't by the absence or presence of price tags on their wares. The same principle works whether you're selling a concept or a vacation: put it in a memo, a manual, or a mural.

TIP 317: Provide Memory Aids.

Listening expert Dr. Lyman K. Steil estimates that the average-knowledge worker listens at an effective rate of 25 percent. Other research shows that after a 10-minute presentation, a typical listener forgets 50 percent of the information heard. After two days, the recall level drops to 25 percent. After a week, the recall drops to about 10 percent. Therefore, you have to help the listener remember your points.

Use metaphors to make concepts easy to recall. Give your listener a personal experience with the concept; that is the idea behind ropes-training for team building in organizations. You can use a mnemonic device for your key points (the three Ps of Universal Services: Prepare, Plan, Promote). You can provide a demonstration model to let the customer get a "feel" for extending his or her memory. Whatever method you choose, work on increasing others' recall of your idea, service, or product.

TIP 318: Use Visuals As Aids, but Don't Let Them Dominate.

Studies by the University of Minnesota and the 3M Corporation, along with an earlier research at the Wharton School, indicate that an audience is 43 percent more likely to be persuaded with visuals than with words alone. Consider a written report, handouts, graphics, or other visuals to aid clarity and recall.

A warning: Anything that's overdone loses its effect. If you underline every word in a report, nothing stands out. If you hang a picture on every wall, no one notices the masterpiece 10 feet to the left of the water cooler. Likewise, if you use a visual for every point, the visuals become the presentation—a serious error. Visuals should never dominate.

TIP 319: Don't Ever Read Your Key Points.

When reading, the all-important eye contact is missing. Rapport suffers. Reading, rather than telling, your ideas destroys your credibility, sincerity, and enthusiasm. The listener always toys with these thoughts: Who generated these ideas? Doesn't she care enough to learn them? Isn't he convicted enough to give them from the heart? Why is he afraid to look me in the eye? Does she doubt what she's saying? Aren't these facts important enough to remember?

TIP 320: Match the Visual, Auditory, and Kinesthetic Patterns.

Neurolinguists tell us that we perceive the world through different senses: visual, auditory, and kinesthetic (the other senses). How do you know your listeners' preferences? Listen to their language for cues:

Visual.   I see what you mean; I just don't see it; he'll take a dim view of that option; that's a shortsighted approach; in my mind's eye; paint me a picture; she's got tunnel vision; and so forth.

Auditory.   That doesn't ring a bell; I keep arguing with myself; outspoken people; call a spade a spade; word for word; spit it out; coming through loud and clear.

Kinesthetic.   Heated debate; makes me uncomfortable; hot-headed; he's so formal and stiff; she's out of touch; hassle-free plan; hang tough; hanging by a thread; nailed him on that point; gut reaction; walk arm in arm on that; lateral moves.

Once you understand your listener's needs, match them with your own language.

TIP 321: Repeat, Repeat, Repeat.

If nothing else works, try the broken-record technique. If you state your message often enough in a variety of ways, somebody eventually will listen. If you hear something often enough, it becomes part of the atmosphere— like humidity. Repetition forms the core of advertising.

TIP 322: Prefer Understatement to Overstatement.

When you overstate your case, the listener raises his or her guard. Everything becomes suspect. A gross overstatement begs a customer to knock the wind out of your sails/sales. With understatement, the other person often takes up your cause for you. Your statement: "We can save a minimum of $10,000 annually." Supporters will often chime in: "And in our situation this year, we saved twice that amount." Your credibility has gone up, not down. Reverse the comments and your estimation loses credence.

TIP 323: Get Past Clichés, Platitudes, and Truisms.

"You can't teach an old dog new tricks." "You pay for what you get." "Haste makes waste." "Let sleeping dogs lie." "He who hesitates is lost." When you resort to summing up your argument with one of the axioms, you give up your most powerful tool. People resist ruts. They'll think you're simplifying a complex problem and falling back on lazy thinking. Come up with your own new slogans and truths.

TIP 324: Don't Beg the Question.

Begging the question means stating the obvious or stating an assumption that sounds as though it doesn't need additional proof. "It's obvious that . . ." "If we continue to collect more information, we'll have more facts upon which to base our decision." "I suggest users perform these tests quarterly because the results will give them further information." "The salvage consultants determined that we should reinforce the welded joints because this was the wisest preventive solution." "More testing may be useful because it may shed more light on the subject."

Persuasive language involves a logical presentation of facts and information, not a fanfare of fancy, overblown pronouncements that are trivially true.

TIP 325: Anticipate Questions.

If you were the decision maker, what would you want to know before giving your approval? Go through the five Ws as prompters: Have you covered who, when, what, where, why, as well as how and how much about your answer? If not, prepare to do so.

TIP 326: Use Others' Questions to Make
Your Own Points.

When someone raises a question, think of bridging. How can you answer and then bridge back to a key point you want to make? *Question:* "How long did you say delivery on the widgets would take?" *Answer:* "Delivery will take about 6 weeks; that's why we need a decision this week." *Question:* "How complex will installation be and what kind of downtime will we have?" *Answer:* "It's complex. And if it's not done right downtime can be 6 to 10 days. That's why I think the credentials of the vendors are critical to our decision. As I mentioned earlier, the technicians at Universal can guarantee . . ."

TIP 327: Notice Whether People Listen to Your Answers.

If you answer a question-objection while the person seemingly jumps to another issue without giving your answer much thought, pay attention to that behavior. That question serves only as a decoy to cover the real reluctance to go along with your proposed idea. When the question is for real, the other person listens and incorporates your response into his or her thinking.

TIP 328: Prepare for the Standard Objections.

Objections in the workplace are, unfortunately, standard: "We've never done it that way before." "We can't afford to." "We can't afford not to." "It's risky." "Let's let somebody else work out the bugs and then we'll see." "We've got too much invested in the status quo." "We don't have the time to devote to it." "We don't have enough people." "We don't have the expertise." "That's somebody else's job." "I just don't think we can make it work." "Our people won't like it."

Plan your response to the objections you know will arise in your discussions.

TIP 329: Recognize the Body Language of Resistance.

Some people voice resistance openly: "I'm not interested." "I don't think the idea will fly." "I can't give it my full attention until next year." Others gesture their resistance: clock watching, foot or finger tapping, playing with objects within reach, doodling on paper, staring out the window or door. Others look for distractions to take them away: phone calls and fires to put out. Some try to make a game of it. They ask unrelated, distracting questions, nitpick your data, and toss out silly comments. Some are openly rude and grow irritable. Some withhold key information and observations so you have to guess what they know. Others just sit patiently and wait for you to "get it over with" so they can politely say no.

Recognize all these signs so you know how far you are from your goal of agreement.

TIP 330: Dig for Unspoken Reservations.

Don't stop at recognizing the signs of resistance. Get them on the table. When people seem reluctant to accept your ideas, be persistent in recovering the reason. You can't respond to an unasked question. You can't calm an unspoken fear. You can't compare options if you have no idea what the other options are. Encourage your decision maker to think aloud so you can either confirm or correct your presentation along the way.

Try statements such as: "Why not?" "How do you think your people will like this?" "Do you think your own customers will welcome this change?" "If somebody comes up with an objection later in the process, what do you think that might be?" "What else would stand in the way?" "Is there anything else that would keep us from moving on this?" "What about other things that would make you reluctant?" "Are there related issues?" "What else stands in the way of an okay?"

Keep pushing until you get the resistance on the table. Silence doesn't necessarily mean consent; it may mean that the obstacles are looming so large against what you say that the listener doesn't see the point in even discussing the matter further. You have to see the hurdles to jump them.

TIP 331: Investigate the Standard Causes of Resistance.

If you're having difficulty getting people to accept your point, take time to investigate their points. Your willingness to investigate and listen goes a long way in demonstrating your integrity and intelligence.

People resist change because it creates uncertainty. Maybe your idea will work and maybe it won't. What if the group invests time and money in the new plan and the old one turns out to be better? That fence-sitting period of indecision creates discomfort.

A second reason for resistance is the not-invented-here insecurity: "Why did someone else, rather than I, think of that idea?" "This is my department; why are you trying to tell me how to run it?" "What's mine is mine." This insecurity is especially at play if the person with the new idea has less experience or time on the job.

Then there's competitiveness. In some situations, if your idea wins, mine loses.

Fourth, there are personality issues: *I don't like you; therefore, I don't like your ideas* or *I'm a negative person—I don't like anything or anybody.* Only after you hear the unspoken concerns and then identify their causes can you set about minimizing resistance.

TIP 332: Brace Yourself Through the Negatives.

Just because somebody is bent on bringing up all the cons to your point or detailing all the pitfalls if you're wrong, don't think all is lost. You don't have to do a point-by-point rebuttal. Many decisions—maybe even most—are made in spite of all the negatives identified and discussed. Brace yourself and wait out the recitation. It's possible, even likely, to lose the small battles at several points and still win the war.

TIP 333: Guard Against Your Own Resistance to Others' Comments.

Do you tune out others while they're still talking and begin to prepare your rebuttal? Are you pouncing on other people's ideas immediately after they're stated? If so, you're not giving those ideas a fair hearing. Even if you've heard the ideas before and know where the person seems to be going with the comment, pouncing too soon conveys a closed mind and an unwillingness to hear others out carefully. Is the pace of the discussion getting faster and faster? If so, the other person, you, or both of you are resisting, not thinking.

TIP 334: Don't Censor Emotional Comments Out of Hand As Irrelevant.

Someone may raise a question that you do not believe is germane to the decision. Don't rush through the concern "to get back to the real issue." Some concerns may not be *logically* relevant, but they may be *emotionally* relevant. For example, the marketing people may bring up a gripe about the way the customer-service people handle angry callers. That issue may have little bearing on how the marketing group pays for long-distance service but may make a big difference in whether the customer-service people keep their jobs. What is relevant varies according to the purpose of all concerned.

TIP 335: Agree Before You Disagree.

To avoid the appearance of not listening to points others raise, hear them out, pause, and then agree with at least something they've said: "That is a related issue, all right. The first thing, however, we need is . . ." or "You have a point. Do you think that should be our primary criteria?" or "You're right about that. I wonder if . . ." They'll tag you as a reasonable, flexible person.

TIP 336: Use the Every-Cloud-Has-a-Silver-Lining Principle.

Your project manager states opposition to your idea to buy brand X pens as gifts to all new hires because of the "exorbitant cost." You concede the point that the brand X pens cost more than most brands, but you point out that the new hires will feel proud that the company has lavished on them such an expensive gift on their first day on the job. Reinterpret negatives as positives.

TIP 337: Ask for the Reasoning Behind Someone's Counterclaim.

Don't argue against the wind. Let's suppose you present a plan for providing computer maintenance service to a customer who says, "It's too expensive." You respond, "Not really, when you consider the X feature." The customer listens and then responds, "But it is much more than we wanted to pay." And you say, "Well, that may be true, but . . ."

You get the picture—arguing over a vague assumption. What does the customer mean by expensive? What is his or her reasoning? How did the customer decide what should be a reasonable price? When you get the answers to those questions, you'll have something specific to work with. If the comment "too expensive" is based on the amount of the customer's budget, you'll know to spend your time figuring out how to help the person finance the service within that budget. If the comment is based on a comparison of your price to that of competitors, then you'll spend your time telling how your service differs from theirs.

Take another example: A boss says, "We can't change that policy because people would get angry." You can't deal with that unless you know the boss's reasoning—why he or she thinks people will get angry.

Of course, be sure to ask for the other person's reasoning in a nondirective, nonchallenging way: "The way we set our price is to determine X, then Y, and then add 10 percent for Z. How did you set your budget figure for this service? Let's see if we're on the same wavelength, or if we're comparing apples to oranges here."

To argue without knowing the basis of assumptions is a shot in the dark.

TIP 338: Check for Reasoning Errors.

Make sure your own reasoning follows logic, and then check for errors in the other person's logic. Here are the most common reasoning faults:

- *Force-fitting an analogy.* Someone uses an analogy to explain how two things are alike—and then they get carried away. "A maintenance agreement on your copier is like an insurance policy on your automobile." Yes, there are similarities that would help someone understand the idea of a prepaid maintenance agreement, but it doesn't follow that the two arrangements are alike in all ways. Insisting that they are to make a point is faulty reasoning.

- *Generalizing from a single case.*   The sales manager in Tupelo feels uninformed by headquarters about the introduction of new products and ad campaigns; therefore, the manager reasons that all sales managers feel uninformed on important new developments.

- *Focusing on all or nothing.*   This reasoning insists on considering all ideas as a package deal. We have to accept all of it or none of it. This product will meet all our needs or none of our needs. We have to reward everyone for perfect attendance or no one for perfect attendance.

- *Stating rather than proving.*   "That manager has been delinquent in dealing with safety issues." Where's the proof? What specific incidents have gone unresolved? "Ferdinand has no ambition to move up in the company." What specifics support this conclusion? Calling a process "primitive" or equipment "state-of-the-art" doesn't make it so.

- *Confusing sequence with cause and effect.*   A demanding controller joins the company August 1 as head of Max's department. Max resigns on August 31; therefore, Max left because he had difficulty working with the new controller. As in this case, chronology may have little or nothing to do with result.

Check for these gaps in logic before someone points them out to you in front of a group and douses your credibility.

TIP 339: Unravel the Thread of "Why."

People believe what they discover for themselves. When someone states an opinion, ask why the person feels or thinks that way. After the explanation, pick out a part of it and ask why. After that explanation, select another thread and ask why. Unless the case is as solid as ice, the person will soon discover some weaknesses in his or her own thinking. Then you will have rooted out opportunity to present your views.

TIP 340: Paraphrase Trivial Objections.

When someone raises a trivial objection, listen carefully. Then, to show them you've listened, paraphrase the objection aloud to them "for clarity's sake." Not only will the other person know you've really listened, he or she will sometimes hear how weak the objection sounds to begin with. The response is often, "Well, never mind. I guess that's a minor concern at this point."

TIP 341: Change Yes-No Issues to Multiple-Choice.

Don't make accepting or rejecting your idea an all-or-nothing proposition. If you agree that some action is better than no action, take care to help your listeners see other choices. If they can't purchase the equipment now to do the printing, are they willing to let you contract with freelancers to get the work done? If they can't give you two operators for the week, can they contribute funds to help you pay for a temporary from outside? If management insists they can't afford to fly their people to the West Coast for a seminar, would they consider conducting a class locally? Would they at least provide videos in the corporate library? Buy a $16.95 book for self-study?

TIP 342: Propose the Let's-Write-It-into-the-Contract Alternative.

Realtors have become masters with this technique. They walk through a vacant house with the prospective buyer, and the buyer says, "Do the drapes go with the house?" The realtor replies, "We'll write it into the contract." Buyer: "How about the fireplace utensils?" Realtor: "We'll write it into the contract."

Try the same approach when your group continues to bring up unlikely what-ifs. "If that happens, we'll stop payment immediately." "If that happens, we can always have them remove the new machine and go back to the old one." This approach minimizes wasted time spent on unlikely scenarios.

TIP 343: Develop a List of Picturesque "Saver" Lines for Recurring Snags.

Speakers have a pocketful of witticisms for common mishaps on the platform. When the microphone suddenly drops on the stand or makes weird noises, they say things like, "Sounds like mating season." "Funny. I brushed my teeth this morning." "Nothing like a live censor."

Likewise, when you anticipate getting bogged down in persuading a team, have some "saver" lines that call attention to a particular problem. Let's say your team always generates a lot of possible solutions but has trouble focusing on specific solutions. You might say, "The grocery store with the most items doesn't necessarily stock gourmet food. I think it's time to stop generating suggestions and start evaluating what we've got."

If your group gets hung up on "who won't like it," try: "Not everyone voted for Abraham Lincoln. I think people who don't now support what we're doing will come around when they see X happen."

If the team argues all the pros and cons and never seems to come to a decision, try: "I'd rather buy a tight pair of shoes than hike the mountain barefoot. Maybe the decision isn't perfect, but let's move on something. We can always make adjustments down the road."

Recapping the problem in such a succinct, picturesque way makes a strong point.

TIP 344: Don't Aim to "Outargue" Them.

As my mother used to say, even if you argue "until you're blue in the face," you will lose if you make the other person feel outdone. You can outtalk, outsmart, outreason, but still fail to gain agreement if the other person doesn't feel good about the decision in the long run. The best approach is to present your point accurately, enthusiastically, and sincerely. Then listen. Know when to be flexible and offer a compromise. Even if you smell blood, don't go for the kill.

TIP 345: When Someone Pushes, Don't Push Back.

Opposition spawns opposition. If you don't believe it, ask a partner to stand face to face with you and align yourselves open palm to open palm. Push gently. You'll notice how the partner pushes back. Push harder. You'll notice the partner increase pressure as you do.

The same principle is at work in persuasion. The harder you push, the harder someone pushes back. So, to neutralize an emotional exchange, as soon as you feel the other side become agitated, let up the pressure. You can even come around to the other side of the table. "Okay, let me stop here and summarize where we are. If I understand you clearly, you think the decision is a bad one for three reasons. First, the X won't work. . . ." Once you stand on the other person's side of the table and take up his or her side, that person becomes neutral again. The pushing stops. You may even want to ask the other side to summarize your key points "for clarity's sake."

The idea is to neutralize the emotional conflict long enough for logic to take its course—should logic be on your side.

TIP 346: Don't Make the Other Person Wrong for You to Be Right.

Ego blinds people to logic. Let the other person save face if he or she wants to agree with you: "Perhaps you didn't have access to the data I just received. . . ." or "The situation has changed drastically since you were last briefed. . . ." or "Despite what he told you, the customer has obviously changed her mind again. Here's her latest wish. . . ."

TIP 347: Minimize Stress for the Other Person.

Putting the other person under psychological stress does not pressure that person to go along with you and "get it over with." Although as parents we might tend to believe differently, kids do attempt to wear us down with their whining and complaining. But studies show that not to be case in the workplace. If people feel pressured to decide something, they'll usually cling to the status quo rather than make a change.

TIP 348: Hold the Sarcasm; Avoid Detractors.

No matter how "outmoded," "primitive," "ridiculous," or "wasteful" the current plan, procedure, or product is, hold your labels and associated sarcasm. People identify closely with what goes on in their departments and within their areas of responsibilities. The reaction is much the same as when you put down others' hometowns. *They* can disparage it all they want to, but they won't permit an outsider to do so.

TIP 349: Avoid Frames As Power Plays.

Emphasizing that you're the celebrity engineer who holds the patent frames you in a more powerful position than your listeners. Reminding the employees in the warehouse that you write their paychecks will not go over well if you're using that position to persuade them to participate on the company softball team. People resent those who rattle their sabers.

TIP 350: Lower Others' Guard with Graciousness.

Alcoholics Anonymous and hundreds of other self-help groups can verify this truth: You cannot motivate people from the outside; their motivation has to be internal. People are more motivated to believe you, help you, or at least get out of your way if they like you. Avoid an adversarial relationship. Be gracious.

TIP 351: Dodge Zaps and Zingers to Get to Your Goal.

Should people not be gracious to you in your attempts to persuade them, keep your goal in mind. As best you can, dodge any personal attacks, any I-don't-like-you statements, any performance deflators. If your goal is acceptance of an idea, approval of a plan, or purchase of a product, then try to put ego aside.

TIP 352: Provide Opportunity for a Trial Run.

Cereal companies don't make us spend $4.89 on a box of new flakes, nuts, and fruit. Instead, they send us a bowl in the mailbox to taste before we have to plunk down our money. Create ways for people to give your idea a low-risk trial before making an irreversible commitment of time, money, or reputation. The lower the risk, the more likely they'll take a step in your direction. Never be afraid of their asking, "What have I got to lose if I go along?"

TIP 353: Note the Difference Between Selling an Idea and Motivating People to Act.

In "selling" something, the focus is on the seller's efforts and success—what's in it for the seller. In "motivating," the focus is on the other person's attitude and benefit—what's in it for the buyer. The subtle difference implies different methods, language, timing, and attitude.

TIP 354: Persuade People to Do Something Specific.

People need an emotional release or a sense of closure if they've come to a logical conclusion. Give them something specific to do, decide, approve. A sales rep once wrote a two-page memo to his management telling about a sale he'd lost due to his customer's counterproposal on credit terms and down payment. According to company policy, the rep had asked for 30 percent cash up front; the customer had countered with an offer of 20 percent down payment. The credit manager refused to approve the deal and the sales rep lost the sale. After a long recitation of the story, the sales rep ended his two-page memo with this recommendation: "We must make it easy for customers to do business with us. We need to wake up to the realities of today's marketplace." As a senior vice president reading that memo, what exactly would you have delegated somebody to do? What would "make it easy to do business with us" mean in this situation? People need specifics to act.

TIP 355: Show Passion.

If you're not sold on your own idea—sold enough to find and organize the facts you need, to develop the strategy to suit your audience, to prepare the presentation, to energize your body, to select the perfect phrasing, to anticipate and prepare for objections—then the decision makers never will be.

5

Holding Your Own
in Meetings, but Working
As a Team

*"Meetings . . . are rather like cocktail parties.
You don't want to go but you're cross not
to be asked."*   —JILLY COOPER

*The ability to express an idea is well nigh as
important as the idea itself.*
                    —BERNARD BARUCH

*Many a good idea has been smothered to death
by words.*   —no attribution

*Sometimes I get the feeling that the two biggest
problems in America today are making ends
meet—and making meetings end.*
                    —ROBERT ORBEN

Meetings can bring the world to peace—or kill 15 hours a week for even the
best time manager. Communicating ideas and creating solutions as a team
take the best of attention and skill. These guidelines will help you lead and
participate in team discussions both to contribute and evaluate ideas.

TIP 356: To Meet or Not to Meet—Study the Question.

How many times have you accepted an invitation to a lunch meeting only to
realize that you spent an hour and a half on something that could have

been done in a 5-minute phone call or a 10-minute memo? The higher you go, the busier you get. And the meetings you attend must count. If you get a reputation for conducting useless meetings, the busiest and best people won't show up.

If you're asked to attend someone else's typically unproductive meetings, defer with one of the following: "Is attendance mandatory?" "I'm unavailable. Is my attendance important enough to change my schedule?" "Could I send a representative?" "Would you mind if I offer my input in writing or by phone?" Others will generally surmise that you expect meeting time to be well spent.

TIP 357: Call a Meeting Only for the Right Reasons.

When you call a meeting, make it significant and be prepared. In a client situation, you may have been working on a deal for months that will either thrive or nosedive on a single meeting. The higher you go in your own organization, the more expectations others have for your abilities to conduct yourself in a meeting—either as a participant or leader. Take things seriously.

Skip the meeting if you have nothing special to discuss, if you don't need others' input, if you have already made up your mind about what you plan to do, or if getting others involved would only complicate your plan.

Do call a meeting if you need to present information to a lot of people quickly and you don't want to write it, if you want input from others on your idea, if you want to gain "buy in" from the team, or if you want to motivate and energize the team about the idea.

So how about the wrong reasons? Meeting as a substitute for work. Rubber-stamping a decision. Complaining. Demonstrating power to make everybody show up. Because joy and misery love company, sorting out true motivations may require some soul-searching.

TIP 358: Set an Agenda.

Some people think that agendas lend too much structure to a meeting, that people can't be spontaneous, or that the atmosphere will be too formal. Nonsense. That's like saying if you plan for a vacation by packing the right clothes, arranging for transportation, and deciding on a destination that you can't relax and be spontaneous along the way.

If you're leading the meeting, set an agenda. Use active verbs, summarize in a sentence the issue at hand, and let the group know what you expect on each issue—"for discussion only," "for their information only," "to collect your data," or "for decision." Whether you stay right with the agenda or take a few minutes' detour, having an agenda will give others a little peace of mind that the meeting is going somewhere.

TIP 359: Start with the Most Important Idea or Issue and Work Backward.

There's a great temptation to begin with the routine matters—the FYI items. But the all-too-frequent problem is that when you save the most controversial and important item until the last, you run out of time. Maybe a Freudian move?

TIP 360: Select Attendees Carefully.

Use the following checklist: Who can provide necessary expert advice? Who will support your cause? Who will oppose your cause? Who will sabotage the project if they don't "get in on the ground floor"? Whose commitment do you need to "make it happen"? There's your guest list.

TIP 361: Own the Setting.

If you plan a clandestine affair, go for a dark bar with soft music. If you want an energized group, go for a well-lit poolside table. If you want an informal chitchat session, try somebody's office. If you want an equal, on-target exchange, look for a conference table in neutral territory. If you want authority and a no-nonsense atmosphere, schedule the boardroom. If you want to play host-and-guest, provide coffee or snacks in a parlor. Whatever your choice and purpose, if you're in charge, be comfortable with and "own" the surroundings.

TIP 362: Stay Out in Front if You Intend to Lead.

Nothing frustrates more meeting attendees than having a supposed leader who doesn't lead. State your role at the beginning and what authority the group will have. Do you intend simply to facilitate a discussion? Will you let them set the process and agenda? Do you intend to tell them how you will discuss each idea and come to decision—consensus or vote? Do you intend to have the final say or will the group have authority to make the final decision? Are you going to keep the discussion moving or abdicate that responsibility to others randomly? Are you going to be a silent observer on each idea or do you plan to put in your two cents worth? Are you strong enough to stop a feeding frenzy should the stronger people begin to attack the weaker person's ideas? When the group starts spinning its wheels, be there with a comment such as: "Where do we go from here?" "What's the solution?" "Which way do you want to go?" "Let's back up and redefine the problem."

You don't have to have all the answers and make all the decisions, but you should be out in front. Either lead or give the responsibility to someone else and get out of the way.

TIP 363: Take Your Seat with Forethought.

Choose seating arrangements as carefully as your meeting site. Where you sit makes a great deal of difference in how you interact with others and how they interact with you. Studies show that people seated across the table from each other tend to communicate more than those seated to the left or right. That across-the-table communication, however, may be adversarial rather than supportive. If you plan to present important ideas at the meeting, make sure that you're comfortable with the surroundings. When you arrive, take notice of where any audiovisual equipment is, what distractions the windows might create, the chance for interruptive phone messages slipped through the door, a ringing telephone, plants that might block someone's view, or a lectern that signals authority.

TIP 364: Take Your Body with You.

Appearances and posture count even when you're in an informal meeting, seated around a table. Yes, rolled-up sleeves, open collar, and stocking feet may be the attire for a "working meeting," but that's not always the attitude to convey. Someone who's "laid back" (meaning loose papers scattered, ruffled hair, sprawling in the chair, hands playing with trinkets and toys) conveys an informal look—and a disorganized mind and agenda. If you have something important to say, look like it. Sit erect. Organize your props and paperwork. Look alert and thoughtful. Your body reflects your mind.

TIP 365: Encourage Participation from Others—
If You Want It.

Some meetings serve only to inform. If that's your purpose, tell the audience what you're going to tell them and be done with it. But if your intention is to generate ideas, get feedback, or come to a decision, you may need to take a more active role in encouraging participation.

Try these techniques: Ask for a show of hands on an issue. Toss out an open-ended question and see who takes the ball. Toss out an open-ended question and suggest that you go around the circle and let everyone give his or her views individually. Present your question or issue in writing, give all members a copy, and ask them to jot their responses quickly. Take up the responses and read them to the group for reactions. Invite nonparticipators by name: "Carl, we haven't heard from you—what do you think?" Finally, you might assign two or three people a devil's-advocate role and ask them to toss out any objections they can think of.

Participation takes effort, and some people are too preoccupied, uninterested, or tired to contribute without encouragement.

TIP 366: Don't Set People Up to Refute You.

If you've already made a decision and intend simply to present the decision at a meeting, say so. If you still have doubt that your decision or planned course of action is the best, say so. But not like this: "I've decided to do X unless someone has a serious objection." Few will have the chutzpah to speak up. If you want to get feedback whether or not you plan to change your mind, try something like this: "I've decided to do X. What do you think the fallout will be from our customers/employees/management?" or "I plan to proceed with Y; what positives and negatives do you think I might have to deal with?"

In any case, don't announce your decision or plan in such a way that people have to "refute" or "oppose" you to give you feedback. If you want feedback and forewarning of the difficulties, make it easy for people to speak their minds.

TIP 367: Don't Use the Group As Camouflage.

Don't use a meeting as a way to make your point with someone else when you don't have the courage to make it directly. Meetings are not battlefields.

TIP 368: Discuss Taboo Issues Anonymously.

If you know certain issues are hot topics and politically dangerous to careers, you have to work hard at creating a safe environment. Consider doing an anonymous survey on the issues and simply "reporting the results" for discussion. Or, you can quote anonymous sources from the grapevine. Say: "Someone has expressed the fear that . . . How do you think we can handle that fear?" "Other people have stated that they don't intend to . . . What would make people feel that way? What suggestions do you have for convincing them otherwise?"

TIP 369: Don't Expect Participants to Pool Their Ignorance.

Some issues, problems, and decisions require information and expertise, not just untrained opinions. If your issue falls into that category, don't bring it up in a meeting format where your colleagues there are uninformed. If you do toss out the idea and they offer their ideas and opinions in a noble effort to help, and you find their "help" inadequate, you'll force yourself into the position of having to ignore what they've said. And if they've wasted time and effort in the process, they're going to be angry. If you want to get input from only those with knowledge or expertise to do so, either go to them privately or call for their input specifically by name.

People feel much more comfortable with—and do a better job of—discussing what they know rather than what they don't know.

TIP 370: Participate; Don't Pout.

Even if you didn't want to attend and "you're there," be there. Listen to what's going on rather than fidget with your paperwork, glance at your watch, or roll your eyes. Your body language can speak volumes to those who think the meeting is important and do want your ideas.

TIP 371: Be Versatile in Playing Several Positions in the Process.

Good meetings require a process. The *traffic cop* makes sure everybody gets a turn to speak, shuts up the monopolizers, and generally ensures that everybody receives fair treatment. The *coordinator* continually brings people up to date as each item is concluded and calls for the next step. The *compromiser* takes an active role in bringing disagreeing people together on an agreed-upon next step. The *commentator* reads everyone's body language and verbal clues to give the group updates on the progress they're making toward their goals and points out where, when, and how the group gets stalled. The *clown* throws out one-liners, either to get attention for an idea or to break tension in the group. On occasion, you'll need to learn to play each role.

TIP 372: Summarize Frequently.

Whether or not you see your official role as the summarizer or leader, if no one takes on that role, do so. To keep the discussion moving on target, somebody has to recap what's been said and point out the next topic for discussion.

TIP 373: Call for a Process Check Occasionally.

At times, the group process will stall. You'll be talking in circles, covering the same territory. You'll hear tempers flare. You'll feel that people are under personal attack. You'll notice that you are deciding, undeciding, and redeciding the same issues. Be the one who calls attention to such breakdowns: "We don't seem to be getting anywhere. Let's see where we got off track. We had started to brainstorm the Y issue. Does somebody have a more effective suggestion for moving us along?"

TIP 374: Remind Yourself and the Group That All Ideas Are Not Created Equal.

In the course of any one discussion, team members may generate several suggestions for dealing with a problem. Don't fall into the trap of giving them all equal billing with something like: "Okay, we have five alternatives on the table. Let's discuss the pros and cons of each." In many situations, only two or three of the many ideas offered are serious contenders. Don't waste your time with all the details of the other, lesser ideas.

TIP 375: Use the "What a Baby!" Response.

Doctors, politicians, and pastors have perfected this technique. The proud father stands outside the hospital nursery looking through the glass at his red, wrinkled newborn. He nudges the doctor beside him, "Well, what do you think, doc?" To which the doctor replies, "What a baby!"

When someone presents an idea that you don't approve of or one that seems inappropriate, don't feel you have to accept it or take time discussing it. After they finish speaking, look at them a moment and say something like: "That may be true." "That's another idea." "Interesting." "Some people seem to think so." "Possibly." "Hmmm." Then break eye contact and move on. That person will rarely know how to take the comeback.

TIP 376: Don't Digress, Ramble, or Sidetrack.

Determine that you'll not be part of the biggest meeting problem of all. Stay on target. If you can't remember the issue, jot yourself a note as the group moves from agenda item to item and refer to it often. Not only is the agenda topic important, but also you should keep track of where you are in the process of dealing with each topic. Are you into the overview? The analysis? The idea-generation phase? Suggesting solutions? Testing agreement on the proposed solutions? Don't be two or three steps behind everyone else.

TIP 377: Omit War Stories.

While they have an audience of admirers, some people fall to the temptation of telling war stories, sharing inside jokes, and recounting wonderful things they once did. Unless time is of no importance to the rest of the group, don't.

TIP 378: Support, Explain, or Reject Only One Idea at a Time.

Poorly facilitated meetings encourage people to dump everything once they finally get the floor. That is, because they have had to wait so long to get airtime, once it's granted they dump their ideas about everything that has been said so far. Don't dump. Unload your thoughts on only one issue at a time and then get off the court. If people learn to trust that you're not going to sidetrack them on several issues at once, they'll let you take the court more often.

TIP 379: Stop a Filibuster.

If one person continues to monopolize the discussion on your idea, use body language to cut that person off. Break eye contact. Lower your eyes to the paper in front of you. Turn your body away from the offender. If necessary, firmly but kindly say something like: "Lisa, I think I understand your viewpoint. Let's hear from somebody else."

TIP 380: Use a Prop to Tag the Motor Mouth.

Now that we're big into incentive awards for team effort, you've probably seen the idea of the roving trophy that moves from winning department to winning department. Try the same idea in a meeting to "subtly" remind motor mouths that they're being repetitive and/or long-winded. A foghorn. A whistle. A bat. A balloon. A broken record. Whatever the object, place it in the center of the table. Then when someone bogs down the meeting, push the prop into that person's space at the table. At its best, it stops the offender; at the least, it generates a laugh and breaks the tension.

TIP 381: If You Don't Have Something to Say, Don't Say It.

Participating doesn't mean you should necessarily feel obligated to comment on every issue. If someone hands you the baton and you have nothing to contribute, pass it on: "I think everybody has already expressed my views." "I don't have an opinion one way or the other." "I don't know a thing about that subject and don't want to confuse the issue." "Thanks, I'll pass." People will love you.

TIP 382: Don't Ask a Question Simply to Ask a Question.

Some team members become uncomfortable with silence. So when a colleague tosses out an idea that is met with silence, some people feel compelled "to get the ball rolling" by asking a question. Don't. If you don't really have a legitimate question and don't care about the issue one way or the other, don't add to the problem by opening your mouth. Hours have been lost by people chasing down answers to questions that should never have been asked and bear little or no relevance to the decision or problem.

TIP 383: Avoid Answering Questions That Nobody Has Asked.

In presenting ideas, try to anticipate others' objections and questions and be prepared with answers. But that doesn't mean you should dump that data without cause. Such thinking leads to talking in circles, digressing, and rambling on with the same information given four different ways. Make your point succinctly. Then pause. If you get questions, pull out your bag of tricks and answer them. If not, don't dump.

TIP 384: Control Interruptions.

The only way to prevent people from interrupting you is to insist on finishing. You can call attention to the interruption verbally: "Pauline, I didn't get to finish. What I was about to say was . . ." "Sorry, but you interrupted me. I had one more item to mention. . . ." "Please let me finish. . . ." Or you may choose to prevent an interruption with body language and voice. Raise your hand to the interrupter and continue to speak at the same or louder volume. Keep talking until the interrupter realizes you do not intend to relinquish the floor.

TIP 385: Don't Assume the Role of Translator.

Example: "I think what Phyllis is trying to say is that her staff is . . ." Trying to "translate" for others conveys very loudly to them that you don't think they voiced their ideas well. It also irritates the group to have an echo effect in the room. Finally, you'll be embarrassed if Phyllis responds that you did not translate correctly. Some people are inarticulate; learn to live with it.

TIP 386: Avoid Letting Others Put Words in Your Mouth.

If you've expressed an idea that someone feels the need to "interpret" for the group, don't let them misquote or misinterpret you. Example: "No, Bill, that isn't exactly what I meant. I meant . . ." "Wait a minute. I said it exactly like I intended to. I'm saying that . . ." "No, that's not what I meant. Maybe I was unclear. I'll try again. . . ." Only you know what you meant to say. Say it directly without an interpreter.

TIP 387: Don't Set a Pattern of Expressing the "Downside."

Yes, you will disagree from time to time and make a valuable contribution by expressing that differing viewpoint. But don't make it a pattern. Offer solutions and encouragement when the others get down, dumb, and defeated.

TIP 388: Know the Difference Between Being Realistic and Being Gloomy.

Have you ever known people who think their view is the only "realistic" one? Their comments begin: "Let's get real here about . . ." "You've gotta be realistic about . . ." "People won't buy that unless it's realistic." "Let's use a more realistic number for . . ." The difference? Realism focuses on the facts; gloom comes from attitude.

TIP 389: Apply the "You Break It, You Buy It" Principle.

Never be the one who tears up everybody else's ideas and then has none of your own to offer. If you criticize the best solutions others have tossed out, you're obligating yourself to present substitutions. According to author Milo Frank, this idea originated with Larry Kitchen, retired chairman of Lockheed. Based on the frequent sign in curio shops "You break it, you buy it," Mr. Kitchen applied the principle to stop people who continually tossed water on others' ideas with their routine negativism. Example: "Joan, since you have serious reservations about the proposal we're discussing, why don't you do a more thorough study of the ramifications of its implementation and bring us an alternative proposal next week."

Caution: The idea is a poor one if your intention is to encourage openness and avoid "groupthink." So apply the principle only to those routinely negative people who run down every idea.

TIP 390: Disagree Without Being Disagreeable.

Never let yourself become a victim of "groupthink," a condition in which group harmony becomes more important than results. If the purpose of a meeting is to generate ideas and get input, by all means speak up when you disagree. Just don't be disagreeable. The difference is attitude.

TIP 391: Strip Ownership from Views.

If you're functioning as a team, you will want to bring all contradictory facts and viewpoints into the open rather than pretend they don't exist. Try to strip away direct ownership and the associated ego to evaluate the ideas independently. "We have a proposal and two viewpoints on the table: one that the plan will take too long; the other view that the cost takes away marketing's veto power. Let's discuss the first objection. What support do we have for that?"

Notice that all names have been removed from the suggestions and viewpoints. Treat conflicting ideas openly and objectively. People hold on most strongly to ideas that haven't been discussed and especially to ones bearing their name.

TIP 392: Use Positive Questioning to Allay
Your Reservations.

When people bring up issues you don't agree with, your questioning can put them on the defensive. However, not to ask the questions and express reservations defeats the purpose of the discussion. To overcome the dilemma, make sure your questioning can be taken only in a positive way. First, demonstrate that you have heard what the other person has said by paraphrasing it, and then lead the person through your confusion or reservations with positive questions: "Jeanine, I understand your position. You want to use contractors because all the projects planned to date call for a specialized expertise that we don't have on board, right? Well, help me understand why your people who have the same degrees as the contractors you've mentioned don't have the expertise. . . . Now, I'm still confused about where we could find the experienced contractors on such short notice. . . . Okay, what would you suggest we do about the up-front payment most will require?"

This line of positively worded questions emphasizes your openness to answers while still expressing your issues of concern. If the concerns can't be answered adequately, the owners of the ideas often conclude that they have defeated themselves because they didn't have the answers—or a good idea, whichever is the case.

TIP 393: Don't Invalidate Others' Feelings.

Examples: "Jim, I don't know why you're so punchy about that." "Jennifer, there's no reason to get so defensive." "It'll be okay, Javier—really, it will." To say or imply that people don't have a right to their feelings makes them robots. People do not live by logic alone.

TIP 394: Legitimize Others' Feelings Without Agreeing.

When you present an idea and hear someone's emotional disagreement, you can legitimize that feeling and then move on. Legitimizing is not the same as agreeing with the comment. Example: "Yes, Phil, I can understand how you might be concerned that X would come across hypocritically to your staff." The speaker hasn't agreed with Phil, but has simply expressed a legitimate concern. Phil will appreciate that acknowledgment and usually quit pressing to make that point.

TIP 395: Lighten Up—The Point Doesn't Have to Be Perfect.

All platforms and purposes are not created equal. Your career will not rise or fall based on every meeting's interaction. If a particular meeting is not necessarily "yours," jump in and participate even though you may not have given it thorough preparation. Spontaneity still succeeds.

TIP 396: Don't Engage in a One-on-One Battle.

Avoid letting a discussion degenerate into dialogue with one other person. Inevitably, others in the group become lookers-on and begin to take sides. Then the opposing ideas become an ego issue and the discussion has a winner and loser. Bad for morale. When you realize that only you and one other person remain in the discussion, say something like: "Well, let's open it up again. Charles, you said . . . and Eugenia, you mentioned that . . ." The idea is to leave the impression that all have contributed to the exchange and that you are conceding to the group opinion.

TIP 397: Don't Harpoon the Idea Because It's a Poor Swimmer.

All creative thinkers and technical wizards are not effective communicators. Be careful that you don't ignore their ideas and responses to your own ideas simply because they did not phrase their ideas well.

TIP 398: Use Another's Question As Your Platform.

An excellent way to get a message across without having to hog the floor is to look for someone's question as a platform—an invitation to speak up. Have your prepared message ready and look for the opportunity to step in when someone raises the appropriate question. You'll be accomplishing your goals on someone else's time.

TIP 399: Be Flexible on the Issues.

We're not talking about flip-flops like the politicians make—whatever the polls support today they "believe" tomorrow. Instead, be open to the facts and flexible in your feedback. The purpose of meetings—most staff meetings anyway—is to exchange ideas. If someone presents facts and sways your opinion, don't hesitate to change your position. That's not being wimpy; it's democratic.

TIP 400: Listen to What's Going On.

Consider listening to be more than the absence of talking. It takes careful attention. And listening increases in difficulty as the number grows from one person to a group of individuals all competing for airtime. Listen and interpret so that you're not the one who's always asking for a repeat of issues already discussed and clarified.

TIP 401: Don't Derail Others' Proposals While They're Still On the Track.

Follow what's going on before you propose something new. If you want to really upset a crowd, let a speaker propose an idea, with all the related facts and analysis, ask for discussion, and get just to the point of calling for a decision . . . and interrupt with a proposal of your own. Your insertion at the wrong time may derail the entire train of thought for the group. Pay attention to the logical process and avoid bringing up out-of-order proposals. After you get past the idea stage and into the proposing stage, let the first proposal work its way through the group discussion and be accepted or rejected before you toss your alternative out for evaluation.

TIP 402: Remain Seated if You Want to Emphasize That You're Tossing Out Ideas "Off the Cuff."

Bringing up an idea while seated plays down your forethought and preparation. It conveys that the ideas are spontaneous and relevant to the issue at hand. Your position says that you're on equal footing with the rest of the group and that you encourage give-and-take. As a result, you'll probably get feedback, pros and cons, agreement and disagreement.

TIP 403: Stand if You Want to Convey Authority and/or Underscore the Importance of an Issue.

When someone "rises to the occasion," the team generally settles back and lets him or her have the floor. The group dynamics change from an informal team discussion to formal presentation. A formal presentation says three things: "I have an opinion already on this issue." "I am well prepared with supporting details." "The issue is bigger and more important than the routine ones we deal with."

From your physically elevated position, your words take on more authority; the group is likely to grant you control of the meeting, even if only temporarily. As a result of all these dynamics, you probably will get less feedback on your idea. Those who support will withhold their comments, thinking that you obviously sound authoritative and need no help in garnering others' opinions. Those who disagree with you may hate to buck authority before an audience; they often save their negative comments for the hallways.

You can sometimes "have it both ways" by presenting your proposal standing up and then taking a seat for the follow-up discussion and turning over the facilitation to someone else.

TIP 404: Opt for a Stool if You Want to Walk the Fence.

If you still can't decide whether to stand or sit, you may want to opt for a bar stool. You convey authority because of the physically elevated position and the "prepared" appearance while creating a relaxed attitude by sitting down.

TIP 405: Take Stage; Don't Just "Drift In."

When you intend to present your own ideas, take stage just as a performer does. None of this "Just a minute, before we go on here. I've been thinking about something." "Maybe this has already come up in earlier meetings, and I missed it." "Don't want to get us off track, but it seems to me we should be looking at this a little differently." "I'm not saying I disagree with what we've already said, but just another, you know, thought about how we could approach it. . . ."

Instead, when you want attention, take it. Sit or stand erectly. Get your papers in order. Project your voice. Use a confident tone. Spit it out.

TIP 406: Grab 'em Fast; Forget the Warm-Up Drill.

Ever since students have been assigned high school essays, teachers have required introductory paragraphs. Business professionals are still stuck in that rut. Forget the introduction when you're offering informal comments. Start at the point of new information or the new idea. "Two comments: The machine will be quicker and easier to run." Then pause and take your cue from others. If they want elaboration, add it. If they have questions, answer them.

TIP 407: Try Being Obscure.

> Try the direct-mail approach. Start with a provocative or intriguing statement to get attention and whet people's appetites for the main course. "So I think maybe we should hire only Ph.D.'s." "I've got an idea—let's beat them at their own game." When the point's "not all there," you'll grab their attention for your elaboration to follow.

TIP 408: Set Yourself Up to Keep the Floor
Until You Finish.

> If you fear that someone will interrupt you before you finish presenting your ideas, preface your ideas with something like the following: "After listening to what has been said, I have four observations to make about the X situation. First, . . ." and then keep enumerating as you go along so that people understand that you're not finished when you take a breath.

TIP 409: Be Conversational; Don't Move into
"Meeting Mode."

> Nobody said formal ideas had to be presented in lecture format. Use your conversational voice, not your lecture tone.

> *Lecture tone:* "I want to inform you that . . ."

> *Conversational tone:* "I just want to let you know that . . ."

> *Lecture tone:* "Please voice your objections if I'm wrong, but . . ."

> *Conversational tone:* "Please say so if I'm wrong, but . . ."

> *Lecture tone:* "The research and development group of which I've been appointed chair, effective May 1, has asked that you be notified that the team is receptive to your proposals about . . ."

> *Conversational tone:* "On May 1, R&D asked me to chair a team to come up with a solution. So, as part of that effort, we need your input about . . ."

TIP 410: Talk *with,* Not *to* the Group.

> Consider yourself in a conversation with more than one rather than "addressing a group." In most situations, that means you'll pause to let others speak or ask questions if necessary for clarification as you move through your ideas. You'll use the "we" and "us" approach rather than "you" and "I." You'll use terms they'll understand rather than lapsing into jargon. You'll

make eye contact with everyone around the table and not read from your notes or stare at the floor, ceiling, or favored ally.

TIP 411: Remember That People Are Most Interested in What's on Their Own Minds.

If you want to grab attention for your ideas, you have to start where people are and lead them to where you stand, not expect them to meet you halfway. What policy is bothering them? What do they fear might happen tomorrow? What frustrates them today? Start there and tie your idea into that concern or hope.

TIP 412: Make Abstractions "Hit the Gut."

Accept the fact that we don't make all decisions from logic. When people get emotional about an issue, accept that emotion, show that you understand it, and then when they regain composure, ask if they can share the reasons for those feelings.

When it's in your interest to do so, play to others' emotions. Abstractions are difficult for people to rally around. Tie them to specifics so that people "feel" an issue. For example, if you want your team to give input to designing your corporate policy about charitable contributions, don't deal with nameless agencies and noble causes. Talk about specific people who benefit from these contributions and specific agencies who will be receiving the money allocated by the policy your team helps draft. If you generate appropriate emotion, "dull" tasks can take on new life and importance.

TIP 413: Don't Plead with Puppy-Dog Eyes.

Your eyes can say you're sincere, you're courageous, or you're confident, but don't let them cry "help." When presenting ideas for approval, don't let your eyes fall into a puppy-dog plea. Those who disagree with you will hop on that body language and drag you through the streets. Present your ideas confidently and then wait for response and approval. If approval isn't forthcoming, don't beg.

TIP 414: Don't Build Your Case—For or Against— On Second-Hand Information.

On important issues, refuse to give second-hand information the same credence as first-hand information. When Helen says that Jack said that Lybert thinks, stop right there. If the information is crucial to the decision, verify it. Make a phone call or postpone the discussion until such relayed information can be verified.

TIP 415: Present Your Proposal Only One Way and Be Specific.

When you're courting several people with differing viewpoints, it's natural to think that the more general you can make your idea, the more "hooks" you're creating for people to latch onto. In that effort, you tend to explain your idea first one way and then another. You use this analogy and that. You think maybe this and maybe that would be part of the final product. Often, the intention with the elaboration is to offer something that will appeal to everybody.

A broad, generally expressed idea, however, usually has the opposite effect: everybody hears something that they disagree with. And you wind up spending more time dealing with the minor details and "what you didn't mean to imply" than you do with the general thrust of the idea.

The group has the sense that your proposal has been thrashed to death, when in reality only the chaff around it has been discarded. Prefer, instead, to propose the idea succinctly, in only one, specific way. Let it stand there in all its glory until people force you to add details by their questions.

TIP 416: Listen to the Counters to Your Proposal Rather Than Planning Your Rebuttal.

Do you recall presidential debates when candidates seemed to have gone to sleep when their opponent took a turn? The same happens in meetings. Don't get so carried away in preparing to defend your ideas when the next person quits talking that you miss what that person says *throughout* his or her full turn. If you do, you may find yourself focusing on an issue that the other person has just conceded, failing to respond at all to the new issues raised. You can't take a time-out while the ball is in the other court. You have to stay alert while the other person serves.

TIP 417: Don't Withdraw Your Proposal Simply for the Sake of Harmony.

Encourage others to express either support or disagreement, but don't let people turn down the idea simply because "someone doesn't like it." Ask for supporting explanation and be sure that everyone either accepts or rejects the idea for objective, logically sound reasons. If you're going to toss out an idea, support it until someone changes your mind or the minds of the rest of the group members.

TIP 418: If You Can't Manage a Touchdown, Try for a First Down.

If you can see that your idea will not be accepted in total, settle for measured success. Suggest that the team give you the go-ahead in a limited way. Ask for a "test run" at some phase of the project "before too much money is spent." All you may need is a little running room to prove that your idea or plan has merit. Don't give up simply because you don't make a touchdown with the first play.

TIP 419: End with Impact; Don't Just Fade Away.

If you're presenting an idea, don't limp away with a sputter. Don't simply drop your eyes, tune out with body language, or let others grab the floor and run away with it. Bring the discussion to closure. Summarize your idea, the pros and cons mentioned, any decision made, and suggest the next follow-up step. Also take responsibility for the fate of the entire meeting. Do your part to make it successful. If the meeting is unproductive and disruptive, decide on the corrective action you'll take next time to change the dynamics.

TIP 420: Don't Sound Like a Broken Record.

Present your idea and support it. After a fair hearing, if the group nixes it, move on. Bring that discussion to an end and meet the next agenda item head on. Nothing irritates others more than having someone continue to bring up a pet proposal or peeve and whine, whine, whine.

TIP 421: Build Support for Your Ideas Behind the Scenes.

Take your model from Congress and the White House on this technique. Just as the President calls individual representatives and senators to the Oval Office for a "briefing," rally support by giving a preview of your ideas before you ever go into a meeting.

You'll overcome the element of surprise that blocks some decisions simply because people don't want to "be rash" and make a decision "too soon." You'll also have the advantage of hearing opposing viewpoints so you can prepare your counter before the formal presentation in the meeting. If you think that people might be hesitant to give you negative views one on one, encourage them with something like: "Help me see the other side of this issue if you don't agree." "If somebody were to object to this idea, what do you think that objection might be?" "What ideas do you have for responding to those who may be unhappy about this?" A behind-the-scenes briefing wins more friends than it creates enemies.

TIP 422: Don't Surprise Your Boss.

Husband and wife, Glenn and Nelda, attended a community auction for a local charity. In a feverish round of good-natured bidding, where several CEOs present began to challenge each other to "dig a little deeper" for a good cause, Glenn popped up to say that he'd pay $10,000 for a canoe trip for six down the Mississippi River. Sitting beside him, Nelda almost gasped aloud. They had agreed before the auction on how much they could afford to give. Glenn's "surprise" angered her as much for his taking the liberty of not including her in the decision as for the large amount she didn't think they could afford.

Bosses feel the same way occasionally. Generally, it's better to present the idea to them privately before springing it on a group and chancing a public embarrassment for them or a reprimand for yourself. The boss may suggest that you "wait on that idea until X happens" or tell you to go ahead and bring up the issue even though he or she doesn't fully agree. Either way, you've followed corporate protocol.

TIP 423: Ask for Input and Approval from Your Superiors.

Don't leave a meeting in which you've presented information or proposed a plan without having a clear mandate for the next step. If response is slow to come, and you want input and honest reaction, ask the lower-ranking superiors for their feedback first. If you want a quick yes-no decision, go right to the top. Ask the senior person for questions, a response, or a go-ahead. After the highest-ranking person speaks, you'll get conformity from there on. There's no use being given "busy work" from the lower-ranking people if the answer from the top will eventually be "no."

TIP 424: Withhold Your Ideas Until Last if You Want
to Encourage Others' Input.

> This strategy makes sense if you're in a position of power to make the final decision. If you state your views first, your team may lapse into groupthink and let the matter pass without expressing concerns or opposing views. When that's the case, toss out the issue, minus your opinion, and ask for others' reactions first. The responses may be more honest.

TIP 425: To Shorten the Decision-Making Process,
Call for a Vote.

> Yes, I know the nice thing to do is to build consensus so that everybody agrees with every decision. On occasion, that never happens. When you feel bogged down, call for a vote. Voting brings the matter to closure.

TIP 426: To Shorten the Decision-Making Process,
Abdicate Your Right to Make a Decision.

> Your second alternative to end frustration when the team can't come to a decision is to call attention to that fact. "It seems that we just don't have enough information to make a thorough analysis. I suggest that we leave the decision to Jack and his department—that they finish their research and then make their decision based on that information." Nobody says you have to accept all authority handed to you.

TIP 427: Call for a Q&A Session at the End.

> Although many people allow questions and answers at the end of oral presentations, some do not think to do so at the end of meetings. Frequently, the questions will be about how to carry out actions or conclusions decided in the meeting. Never leave a meeting with fog still hanging in the air.

TIP 428: Thank Others for Their Contributions.

> Even bad ideas have some merit. "Thanks, Joel, for bringing up the analogy of the socks. That provided a simple way to look at things." If the ideas were helpful, new, insightful, resourceful, supportive, convincing, relevant, or any combination of the above, say so. Commendations keep them coming.

TIP 429: Play Santa.

People work harder and quicker for rewards. Figure out ways to reward yourself and team members for contributing ideas and solutions. After you've made a quick, effective decision, suggest a reward: "We put that issue to bed in 10 minutes. Let's grant ourselves a 5-minute caffeine break." "Great. We have everybody on board and feeling positive about this plan. Let's pig out and order pizza." "Well, we've just worked out the last detail to make this idea fly. I say we all take part in the presentation to the board. Everybody should share in the glory. What do you say?" The reward doesn't have to be big—a shared bag of Snickers, a break, time off, recognition for individual contributions to the group, a verbal pat on the back for the team. It's the idea that counts.

6

Listening Until You Really Hear

*Know how to listen, and you will profit even
from those who talk badly.* —PLUTARCH

The road to the heart is the ear. —VOLTAIRE

*A good listener is not only popular everywhere,
but after a while he knows something.*
—WILSON MIZNER

*Conversation in the United States is a
competitive exercise in which the first person
to draw a breath is declared the listener.*
—NATHAN MILLER

*It is a secret known to but few of no small use
in the conduct of life, that when you fall into a
man's conversation, the first thing you should
consider, whether he has a greater inclination
to hear you, or that you should hear him.*
—SIR RICHARD STEELE

No one ever listened himself out of a job.
—CALVIN COOLIDGE

*Everybody wants to talk, few want to think,
and nobody wants to listen.*
—no attribution

One advantage of talking to yourself is that
you know at least somebody's listening.
                                    —anonymous

Let every man be quick to hear, slow
to speak. . . .   —NEW TESTAMENT, JAMES 1:19

Listening means the difference between passing or failing a test, making or losing a sale, getting or losing a job, motivating or discouraging a team, mending or destroying a relationship. But listening has gotten a bum reputation as a passive state. Not so. Listening is simply the precursor of successful activity.

TIP 430: Decide That You Want to Listen.

Many people listen poorly simply because they have no intention of listening well. They're preoccupied with themselves. They're too busy talking so that they can feel understood. They're focused on getting what they want done or heard; they have no time to be interrupted by someone talking to them.

Parents, teachers, and other authority figures confuse us with other poor listening habits and clues. These adults send us wrong messages about listening with comments like, "Don't pay any attention to her." "Just look away and he'll leave you alone." "Just pretend you don't notice and he'll stop." "You can't believe everything you hear." "Don't let the bully know it bothers you." "Forget what he says; he didn't mean it—he's just angry." "He just talks a good fight—blows smoke. Nothing will come of it." "Tell her what happened. If she doesn't listen, that's her problem."

No wonder kids doubt their ears and eyes and can't decide whether to listen or not.

Have you ever heard people say they don't have time for something—golf, or walkathons, or church, or dinner with a friend? Not true. We all have the same 24 hours each day; what they mean is that something isn't important enough to them yet to make time for it.

The same is true for listening. We will find ourselves poor listeners until we make up our minds we want to become good listeners. Listening requires conscious effort and a willing mind. It's a decision to take an action.

What's the payoff? Listening keeps you informed, up to date, and out of trouble. It increases your impact when you do speak. It gives you a negotiating edge, power, and influence. It makes other people love you.

Listening is a gift to yourself and to other people.

TIP 431: Listen with a Clean Slate.

Good listeners welcome new information and new ideas. Good listening does not require building a wall to screen out ideas and people that have as their purpose to change you or the things you believe. Rather, listening means standing on level ground, listening as though you were a doctor gathering new symptoms from a patient or a pilot in touch with the control tower during a storm. Excellent listeners expect to grant differences, grow their views and values, and gain insights.

TIP 432: Clean Your Listening Filter.

There are some announcements we've trained ourselves *not* to hear. When the TV sports commentator says, "Let's pause now to let you hear from our sponsors," you take that as your cue to get something to eat. The digitized voice on the airport tram says, "Please stay clear of the doors; they are about to close." The mysterious voice on the parking lot of rental car agencies instructs: "Please leave your keys in the car and note your gas mileage; before leaving your car, please check the car for your personal belongings. . . ." At times you do not hear these routine announcements at all.

We all have built-in filters to save us time in listening. The trick is in identifying the ones we should keep in place and the ones we need to clean or remove. Executives may filter any advice given by an outside consultant. Bosses may filter any suggestions given by employees. Customers may filter any advertisements from a company that has disappointed them in the past.

Some filters save time; others prevent opportunity and understanding. Continually upgrade your list to determine which are which.

TIP 433: Recognize That Listening Is Not Waiting Your Turn to Talk.

Salespeople are often surprised to find that listening is one of the key ingredients of the most successful performers and the downfall of the poor performers. For them, awareness is half the battle. The same can be said of listening by most other professionals. Once you become aware of the benefits of listening and the pitfalls of not listening, you're a long way toward making improvement. The absence of talk is not the same as listening.

TIP 434: Avoid "Listening" As a Retreat.

Those who are afraid to speak their mind on an issue, those who don't want to risk being wrong, those who are tired, those who don't want to "get involved and make connections"—those people often pretend they're listening. They may be looking at you, but they're not listening; they're just not talking. When you recognize the habit or attitude in yourself, be aware of the difference between that and real listening. Listening takes energy and requires reflective talking; retreating is a mental recess. People you're "listening" to and encouraging to continue with a slight nudge of a question ever so often will not be fooled. They may continue to carry the conversational ball along for you, but afterward they will feel let down, if not resentful.

TIP 435: Listen with Compassion.

Some people listen with a superior tone, a critical spirit, or aloofness. In addition to speaking this way, they listen with the same attitude: eyebrows raised, scowling mouth, glaring eyes, folded arms, smirking lips. Such does not encourage people to open up and speak their mind. Nor does it free them to think reflectively about themselves and change the way they're acting or feeling.

Don't confuse compassionate listening, however, with simply giving verbal reassurances: "That's all right. You couldn't help reacting that way." "Well, don't worry about it. Things have a way of working out." "I know what you mean—bosses are all alike; you can't trust them to be fair." These responses are not helpful at all. They tend to brush the listener's feelings aside and imply that he or she isn't a good judge of what's worth worry or work, what's a problem and what's not, what action to take or not take.

Compassionate listening provides something more than glib assurances. It empowers people because it enables them to lower their defenses, share themselves, and find their own solutions in an accepting atmosphere.

TIP 436: Listen for Feelings As Well As Facts.

Noted clinical psychologist Carl Rogers believed strongly that a patient's healing could be greatly speeded up by the simple act of having an analyst who really cared. "If I can listen to what he tells me, if I can understand how it seems to him, if I can sense the emotional flavor which it has for him, then I will be releasing potent forces of change within him."

Far too many people pay an analyst for what friends should and could do if they practiced listening for emotions. Letting the other person know that you understand the emotion behind his or her words gives the satisfying sense of *really* being understood.

TIP 437: Listen for the Context.

When we read a news story where a cousin shoots an uncle over a card game, the incident shocks us because of the enormity of the deed in response to the provocation. In such incidents, we can be sure the immediate act was not the whole of the situation. Words and feelings always have a context. A friend says to you: "There are so many rumors going around in my company that you never know from one day to the next if we're going to be merged, acquired, or just laid off. I'm not sure whether I'd be canned or not. So I can't decide about buying that house. We'd have to do some remodeling, for sure. The mortgage payments really will stretch us, and if Jill decides to switch careers, that'll affect our cash flow severely. I'm totally puzzled about the next step."

With this comment, you have a broad context to understand the whole situation: the rumors at work, the spouse's job uncertainty, the remodeling necessary. But what if the friend said only: "I can't decide about buying that house. We'd have to do some remodeling"? You might respond by talking about the pros and cons of the house—the location, the down payment, the interest rate, the condition of the inside. And you'd be way off base about the total meaning.

Words do not mean much outside the context of someone's experience and situation. Probe for the context so you can listen adequately and respond appropriately.

TIP 438: Listen for What Is Not Said.

Why did the talker decide not to tell you a particular fact? Why did the boss not mention delay on the related projects? Why did the customer not mention volume discounts when he or she always buys on price? What's not said can be as revealing—and as important—as what appears in the headlines.

TIP 439: Paraphrase; Don't Parrot.

Reflective listening has been misunderstood. When psychologists first introduced the concept, many people understood it to mean simply repeating to the talker what he or she said, as if it were an attempt to prove you heard. The purpose was lost. The idea of paraphrasing is to show talkers that you fully understand their meanings—not just hear their words.

The difference is enormous. By paraphrasing their views, you give talkers a chance to reflect on what they've just said, to make sure that's what they mean, maybe even to change what they think or feel after hearing it again.

Here are paraphrasing responses: "If I understand you correctly, you're saying . . ." "You really mean that . . ." "As you see it, . . ." "From your perspective, . . ." "Let me see if I get where you're coming from on that—you think that . . ." "What I hear you saying is . . ." "Am I hearing this right? You think . . ." "So to sum up then, you feel . . ."

An Example of Reflective Listening/Paraphrasing

DAVID: I've told Angie a thousand times to get first-class letters out the same day that somebody in this department writes them. And the summaries I've given her to do are inaccurate again. I asked her for the raw numbers and she spent two hours averaging them all. Then she doesn't know why she's got so much to do. Complains that she can't get everything done!

JUAN: So you feel pretty exasperated with her performance, right? It's putting the whole department in a bind?

DAVID: That's an understatement. We have invoices that don't go out. We have customer letters that don't go out. We've had to spend money on temporaries twice this week because she's so far behind.

JUAN: You think that if Angie would follow instructions better you wouldn't have had to hire temporary help?

DAVID: Well, I'm not saying that exactly. I don't know whether we do or don't need to hire anyone else. I can't tell if the job really is too much for one person or if Angie just can't handle it. If she followed instructions better and at least did things right, then I'd have a better handle on the real workload.

JUAN: You'd then know how much of the problem was due to rework caused by Angie and how much of the problem was that there's just too much to do.

DAVID: Exactly.

JUAN: So at this point, I guess you're feeling a lot of pressure from the customers who don't get answers or invoices and the rest of the guys around here that are complaining to you about Angie. And if Angie's complaining that she's overworked, you've got everybody unhappy.

DAVID: No, I don't think Angie really feels overworked. She just says that. I think she realizes that she's not performing up to standard. The workload issue is just an excuse.

You get the idea. Juan has paraphrased on three levels: the words, the feelings, and the implied words and feelings. Of course, paraphrasing is not called for on all occasions. Here are occasions that do call for such in-depth listening: When you or the other person experiences strong feelings and wants to talk things over. When you or someone else has a conflict to resolve. When someone needs new ideas or wants feedback on ideas. When you're inclined to disagree with or ignore what someone wants you to accept.

All conversations are not created equal. Be choosy about which ones require this effort. Then give those important conversations all you've got. Paraphrasing helps the talker feel understood, think openly, hear and verify what he or she is really feeling and thinking, and reflect on what to do next. Paraphrasing electrifies both people involved.

TIP 440: Attend with Your Entire Body.

As part of an exercise in our communication workshops, we have a participant-speaker address the group. Then, while that speaker goes out of the room to prepare, we ask the group to help with a little demonstration that the speaker doesn't know he or she is a part of. We ask the audience to give the speaker a couple minutes to warm up and then to start to act disinterested. Some people lean forward with their head propped in their hand, resting on an elbow. Others lean back in their chairs, hands behind their heads. Some shuffle through purses or pocketbooks for a mysterious item. Others began to gaze out the window. Most break eye contact with the speaker. Nothing is overtly rude, just subtle.

In less than a minute's time, the speaker gets flustered and even angry, totally unaware of what the audience has been instructed to do. When they begin to see the signs of inattention, some speakers will began to talk faster and faster and louder and louder. Others will stop, start again, stop, then lose their train of thought completely. Some will begin to pace around the room more feverishly and gesture more dynamically. They don't know exactly what or why, but they understand that people are no longer listening. The experience dramatically illustrates for the group the importance of a listener's attentive body language.

People want you to sit or stand in an alert position, lean toward them, stop rummaging with your paperwork, and look at them when they talk to you. Your whole body has to listen.

TIP 441: Invite People to Talk by Commenting on Their Body Language.

Shy people may need encouragement to talk to you, particularly when they're unsure if you'd be interested in what they have to say. A good way to communicate to them "Hey, it's okay, I'm ready to listen" is to comment on their body language and then listen to their response: "You look puzzled." "You look excited—your eyes are flashing." "What a smile—what gives?" "Lost your best friend or your dog? You look down." Although the person may not take your cue, he or she has had an open invitation to respond with meaningful conversation.

TIP 442: Play "What if" to Encourage Reflection.

Have you ever had a coworker come into your work area and say, "Hey, I got a problem. I need some help." Then as she starts telling you the problem, she suddenly says, "Wait a minute. That's an idea. Never mind," and dashes out. She has solved her own problem by just hearing herself talk about it.

Having someone listen gives us an acceptable reason to talk to ourselves out loud. And talking about the problem as if you are explaining it to another person clarifies details, identifies issues, and raises possible solutions.

On such occasions, help others think aloud by asking "what if" questions. It's not that you have the answers—they do. Your helpfulness comes in listening to them and then helping them reflect or think differently about what they've said.

TIP 443: Respond to the Feelings, Then the Facts—Not the Reverse.

"Calm down, calm down. Tell me what happened." Although it's a typical response, that's not the best approach when someone is angry, frightened, or frustrated. Uncork the emotion first, then ask for the facts. Customer-service reps understand the concept in dealing with irate customers, parents understand the concept in settling sibling battles, and ambassadors understand the concept at the negotiating table.

Disregarding this concept can cost a sale or a customer. For example, a hotel guest calls down to the front desk and says, "There's a husband and wife next door having a knock-down, drag-out fight. They're yelling and screaming. Would you see what you can do about it? I'm trying to get some sleep." The desk clerk says, "We can move you to another room, if you prefer."

Wrong move. That's an obvious solution. But the hotel clerk would have done better to respond to the feeling, "It's late, and I'm sure that's very disturbing. We'll call their room and take care of it." The "solution" response presumes a superior position, as if the other hotel guest hadn't thought of moving to another room. Not only does the response sound unfeeling, it sounds like a put-down.

Questions, comments, explanations, and observations come a lot easier and clearer *after*, not before, the emotional release.

TIP 444: Be Careful About Attaching Any Labels to What You Hear.

People may experience the same situation and use different words to describe it. What one listener calls "worry" another calls "concern." What one calls "petulant" another calls "feisty." What one labels "angry" another calls "afraid." "Shyness" can be mistaken for "aloofness." Once you've labeled the feeling expressed to you, you tend to direct all else under that umbrella. Be sure the labels don't take you off track.

TIP 445: Take Off-the-Subject Comments As the Subject.

In the middle of conversation, when someone makes a remark that seems off the topic at hand, that comment is irrelevant. But that irrelevancy often provides a big clue about what's really on the person's mind. Consider dropping the topic at hand and taking up the new subject. You'll help the other person get the pressing problem "finished."

TIP 446: Overlook "Trigger" Words to Get to the Real Message.

When you hear emotional words, derogatory words, profanity, or politically motivated words, try to get past them to the real message: "bureaucrat," "lazy," "windbag," "hustler," "unfair," "gross negligence," and so forth. If you get hung up on the speaker's word choice, you may miss the primary message. Hear the person out. Then you can always go back and correct the word choice mentally.

TIP 447: Recognize "Stoppers" Before You Deliver Them.

When someone starts a serious conversation with you, your reaction will either encourage that person to keep talking or stop him or her cold. Stoppers: ordering, commanding, threatening, moralizing, advising, lecturing, criticizing, blaming, shaming, diagnosing, interrogating. If you doubt these tones and words will stop a conversation, recall the last 10 unpleasant ones you've had.

TIP 448: Avoid Me-Too Interceptions.

"I don't know what I'm going to have to do with my teenager; he's totally irresponsible when it comes to money." Response: "Oh, do I ever identify with that! I've mentioned that my oldest is a junior at the university. Out in an apartment on his own. Well, the other day he calls me up and says . . ." Before you know it, the situation has been reversed. The person who introduced the subject and wanted to express his frustration is now the listener for the other person's saga.

Yes, empathetic listening means that we share common experiences, but the key is timing. The first talker was cut off before being able to tell about his situation and fully express his frustration. Don't intercept the conversational ball.

TIP 449: Use Silence to Encourage the Talker.

Recruiters understand this as their best tool to find out more about a job applicant. Silence makes some people uncomfortable, and they will do anything to fill it. Whether making someone uncomfortable so they will chatter on with revealing information or inviting a friend to unload, silence encourages talk.

TIP 450: Probe with Open-Ended Questions.

Probe someone's comments with questions that begin with the five Ws: Why is that so? When is that true? Where is that true? With whom is that true? What is true? How is that true? How much is involved? Don't become an interrogator with yes-no questions; closed questions put you too much in the driver's seat. Instead, with open-ended probes you encourage the listener to explore both feelings and facts for errors and insights.

TIP 451: Be Wary About Listening for What You Want to Hear.

My entrepreneurial college-age son recently asked his stepfather if he could use part of his office building for teaching country-western dance lessons. His stepfather replied, "I have reservations about that, Jeff. I'm often working late at night, and having people here would be distracting. And the cleaning crew that comes in might not always clean up after them—I don't know exactly what time they make it to our building. And the tenants next door have a silent alarm that even our own employees set off when walking through the lounge after hours—and they know it's there. Dancers in here would be setting it off and the police would be having to come out. And I wouldn't want people just milling around through our workstations."

"But couldn't you move those wall dividers over into the big open area and keep people out of the workstations?" Jeff asked.

"Well, I don't know. I guess that's a possibility. . . . What nights are you planning to give lessons—I'm up here late working every night but Wednesday."

"I haven't decided on a specific night yet," Jeff answered.

End of conversation.

My son came home and told me that his stepfather said it was okay for him to have the dance lessons in the building—as long as they were on Wednesday nights and as long as they used the partitions to keep people out of the workstation areas.

We hear what we wish to hear.

TIP 452: Be Wary About Not Listening for What You Don't Want to Hear.

A regional manager of a construction firm had a long talk with his vice president to express dissatisfaction with what he considered were misleading comments made to customers. "You tell customers we're not just a contractor—that we have our own manufacturers for the cabinetry we install in the office buildings. But a warehouse with a table saw is not a manufacturer. I don't like misleading people." The vice president soothed the manager's convictions with promises that they had plans to get into the manufacturing side shortly.

As time went on, there were other such discussions. The regional manager told the vice president he was upset about late commission checks and unnecessary requested travel. Each time the vice president soothed his feelings, agreed that things were not as they should be, and promised improvements.

Six months later, when the regional manager offered his resignation, the vice president looked shocked. "You pull in more business than all the other regions put together. You can't leave. What will it take to make you change your mind? How much raise do you want?"

Whatever the specific mindset—they're worried, upset, misguided, uninformed, or dumb—people don't hear what they don't want to hear.

TIP 453: Avoid an In-and-Out Pattern.

Because we listen four to six times faster than someone talks, wandering ears become a temptation. We fade in and out just like channels on a TV. Become aware of this habit by forcing yourself to do something constructive with the extra listening time: Chunk the information and learn it as you hear it, make notes, or analyze comments. Just stay tuned.

TIP 454: Listen All the Way to the End; Don't Assume.

Doctors and their patients provide the best illustrations of this common weakness. After the doctor has seen three patients during the morning, all complaining about vomiting, diarrhea, and upper respiratory problems, the fourth patient gets half an ear. The doctor begins to write out the prescription while the patient finishes the symptoms. I would venture a guess that our health-care system pays for a great many unnecessary medical procedures and tests exactly for this reason.

Listening costs less than testing. The one word "not" can make a whopping difference in someone's meaning. That's why shipping departments find it necessary to print statements in this manner: "This is a packing slip, *not* an invoice."

If you catch yourself interrupting someone with, "I know just what you mean. . . . Yesterday, the same thing . . ." be careful.

TIP 455: Decide When Not to Listen Reflectively.

Just because somebody talks to you does not mean it's in his or her best interest or yours to listen reflectively. If a speaker is so eager to get out his or her story that he or she doesn't stop for your paraphrases, then your doing so would be an interruption. If the speaker just wants to vent emotions, you may choose not to listen and not to paraphrase abusive comments to you. If speakers have difficulty expressing themselves, to paraphrase might interrupt their thoughts and they might begin to let you "talk for them." If the speaker is simply passing along information, there's no reason to paraphrase unless you yourself want to verify what you heard for accuracy sake. Finally, small talk requires only a small-talk response.

Make reflective listening a conscious choice, depending on the circumstances.

TIP 456: Eliminate Physical and Psychological Noise.

Taking calls on my kitchen telephone presents a number of challenges: The washer and dryer from the nearby laundry room. The dishwasher in midcycle. The TV in the adjoining family room. The radio through the intercom. And a conversation left in midsentence with a husband using sign language to finish. These background noises and concerns prevent my hearing clearly when I use that phone.

The problem is that background noises we've become accustomed to prevent our hearing, and we're not even aware of them sometimes. In the workplace, we have printer noise, music over the intercom, coworker conversations, and ringing phones. We don't realize how much all this noise affects our concentration. If you want a comparison of what you can accomplish without all that noise, try staying after hours or arriving early before the noise starts. Compare your concentration with that during peak noise hours.

TIP 457: Make Up for the Listening-Talking Differential.

According to various researchers, we can listen about four to six times faster than we talk. Therefore, when someone talks to you—either formally in a presentation or in casual conversation—your mind may dawdle along the way and not miss much—or miss a great deal. The difference has to do with what you do with that extra time. If you're not careful, you can use that extra listening speed to let your mind wander off onto another subject. In fact, you may even run three or four channels at once: listen to what the checkout clerk is asking about the price of bread, think about what you're going to have for dinner, worry about catching cold standing under the ceiling fan, and write out a check for the groceries.

In certain instances, that may be an efficient use of your time. However, if the talker merits your attention, you can use the extra thinking speed to listen well. You can make notes. Or you can evaluate what you're hearing: Why is the person saying this? When is this true? Where is this true? Why is this true? How is this true? Why is this important to know? How can I use this information? How should I respond? That evaluation makes efficient use of your extra listening speed. Finally, you can use this extra time to fix what you're hearing into long-term memory. Chunk it into pieces, develop a mnemonic device, outline it with key words, or just repeat it to yourself—use any of these methods to fix the information in your mind so that it stays put.

TIP 458: Make Notes on What You Hear and Don't Be Afraid to Ask People to Repeat.

When angry customers call to tell you about a problem—or even mild-mannered, happy customers to tell you about a situation—don't be hesitant to ask them to repeat key facts or details. Say something like, "Would you repeat that attendant's name please. . . . Okay, now let me repeat these key facts to you again to make sure I have everything correct. I want to make sure I have all the essential information so we can get a quick resolution."

They'll want the account to be as accurate as you do.

TIP 459: Don't Take Copious Notes.

If you have to err one way or the other, take fewer notes rather than too many. If you try to write down everything someone says, you will invariably miss some things. And not only will you miss some words, but with your eyes glued to your page and your mind intent on getting the words down you'll miss pauses and nuances of meanings, voice inflection, and body language that helps you interpret the words. Fewer is better. Less is more when it comes to note-taking.

TIP 460: Ask for Clarification of Instructions.

Everybody needs feedback: bosses, parents, presidents. When the machinist gives the new-hire instructions to operate the lathe and finishes with, "You understand?" The typical new-hire will respond, "Yeah, I think so." Why is that? (1) People think they understand and don't know they don't understand until there's a mistake. (2) People don't want to look stupid by admitting they don't understand. (3) People don't want to waste other people's time by having them repeat themselves. (4) People don't want to appear to be criticizing the way the other person gave them the instructions by admitting the instructions were unclear.

For whatever reason the hesitancy, forget it. Ask. You're doing the instruction-giver a favor by verifying that you understand and by asking clarifying questions if you do not. People will find it much easier to repeat themselves up front, if necessary, than to repeat themselves later while trying to undo, redo, or make do.

TIP 461: Listen to Difficult, Complex Information As It Relates to You.

Seminars, symposiums, and staff meetings may all include information that you consider dull or even complex. During these times, you may give your mind permission to go on recess. But is that in your best interest? If so, be my guest. If not—if you really need to know the information, but you find listening a chore—practice discipline. We're used to "absorbing" information through entertainment on TV, radio, or CD without having to work for it. Listening to things that require concentration takes effort.

Try jotting down key points. Not comprehensive note-taking, but keyword or key-point note-taking. It forces you to pay attention and look for the structure in the information you're receiving.

Also, look for personal application in what you're hearing. If you were about to be sent up in a space rocket, you'd probably find it easier to listen to instructions on using the oxygen mask than if you intended to spend the weekend lounging in front of the TV. Always dig for the WIIFM (what's in it for me?). Why do I need to know this? How can I use this information? If you're a salesperson trying to learn new product specifications, visualize the paycheck because of your knowledgeable response to a customer's technical question. If you're hearing why management decided to set up a certain retirement plan, visualize yourself having to explain it to your spouse. Look for purpose. Whet your appetite.

TIP 462: Know When to Listen Analytically.

When someone dumps his or her feelings about a broken love affair, you need to listen reflectively—to hear the feelings along with the facts. On the other hand, as a manager you have to learn to listen analytically. You may have to take the lead in helping the other person sort fact from fiction, to discern hidden agendas, to develop creative alternatives to problems, and to evaluate those alternatives.

Good management demands knowing when to listen and paraphrase versus when to listen and analyze.

TIP 463: Overcome Personal Bias to Evaluate Effectively.

Although difficult, recognizing the need for objectivity on occasion improves our reception to messages. Be aware of stereotypical thinking and negative thinking; otherwise, your reactions and the resulting situation become self-fulfilling prophecies.

TIP 464: Sift Out Propaganda Techniques As You Listen.

The *bandwagon* approach invites you to accept an idea or take an action just because everybody else is: "This has been our most popular desk chair" or "Here, listen to what Mr. Smoe says about this plan."

The *all-or-nothing* persuader insists that you must accept everything about an idea or reject it in total. Either you take the plan in its entirety or forget it. Either you buy the product and all related services or it won't work at all.

The *generalization* leads you to come to a conclusion based on a single or a few incidents or facts. "John Smith is an engineer who can't write well; therefore, no engineers write well."

The *like-one-like-'em-all* pitch links the new to the old, with the intent of giving your one idea a free ride. "You loved hearing Roland speak last year? Then you're going to really like Fred" or "You remember how well this process worked last year? Then we can set it up the same way this year."

This next propaganda technique is more subtle: *I call 'em like I see 'em.* The persuader hopes to color your thinking simply by his or her word choice: "This outdated system . . ." and before long you find yourself thinking the system is outdated. "This leading-edge technology . . ." and soon you find yourself thinking of that company's technology as the wave of the future. All because the persuader labeled things so.

The *card-stacking* persuader tells you only the facts that he or she wants you to hear, selectively omitting others that would give you both sides of the picture. And every argument seems right until you hear the other side.

Finally, the *evangelistic* persuader uses hot, emotion-evoking, descriptive words to stir people to action. "Are you going to let those rich tycoons sitting in their ivory towers with their $1000 pin-striped suits kick you while you're down?"

Think critically to avoid being taken in by these indirect tactics and inconclusive arguments.

TIP 465: Analyze the Persuasive Tone As You Listen.

When you're about to be "sold," your defenses go up. Why? It's not so much that people mind buying an idea as that they mind having someone think they've been deceived by someone's tone or manner. Listen critically for the following attitudes:

Good ole buddy. This persuader makes you feel that because you're a long-lost friend he or she is going to give you the real scoop—the inside story that the person wouldn't tell just anybody.

You and I are different from those other folks. This persuader pushes to find things in common with you—we have the same hometown, we both have toddlers, we both like to drink at Grady's Bar. And it follows that if there's a strong identification, you'll buy what the persuader is saying. Why? Because you two fall into a different category than "average folks" so you'd better stick together.

You're so wonderful. This persuader loves your office, your kids, your management philosophies. How could you not go along with someone who thinks you're wonderful, talented, and lovable?

Let me enlighten you. This persuader wants to educate you so that you can see the light and understand those complex things he or she has mastered. The person shows such "patience" with you.

If any of these tones and attitudes come through, listen past them to the real message and action to make sure you're not persuaded by the tone rather than the ideas themselves.

TIP 466: Use a Checklist to Avoid "Morning After" Remorse.

If you frequently find yourself with buyer's remorse—whether buying a product or an idea—hone your critical listening skills with a checklist. Before making a quick decision, ask yourself these questions:

- How credible is this persuader?
- What are his or her credentials?
- What does this persuader have to gain or lose?
- What is the major premise here?
- Is there supporting evidence?
- Is that evidence logical and conclusive?
- What is fact and what is opinion?

- What other information do I need before deciding?

- Why does this idea appeal to me logically?

- Why does this idea appeal to me or repel me emotionally?

- Why do I need to decide quickly?

- Why am I trying to delay this decision?

Listen critically to stay on the straight and narrow. Many a buyer and decision maker wishes he or she had pulled out this checklist "the morning after."

TIP 467: Summarize What You've Heard After Lengthy Sessions.

In addition to paraphrasing as a conversation unfolds, summarize at the end to make sure you have understood the key points covered and any next-action items. Writers add a summary paragraph or chapter at the end of their articles and books to make sure they've hammered home their theses. Meeting leaders recap major conclusions at the close of formal meetings. Telemarketers outline the next steps of action before they hang up. But for some reason, if people have talked one on one, face to face, they forget the need to do the same thing. Summaries provide one last chance for clarity.

7

Asking the Right Questions Without Being Intrusive

Judge a man by his questions rather than by his answers.   —FRANÇOIS MARIE VOLTAIRE

It is harder to ask a sensible question than to supply a sensible answer.
    —PERSIAN PROVERB

No man really becomes a fool until he stops asking questions.   —CHARLES P. STEINMETZ

Better to ask twice than to lose your way once.
    —DANISH PROVERB

The man who is afraid of asking is ashamed of learning.   —DANISH PROVERB

It's better to know some of the questions than all of the answers.   —JAMES THURBER

It seems that when a fellow claims to know all the answers some fool comes along and asks the wrong questions.   —no attribution

Children grow up asking questions. The better their questions, the more challenging and important the answers we give them. Questions embody a child's creativity, serve as an aid to learning, cause others to reflect on the meanings of things, irritate those cooped up with them for long periods of time, and embarrass parents in front of friends and strangers. As adults with questions in the workplace, we run into the same concerns, issues, and irritants—for better or worse.

TIP 468: Know Your Purpose in Asking Questions.

With purpose comes organization. You can go from the broad and general to the narrow and specific. For example, if you're interviewing someone for a job, you may begin with a broad, general question: "Tell me a little about your last job—what you liked or disliked." As the applicant begins talking, you'll follow up with more specific questions generated from the earlier answers: "So why do you think you were so successful at selling the widgets when others couldn't meet quota?"

On the other hand, you might decide to go from the narrow and specific, easy-to-answer questions to the broad and general. "How long were you at the last job?" "What was your title there?" "Did other people work with you on those projects?" Then broader: "What are some of the difficulties you think arise in working in teams and being held accountable for others' results?"

On other occasions, you may want to ask unrelated questions in a random fashion, such as when surveying customers about price points or asking team members what projects they want to tackle next.

Broad, general questions give the asker more latitude to explore and gather information he or she didn't know to ask about. They also give listeners great latitude in leading where they want to go. By contrast, specific, narrow questions give the asker more control, but sometimes less information. Specific, narrow questions can be either easy to answer or difficult to answer if the answer puts the listener on the spot.

With questions to a client, a coworker, or a complainer, know your purpose.

TIP 469: Decide Whether to and When to Lead.

"Isn't it obvious that the MIS department needs these figures by the end of the week?" clearly says that you expect the listener to agree with you. As a result, the listener may feel pressured or trapped. In other situations, however, you may need to lead a customer or coworker to a decision or a quick response: "You probably want a matte finish, don't you?"

Here are other reasons to lead with questions:

- *Lead a customer to clarify.* "Can you elaborate on what you mean by inadequate turnaround time?"

- *Lead a customer who is digressing.* "Yes, you mentioned the filter earlier. You started to tell me something about the missing label, didn't you?"

- *Lead a customer who keeps going in circles.* "Okay, let me see if I have things straight to this point. You said the delivery driver arrived at noon. That he didn't have the right tools to install the machine. And that he waited out on your deck for one hour until his backup driver arrived. Now, was there any other wasted time that you noted and wanted us to deduct from your repair bill?"

- *Lead a customer to generalize and get to the point.* "So your main concern is that the bill should not reflect time spent due to the driver's incompetence?"

- *Lead a customer to be specific.* "You said the driver was discourteous. Did he yell? Act sullen? Refuse to give you his name?"

- *Lead a customer to clarify seemingly conflicting facts or statements.* "Your colleague said he arrived at noon. I understood you to say he arrived at 2 o'clock. Which time is correct, or did I misunderstand one of you?"

- *Lead a customer to give you feedback.* "Do you think you will go ahead with the February order if this repair is completed on time?" "What other concerns do you have about awarding the contract to us?"

- *Lead a customer to agreement.* "I've decided to delete all the service charges. Will that be acceptable to you?"

The leading question is not bad or good within itself; simply realize its purpose and its effect. On occasion it may sound patronizing; on another occasion, efficient.

TIP 470: State the Point of Your Question.

For best results, give questions a context. A trade-show manager asks his assistant how much small, plastic trash cans cost. His assistant calls eight stores to put together a list of potential suppliers of trash containers, with the available sizes and prices for volume purchases. When she reports back to the manager with her list of suppliers, he comments that they're all too expensive for the one-time use he intends—to place them in the exhibitor booths for the upcoming trade show. When he amplifies on his purpose, the perturbed assistant explains that her next-door neighbor runs a cleaning service. And that cleaning-service company will supply trash containers with their janitorial service for a fee less than the cost to purchase the containers.

Once again, wasted effort. The manager didn't give the bigger picture that prompted the question.

Explain why before you ask. Context makes a big difference. If people know why you're asking, they may supply helpful information that you haven't even thought to ask.

TIP 471: Ask Closed Questions to Gain Agreement.

Closed questions call for a specific, limited answer, not an expansive one: a word, phrase, or simple sentence. Salespeople learn firsthand the hazards of giving customers too many choices, because they can't make up their minds. Instead of "What color staplers do you want?" they ask, "Do you want those in black, gray, or putty?"

When you're in a hurry to get agreement, try the same technique with your boss or coworkers: "I need to talk with you about the Compton project. Would Tuesday morning or Wednesday after 2 o'clock be better for you?" To a customer try, "Would you prefer that we send you a refund check now, or credit your account for next month?" Closed questions focus others' thinking and bring them to decision quickly. When you want a specific answer, ask a pointed question.

TIP 472: Ask Open-Ended Questions to Gather Information.

Open-ended questions usually cannot be answered with a simple word or two. Such questions begin with who, what, where, why, when, or how. They give listeners a wide range of responses. Examples: "How do you think the client will react to this proposal?" "When do you think would be the best time to survey our employees?" "What things should we be wary of when we change suppliers?" "Where have you had the most success with this procedure?" "Who do you think could benefit from this new information?" Open-ended questions provide you with the most information.

TIP 473: Ask Others for Opinions Rather Than Facts if You Want to Draw Them Out.

Requesting a fact limits a person's thinking. He or she generally answers with the fact and grows silent again. If you want to have the person expand so that you can gather a wide range of information and impressions, suggest a topic rather than ask a question: "Tell me what you think about the way the President is handling the economy." "What do you know about nuclear energy—have you given it any thought for heating your home?" "How about employee morale around here?"

TIP 474: Avoid a Cliché Question if You Don't Want a Cliché Answer.

Don't blame others if they're not talkative if the only stimulating questions you use are clichés. "How's it going?" usually elicits a response like, "Okay, I guess." The same is true for these clichés: "How are you?" "Is it morning?" "Did you have a nice weekend?" "What's up?"

TIP 475: Ask Even if You Don't Expect an Answer.

We learn this trick from reporters and lawyers. Even if you don't expect an answer, you can ask a question just to see how the other person reacts and how he or she refuses to answer. The attitude revealed may be as important as the information released. You get information without getting a formal answer. This technique can be useful in negotiating and learning where the limits of information exchange fall.

TIP 476: Act as Though You Expect an Answer.

It's amazing how many people pose question after question in their conversations, as if they were rhetorical, and never pause for an answer. When you ask a question and then rush ahead with an answer yourself or move on to the next topic, the other person notices the pattern and decides you don't intend to take any answer seriously. Nervousness also plays a big part in someone's talking right through where the pauses should go. Be aware of that habit; ask, pause, wait.

TIP 477: Make Sure Your Body Language Encourages an Answer.

Have you ever watched someone toss out a question as though it were a green light for another person to proceed with the conversation while the questioner attended to something more important—like the papers on his or her desk or the conversation going on beyond the talker's shoulder?

Your body language either supports or undermines the intention of your question. The responder needs some sort of support: a nod of agreement or a follow-up question that demonstrates you have listened to the first answer. Do you smirk at what you consider inadequate answers? Glance away as if other things are more important at the moment? Ask dumb follow-up questions that indicate you weren't listening to the first answer? If so, tell your body that you're interested in the answer to the question your mouth just asked.

TIP 478: Remember That Wording Makes a Great Deal of Difference in the Answer You Get.

Official pollsters will be the first to point out that the wording of questions is extremely important in survey results. For example, multiple-choice questions that mention alternatives will elicit more people who agree with the alternatives than questions that do not suggest alternatives at all. "Knowledge" questions get fewer responses than opinion questions. Positively worded questions generate more positive responses than negatively worded questions.

If the question you intend to ask is an important one, take great care in how you word it. If you don't have time to read body language and rephrase it on the spot, write out your question and practice it before you get an audience with the decision maker or other person who holds the key to your future.

TIP 479: Don't Give Overlapping Alternatives.

If you want to walk away with a clear understanding about expected action, avoid ambiguous questions with "and/or" and "both/and" implications. For example, in a staff meeting a manager poses this question: "Do you think the team is moving along all right in drafting the new procedures, or do you think we should look into hiring a consultant for analyzing and drafting some of our processes?" It is entirely possible that some people in the staff meeting could answer, "The team is doing well and, yes, it would be a good idea to hire an outside consultant." More than likely, however, the staff members will take one or the other of the alternatives posed in the question: either that the team is doing well enough alone or that the team needs input from the consultant. If the staffers mention hiring the consultant, the manager may gather the impression that they think the team isn't handling the task well. That would be a wrong conclusion drawn from such a response.

Another example: "Do you want to go to Hawaii for the sales meeting, or would you enjoy something closer in Canada?" The answer could be, "I'd love to go to Hawaii and, yes, I'd enjoy a shorter trip to Canada." If the person answers, "Hawaii sounds great," that doesn't necessarily mean Canada is an undesirable choice or even second choice. Take care in structuring questions so that you know the difference between "either-or" and "both-and" responses.

TIP 480: Clarify Whether You Want Evidence or Opinion on Speculative Issues.

For example: "If we raise our prices on this item, what effect will it have on our customers?" Do you want the other person to give you evidence—comments from prospective customers about price, market trends in pricing, rumors about the plans of competitors? Or do you want an opinion about the effect the other person thinks the price increase will have? Unless you clarify your expectations that opinions (even unsupported ones) are welcome, you're likely to get few answers about the future.

TIP 481: Frame Off-the-Hook Questions When Asking for Favors.

If you're dealing with subordinates or if you don't want to impose on a friendship, phrase your questions so that people know it's okay to say no. "We probably should stay open over the holiday—but I suppose you probably already have plans other than work, right?" or "We need someone to pick up the gift for Tseuko's retirement luncheon. Is everybody in a big hurry or would someone have time to stop by the mall?" Such phrasing lets people off the hook without making a big deal of turning you down.

TIP 482: Ask Questions to Convey to Others That You Value Their Input.

Asking questions should be a promise to pay attention to the answers. Make statements if you don't want input. Of course, listening is no guarantee that you will use every idea or piece of data received, but people will watch for a pattern. When you do want to solicit opinions, follow through by listening and evaluating them. Just going through the motions creates hostility.

TIP 483: Establish Rapport by Asking Questions.

Most people like to have others show interest in them. When you seek out another's opinion or ask about someone's experiences or interests, you're complimenting them. That warmth builds rapport.

TIP 484: Solicit Feedback by Asking Questions.

It's a mistake to think that because people give you no contrary feedback they are in agreement with your approach, your philosophy, or your action. People feel intimidated by those in powerful positions and by others who can help or harm their careers. As a powerful person, when you want feedback, it's often up to you to solicit it repeatedly with questions: "Does the idea of working 10-hour shifts appeal to you in any way?" "What would you consider creative incentive awards for achieving our quarterly goals?" "How do you think we performed on the last project?" Just because you ask questions doesn't mean you'll get honest answers, or even any answers. But asking no questions and leaving feedback to chance almost ensures there will be none.

TIP 485: Encourage Buy-In Action by Asking Questions.

If you have colleagues who can't seem to meet deadlines, let them set their own. When faced with soliciting their cooperation or information on a new project, instead of stating the deadline, ask them to set the deadline. "John, please let me know what day I can expect the printout on the Carlton site." When people set their own deadlines, they are more likely to meet them.

Here are other examples that encourage people to participate and buy into group action or decisions: "Do you think this plan will work?" "Can we count on your help?" "Does this approach make sense to you?" "Which of the two alternatives do you think we should try first?" "Are you willing to give this plan a try?"

TIP 486: Ask Questions to Lead Others to Analyze Their Own Suggestions.

An employee speaks up in a meeting with this suggestion: "Why don't we go ahead and print 100,000 copies of the brochure since we'll be doing more mailings later in the year?" Rather than snap back with, "Because our test mailings will determine whether we need to change the copy," lead the employee to evaluate his or her own suggestion by questioning: "Will later mailings go to the same prospective buyers? If so, will they respond to the same copy?" or "How much would we save by printing all 100,000 copies now as opposed to the expense of two print runs?"

The questioning route helps employees learn to analyze suggestions without your intervention, giving them confidence in their abilities for later situations and giving them the impression that you're not closed to all suggestions.

TIP 487: Analyze Your Own Ideas with the Five W Questions.

One of the best guides for analyzing a new idea thoroughly is to set up the five Ws as a framework for thought: *why* it would work, *where* it would work, *who* would be involved, *when* it would be useful, *how* it could be implemented. Pose these prompting questions to yourself or to others involved in the analysis.

If the answer is unfavorable, rephrase the questions before you give up on the idea: *Why* did the process not work for us? *What* could we improve to make things work better? *What* results did we want that we didn't achieve? *Who* else could benefit from joining us in the process? *How* do we want to do it next time? *What* can we learn from this effort?

TIP 488: Stimulate Creative Thinking with What-if Questions.

You can lead people to reflect on the unknown of various events or circumstances by posing what-if questions: "What if we held elections only once a decade rather than every two years?" "What if we cut out commissions all together?" "What if we make this project a charitable contribution?" "What if we could get the customer to pay us up front?" Strangely enough, most of us don't put ourselves on the spot often enough to come up with creative solutions. Yet, when posed with such questions from others, we take the challenge. The result is often insightful answers that benefit both people.

TIP 489: Plant Your Own Ideas with Questions.

"Has anybody given serious thought to bypassing the marketing department with this campaign?" "Is it realistic to think employees will not mind lengthening the workday 10 minutes?" "How would it work if we combined the flyer and the catalog in one envelope?" "What would happen if you went back to your own supplier and suggested the change?" With such questions, you've planted the idea in a low-risk way; others can take it or leave it without your having to defend the position or sell it actively.

TIP 490: Persuade People by Asking Questions.

"Do you think your career could benefit from exposure to this training?" "If you were to seek such a lateral move, what experience could you pick up along the way that might help you get to the next level when something opens up?" "How would a customer react to your offer to provide the service at no charge—do you think he or she might be more inclined to ask us to bid on the other projects?" All of these questions frame a benefit for the listener. You may help others "suppose": "Let's suppose you accept this transfer; what other responsibilities might come your way?" You may help them justify: "How could you justify the extra cost involved in the move—didn't you intend to try to refinance your mortgage anyway?" Help them compare or contrast: "If you accept this job, will you be in a better or worse position to move to headquarters than if you stay here another 18 months?"

By the very phrasing of such questions, you are encouraging the other person to consider the merits or probability of a situation. And people give more credence to what they themselves say with their answers. The secret to being persuasive is getting others to answer the right questions.

TIP 491: Ask Questions to Uncover Resistance.

As any salesperson knows, having a silent prospect doesn't necessarily mean that he or she is ready to buy. What the prospect doesn't say can hurt your efforts. When you propose an idea in a meeting or offer a suggestion to a boss and the response seems to be a stall, ask questions. Uncover the resistance to the idea so that you can get it out in the open and deal with it.

TIP 492: Move People from the Emotional Level to the Analytical Level (or Vice Versa) with Questions.

For example, someone comments to you: "I'm really upset about the news report on the accident and public opinion polls that say most people blame our company." You can respond with a statement or a question, depending on your intention. Empathetic statements: "Yeah, I can see why." "It could be bad for stock prices." "It's going to be rough talking to neighbors and customers who call in." Any of these empathetic statements will encourage the other person to elaborate on the feelings.

On the other hand, you might respond with a question: "Why do you think reporters always try to focus on controversy?" "Do you think they've really investigated all the details about the accident at this point?" "Why are you so worried—do you have to deal with customers face to face?" With any of these questions, you're calling for a rational answer. You're asking the listener to move away from emotions and dig into their analytical sphere for answers and explanations. If your intention is to get away from emotion, ask a question. If, however, you want to be empathetic and allow the others to vent feelings, make statements that show you accept and understand their feelings.

TIP 493: Resist Demands or Commands by Using Questions.

If you don't think you can be straightforward with authority figures, force them to rethink their demands or commands with questions such as: "Are you aware that it will take me about three days to collect this data?" "Are you sure that the client really needs this report?" "Could you write out the instructions so that I understand fully what's involved before I begin?"

TIP 494: Find Commonalities with Questions.

A large part of building rapport with colleagues involves finding things you have in common. Questions move the process along—especially if they're broad enough to allow expansive answers. The broader the questions, the more chance you'll discover connections: "What's your background in the industry?" "What part of the country do you like best?" "How do you feel about the quality initiatives the company keeps pursuing at such expense?" "Do you feel as confused as I do about the new family-care options they're offering us?"

TIP 495: Reduce Your Anxiety by Asking Questions.

Fear of the unknown grips all of us from time to time. Posing our fears as questions to colleagues has a calming effect on our own mind. On the surface, the questions seem to gather information; in reality they collect others' reactions to the same situation. "Does anybody know if that noise means trouble?" "Are we the only people gullible enough to volunteer for this committee?" "Has anybody polled our customers to see what the reaction will be when we tell them the price increases we're planning for next year?" In other words, by asking if others join us in our fears we find comfort to go along as planned or courage to resist.

TIP 496: Use Questions to Stall.

You can almost always stall a decision by asking for more details, more data, more analysis, more options, more explanations, more benefits, more comparisons, more testimonials, more objections from your subordinates or colleagues. As long as people are chasing down answers, everyone is stalled in coming to conclusions.

TIP 497: Use Questions to Guide Conversation.

When you ask a question, you redirect conversational traffic to a new topic. As long as you aren't demanding and insensitive and don't sound like an interrogating district attorney, questions for this topic-changing purpose sit well. Just be sure to use open-ended questions that give the responder plenty of latitude to take off in several directions.

TIP 498: Pose Questions As Fun.

Consider how many people like to answer questions "just for fun." Notice how many radio stations pose questions as games for their listening audiences: "What was your most embarrassing moment?" "Who was the most famous person you met and what was that person like?" "What were Bobby Jo's hottest hits in the seventies?" Or consider the people you see bent over crossword puzzles or the popularity of quiz games on TV. In our communication workshops, we toss out a question and have people debating the answer for three days during lunch and breaks. People like to use their minds constructively.

Help them by posing questions for fun and for reflection. Toss these out in your small circle at the next cocktail party: "So tell me, who remembers the number one pop hit of last year?" "How many CEOs running the *Fortune* 1000 companies would you guess are under 40 years old?" "Opinion poll here: What star has had the biggest influence on the movie industry to date?"

TIP 499: Use Questions As a Display of Control.

The person who asks the questions stands at the helm of the ship. We allow only those in the appropriate positions of power over us to impose on us by guiding our topics, our discussions, and our analysis with questions. The person who decides who gets to ask the questions and then decides which questions are relevant and which are not controls the group. This principle works for emcees, panel moderators, lawyers, and judges. In the United States, we question and answer by consent.

TIP 500: Use *Why* Questions with Care.

Questions in a neutral tone that ask "why" about events cause little problem: "Why is the floor tile on backorder?" But asking "why" questions about people puts others on the defensive, especially if they already have a tendency to be defensive. "Why did you miss the meeting?" can be a straightforward call for information from a person who is surprised that you missed the meeting and knows you must have a reasonable explanation. On the other hand, "Why did you miss the meeting?" can be a blaming statement meaning "You shouldn't have missed the meeting—what do you have to say for yourself?"

Most people resist *why* questions that evaluate and judge reasons, motives, and intentions.

TIP 501: Avoid Trapping People with Questions.

A father comes home from the office and asks, "Johnny, how many times have I told you not to leave your bike in the driveway?" Does the father want a number? Hardly. His point is clearly that Johnny should have the message by now. We've watched too many court trials in the movies not to feel the rush of adrenalin when the prosecutor is moving in for the kill. With the unwary witness on the stand, the lawyer lays the groundwork with "innocent" questions to which the witness gives false answers. Then the prosecutor comes through with the real zinger question and the witness realizes he or she has been caught in the lies.

In the office, such questions sound like this: "Have I not made it clear that these expense reports are due on the fifth of the month?" "Did you miss the staff meeting where we discussed that issue?" "Did you not know that the customer expected to have this merchandise arrive undamaged?" "Don't you feel any concern at all for the outcome?" "You do want to make the sale, don't you?" The question is meant either to entrap the person or make the person feel foolish however he or she answers. Give people freedom to express disagreement or to refuse to take the either-or choice.

On occasion, you do already have the answer to a question and need to ask others to verify that you're correct. If that's the case, tell them what you're doing so they won't feel trapped with game-playing. For example: "Susan, why don't you tell me what happened out on the dock when the truck pulled up to unload. I already have a couple of witnesses who have told me what they saw, but I'd like your perspective on the incident."

TIP 502: Avoid Questions That Accuse.

"What did you think would happen if you let this situation rock along without notifying me?" accuses the listener of ulterior motives—or stupidity. Other accusing questions: "Why did you not write a letter to begin with?" "How do you know that's true?" "When did you expect to verify the client's order?" "How did you think we could process that many orders in one day?" "Who did you think was going to pay for that kind of promise to the customer?" Better simply to make a statement about what you think would have happened if the situation had "rocked along" or ask neutrally for the other person's viewpoint: "Did you consider notifying me, or did you think that was unnecessary at this point?" "Do you think the customer will be willing to pay for this extra service you promised?"

TIP 503: Don't Demand with Questions.

"When are you going to call that committee chair back and tell him you don't have time to participate and do your job here?" "How can you even consider taking vacation that week when we have such a short deadline?" "Where can you possibly think of finding a replacement at such a late date?" "Why can't you develop the proposal yourself with our boilerplate?" Such questions make demands rather than call for answers. To use them simply makes the other person wary of other questions on other occasions.

TIP 504: Don't Use a Question as a Dare.

"Well, when are you going to do something about it?" "What are you going to do about it?" "What do you mean by that kind of comment?" "Are you implying that I'm incompetent in my job?" Any of these questions dare the other person to be honest with a response. They "needle" the person to take action or risk the relationship or other consequence if answered.

TIP 505: Don't Design Multiple-Choice Questions When Both Choices Are Wrong.

"Are you so far behind that you thought it didn't matter that one more form wasn't turned in, or were you going to claim it got lost in the mail?" Of course, either alternative puts the other person in a bad light. People don't like multiple-choice questions when all choices make them look bad.

TIP 506: Don't Use Show-Off Questions.

"Did I tell you about having lunch with the CEO last week at the sales meeting?" "After reading several of the most recently published articles about nuclear fission, I'm wondering what you think about Clarendon's theories?" Such questions are brags or attempts to show off the asker's own expertise—not a true question that gathers input. Most people identify such purposes and resent them rather quickly.

TIP 507: Don't Overpower the Opposition with Questions.

To wrap up a discussion in staff meeting, the manager says, "We're already half an hour later than I hoped we'd be in coming to a decision. If nobody has a serious objection to that campaign theme, we'll move on. Any more objections?" The effect of that question is much like a speaker announcing, "Well, it's time for a break—unless somebody has a question?" Who in their right mind will incite the group in bad need of coffee and a bathroom break? In effect, such I-plan-to-do-this-unless-you-fail-to-follow-my-cue questions kill any honest feedback or alternative ideas.

TIP 508: To Express Opinions, Make Statements Rather Than Hide Opinions in Questions.

Instead of asking, "Isn't the MIS group taking a long time to forward those documents?" state your opinion: "I think the MIS group is taking a long time to forward those documents." With the question format, you might get a "no, not necessarily" response and then you'll be put in the position of either having to drop the issue or to argue with the person who responded with the opposite view. Instead of "Do you like the way I set up these tables?" say "I hope you liked the way I set up these tables." With a statement, other people can choose to respond and agree or remain silent and not put you or themselves on the spot.

TIP 509: Use a Pause Instead of a Question.

When you want to encourage the other person to continue to elaborate but don't want to give the impression of "cross-examining," try the pregnant pause. Many people feel uncomfortable with a pause and will do just about anything to fill it. After the other person stops talking, pause for 3 to 5 seconds and allow him or her time to continue with other details.

TIP 510: Use the Echo Technique.

When you want to encourage people to continue talking, repeat the last word or phrase they've just said as a question. They'll take the lifted voice as a cue to elaborate. For example:

SHARON: . . . so I'm undecided if the transfer will do me any good.

BOB: Will do you any good?

SHARON: You know—if it will count as technical experience should the Boston job open up later in the year.

BOB: "Later in the year?"

SHARON: "Well, maybe by December. Or it could be January before it's open, but soon anyway. I'm just afraid I don't have the patience."

BOB: "Patience?"

SHARON: "To work with Brenda and Harry. They're both such perfectionists."

BOB: "What do you mean by perfectionists?"

SHARON: "They just never sign off on a project. They've always got to modify just one more thing. They never make a development deadline."

You get the idea. The echo technique gets elaboration by default.

TIP 511: Remind Others That It's Okay Not to Have Answers to Your Questions.

Sometimes a question meant to provoke thought is taken as a serious question that must have an answer. When the others mull over the issue and toss out answers that you refute or punch holes in, they begin to feel stupid, frustrated, angry, trapped, or wrong. Your question may put a damper on the entire meeting or party. When you see that happening, rush to explain that you don't expect them to come out with a rock-solid answer—that you intended the question to generate ideas, nothing more.

TIP 512: Adopt the Ben Franklin Perspective.

Ben Franklin, a philosopher without the formal training, demanded that people think. He questioned everyone about everything—scientists, community founders, medical professionals, public educators, and administrators. What-ifs made his world go around. If you want to challenge the status quo, charge up your staff meetings, or spark your social life, ask questions. You'll force people to justify or change views, to think creatively, to gather new information, and to expand their horizons.

8

Answering Questions So People Understand and Remember What You Say

It infuriates me to be wrong when I know I'm right.
—JEAN-BAPTISTE MOLIÈRE

There are no embarrassing answers—just embarrassing questions.
—CARL ROWAN

An educated man is one who has finally discovered that there are some questions to which nobody has the answers.
—no attribution

It's frustrating when you know all the answers—and nobody bothers to ask you the questions.
—no attribution

When somebody says, "That's a good question," you can be pretty sure it's a lot better than the answer you're going to get.
—FRANKLIN P. JONES

Answers to questions can take ideas from proposal stage through successful implementation; they can soothe broken relationships; they can provide

181

instruction and advice. But answering questions correctly, confidently, competently, completely, consistently, compassionately, and concisely is no easy task. With the proper structure, substance, and style, you can prevent your answers from becoming off-track ramblings.

TIP 513: Use the SEER Technique.

Does this after-game interview between jock and reporter sound familiar? "What was your single biggest mistake in today's game?" the reporter asks.

"Well, we had problems, that's for sure. Some difficulty running the ball, that's for sure. The other side was out there where we should have been. We made some mistakes all right. They cost us some points. Our passing was just so-so. And blocking was a problem. They just beat us—that's all there is to it. They outplayed us."

So what's the biggest mistake? Who knows? The same rambling occurs when politicians meet the press or bosses confront employees about performance. To avoid having your listener walk away with a vague sense of "nothing said," try using the SEER technique, a format we devised to train executives to use in our oral presentation workshops.

The SEER technique is an organizational format for structuring your answers so that the answers are clear, concise, authoritative, and memorable*:

S (Summary)	Give a one-sentence summary of your answer or position.
E (Elaboration)	Elaborate on that answer with the appropriate details: who, when, where, why, how, how much.
E (Example)	Give a concrete example to make the abstract ideas clear, usable, and memorable.
R (Restatement)	End with a one-sentence restatement of your answer or position.

Here's an example. Your prospective customer asks, "Does your company really care about the small customer?"

Summary. Yes, most definitely, we care about small customers. They keep us in business.

Elaboration. In fact, 70 percent of our volume comes from accounts that we've labeled "small business." We'd rather have 100 customers doing $50 to $75 a month with us than to have one customer doing half

*Reprinted from *Executive's Portfolio of Model Speeches* by Dianna Booher.

a million a month. That's our perspective. We think we get a broader grasp of the industry by dealing with a large variety of small accounts. Why, we even print a special catalog just for small businesses, showing products and services they specifically need. They even have their own 800 number for telephone support.

Example.   Just last week, a VP of operations at Universal, Inc., one of our accounts, told me that because we had learned so much about their business just by selling to them they decided not to hire a permanent purchasing agent. Instead, they've contracted with us to place their orders for related products supplied by other vendors. It's a real partnership. We'd like to do that with all our customers.

Restatement.   So, yes, we do care about our small customers.

Framing your answers in this structure, you'll find that others understand your main point, and more important, remember it.

TIP 514: Use the Genesis Technique.

If you're asked a question and no immediate answer comes to mind, you can always use the genesis technique: start back at the beginning of time and talk until your mind focuses on a specific answer. Question: "How did you arrive at the exact commission rates for the sales reps?" Answer: "When we began to set compensation policy for all our employees, we tried to look at the entire package—salary, bonuses, incentive awards, fringe benefits like company-car use. We tried to investigate which were most valuable to employees. When we surveyed sales reps, we . . ."

Eventually, the answer will hit you and you can continue on target. Such a long-winded, roundabout answer may annoy people, but that may be preferable to drawing a blank on issues you're supposed to know as well as your own name.

TIP 515: Answer One Question at a Time; Avoid Multiples.

When someone asks you multiple questions in one large chunk, you have several choices: (1) Answer all of them. (2) Pick one or two to answer. (3) Lump them all together and give a general answer. Examples: "You've asked three good questions. For the sake of time, let me deal with only the last one. . . ." "Whoa—I don't know if I can remember all those. Let me pick out a couple to respond to. . . ." "Your questions really all point to one concern, I think: Do we know how to Y? I can answer in a word—yes."

TIP 516: Remember That Few Answers Are "Off the Record."

When someone catches you in the hallway and asks for your "honest opinion, off the record," don't count on its being held in confidence. Even if you respond to the question with a shrug or nod, you might be surprised to hear what you "agreed with" according to the next day's rumors. It's best to take such questions "on the record" in front of a group so that you have witnesses to your response. For example, during the break at a staff meeting, George asks, "So, do you think we'll really ever get management to respond to our suggestions?" Response: "I imagine that's on everybody's mind. When we reconvene, let me bring that issue up to answer for everybody." And do so.

If you really don't want the question to surface in front of the group, ask George to bring it up himself in front of the group and hope he won't because he doesn't want his name attached to the question either.

Or try one of these responses: "That's a question I don't have authority to answer. Why don't you write it down and I'll present it to my boss?" or "I wouldn't want to speculate on that because I don't have all the facts and could be wrong. You'll have to ask someone else."

TIP 517: Probe for the Real Interest or Concern Behind Hypothetical Questions.

With a hypothetical question, you have three choices:

1. You can decline to deal in speculations. "I'm sorry, but I don't want to get into what-if situations that we may never have to face" or "I think any speculation would be meaningless on this issue."

2. You can speculate, waving a big red flag identifying your answer as purely hypothetical. "I will give that question a stab. Let me remind you that I think such a situation would never, never happen under the plan we developed. However, in that highly unlikely situation, we'd try to . . ."

3. You can probe for the real issue behind the question and deal with that issue or concern. Question: "If Jim's diagnosis had been cancer, would we have made an exception?" Answer: "Is your concern with that question that we haven't thought the leave policy through fully? If so, I can assure you that we have considered the treatment of patients who might be off work indefinitely. In those cases, . . ." You would simply refuse to deal with Jim's individual case.

Always consider the danger of answering hypothetical questions. Even if you answer them satisfactorily, if the asker's intent is to trap you, the questioner will continue to change the details on the hypothetical question until you are backed into a corner. If your first response is satisfactory, the asker will respond with, "Yeah, but what if Jim . . ." You answer again with the new details. Then the questioner comes back with, "Yeah, but what if then Jim decides to . . ." You can almost never win. If the asker intends to do so, with hypothetical questions as bait, he or she can reel you into the net or keep you on the line forever.

TIP 518: Expand Your Options on Forced, Two-Option Questions.

Don't let others design your multiple-choice exam. Expand your options. Question: "Do you think we can win the bid if we come in under $50,000?" Answer: "I don't think price will be the deciding factor. The customer's impression of our credentials will be an equally important factor, I think." Other examples: "The question is more complex than either a yes or no answer." "If you ask me, we've got more options than either A or B. We might even consider C."

Stay in control and don't let others force you into a limited answer if the limited answer won't do justice to the issue.

TIP 519: Help the Questioner Bogged Down in a Rambling, Long-Winded Question.

Body language goes a long way in helping people spit out questions. You can start to back away from them, and they'll subconsciously speed up and get to the point because they see you "leaving." Or you can slowly move toward them with outstretched hand and nodding head, and they'll subconsciously speed up, seeing that you're "rushing" them.

If body language doesn't work, help the person phrase the question by breaking in with one of the following: "Okay, I think I understand your question now. My answer is . . ." or ". . . so you want to know if X happens? Well, my answer is . . ."

If the individual keeps talking without ever seeming to come to the question, you can call for the question directly: "I'm sorry. I didn't understand a question in what you said. What exactly is the question?"

If someone is quite involved in a monologue, you can interrupt the monologue with a short question of your own to which the person can give a one-word or one-phrase answer. When he or she stops the monologue to answer your question, you have regained the floor.

TIP 520: Stop Your Own Monologue Answers.

Long-winded answers irritate as much as long-winded questions. If you intend to wax on about an issue, seek a group platform where the audience knows you intend to give a speech and grants you the privilege. If your answer runs longer than 30 to 45 seconds, you're no longer in a dialogue; it's a monologue. If you feel you're going on too long and haven't finished what you intended to say, pace yourself by stopping to ask the other person for some reaction to what you've just said—do they agree, disagree, not care, have different information? Then, after you listen to their comments, deliver your next point on the earlier answer.

TIP 521: Assume the "Dumb" Question Has a Connection You Don't Yet Understand.

Assume what sounds like a dumb question has a connection that you don't yet understand and ask for clarification. If you brush it aside and then have someone point out to you the relevance of the question to the issue, you'll look foolish yourself. If the question seems "out in left field," irrelevant, or plain dumb, clarify: "I'm sorry, but I don't quite understand how X relates to Y. Would you explain the connection?" "I'm confused. What prompts the question?" "We missed the point, I guess. We are discussing Y, and I don't understand why Z would be an issue."

If the person clarifies and the question is pertinent, you've saved yourself some embarrassment. If the person concedes that the question is off base, you've saved yourself some time. If the question is in fact dumb, answer it briefly if you can and circle back to the main issue without embarrassing the asker.

TIP 522: Unload "Loaded" Questions.

Identify the hot words—those with negative connotations—and restate the question before answering it. Or, if you don't choose to repeat the question, respond to the question minus the negative words.

Example: "Why is management being so *stubborn* about lifting the ban?"

Answer: "Are you asking why management has not set a definite deadline for lifting the ban? I think partly we're concerned that . . ."

Example: "Are you saying that we're too *stupid* to make that decision ourselves without going to a supervisor for approval?"

Answer: "The reason we're asking you to go to a supervisor for approval is that this brief delay of even 15 seconds while you leave the customer alone at the counter allows time for . . ."

Don't let the offensive, negative words hook you into responding negatively to an important issue. Neutralize, neutralize.

TIP 523: Turn a Negative Question into a Benefit Statement.

A customer asks, "Why do you have so much red tape associated with these service agreements?" "Benefit" answer: "Why does having a list of all the company liaisons benefit you? Well, let's say Kathy in your word processing department calls for service. Within seconds, we can check the file, verify her as an authorized contact, and answer her question while she's on the line—without waiting for a callback. Your doing the paperwork up front in providing us names of liaisons saves you time when you have a problem and need service immediately."

TIP 524: Challenge Questions Based on Misinformation or Invalid Assumptions.

Question: "Given the huge sums of money we've spent on market and trend studies in recent years, why haven't our earnings matched those of other investors on real estate in the local area?" That question contains four assumptions that may or may not be true:

1. The company has spent "huge" sums of money.
2. The market and trend studies contained accurate and helpful information.
3. The company's earnings did not match those of other investors.
4. The other investors presented accurate numbers and those numbers were based only on real estate investments in the local area.

With such a question, you can either accept, qualify, or reject any of the assumptions or facts, then answer the "leftover" question if you care to do so. Answer: "First, I don't consider $4000 'huge sums of money.' Second, those studies were based on old information and did not contain much with regard to our industry. Third, you're correct in that our earnings were one percentage point lower than our competitors' earnings. And, finally,

I'm not sure their figures included only local real estate. Nevertheless, the question remains, why were our investment returns less than we had hoped? First, . . ."

TIP 525: Define Terms and Agree on Criteria Before You Give "Value-Based" Answers.

Two meeting planners spent an hour debating the best site for an upcoming annual sales and awards meeting. The first meeting planner argued that Orlando was the best choice because of the nearby attractions for families accompanying the salespeople. The second meeting planner insisted that Dallas was the best site because of its central location and airport. Neither stopped to define how they were defining "best" site. What exactly did the criteria include? Cost, tourist attractions, weather, travel time required, local accommodations? Had they been clear up front in defining and agreeing on criteria, answering the question of the "best" would have been much easier.

Carefully come to an understanding on questions phrased like these: "What is the most favorable? Cheapest? Quickest? Highest quality? Most prestigious? Honorable thing? Ethical? Profitable?" Define, then answer.

TIP 526: Help Questioners Meet Their Objectives with Their Showcase Questions.

When people ask questions simply to show off their own expertise, oblige them if you have the time. Question: "Tell me what differences you see in the quality principles set forth by the gurus Deming, Juran, and Crosby." Answer: "Actually, I haven't made a study of the uniqueness to their individual programs. You seem well versed on the subject. What differences do you see?" They love you for the showcase opportunities, and you're off the hook.

TIP 527: Diffuse Hostile Questions.

Myles Martel of *Mastering the Art of Q and A* has expressed it well: "Composure can speak as loudly—or more loudly—than content." You have only to ask people which political candidate "won" the various presidential debates to verify that truth.

Hostility comes in three flavors: (1) questions that show hostility toward you as a person, (2) hostility reflected in the situation, or (3) the asker's personality. If the hostility comes from the pressure of a situation or from a typically hostile person, diffuse it by removing the "hot" words and then answering the concern in a straightforward manner. If the attack is personal, try to put your ego aside, omit the negative comments or words, and answer with facts as you see them.

Example: "Don't tell me that with *your limited expertise* in the field, you're going to handle our account yourself?" Answer: "You are correct in that my academic training has been in psychology rather than in finance; however, I have been managing financial portfolios for large clients for the past 20 years. The performance of these funds has matched or surpassed those results of all our other investors. If your concern is my experience in global funds, I can give you the statistics on those accounts specifically. And I can assure you that should I ever find myself in a quandary over a decision, I would not hesitate to bring the issue up in our daily staff meetings, which are set up just for that purpose for all our representatives."

Give a straightforward answer dealing with the facts. If you meet hostility with hostility, you lose. If you match hostility with graciousness, you win in the mind of all observers.

TIP 528: Bridge from the Questioner's Agenda to Yours.

If you don't want to answer the question you're asked, bridge to your own points with one of the following: "I appreciate your question, but more to the point in our organization, I think, is the issue of X. The X issue involves . . ." or "A more fundamental issue than that in your question is . . ." or "The larger question than the one you raise is . . ." Chase your own rabbits.

TIP 529: Bridge from the Abstract to the Specific or from the Specific to the Abstract.

You may or may not want to match the intensity of the question with your answer. Bridging is your escape route. For example, if the questioner asks you a broad, general opinion question, you can answer with a specific, factual question.

Question: "So what do you think about the President's new tax plans?" Answer: "Well, I know I don't like paying 5 cents a gallon more every time I pull into the service station." Or you can reverse the situation. Question: "Why do you think employees have not been more responsive in signing up to participate in the tutoring programs we're sponsoring in the community?" Answer: "Volunteerism in the United States isn't what it used to be."

TIP 530: Use Cliché Answers with Care.

Say someone approaches you in the company cafeteria and asks, "So how is the Fullerton deal moving along?" You answer: "Pretty good." Similar answers to similar questions follow these lines: "Same song, second verse." "So-so." "It's still on target." "Fair to partly cloudy." "We're hanging in there." All such clichés create distance. If the other person has asked the question as a show of interest or wants straightforward information, he or she will be put off. If you routinely deflect honest questions with pat answers, people will stop asking about your concerns, feelings, and opinions. They'll decide you do not want to communicate sincerely with them.

TIP 531: Know When Flippant Answers Are Out of Line.

Having a sense of humor is an advantage in any situation, but flippant answers about serious issues or during a time crunch frustrate people. Some people find themselves tossing out humor when they can't face issues squarely. Try to identify those times when you're using humor as an avoidance technique. Recognize that even humor, however generally welcome and refreshing, has a time and place.

TIP 532: Don't Bomb When a BB Gun Will Do.

Some people tend to overanswer when asked a simple question and get a reputation for that sort of thing. Nine-year-old Matthew, sitting in front of the TV one night, asked his father: "What does centrifugal force mean?" Dad: "Go ask your mother, I'm busy." Son: "That's okay. I don't think I want to know that much about it."

Why do people respond to a question with a bomb when a BB gun would do? Some talk until they come to an acceptable answer. Others react to their ego-need to show off vast knowledge on the subject. Others aren't sure their answer is clear, so they keep explaining until they get some feedback that shows understanding. Others give a lengthy answer because they fear a brief answer would sound curt. Some people feel defensive or consider their answers inadequate, so they keep attempting to justify their positions. Still others don't fully understand the question, so they talk all around the issue, hoping to say something pertinent and helpful. Whatever the reason for overanswering, use the BB gun on first attempt. Leave it to your listener to ask for a more in-depth answer.

TIP 533: Don't Ignore Questions to Avoid Confrontation.

When people ask questions on controversial issues or make statements that you disagree with, it might be easier to ignore them and the issues rather than to risk a confrontation—easier, but not best. Giving no response at all leaves the other person feeling slapped in the face. Instead, state your disagreement generally and then change the subject if you want to avoid the issue. Example: "Roberto's comments were really out of line in the meeting this morning, don't you think?" Answer: "Actually, I thought what he said was appropriate. But I haven't given it much thought since the meeting. I've been really involved in that project due tomorrow. I'm working on . . ."

TIP 534: Give Multiple Answers Without Claiming Any as Your Own.

If someone asks you the best way to solve a problem, you can toss out several possible solutions without committing to the one you prefer. Example: "How do you think we can guarantee to the customer that we will not miss any interim deadline on this multiyear project?" Answer: "One way might be to cotrain a backup crew. Or we might want to use a subcontractor during certain phases and run the work in tandem. Or we might ask the customer to supply liaisons at crucial decision points. We've got several options."

TIP 535: Fog the Issue with an Irrelevant Point.

If you don't intend to give a clear, straightforward answer, you can confuse the issue by bringing up an irrelevant point with a statement or question of your own. Example: "Why does this community refuse to approve a sales tax increase that would support the kind of parks and recreational facilities the citizens seem to want?" Answer: "Some people cannot understand the need to plan for the future—they don't even have their own retirement savings plans. How can you expect them to plan for the city?" Example: "Do you think the flextime policy will be a big morale booster for the staff?" Answer: "The snarled traffic will still be the biggest problem in their getting to work on time."

TIP 536: If You Intend to Be Clear, Ask for Explicit Confirmation and Feedback.

Simply because you give an answer doesn't mean that the answer was understood, even if you conclude it with something like "Is that clear?" or "Do you understand?" Most people will nod and answer affirmatively. To say otherwise would be tantamount to saying "No, I'm stupid—I don't get it" or insulting you with "No, your answer wasn't clear."

Instead, ask for more explicit feedback to make sure the person understands: "Is that information helpful?" "Did that overview give you enough background to begin the task?" If you want to make very sure you are understood, you can ask for even more specific feedback: "Let's see how clear I was. Based on the information I just outlined, what do you think would be your first two or three steps in implementing this policy in your department?" The answers will confirm whether your original comments have been understood.

On occasion, you may not want to answer a question at all. Routinely asking, "Did I answer your question" or "Is that clear?" may get a response such as "Not really" or "No, what I really wanted to know was . . ." You'll be left looking incompetent, foolish, or, at best, on the spot trying again with an answer you don't want to give.

TIP 537: Forget Feedback if You Want to Show Confidence in Your Answer.

In situations with your superiors, to end a question with "Did I answer your question?" or "Did I cover what you wanted to know?" makes you appear insecure, lacking confidence in your ability to answer. Give the best answer you can and wait for your superior to assume his or her question was unclear or inadequate. If the question is rephrased, make another attempt to answer it.

TIP 538: When Piggybacking Someone Else's Answer, Frame Your Comments Tactfully.

For example, in a meeting, your human resources director has answered a question about compensation packages and has omitted an important point; you feel the need to add your answer. Here's a no-no: "Elaine left out an important point that I want to mention." Better: "I want to add a point to what Elaine explained." Best: "Elaine's answer brings up another consideration. What we plan to do about X. Let me mention that briefly. . . ."

Your piggyback answer should not make the previous answer seem inadequate or wrong.

TIP 539: Set Boundaries for Which Questions You Will and Won't Answer—And Stick to Them.

A doctor sets limits on his or her expertise with a difficult-to-diagnose case. "If the tests show that the problem is X, I can help you with medication. But if the X rays indicate Y, I'm going to have to send you to a podiatrist for more testing." You don't respect the doctor any less for setting the boundaries; if anything, you're glad he or she is honest about the limits of expertise. You may have similar limits—because of a lack of expertise or simply because you prefer not to share it. Say so. "In this meeting, I'd rather not go into issues of costs. I'm here to respond to technical questions about how the system works." And if a question about cost surfaces later, stick to your limits: "As I mentioned earlier, I am not prepared to discuss costs." People will respect your boundaries if you yourself do.

TIP 540: Before Giving Any Answer, Consider the Costs and Opportunities.

When your answer may be crucial to your future, run through a mental checklist: What prompts this question? Do I fully understand the question? What am I risking with an answer? How clear do I want to be? What information should I share? What information would be best to withhold? How will my tone affect the response? What does the body language of the asker communicate? What do I want to communicate with my own body language? Which is the most important in this response—style or substance? What goals do I want to reach with my answer? What opportunities does answering this question present for me? All of these questions should flash through your mind in 1 to 2 seconds as you prepare to answer. That brief pause can be the difference between results or regrets.

TIP 541: Use Verbal Stalls with Care.

As a lecturer or instructor, you may have learned to reinforce questioners or give yourself thinking time with comments such as "That's a good question" or "I'm glad you brought up that point." But when talking one on one, these comments may sound patronizing. And comments such as "As I mentioned earlier today in the staff meeting, . . ." can sound like a verbal slap on the hand and a reprimand for not listening. They destroy rapport with your listener. Be silent with a reflective gaze rather than stall with judgmental phrases that sound as though you're about to hedge, make something up, or respond with great reluctance.

TIP 542: Remind Yourself That You Don't Have to Answer Every Question.

Growing up, we had to answer every question the classroom teacher asked, and that feeling of "must" still hangs on. There are several ways you can deflect a question you don't want to answer, with or without giving a reason: "If I understand your question correctly, you're really asking if . . ." and give your own interpretation. "Your question prompts me to ask you something first. Is . . ." "I think the real question is not X but Y." "Let me phrase your question a little differently before I answer it. . . ." "I'm sorry, but that information is confidential." "I'd rather not answer that question, if you don't mind." "I think that question doesn't have an answer." "The answer to that question would be purely speculative."

You can also use humor to deflect a question: "What a question—do you want to get me fired?" (said with a light tone). "Don't we all wish we had the answer to that one—I'd settle even for half an answer." "Asking the questions is the easy part; answering them breaks me out in a cold sweat." "You must have spent all night phrasing that question; give me a couple of weeks to come up with an answer, will you?"

If you're unsure whether the questioner has manipulative intentions, you can always ask the reason for the question or explain your reluctance in a straightforward way: "I'm curious. Why do you ask that question?" or "As you might imagine, that question is difficult to answer. If I say X, you'll think Y; and if I say Y, I'll look uncaring. I don't think I could win with any answer to that question" or "Under the circumstances, I don't think I want to answer that question" or "Such a question makes me a little uncomfortable. I'm not in a position to know all the related facts."

TIP 543: Remember That the Whole Performance Counts.

When it comes to questions, style is equal to substance. Your competence can be communicated in the clarity, resourcefulness, and conciseness of the content; in your delivery of the answer—with courtesy, confidence, composure, concern; and finally, in the results you achieve with your answer. Substance plus style equals success.

9

Saying No and Giving Other Bad News Without Leaving a Bad Taste in Someone's Mouth

The worse the news, the more effort should go into communicating it. —ANDREW S. GROVE

None love the messenger who brings bad news. —SOPHOCLES

Many a manager has planned a trip across country for the week simply to delay giving bad news to his or her staff. Saying no to an idea, proposition, or request from a customer, salesperson, parent, or partner creates knots in the stomach and costs hours of sleep. And the damage done in the delivery can be far worse than the answer itself or the discomfort of the person giving the message. Saying no will seldom be easy, but with the following tips, you may find the task less painful and more productive than imagined.

TIP 544: Be Clear About Your Own Priorities.

Some priorities stay near the tip of your tongue; you know you don't want to be a part of this and you know you do want to be a part of that. Your values constitute your basis for saying yes or no in every request for your help or your time. And for the bigger issues, you can ask the age-old question, "If I had only six months to live, would I take on this project?" That thinking will help you focus on the important, time-consuming, life-changing commitments.

Unfortunately, everything else falls in between the definite yeses and the definite nos. If your most distressing indecision about your time and your money come at work, take some time every few months to focus on your own career and personal goals. Write them down. That list will help you focus and weed out the requests that deserve a "no" response.

TIP 545: Recall the Three Ways to Say "No," and Make a Conscious Choice.

You can say "no" with an uncaring attitude: "No way will I let you borrow my car. Go rent one yourself." You can say "no" passively, hiding behind an excuse that is not the real reason. "I can't. My manager has me so involved in another project that I can't look up." Or you can *say* "yes" and *do* "no." That is, you can seem agreeable and agree to do something and then not come through at the last moment. The last way is the easiest—at the time. But in the long run you disappoint the person more deeply and often cause more severe problems than an honest, earlier "no."

TIP 546: Ask for Time to Think.

Don't say "no" simply because you have been caught off guard and can't phrase the negative in a tactful, acceptable way. Even if you know you intend to say "no," it's perfectly acceptable to ask for time to think about your wording. "Let me think about that and get back to you." "Nos" rarely have to be immediate.

TIP 547: Forewarn People When You Have Devastating News.

When delivering an unexpected bad-news message that will certainly be a shock to someone's emotional system, warn that person by simply saying the words. "I'm going to have to give you some bad news." Such an outright statement lets people prepare physically and emotionally for the upset. During this adjustment time, their bodies make the necessary preparation for handling the shock.

TIP 548: When Writing, Be Positive or Neutral
in Introducing the Bad News.

> When you find it necessary to write your "no" message, you do not have the
> benefit of the rapport established by personal contact—a warm smile and a
> firm handshake. When writing, begin by trying to establish that rapport by
> simply bringing up the topic in a neutral or positive way. If you're going to
> have to tell a subordinate you have decided not to grant the transfer, you
> may begin with a neutral opening: "Bill, I'm responding to your request
> that we consider you for the opening in the La Jolla office." This neutral
> opening of the topic sets the stage and a matter-of-fact tone.

TIP 549: State the Reasons or Your Criteria for Making
the "No" Decision if You Are in a More Powerful Position
Than the Other Person.

> If you must tell others "no" and you want to help them understand your
> decision, give your reasons or your criteria before you state the "no." By the
> time they have listened to your explanation of the criteria upon which you
> based the decision, they will have already "read between the lines" to know
> you will be saying "no" at the end. This arrangement softens the tone of
> your "no" and allows the other person to retain composure and save face in
> making an appropriate, accepting response.
>
> Example: "In any transfer decision, we consider several things: tenure in
> the present position, total performance in similar jobs, costs of relocation,
> trained replacements of those who might want to move. In your case, the
> cost of relocation has been of major concern." By the time, you get to the
> "no," the listener will know it's coming. As a result, the decision will not
> sound so arbitrary and cold; the criteria explanation provides a cushion.

TIP 550: Remember That You Generally Do Not Have
to Give a Reason for Your "No."

> You do not have to give explanations, but if you know the person making
> the request well, you probably will want to do so. An explanation is not the
> same as an excuse. An excuse involves making up something that sounds
> logical but is not the real reason. A real explanation includes your own
> choice and control about what the other person has asked. "Yes, we do have
> money in the budget for a few year-end bonuses. But I've allocated the
> money elsewhere. I've decided to use the money for additional training on

the equipment." You have not shunned your own responsibility in the decision, just explained your refusal.

People have a right to ask you to do almost anything—and you have a
right to say "no." Examples: "I'm sorry I can't explain my decision, but the
answer is 'no.'" "Under normal circumstances I'd be happy to help you,
but this is bad time for me." "I can't participate." "Sorry, but I've decided
that would not be in my best interest." "After careful thought, I've decided
not to participate myself, but I wish you the best in the undertaking."

TIP 551: Be Firm, Fair, and Nonjudgmental
in Your Response.

If you're saying "no" because you do not approve ethically or morally of
something the other person has asked you to do, it is usually best to be nonjudgmental and succinct in your response. Do not feel compelled to pass
judgment on their request: "No, I'd rather not participate." "No, I don't
feel comfortable supporting that position." "I've decided not to attend for
personal reasons." "After careful thought, my answer has to be negative.
And I'd rather not share my reasons if you don't mind." "No. Thank you for
your consideration in asking me to join you, but I've decided not to."

TIP 552: Phrase Your "No" as Positively as Possible.

Wording a "no" requires tact. Positive wording to minimize the damage to
someone's self-esteem takes the most tact of all. Examples: "We don't have
time to include you on the program" versus "I really regret that we're not
going to be able to take advantage of your expertise on this subject." "We're
not going to be able to do business with you because your price is just too
high" versus "I wish we could have found a way to do business together. I'm
sorry price had to be our major consideration on this contract."

TIP 553: Learn to Say "Yes, and"
Rather Than "No, but."

I once asked a systems analyst if his company typically assumed any and all
liability for the performance of the computers they installed and the service
they performed. His answer was, "Yes, we'll do *anything* the client wants—
at a price. Believe me, they will pay for our assuming that risk. If they
insist—and pay for it—we'll find a way to say 'yes.'"

When you'd like to be in a position to say "yes," check the limits to see
what's negotiable. "Yes, we can do it, and here's what it will mean. We'll have
to have temporary help or leave X undone or forget about doing the usual Y."

With your boss's requests, bump against the requirements of the job to find ways to say "yes": "Are you absolutely certain the project has to be finished on July 15?" "Can we use our best guess if we can't locate the actual numbers by then?" "Can you find someone else to cover for me in California if I make the meeting for you in Dallas?"

"Yes" makes everybody smile. "Yes, and here are the details to make that work."

TIP 554: Be Dramatic with Your "No."

Sometimes you can celebrate your "no" as a major decision in life. Be dramatic with theatrics and props, if necessary, to make the point that you have "won a personal victory" by the careful process of coming to "no." Example: "Ta-da. You're looking at the new West Coast regional director. After three pepperoni pizzas and two bottles of No-Doz this weekend, I forced myself to make a list and check it twice to find out who's naughty and nice. I've decided that the regional director's job is it. That's where I want to hitch my star. Unfortunately, that means I have to say 'no' to your offer here. At first, I was torn between the choices, but now I feel good about the decision. I'm set free. A direction at last. Please understand my decision." With such fanfare, the requester often feels as though he or she should celebrate with you for having come to a difficult decision. At the least, he or she will know the answer is definite.

TIP 555: Use the Broken-Record Technique.

If someone refuses to accept your "no" and continues to harangue, give thought to phrasing a one-sentence "no" statement and use only that sentence over and over. Don't be sidetracked if the person brings up other benefits, mentions other issues, or makes other concessions. Say your one sentence again and again in a matter-of-fact tone. Example: "Would you trade weekends off and work for me July 15 and 16?" Answer: "I'm sorry I can't. I'm planning to attend a family reunion then." Requester: "But I traded weekends with you the last time you asked." Answer: "I know. I'm sorry. But I'm planning to attend a family reunion that weekend." Requester: "I'd pay you double time." Answer: "I can't. I'm attending a family reunion that weekend." Be firm, calm, courteous. It will end.

TIP 556: Use the Sandwich Technique.

Begin your "no" with a positive or neutral statement about what the other person has asked you to do. That shows the person you have listened well.

Make the second statement the "no" part of your message. End with a neutral or positive statement about the request or situation to show that you have no hard feelings because you were asked and that you feel no guilt about saying "no." Example: "I understand why an early copy of my report could be useful to you in tomorrow's decision. However, I can't release the sales numbers until the close of business today. I do hope the meeting goes well because that decision will have a big impact on both your division and ours."

TIP 557: Give the Raincheck "No."

When you want to make sure the other person knows you have a legitimate reason for saying no rather than an excuse, and when you want to encourage further requests, offer a raincheck: "What an opportunity for on-the-job training! If it were any other week, I'd love to accompany you on the tour. Please put my name at the top of the list the next time you have an opening."

TIP 558: Offer Alternatives.

If you can't offer to help the other person with his or her request, suggest alternatives. Consider the results the requester wants and think of other ways to meet those needs or criteria. "I can't attend, but maybe you'd like to have my assistant attend and offer insights on the project." "We can't do the project in-house to meet your deadline, but I can give you the name of an excellent freelancer who might be able to work your project in on short notice." "We can't get our delivery truck out there today, but I could ship the items overnight express so that you'd have them before the 2 o'clock meeting with your boss." Any such offers convey to the other person concern over the situation.

TIP 559: Mention Any Conditions Under Which You Might Change Your Mind.

If your answer is not definite and irrevocable, let the other person know that; it softens the message. Example: "If you decide that you don't need the work completed until next week, let me know and maybe I can reschedule my tasks at the end of the month." "If you can get by with pen-and-ink drawings, I'd certainly take on the project for you." "If you decide to change your terms, please talk to us again about your products."

TIP 560: Let the Facts Speak for Themselves; Show Rather Than Tell.

When delivering bad news about a situation, show up at the meeting with the numbers and results in black and white. Show them rather than tell them. This tactic distances you from the situation. If the individual or group doubts your bad news, welcome their comments about doing their own investigation. In fact, express the hope that they are right and you are wrong; if your information comes into question, encourage them to seek other expert opinions.

TIP 561: Find One Kernel of Good in the Bad.

Emphasize any positive twist at all. Point out that it's better the company "found out the truth now rather than lose another $50,000 down the road." Mention that at this point they've spent "only two weeks on the project—it could have been two months." Maybe they will "take comfort in the fact that your division is one of the first to know and will not be caught by surprise like others." Suggest that all has not been lost—there may be information or insights that can be salvaged from the experience. Look hard for the grain of good.

TIP 562: Sit on the Other Side of the Table.

Identify yourself psychologically with the group who is hearing the bad news. Position yourself as one of them so that you will not be beheaded as the bearer of bad news. "I am as disappointed with the situation as you are." "I had hoped that the figures would be different." "I'm just as puzzled as you are about where we go from here." Don't be the scapegoat.

TIP 563: Deliver the Worst News in Person.

Don't hide behind messengers and mediums—E-mail notes, letters and memos, committee announcements, press releases, or rumors. The worse the news, the more important that you deliver it in person. Not only will the individual or group be disappointed at the bad news, they'll resent your lack of courage in delivering it face to face. Courage shows up most in the midst of adversity.

10

Apologizing (and Accepting Apologies) Without Groveling or Grit

No persons are more frequently wrong than those who will not admit they are wrong.
—FRANÇOIS DUC DE LA ROCHEFOUCAULD

Apologies only account for the evil which they cannot alter.   —BENJAMIN DISRAELI

The three most difficult words to speak are, "I was mistaken."   —no attribution

To err is human, to forgive, divine.
—ALEXANDER POPE

Some people apologize too often; others, too seldom. And in either case where apologies are called for, most people would rather receive them than give them. The biggest rebuff of all comes in having an apology shunned and tossed to the wind. Yet, apologies have great effect. An apology or acceptance of an apology can be the glue that makes teams work, makes managers productive after a mistake, and enables leaders to get up after they've fallen.

TIP 564: Decide What Apologizing Means in Any Given Situation.

In a communication workshop for a corporate client, a participant made this comment: "We never apologize in this company." He went on to explain that the company lawyers adamantly refused to allow any individual representative to write a letter to a customer in a "sticky" situation without having the legal department review the letter. From this company's perspective, apologizing meant accepting liability for whatever the situation or outcome.

To some people, on the other hand, apologizing means simply: "I'm sorry there's a problem." They apologize profusely only to avoid more serious difficulties or to win favor because it's expected. Others think apologizing means assuming an inferior position, and find that hard to do.

According to the dictionary, apologizing means an expression of regret for some fault, failure, insult, injury, or outcome, but it does *not* mean accepting *responsibility* for an outcome or failure.

Therefore, you can choose to attach either significance to any particular situation—from expressing liability to avoiding it.

TIP 565: Apologize Specifically.

The most frequent cliché in apologies is the blanket statement: "I'm sorry for any inconvenience this may have caused you." That comment only makes angry people angrier. "For *any* inconvenience" implies that the speaker hasn't given any thought to how the person might have been inconvenienced. The choice of the word "inconvenience" implies that it was "no big deal." "This *may* have caused you" implies that the situation may have caused no problem at all. In other words, translate the sentence this way, "I don't know or care how my actions could have inconvenienced you, but if they did, here's a blanket 'I'm sorry.' "

Instead of that blanket, inappropriate wording, be specific. Let the person know that you understand either the difficulty of the situation or the hurt caused by your actions or words. "I'm sorry for the delay in responding to your call; I know you were in a hurry for the information." "I'm sorry the package didn't arrive until Friday. I know we had promised you'd have it by Wednesday, and because of our late shipment, your own customer orders have been delayed." "I regret your having to make three long-distance calls to track down the information." "I failed to notify you of the additional charge. You're right, I should have done so. I apologize for that." "You were expecting a complete report today, and now without it, you'll be delayed in making the final committee decision. I'm sorry the report is still incomplete." Such statements may or may not accept responsibility, but they do let the other person know you are aware and concerned about the outcome.

TIP 566: State Any Corrective Action You Plan to Take
or Have Taken Rather Than Reminding Someone
of the Problem or Issue.

You can take the wind out of an angry person's sails by stating immediately that you have corrected a mistake or problem. In other words, move to the "punch line," the most important concern, to let others know they no longer have to fight to get the problem addressed. Once the issue is settled to their satisfaction, there is less will to continue to discuss the details or disagree over whose fault something is. The other person's primary concern is a resolution.

TIP 567: Explain the Reasoning
Behind Corrective Actions.

Giving an explanation of how a mistake happened adds credibility to your corrective action. Let's say you have car trouble and take the car into the repair shop. When you return to pick up the car, you ask the mechanic what he found wrong with it. He responds, "Well, we thought it might be the starter, and put a new one on. But that didn't seem to be the problem. Then we checked the spark plugs—they were okay. We never did pinpoint exactly what was causing the problem, but it seems to be running all right now." Do you feel confident about driving that car out of the repair shop? Of course not. If the mechanic can't tell you what's wrong with it, you're not sure he has repaired it.

On the other hand, this explanation sounds reasonable: "I checked with our mail room about why your package did not reach you on time. And Terry said that unless packages have an 'express' tag on them, they may remain in the mail bin for two to three days when they're understaffed and can't find time to box them. Therefore, I've made the following changes in procedures so that you will receive future shipments promptly. . . ."

If you can't state how something happened or can't explain your reasoning when you made an error in judgment, other people cannot be sure you'll handle future situations any better. An explanation lets them know that you care enough to investigate and that you have gained insight from your investigation or reevaluation of the situation. Your explanation adds credibility for the future.

TIP 568: Avoid Making Excuses if the Mistake Was Due
to Your Carelessness or Insensitivity.

When the situation is due to obvious carelessness or insensitivity, an explanation doesn't help. It sounds like an excuse. And your excuse will only elicit new accusations about the problem and escalate the whole affair. Own up to the insensitivity or the behavior without excusing what you said or did: "You're right. I have been late to the meetings for the last several weeks. Everybody is busy and everybody has to fight traffic to get here. I simply didn't plan to leave early enough. I kept you waiting and I'm sorry."

TIP 569: Express Regret for the Results
an Inadvertent Mistake Caused.

Recently, we were training three new employees in our office, and I had worked out a complex training schedule for each, marking certain in-house classes they were to attend on a master calendar. Then I dropped a copy of the master calendar in each employee's in-box. On several occasions, when a question arose about when someone was to be out of the office, I reminded the administrative assistant that that information was on the training calendar. "Didn't you get a training schedule?" I asked, to which she answered "yes" each time. On the third such mix-up, we discovered the miscommunication. I was referring to the calendar showing scheduling for training new employees; she was referring to the wall calendar showing training workshops for clients! A classic, inadvertent "mistake."

Even though your mistake or misjudgment may have been unintentional, the repercussions for the other person may be just as severe as if the mistake were a direct affront.

Even if you could not have foreseen the problem your actions caused, you can express regret for the results: "I changed the meeting room at the last moment to escape the outside noise from the renovation crews. I'm sorry you were unable to find where we had moved and missed the meeting. I never thought of leaving a message with the main receptionist because I didn't know you had planned to attend. You must be frustrated, however, to miss the meeting after driving an hour to get here. I'm sorry we were unable to get the message to you." Such a statement doesn't admit blame, only regret at the situation.

TIP 570: Be Sincere.

Apologies from some people sound more like a demand than anything. "Look, I said I'm sorry. What else do you want?" To be effective, an apology has to be more than an attempt to demand that the other person "forget it" and move on. Some see an apology as a perfunctory line, offered only when they see no other way to get the action moving again. Apologizing means regret over the situation and an intention not to repeat the performance that caused the problem. It's not a demand to "forget it."

Sincerity comes through in tone, body language, and word choice. For example, your boss stands with hands on hips facing you with a grimace: "Look, I'm sorry I didn't tell you the due date was tomorrow. I've got fifteen irons in the fire, okay? Griping about working late isn't going to get it done any faster."

Sincerity sounds like this: (Boss standing beside you with dejected, downcast eyes) "I'm sorry. I should have told you the due date was tomorrow. John told me and I failed to pass it on. What can I do to help you get it done?"

TIP 571: Reestablish Rapport on a Neutral Subject.

Like lovers who kiss and make up, coworkers or friends need to "sign off" on the difficulty and move ahead. A good way to do that is to make an additional comment or two on a neutral subject before ending the conversation. That final effort on a new topic, or at least an unrelated detail of the current topic, serves as the final handshake and puts a relationship back to normal. This closure helps to prevent any awkwardness at the next encounter.

TIP 572: Avoid Apologizing to Gain Sympathy.

The too-frequent apologizer is a second cousin to the person with low self-esteem who continually delivers put-downs in hopes that the other person will refute them with a compliment. Bleed according to the pain caused. If your actions or words caused severe problems, apologize profusely. If your actions or words caused only a minor inconvenience that was understandable in the circumstances, a brief apology will do. People who apologize too frequently sound as egotistical (centered on self, even if with a poor self-esteem) as those who never apologize for fear of appearing weak.

TIP 573: Consider Apologies an Important Way to Build Rapport.

Researchers tell us women tend to apologize more often than men. Why? Because women enhance their self-esteem from their relationships. When relationships are broken, women feel the impact more severely. Men, on the other hand, may apologize in a more matter-of-fact, take-it-or-leave manner. They consider it a ritual more than pinpointing of fault. Others think apologizing weakens them or puts them in a less powerful position. They may think others will lose respect for them, they'll be made to "jump through hoops" if they own up to the error, and if they pretend nothing has happened, no one will be the wiser. Nonsense. Don't overlook the opportunity to repair a damaged relationship with an apology.

TIP 574: Accept Apologies Graciously.

Although an apology may not be enough to soothe your wounded pride or to make up for the catastrophe it caused, accept whatever is offered. "Your apology is accepted." "Thank you for mentioning the incident." "I accept your apology." "All right. Let's just forget it." "Okay. Accepted." "I appreciate your talking to me about it." Any of these comments acknowledges the other's efforts to rebuild the relationship and confirms your willingness to move ahead to other concerns.

To match the apology with your own restores balance also: "Forget it. I also should have double-checked the status." Or: "Accepted. And I apologize for not notifying you of the damage earlier."

Even if you don't match the apology offered because it seems inadequate or insincere, accept the attempts, however feeble, graciously. You'll help the other person save face and eliminate a stumbling block should your paths cross in the future.

11
Criticizing Without Crippling

The difference between coaching and criticism is your attitude.   —no attribution

He has a right to criticize who has a heart to help.   —ABRAHAM LINCOLN

There are people who take the heart out of you, and there are people who put it back.
                    —ELIZABETH DAVID

A smile in giving honest criticism can make the difference between resentment and reform.
                    —PHILIP STEINMETZ

Tact is the art of making a point without making an enemy.   —HOWARD W. NEWTON

When I complain, I do it because "it's good to get things off my chest"; when you complain, I remind you that "griping doesn't help anything."   —SYDNEY HARRIS

People ask you for criticism but they only want praise.   —SOMERSET MAUGHAM

The art of managing people is stepping on their toes without messing up their shine.
                    —anonymous

Unlike apologies, criticisms roll of the tongue quite easily—to those people not directly involved in the situation. The difficulty surfaces when we intend to give *constructive* criticism rather than *destructive* criticism *to the person needing to hear* what we have to say. The true measure of giving successful criticism, however, is not intentions but results. The other person can't see intentions; he or she hears only the words. The following guidelines can help you match words to your intentions.

TIP 575: Identify Your Motive for Criticizing.

Positive reasons for criticizing include commitment to and concern for another person and a sense of responsibility to have things done "right." Negative reasons for criticizing include poor self-esteem and the resulting attempt to build yourself up at someone else's expense or as a defense or excuse for your own failures. If those two statements can't help you sort out motives, try the following, more detailed checklist:

- Will this criticism make you look better?
- Will you enjoy or dread giving this criticism?
- Do you want to demoralize the other person?
- Do you want to condemn or guide?
- Do you want resolution or more conflict?
- Is the issue a personal matter with you?
- Do you criticize habitually?
- Are you open or manipulative in your comments?
- Do you feel critical simply because you're in a bad mood or feeling depressed?
- Are you the best one to give this criticism?
- Are you giving the criticism to appease some third party?

If you don't like the answers to any of these questions, consider waiting to give the criticism until your motives are clear.

TIP 576: Check for Criticism Preferences.

When you're beginning a long-term relationship—either as a family member or as a boss-employee—have a frank discussion. Ask if the other person anticipates making any mistakes over the next few months or years. Most people, of course, will admit to that probability, usually with levity. Ask them, then, how they'd like to handle the criticism or feedback. Would they prefer you be direct or use a softer, less-direct approach? Would they prefer you wait until the end of the day or talk early in the morning? Would they prefer you talk on site or talk away from the office or home?

In addition to the obvious benefit of knowing preferences, when such discussions become inevitable, you can remind them of this earlier conversation and point out that you've tried to comply with their preferences. That in itself sets forth a caring, but matter-of-fact, situation.

TIP 577: Realize the Stress of Hearing "I'd Like a Word with You."

Do anything you can to reduce, not create, more stress for the person about to receive criticism. Keep your tone as matter-of-fact as possible, without the high school principal effect. At the beginning of the conversation, preface your remarks to let the person know the severity of the discussion. If your discussion is going to end in a formal reprimand, you don't want to start off with chitchat. But if the criticism is a one-issue agenda and of the more routine nature, say so at the beginning. "Kate, I'd like to take about twenty minutes to talk to you about the way we're shuffling these packing slips between departments. I want to share with you my perspectives and get yours and see if we can come up with a better process."

In other words, lay out an overview of the parameters of the discussion, the time involved, and the hoped-for outcome. Take the pressure off about the unknown so the person can concentrate on the major problem and resolution, minus the anxiety.

TIP 578: Watch the Red-Pencil Mentality.

This term used by Sidney Simon in *Negative Criticism* refers to what some seem to perceive as their mission on earth—to point out all the errors for all the world to see. This attitude becomes a compulsion, like a housewife who can't pass a picture frame without straightening it. Before you're tempted to red-pencil somebody, try to recall the sense of pride with which you turned in an English composition that had been typed with perfect margins and appropriate commas. Do you remember the disappointment when the professor passed your graded paper down the row for all to see your errors cast in red ink? Why do that to people? Is the criticism really worth voicing?

TIP 579: Separate Fact from Opinion As You Gather Your Thoughts and Information.

"Jill, you're lazy" is opinion. "Jill, you have processed only 28 application forms today; your quota is 48" is fact. Particularly if the "facts" are coming from another department, make sure you probe enough to distinguish which is which. Did the customer actually *say* that Stan hung up on her, or did the customer say Stan was rude? Did Bill *say* the report was too late to do any good, or did Bill say the report was submitted three days late?

Know which is which—fact or opinion—and be ready to point out the difference. The receiver of criticism will seldom dispute facts, but will often ask for support of opinion. In either case, you want to be able to cite the appropriate information.

TIP 580: Make Sure You Know What You're Talking About.

Ask yourself if you have all the facts, figures, and circumstances of a situation before you bumble into a hornet's nest to offer criticism. You'll back out of such a discussion with a big sting if you haven't done the preliminary investigation. Even then, double-check. It's too easy to put three facts together and come to the wrong conclusion.

TIP 581: Screen Yourself Before Being "Frank" and "Telling the Truth."

The "truth" will not necessarily change the world—or another person. Remember that "truth" is often subjective, and "frankness" may be a code word for insult. Examine your motives for criticizing. Determine the intentions of the person who "needs the truth." Then consider discretion. What are your ultimate goals for your relationship with this person? The greater priority may be preserving that relationship rather than preventing a reoccurrence of some minor incident.

TIP 582: Consider the Positive Results of the Exchange: Improved Mental Outlook, Improved Relationship, New Insight, Possibility of Effecting a Change.

Before you decide to offer criticism, think about the positives of the situation. Will people feel better about improving themselves, a process, or a plan? Do they generally seem to want feedback and make an effort at self-improvement? Will your offering this criticism actually improve your relationship with them? What new insights might you both gain from a frank discussion? What are the possibilities for improvements in how you both interact and accomplish your work goals?

In other words, focus on the positive aspects of what an open discussion will bring to the table. These are your incentives that will give you confidence with what might be an uncomfortable discussion.

TIP 583: Consider the Negative Results of the Exchange: Mental and Emotional Outlook, Time Involved to Help with the Change, Probability of Effecting a Change, a Severed Relationship.

Forget trying to change the people who are manipulative and maliciously destructive, those with a conflict in values, those without the mental capacity to master a task, those addicted to drugs, and those with mental problems and low self-esteem. These mental and emotional problems indicate that the time spent in criticizing will be fruitless. These people either can't or won't change.

A second concern is time: Do you want to spend the time it will take them to change? Finally, will your help produce the change? Ask yourself how many times this person has probably heard the same criticism? Has he or she done anything about it?

The answers to these questions will tell you whether your time and effort will pay off. If not, withhold the criticism and either figure out how you can minimize contact with this individual or how you can get your work done without this person at all.

TIP 584: Consider Whether You Could Foster the Same Change with Praise Rather Than Criticism.

After you have determined that there are positive reasons to go through with the criticism, use one last screen: Could you get the same effect with praise? Without setting up a phony situation, could you entice the person to do a particular thing differently by rewarding or praising the desired behavior as opposed to criticizing the less-than-desirable behavior?

TIP 585: Make Sure You're Not Doing the Same Things You're Criticizing.

We tend to react to attitudes, weaknesses, or traits in others that we dislike in ourselves. And the receiver of any criticism will be the first to point out any inconsistencies.

TIP 586: Rehearse Your Criticism.

Take the time to plan what you're going to say: Organize your comments. Decide how to word them. Practice the proper tone. Decide where and when you're going to conduct the discussion. Remind yourself that the reason for giving the criticism is not to hurt others, but to help them correct performance. Focus on the fact that after the criticism, both you and the other person will be better off for having made the improvement.

As with any other difficult task, preparation boosts your confidence and your effectiveness.

TIP 587: Select the Appropriate Emotional Timing.

Make sure neither you nor the receiver is angry, irritated, or impatient. You want to maximize the chance of catching the other person at a peak of emotional strength so he or she has the self-confidence, control, and motivation to accept your comments.

Your emotional state as criticizer is equally important for success. If you give criticism when you're angry, the receiver is likely to slough it off with "When she calms down, it'll blow over" or "She's just blowing this all out of proportion. I'll just lay low until she gets over it." Both giving and accepting criticism take emotional strength; find the peak time.

TIP 588: Select the Proper "Real Time."

In addition to the emotional climate, timing also includes "real time." Giving criticism at the end of the day just before employees go home allows them time to regain composure overnight and minimizes the time lost for productive work after the discussion when they're upset over the criticism.

On the other hand, sometimes giving the criticism earlier in the day allows people opportunity to see and feel from your back-to-the-routine manner afterward that life will go on, that you intend to move on with current tasks, and that your relationship has not been altered substantially. In other words, they won't have time to brood; they must move on with their day's tasks and function around other people.

Know your audience and the potential impact on that person's recovery rate before deciding on the appropriate time of day. The most crucial aspect of "real time" is that your criticism is prompt enough to prevent the receiver from making another mistake.

TIP 589: Criticize in Private.

Praise in public; criticize in private. Consider not only the actual time of the discussion away from others' ears, but also the surrounding circumstances and appearances that create rumors. "Get a hold of Keith and tell him I want to see him in my office before he goes home today" said in an angry tone to your secretary may be a broadcast to the world. At the least, Keith will probably know the secretary knows and will fear others have overheard the edict also.

The humiliation of being confronted in front of peers or customers will shut down any and all communication lines.

TIP 590: Avoid Beginning with a Trapping Question.

Do you remember your father asking you at the dinner table, "Johnny, how many times have I told you not to leave your bike in the driveway?" Did he really want to know how many times? Of course not. And even if you smarted off with 2349 times, that wasn't the point anyway.

Workplace versions of those childhood trapping questions sound like these: "Do you think this product is going to sell itself?" Or: "How many times have we discussed in staff meetings the importance of taking complete phone messages?" Or: "Do you recall my warning you earlier that you need to watch the tax consequences of these revenues monthly?"

A trapping question produces only a defensive stance. And more important, you'll be discussing the answer to that question rather than the real issue and solution.

TIP 591: Remove Threats from the Criticism.

A threat sets up a condition about continuing the relationship or creates fear about consequences and future work. When a person fears, he freezes. No one performs best in fearful conditions. Thinking becomes muddled. Timing becomes questionable. Tempers flare.

TIP 592: Avoid an I-Told-You-So Tone.

When tempted to use this tone, remind yourself of the implication. Such a tone confirms the correctness of your own position rather than focuses on change in another's behavior. It says: "I was right all along." A more productive focus is: "I'd like you to be right in the future; so in order to do that, you need to change."

Granted, you are not trying to create a pleasant, happy atmosphere; criticism delivered in that tone would be perceived as phony. But you can be straightforward, businesslike, direct.

TIP 593: Criticize Specifically, Not Generally.

General criticism cannot be substantiated or corrected. Most often it is ignored. But the words hang there, festering. In identifying the specific things you want to correct in another's behavior, you improve your effectiveness several ways:

First, you gain credibility. When the receiver calls your hand on a sweeping generalization about her behavior and you can't offer immediate specifics to back up what you say, your criticism loses validity. Often the person dismisses what you say as "hogwash."

Second, you both automatically focus on concrete actions to improve the situation.

Third, the criticized person must define the behavior in the same way you do. For example, with a generalized criticism you might say: "Heidi, you just don't seem to care about your work." (You mean Heidi is frequently late, takes long lunch breaks, and never stays after hours to finish projects.) Heidi responds: "What do you mean I don't care? I even called in on my vacation last week to see if Jason had any questions." (Her interpretation of "care" is different.)

To summarize: Specific criticism (1) forces the receiver to define acceptable behavior and performance, (2) focuses on concrete, corrective action, and (3) adds credibility to what you say.

TIP 594: Criticize the Viewpoint or the Behavior,
Not the Person.

Try: "I asked you to let me know if the report would be finished on time, and you did not notify me that it would be late." Not: "You're simply undependable when it comes to doing what you say you will."

Try: "I think you mishandled that customer situation. You didn't try to reschedule the appointment, and you didn't offer to deduct the shipping charges. You failed to offer either option and both are within your power." Not: "You seem scatter-brained. You don't think. You don't follow procedures."

Try: "You didn't let me know the equipment wasn't working properly and that you needed it repaired by next week." Not: "You're inconsiderate and uncooperative when it comes to supporting our department's projects."

People can discuss viewpoints or behavior and verify facts; they can even verify interpretation of those facts. But they'll rarely agree to personal labels, much less agree to make a change. How, specifically, does someone become "less scatter-brained" or "more cooperative"? Can they do that by next Friday?

TIP 595: Focus on Observable Behavior, Not on Conclusions About That Behavior.

Discuss what you saw or heard before you label that talk or action. After you voice your observations, the person criticized can verify that your observations are correct. Then, after that verification, you can label the behavior as "right," "wrong," "rude," "incompetent," "in poor taste," or "offensive." And even after you label that behavior, express such labels as your opinions, not facts. Those labels often lead the other person to explain intentions and "compare feelings" or "conclusions" with you.

Try wording like this: "I can appreciate why you felt it necessary to do X; but here's what I expected" or "I can understand your reasons; my reasons are different" or "I agree with some of what you said, and I still have concerns about Y," or "That's true; here's another ramification of that action, however."

In other words, in a meeting of the minds, state the criticism as flexible, under consideration, and subjective. The result is a more amiable, constructive dialogue rather than a conflict of emotions.

TIP 596: Don't Turn Comments About Work Problems into Major Character Flaws.

If you're talking to people with low self-esteem, they themselves have a way of taking even the slightest correction of their work into poor pity-pitter-pat. "Rosalinda, you've missed several meetings, and I'm concerned that you're not going to be up to date enough on these projects to anticipate our staffing and equipment needs. One week you're 'up' and with us and excited, and the next week, you seem preoccupied." Rosalinda's response: "So you're trying to tell me I'm manic-depressive? Or that I intentionally sabotage your projects because I'm envious of your authority—is that what you're really implying? You may be right."

Don't let that happen. Tell others to discuss any such personal issues with their analyst at $200 an hour, and instead stay focused on the work problem.

TIP 597: Bring the Criticism "Forward."

Don't talk about what people *did* in the past; instead highlight what they *are doing*. The difference is enormous. What someone did in the past sounds irrevocable, unchangeable, damning. What someone is doing emphasizes transience rather than permanence; if he can change or improve it, there's a hopeful attitude. Yes, of course, you have to mention past behavior, but link that behavior into the big-picture trait, habit, or process that can be changed.

TIP 598: Don't Ask Why.

"What" questions focus on someone's values, intentions, and results. Yes, a "why" question may lead to insight and understanding that both of you need, but more often than not, it leads to a defensive discussion of motives. Ask yourself why you want someone to blame. Will you handle the situation differently if you can place the blame on a person? If not, asking "why" is often fruitless. Instead, ask something like: "What happened?" This question removes personalities and fault. You may or may not agree with the motives, but in any case, with "why" questions, you'll almost always be off track in changing the observable behavior.

TIP 599: Use "I Need/Want/Expect" Phrasing When Possible.

Thomas Gordon of the Parent Effectiveness Training program first suggested these three steps: (1) Say clearly how you feel, what you want, or what you expect. (2) Describe the observable problem or behavior. (3) Explain the consequences or results of the behavior.

Here's an example: (1) "I feel rushed when in a one-week period I'm given four or five proposals to which I'm supposed to plan graphics. (2) When I have to 'beef up' that many documents, I find myself just grabbing graphics from the clip art and not really giving the concepts much thought. (3) Then the proposals go out to our clients half-baked. They're just not up to the standards we've set." With this three-part statement, the focus is on the action and consequences rather than on who's doing what.

Not: "You need to be doing these faster." But: "I need these proposals done faster."

Not: "You should make appointments ahead of time with the clients rather than cold-calling." But: "I expect our service people to make appointments ahead of time with clients because our clients can't set their work schedules around us when we just cold-call them to do routine maintenance. As a result of our people not making definite service appointments, we've lost two accounts this month."

Phrasing determines the difference in many reactions.

TIP 600: Don't Compare People.

Adults in the workplace hate comparisons as much as siblings do. If you supervise others, compare their behavior against your expectations. Or compare against a person's own stated goals. Or compare against the standards set to earn rewards. Or compare against mutually-set objectives. But don't compare one individual's work to another's work—past, present, or sainted.

"When Dorothy was in this job, she always sent us managers an annual needs-assessment survey. I think that was a more precise way to collect the necessary information." Such comments don't win friends—or motivate changes.

TIP 601: Include Credits with Your Criticisms.

Try to keep balance in your observations. What is the person doing right? What do you admire? What positive changes has this person made? People tend to do more of what they're doing right than to do less of what they're doing wrong.

In what order does one give the credits and criticisms? There are both schools of thought: giving the credits first, or giving the criticisms first. The problem in giving the positives first is that the person doesn't really enjoy them because of anxiety in waiting for the negatives. The drawback to giving the criticism first is that if the negative discussion gets out of hand, neither of you may be in a frame of mind to share the positives. Although you'll be ending on an "upbeat note," the receiver may be so "hung up" on the criticism that he or she can't hear the positives at the end.

A third structure is to focus only on action—ways you'd like to see the person improve and then what he or she is already doing right. People would much rather work on "self-improvement" goals than on "problems" to be solved. This arrangement also ends on the positive affirmation.

A fourth alternative is to give both praise and criticism in balanced proportions—but at different times. For some people you can give 99 compliments and one criticism and the criticism will outweigh all the 99 positive comments. Choose one five-minute time in the morning and offer your praise. The next day, offer your criticism. They're balanced, but not in the same setting.

Which structure to choose? Let the subject of your criticism and the anticipated reaction of the receiver determine the format.

Criticism originally meant to give an objective appraisal of ideas, plans, or work. Book or movie critics discuss merits as well as demerits of a manuscript or play. Somehow in the workplace, however, the term criticism has taken the negative meaning only. When you give criticism, why not change that perception with a balanced discussion? Communicate your observations in such a way that the person benefits and can use your comments for long-term improvement for all concerned.

Even all-stars and substitutes have good days and bad.

TIP 602: Lead the Person to Do a Self-Critique.

When we train a participant in one of our oral presentations workshops, we like to lead them through the process of self-critique: What did you think went well in your presentation? What didn't go as well as planned? If you could present this information a second time, what would you do differently? Finally, what would you like me (as instructor) to watch for and offer more critique on during your next performance? It always amazes me how accurate self-critiques are. And what's more, people believe their own critiques more strongly than they believe those from the instructor.

Try using the same principle by leading your employees to do self-critiques of their performance on particular projects.

TIP 603: Assume Some of the Blame Yourself.

If you can do so honestly and if you have the ego-strength to meet the other person more than halfway, this approach will certainly generate a welcome response. "I certainly can share in any blame for the vendor-selection process; I know I've been traveling a lot lately and probably was not around enough to give you opportunity to bounce ideas off me for issues that affected both our departments" or "Maybe I was too fuzzy in the last staff meeting about exactly what I planned to do with those printouts. In any case, they're not set up in a usable format."

Let the receivers of the criticism save face by your sharing any blame that needs to be assessed. It takes the pressure off them to defend themselves and make excuses.

TIP 604: Substitute Problem Solving for Criticism When Possible.

Offering to approach the situation as if it were a problem that merits cooperation shows a cooperative, positive attitude. Confirm that you have mutual goals, and spend your time developing alternatives to get what you both want. Your conversations will probably end up with transitions like these: "So what are the alternatives?" "What suggestions do you have for . . . ?" "I'm open to suggestions."

TIP 605: Couch Your Criticism as a Request for Help.

This approach is most effective with bosses or peers. Outline what effect a certain behavior is having on you and what the consequences are, and ask if they have suggestions for how you should handle the situation. In effect, you have asked for permission to criticize by your invitation to them to "discuss a problem" with you.

TIP 606: Criticize Only One Thing at a Time.

People cannot recreate themselves, their jobs, their habits, and their processes by trying to do everything at once. None of us has the luxury of emptying out all the file cabinets or databases to start over, but we could clean out the inactive client files in a reasonable time. Let people focus on one improvement until they master that area. Then offer another goal—and carrot.

TIP 607: Relate Your Criticism to Some Goal of Theirs.

Try to point out how the observed behavior thwarts a mutually shared goal. People put more effort and emphasis on correcting things they can see have a positive benefit for them. And that benefit doesn't have to be intrinsic. To correct problem X doesn't have to make them healthier, happier, or sexier immediately and directly; the benefit of correcting the behavior may simply be to get a higher performance rating, which will result in a bigger raise later. The resulting raise may bring health or happiness—depending on how they spend it. The benefit in that case is an indirect one.

TIP 608: Criticize to Some End.

The worst kind of criticism to take is that on which you can take no action. People can't change their height, their family, or their history. The criticism should end with some specific goal to move toward improvement. Criticism on unchangeable things frustrates and demoralizes people. At worst, they'll feel powerless, confused, and hopeless. At best, they'll simply shrug their shoulders at the silliness of expecting them to change the unchangeable and ignore the criticism altogether.

TIP 609: Describe the Behavior Change or Action You Want Others to Take as a Result of Your Criticism.

If you tell employees you want them to deliver better customer service, what does that mean? Answer the telephone on the first ring rather than the third? Double-check the spelling of the customer's name on letters? Make home deliveries? Respond to service calls within two hours? Smile more often?

Here are the kind of vague improvements that frustrate people and defy change: "Demonstrate a better attitude." "Do something about the morale around here." "Eliminate these miscommunications between departments." Instead of the vague "goals" alone, *describe* the "better attitude" you expect. *Describe* the "morale" improvement. *Name* the "miscommunication" you want eliminated.

If you can't describe the corrective action or improvement you want, you probably won't get it.

TIP 610: Monitor the Pace of the Conversation.

When you're tense in giving your criticism, you tend to talk faster and faster. That rapid speech makes the receiver feel interrogated, lectured at, and run over. As a result, the receiver may sit dumbfounded, overpowered, and unable to respond. When the receiver can't respond, you have no idea whether your message is being received—if the other person acknowledges awareness of a problem and intends to correct it.

So to slow your pace and relax your delivery manner, take deep breaths. Pause frequently. Break eye contact. Fiddle with a prop, such as your glasses, your soft-drink can, or your computer. The idea is to slow yourself down enough to give the other person an opportunity to absorb and respond to what you're saying.

TIP 611: Check Your Response to the Receiver's Comments.

If your words are angry or your demeanor is superior, scowling, condescending, or closed, you will most likely turn off any real communication with others you're criticizing. They will reject you as a person and therefore reject your criticism. The goal is to give criticism in such a way that others respond to it and make a change. An angry, rejecting demeanor shuts down that possibility. Play the part of coach rather than cop.

TIP 612: Summarize Key Points and Actions for Correction.

If the discussion has been lengthy, help the person attach the right importance to everything that has been said. The receiver may have overreacted to parts of your message and missed other key points altogether. It's helpful to recap at the end and outline the steps of action: "So we've discussed the problems we have in the lab when the power goes off without warning, the difficulty with getting the machines repaired, and the safety concerns with contract laborers from your department just walking through the lab at will. You've agreed to talk to the temporary people about their wearing hard-hats. And I have volunteered to write a memo to the facilities people about the outages." Everything is put in perspective.

TIP 613: Don't Ask if the Person "Understands" What You've Said.

The person will answer in the affirmative, because to say otherwise would imply he or she is stupid or that you've been unclear. But more important than that, it communicates a parent-child, patronizing tone. If you do want to verify that the receiver understands, ask for "confirmation" of the key points and suggestions for improvements.

TIP 614: Recognize When Enough Is Enough.

After you've made your point, illustrated your point, asked for and discussed the receiver's response, and identified specific actions to be taken or behavior to be changed, stop. There is nothing but resentment to be gained by repeating yourself.

TIP 615: Decide Who Should and Shouldn't Know What.

Work on deciding how you will put the incident or problem behind you and continue with the relationship. How will you explain changes to other people? Who will or will not be told anything about the discussion? How will you conduct yourselves around each other?

TIP 616: End Criticism with Encouragement for the Future.

Particularly if the person responds well to the criticism, comment on that upbeat, can-do attitude. Stress cooperation and mutual goals rather than conflict, blame, and defeat. Communicate your confidence that that person can change or improve behavior. As Deep and Sussman (authors of *What to Say to Get What You Want*) point out, "All saints have a past, all sinners a future." Even movie moguls have bad rehearsals and unfavorable reviews. Your goal is to have a box-office bonanza.

12

Taking the Sting Out of Criticism Leveled at You

Thank not those faithful who praise all thy words and actions, but those who kindly reprove thy faults. —SOCRATES

One of the surest marks of good character is a man's ability to accept personal criticism without feeling malice toward the one who gives it. —O.A. BATTISTA

It is the peculiar quality of a fool to perceive the faults of others, and to forget his own. —CICERO

Adverse criticism from a wise man is more to be desired than the enthusiastic approval of a fool. —AMERICAN SALESMAN

Most people would rather defend to the death your right to say it than listen to it. —ROBERT BRAULT

A remark generally hurts in proportion to its truth. —WILL ROGERS

Men occasionally stumble over the truth but most of them pick themselves up and hurry off as if nothing had happened. —WINSTON CHURCHILL

One way to avoid criticism is to do nothing and be a nobody. The world will then not bother you. —NAPOLEON HILL

Whether from a boss, a peer, a friend, or a family member, criticism smarts, no doubt about it. So how do you respond to it emotionally, evaluate it objectively, use it constructively, or discard it appropriately? The following tips may smooth the rough spots.

TIP 617: Consider the Value of Criticism.

Criticism has been given a bum rap in society, possibly because there are so many different kinds of criticism that can come our way. We can be criticized for something that was not our fault; for something that we have no control over; for being smarter or performing better than someone else and making that person jealous; for deliberately doing something wrong; for unintentionally doing something inappropriate; for something that is true about us; for something that is untrue about us; for our intentions, actions, results, appearance, attitude, personality, or job performance. It's difficult to lump all these kinds of criticisms together.

But consider the value: It is a form of communication—although a negative one. Sometimes negative communication from someone is better than no communication at all. It is a source of information, and it can be your best motivation for self-improvement. Criticism leveled at you is ultimately yours to use—either to disregard or benefit from it. If the criticizer is a boss, coworker, or family member, try to think of that person as a coach and you'll be much less resentful. If that person's intention is to help you improve, try to forget the framework for the comments and latch on to the benefit.

TIP 618: Remember That Even the Best Get Criticized.

Many people find comfort in a group. If you're among the criticized, you're in good company. Religious leaders receive criticism even if living on bread and water to feed the poor. Heads of state receive criticism, even though at least half the voters at one time considered them worthy of office. Doctors are sued for not making a timely diagnosis, even though a patient may suffer from a rare disease. Famous athletes get booed when they don't live up to their previous feats and track records. Movie stars are forgotten if their last performance flopped at the box office. CEOs receive criticism if the company does poorly, or if it does well—investors want to know why they couldn't have done better in such economically favorable times.

No one is immune; criticism is our national pastime.

TIP 619: Think Twice Before You Invite Criticism by Habit or Attitude.

Few people go through life with such tough skin that they don't care whether others approve or disapprove. Not that they live their life with others' approval as a guiding force, but most mentally healthy people notice and care when others are displeased with their behavior. There are several surefire ways to invite criticism on the job and at home: being unprepared, being poorly organized, failing to do what you promised, putting other people down, running over the rights of others, always demanding your own way, being confrontational in tone or manner, failing to be clear about your expectations of others, being inconsistent, asking for others' opinions and then always ignoring that advice, doing sloppy work, disregarding or being oblivious to what is going on around you, disregarding the social or work norms in behavior, speech, or dress. People unaware of any of these expectations or averse to them may as well get used to criticism. They're asking for it. They either have to change that behavior or decide that criticism will be a fact of their lives and learn to shrug it off.

TIP 620: Determine if the Criticism Is Intended to Be Constructive or Destructive.

You can often tell if a person intends to destroy you with a comment or intends just to bring about some change. Pay attention to the word choice, the emotion, the body language, and the specifics of the comments.

Did the person say you were always late or call you lazy? Did the criticizer sound as though he or she had planned the comments in a logical and thoughtful way, or did the criticizer just blurt them out in an emotional rage? Did the body language show control or simply anger? Did the criticizer back up what he or she said with specific descriptions of your behavior and have specific corrections in mind, or seem foggy about what changes you were supposed to make?

What could be the criticizer's agenda? To score points at your expense? To build or protect his or her own self-esteem? To impress onlookers? To vent anger at you because he or she is afraid to show anger at the person causing the trouble? To hurt you?

Finally, ask yourself about the subject of the criticism? Are the comments about your personality, lifestyle, or appearance an attempt to control you or make you feel guilty? Or, is the subject about a mistake, something regarding a problem to solve?

The answers to these questions will tell you whether the criticizer's primary intention is to hurt you or to improve a situation. If you're still in doubt, try asking the person directly about intentions: "Did you simply want me to know how you felt about me, or did you want us to try to work out the problem?"

One caution: Some people are inept at offering criticism. They will choose the wrong words, become emotional, and focus on the problem rather than the solution only because they are incompetent. You'll have to use your best judgment in determining their intentions. Don't attribute to them ill will when their problem is ignorance.

TIP 621: Give People an Invitation to Criticize Only if You Mean It.

If you routinely ask for criticism, don't be surprised if you get it. "Just let me know if you'd prefer me to do this another way" or "Am I preparing the report in the most useful format? If not, let me know" or "If you see any problems with the way I plan to tackle this upcoming meeting, give me a call." When you ask for comments, people rarely point out what you're doing right. Instead, they feel compelled to tell you what you could do better, quicker, faster, easier, or smarter. So if you don't really want criticisms or suggestions, don't give others a license to dump them on you.

TIP 622: Consider the Setting Before You Decide How to Respond.

If you're in a large group when someone offers a critical comment, you may decide to let the remark pass so as not to make a scene and prolong attention on the issue. Quickly state the facts or your position, and change the subject. If you're in a situation where the outcome could be crucial to your future (such as in a staff meeting with your boss), you may want to take more time to correct a false impression and state your position on an issue, or give the facts about what actually happened.

If, however, you're one on one with someone and have the liberty of time and privacy, you can discuss the criticism thoroughly until you come to some resolution. Control and conscious choice are the keys to an effective response.

TIP 623: Arrange to Have Criticism Leveled on Your Own Turf.

If you know there's a problem when the boss or coworker says he or she wants to "talk to you about something," suggest your own office. You can control the timing and the privacy. And unlike the feeling of punishment when as children we were called to the principal's office, there's something about familiar surroundings that gives you a sense of control and dignity.

TIP 624: Stifle an Immediate Denial.

Denial as adults is just as normal as that of children in these chants: "You did." "I did not." "Yes, you did." "No, I didn't." "Did too." "Did not." When someone levels a criticism, stifle the urge to close the person down with such responses as: "You don't know what you're talking about" or "You're wrong and I don't want to talk about it any more" or "That's none of your business" or "You're just jealous."

TIP 625: Squelch the Urge to Counterattack.

This response is probably the most natural. When the criticizer offers comments on your behavior, you return the favor. Criticism: "This manual was done much too hurriedly. You've left out some of the most important procedures." Counterattack: "Well, you're not such a polished writer yourself. That memo you sent out last week confused the heck out of everybody." When the pattern is to "top" the criticizer, the original issue gets blurred in the process.

TIP 626: Stifle the Urge to Rationalize.

Rationalizing is using a perfectly logical excuse for your actions—but not the real reason. For example, someone criticizes you for being late to client meetings downtown. You know you lose time by sleeping later than you should, but you claim it's the heavy traffic and unexpected accidents on the freeway that prevent your on-time arrival. Such rationalizing is usually acceptable to the other person, but untrue. Rationalizing becomes a habit—and never solves a problem.

TIP 627: Don't Project the Blame onto Someone or Something Else.

Here's how such projections go: If you write a weak report, you claim it was the fault of the manager who didn't give you enough information. If you smudge up the printing job, you claim it was because of an antiquated printing press that "goes haywire." If you take poor photographs, you decide it was because of bad film, poor lighting, or the wrong kind of camera. The lead-in to most of these projections is "yeah, but..." Listen to kids; they're experts at "yeah, but he/she/they..."

TIP 628: Avoid Superficial Acceptance.

Some people toss aside criticism with little real thought about change or prevention. They verbally agree, but continue with the action or pattern with no thought for change: "Sorry 'bout that!" "Uh oh. I blew it." "Can't win 'em all." "Better luck next time." "If that's the biggest mistake of my life, I'll be sainted some day." Such a pop-off may get others off their back for the moment, but it doesn't resolve a recurring problem.

TIP 629: Don't Pretend It's "No Big Deal."

Do you remember back in high school when a friend didn't win the student council election? Her response may have been, "It doesn't matter. I really don't think I would have had time to do all the committee stuff anyway." Avoiding hurt by pretending indifference allows someone to save face, but it doesn't change the criticism or the situation that evoked it. Withdrawal or passive acceptance can become a habit-forming response to all of life.

TIP 630: Don't Go Home and Yell at the Dog.

Psychologists call this reaction "displacement." That is, you're angry with a customer who says you're not servicing her account properly and threatens to take her business elsewhere. Instead of dealing with the problem, you go home and yell at your spouse, your kids, or your neighbors to vent your frustration.

TIP 631: Guard Against Overreaction on Your Sore Spots.

Be honest with yourself about your own hot buttons. If you're always late and you know you're always late and you hate being late, chances are that when somebody criticizes you for being late, you're going to overreact. You're going to fly into a rage, yell, scream, deny, or counteract by accusing them of something else. Why? Because they pinched a sore spot—something you yourself don't like about your behavior or attitude. Part of the expressed rage is rage at yourself. Instead, breathe deeply, wait for control, and react in a way appropriate to the specific comment that was offered. Otherwise, you'll have an escalation on your hands that you or the other person never intended and that you cannot explain or defend. It will be a totally unreasonable response.

TIP 632: Maintain Your Emotional Equilibrium.

When criticism is unexpected and swift, it's like a punch in the gut. Humiliated, we don't speak up to defend ourselves or state an opposing view because we're embarrassed to find ourselves in the situation at all. Particularly, if our integrity is questioned, we're hurt or angry that someone has brought up the issue at all. Tears well up. We yell or curse, throw things, slam doors, slap desks, slam down phones, or stalk out of meetings. Or we do the opposite: turn inward with undeserved self-blame and become depressed or resign ourselves to the fact that we have to "put up with" the situation.

All such responses are inappropriate as either short-term or long-term reactions. Instead, take time to calm down. Breathe deeply or play with a prop like your glasses or your computer. If time, take a brisk walk, hit a golf ball, or otherwise change the surroundings. Do whatever it takes to regain your emotional balance and think clearly with deliberate action rather than reacting inappropriately.

TIP 633: Be Willing to Accept Responsibility Without Accepting Blame.

The higher you go in an organization and the more powerful you become, the more frequently you will receive criticism for things you did not have direct involvement in or responsibility for. That principle is always true when you're representing your company to an outsider. To a customer, *you* are the company.

Have some of these stock phrases ready when you must take responsibility without blame: "I'll check into that situation, determine what happened, and correct the problem." "I'm not sure who handled that project, but I'll see that your concern is addressed." "You're correct. Such a situation should never have happened." "This result is disappointing. There must be a solution—I'll do my best to find it." "I agree that we have to change things to improve X."

To assume a position of power requires broad shoulders. Can you imagine the CEO of a billion-dollar corporation responding to criticism about poor performance of the company with a comment like, "Well, it's not my fault; they did it"?

TIP 634: Avoid Taking All As "Absolute Truth."

Many criticisms are subjective opinions: "You don't respond enthusiastically when your team's ideas are accepted for an award. What's the matter—aren't you a team player?" Or: "You don't seem motivated to improve. You don't take any initiative for your own self-development." Those are subjective statements. Only you know if they're true.

If others are unable to offer convincing evidence of their position, don't feel compelled to take their assessment as gospel truth. Even if they're in a position of authority, that position does not give them a corner on absolute truth about your motivations or attitudes. Some things are not observable or measurable by others. Don't let attempts to label those feelings or motivations devastate you.

TIP 635: Separate Opinions from Descriptions.

Opinions about what you're doing are subjective; descriptions are factual comments about what you said or did. When someone gives you opinions, ask for details as support to determine if their opinions are accurate. If someone says you're "lazy" or that you "don't care about your job," or that you "have a bad attitude," then you need to know specific actions and behavior that create such an impression. Ask for examples. If necessary, guess what the person is referring to and ask for confirmation.

Example of criticism: "You never follow instructions. Sometimes I wonder where your mind is. You seem out to lunch half the time. Preoccupied. What's bothering you?"

Ask for specifics. "What instructions are you referring to? On which projects have I not followed instructions? Which instructions did I not follow?"

Offer specifics and ask for confirmation. "Are you talking about the travel arrangements for the last two conventions?"

Ask for more elaboration of any kind. "Do you think we could have found a cheaper fare? Is that your concern? Do you notice specific situations where you think I'm more or less capable of following your instructions? Do you think we have more confusion when the task is a hurried one? Or, do you mean even on daily projects?"

With specifics, you can correct someone's assumptions about those situations or change those actions. But it's next to impossible to respond appropriately to a subjective opinion without collecting the person's supporting detail.

TIP 636: Listen to Someone's Criticism Without Interruption.

If you interrupt someone at the first negative comment or during the first comment you disagree with, the exchange quickly escalates into a full-blown argument. Instead, let the other person finish completely what he or she intends to say. Then ask questions, collect details about opinion statements, and finally present your own interpretation of the facts or your own position.

TIP 637: Consider the Source.

After you've taken the first step of identifying others' intentions—are they destructive or constructive?—then consider the source of the criticism in more detail: Is this person qualified to judge your action, attitude, performance? Does he have the appropriate academic or job training, the experience in similar situations, and the opportunity to compare your actions with those of others? Is she basing her comments on an isolated incident, or has she observed you over a long period of time? This assessment should tell you how much faith to put in the comments.

When the source of the criticism is vague, probe further. People who don't like confrontation often couch their own comments in claims such as, "I've heard others say that . . ." or "Rumors around here are that . . ." or "People are upset because . . ." Probe for the true source of such comments: "It would be helpful to know how much credence I can put in that comment. Exactly who is saying that?" "I could figure out the basis of that feedback if I knew where those comments were coming from." "Without knowing who has actually said what specifically, I can't really take any corrective action. I need specifics." When the source is identified, then you can evaluate the comment appropriately.

TIP 638: Consider the Emotional Climate.

When others criticize you, evaluate the sincerity and validity of their comments by gauging their emotional setting at the moment. Are they angry at someone else? Are they afraid of the consequences of a particular action? Are they upset because of a missed deadline? Do they fear they'll look bad because of your action? If any of the extra pressures are part of the climate, let others cool off and handle the immediate situation before taking their criticism at face value. Bring up the issue again when they've calmed down and reassess their comments to see if those comments are less severe.

TIP 639: Ask Yourself if Others Have Made the Same Observations.

Before disregarding someone's criticism as unfounded, consider whether you've heard the same comments from other sources. If your boss has commented on your "procrastinating with your projects," has your spouse also complained that you've been promising to clean out the garage since last summer? Have your kids complained that you keep saying you'll take them to the ballpark but never find time? Has the United Way chairperson called several times to ask for the list of names on your subcommittees? Does the paper carrier have to come by two or three times each month to collect your payment? Do you have late charges assessed for overdue bills? Have colleagues "gone ahead on their own" while waiting for you "to get back to them"? Take a hint.

TIP 640: Agree with the Criticism.

Yes, sometimes we say or do inappropriate things and if we're honest, we'll have to agree when someone comments on them. The boss says, "You're late with your status report again." Kelly responds: "You're right. It was due last Friday. I always seem to try to make a few more appointments on Friday than I can realistically handle and then wind up with insufficient time to do the report at the end of the day." The conversation will probably end there. The other person often just wants acknowledgment that there is a problem and that you accept responsibility.

If, however, Kelly responds: "Yeah, it was late, but I was just trying to make a few more calls. You want us to meet quota on the calls, don't you?" the boss would probably respond, "Yes, but this report has nothing to do with meeting quota. We've got to have the report for planning purposes. Other people manage to get theirs in on time." And the conversation would have escalated from there.

What could be simpler? State that you agree with the essence of what was said (even if you don't agree with the comments in their entirety), and state what you will do differently. The pressure is off immediately. The other person doesn't feel compelled to keep pointing out the problem, and you don't feel compelled to keep refuting it and losing credibility.

A second way you can agree is to state that you understand what the other person is saying. This doesn't mean you agree with what that person has said; it means you have listened well. "Okay, I think I know where you're coming from. You've seen me reprimand two or three of my telemarketers for forgetting to mention this month's special and you think I don't give enough praise because you've never heard me comment on what they do well. Is that what you're saying?" Get their confirmation that you have correctly interpreted their comments. Then state your own view of the situation, which may or may not be the same. For example: "I don't see my behavior in that light. I know there can be different perceptions in situations like this. Here's my view of what happened . . ." or "I think we probably have a fundamental difference of opinion about how those situations should be handled. I'll keep your comments in mind next time." In either case, you have accepted, not interrupted or argued with, the criticizer's comments.

What if the other person's perceptions are blatantly wrong? You have a third option for agreeing: Agree with the person's right to an opinion. State something like this: "I understand that you think my strategy with this client is wrong. You want me to try to submit a proposal for the equipment and you think I've been dragging my feet. I disagree that a formal proposal is the best way to handle this account, and I've given you my reasons. But I accept your opinion. Which way would you like me to handle it—your way or mine?"

Finally, you can agree in principle. That is, maybe the other person has compared your performance to an abstract ideal that no one could meet. You can agree in principle on the goals or the desirability of certain action or performance in a perfect world. For example, someone has criticized how you have handled an irate customer. You might respond: "Well, I agree that with signs posted about these policies, our customers would be more likely to accept our position about needing a deposit" or "Well, I agree we shouldn't let a customer leave angry" or "You're right. It would have been better if I had thought to remind the customer that his company had paid these deposits in the past."

Agreeing with the other person's criticism or agreeing that the other person has a right to express a critical/opposing opinion is a powerful response.

TIP 641: Ask for Thinking Time.

If you're unsure whether you agree or disagree with someone's criticism, ask for time to think: "I understand what you've said, but I'm not sure I agree with your interpretation of the facts. I'd like some time to think over what you've said. Could we talk again later this afternoon?" This reflection time will allow you to present your own position in a much more thoughtful, logical way and will add credibility to your response because it's not a "gut reaction" but one that you've considered fully. Such a discussion also minimizes the chance for escalation.

TIP 642: Express Regret About the Results of a Situation.

Even though you may not be the cause of something the criticizer mentions, you can always express regret for the situation. "I know you were expecting the shipment on Friday. I'm sorry you were delayed in finishing the project." You did not say you were responsible, only that you understand the frustration of the other person's being delayed. "I understand the client may cancel the contract over this issue. I hate that. They've spent thousands of dollars with us. It's too bad he insists on that kind of volume discount." You did not say you mishandled the account, only that you regret the client is threatening to cancel. There is a big difference. Empathy with a situation costs nothing and paints you as a reasonable, understanding person.

TIP 643: Limit the Application of the Criticism to Your Goals While Discarding the Unusable.

Changing takes time, energy, and attention. If someone has criticized you for something other than a simple mistake—such as your lifestyle, your attitude, or your personality—then change will take considerable effort. Evaluate the payoff before you decide to tackle such monumental change. What are your personal goals?

For example, if the criticizer has said you're a selfish person, do you care? Do you want to become a more giving, generous person? If that's not a personal goal, forget the criticism and save your energy. If the criticizer says you're messy and disorganized, and having a messy, disorganized desk doesn't bother you, forget the comment. Accept their opinion, state that disorganization is causing you or others no problem in life, and then forget the comment.

TIP 644: Thank the Criticizer for Helpful Comments.

When you know others have your best interests at heart or when they are criticizing you for a simple mistake, accept the comments graciously. Yes, maybe people could offer the comments in a more positive way, and yes, maybe people have failed to acknowledge their own part in a difficulty, but if their comments have benefited you in some way, say so: "Thank you for letting me know this was a problem rather than just taking it to my boss. I appreciate your coming to me first." "I appreciate your perspective on how the situation should have been handled. I'll give it more thought in the future." "Your points are well taken." "I can see how that situation might cause real grief with a bigger customer. I'll be more careful." "I know this discussion was difficult for you too. I appreciate your caring enough to mention the issue to me." That's class!

TIP 645: Ask How the Other Person Would Have Handled the Situation.

In a matter-of-fact, not belligerent tone, ask a boss or peers who criticize you how they would have handled a similar situation. Then listen. If your purpose is to argue with their answer, you'll only escalate the situation. But if your purpose is to learn from their comments, you'll present yourself as a reasonable, self-assured, open individual. And, at the least, if the criticizer can't respond with concrete suggestions, your asking and their reflection may change their perception about your competence in the situation.

TIP 646: Change the Mistakes You Alone Control.

If the criticism involves a mistake, simply go about finding ways to solve the problem. Everybody is entitled to make honest mistakes; everybody is obligated to correct them when they're pointed out.

Move into the problem-solving mode rather than wallowing in the mess with: "But nobody told me." "But the situation changed." "Yeah, but I didn't mean to." "How was I supposed to know that X would happen?" "Your instructions were unclear." "You couldn't have done any better yourself." "Life isn't fair." "Nobody appreciates what I do around here."

TIP 647: Rechannel Your Emotions to Concentrate on Your Mission.

Channel any emotional energy from the criticism into action. What are you about? What are your goals with the project, the job, the position? That anger from an unjustified criticism can be put to good use with positive action. Psychologists offer the same advice to those suffering from a tragedy. The parent whose child is murdered by a drunk driver works through grief by serving on a citywide campaign to tighten the drunk-driving laws or organize an escort taxi service for New Year's Eve parties. The same principle can work for you with criticism. Put that emotional energy into proving the other person wrong or into improving your skill, attitude, or behavior.

TIP 648: Agree on a Plan for Change and Set Timelines.

If the person who has offered the criticism is an authority figure whom you must please (boss, team leader, chairperson of a committee), then after your exchange of viewpoints or positions, agree to a new course of action.

There's not much chance of improvement when you end a meeting without a clue as to what or how to do things differently. What will it take to improve the situation? Ask for specifics, or offer specifics to see if they're acceptable to the other person. Gain agreement, and set timelines.

TIP 649: If You Can't Change, Cancel Bitterness as an Alternative.

If someone comments that because of your height you don't command respect as a leader, you're going to find yourself in a tough spot to grow a few inches. If someone suggests that because you haven't had broad managerial experience you're unable to supervise your unit, you're going to find it difficult to reconstruct your work history. Instead of growing bitter at the comments, judgments, labels, and prejudices, choose another alternative. Either determine how to prove the person wrong, change your goal, or decide that person's assessment doesn't count. Bitterness over what you can't change creeps into the crevices like a cancer until it colors all your interactions with others.

TIP 650: Keep Yourself Physically and Spiritually Strong.

Our emotional stability for dealing with complaints is closely related to our physical and spiritual condition at the time. If you're feeling lousy with a sinus infection, irritable because you haven't gotten a good night's sleep in a week, or depressed because of your lack of worthwhile personal goals, criticisms will cut deeper than normal. Guard your outlook on life and your physical ability to meet challenges.

TIP 651: Recall Your List of Strengths.

If you're not a great supervisor, remind yourself that you're a great father. If you can't sell or learn to sell, then remind yourself how well you organize other tasks. If you can't speak well before large groups, recall how well you give advice one on one. If necessary and if you work for an overly critical boss who focuses on the negative with little attention to the positive, write out a list of your strengths and post them where you can refer to them quickly in moments of high emotional crisis. Focus on your strengths if you lose your equilibrium. Strive for balance.

TIP 652: Don't Take Yourself Too Seriously.

Do you really expect yourself to be perfect? Do you really expect yourself to go through life without having anyone differ with you or express a negative opinion of you or to you? Whatever the matter, is it a life-or-death issue? Will it make a good story to tell your family and friends? What difference will it make a year from now? Play the worst-case scenario. If you can live with that worst case, forget it. Have a good laugh at your own expense.

13

Giving Advice or Feedback Someone Can Really Use

Men give away nothing so liberally as their advice.
—FRANÇOIS DUC DE LA ROCHEFOUCAULD

Advice is seldom welcome, and those who need it most like it least. —SAMUEL JOHNSON

Nothing is more confusing than the fellow who gives good advice but sets a bad example.
—no attribution

Advice after injury is like medicine after death.
—DANISH PROVERB

Asking for advice is how some people trap you into expressing an opinion they can disagree with. —FRANKLIN P. JONES

Be careful when you give advice—somebody might take it. —no attribution

Unlike giving criticism, most people enjoy giving advice. Heartfelt advice about issues of vital concern ooze out like so much salve in a tightly compressed tube. The difficulty comes in determining if the person wants to be healed, anointing the right sore spot, making sure the medication is appropriate to the problem, and recapping the lid after the initial diagnosis and treatment.

TIP 653: Know Your Own Motives
for Offering Advice or Feedback.

People like to give advice and feedback for any number of reasons: to bolster their own egos; to show off their knowledge or wisdom; to control others; to "prove" something; to "get back at" other people who won't have their privileged advice; to help; to lessen another's pain or learning curve; or to show empathy and support.

Some of these reasons are praiseworthy; others are not. Knowing your own motivations helps you "cap the flow" when tempted to spew off advice too frequently.

TIP 654: Don't Sneak Advice
into Informational Statements.

Why isn't advice always welcome? It often makes others feel wrong, dumb, or inadequate, and thus defensive.

Advice: "I think you should go ahead and start the meeting."

Information: "It's twenty past seven."

Advice: "Don't you realize that if you're going to get a summer intern in your department, you'll have to put in a request by February?"

Information: "Most summer interns are placed by February."

Advice: "I'd think twice before asking Gerald to head that campaign."

Information: "Gerald headed our campaign three years ago, and he resigned right in the middle of it without even giving us an explanation."

Other harmless forms of advice creep into our conversations when we may think we're actually comforting someone. We make comments like: "Just take it easy and relax. There's no reason to worry." Although the intention is noble, the result can be that the friend thinks you're not taking his or her situation seriously. If such impromptu advice drips from your lips, try to catch yourself in midsentence and retract.

TIP 655: Nudge People to Ask for Advice,
but Be Willing to Wait.

You may edge into advice if you see that the other person has a real problem or difficulty: "I noticed that the phone call from your boss upset you. Do you want to talk about it?" "It seems you've had to redo these reports several months now—do you want to brainstorm ways that we might improve the lay-out to begin with?" "Hey, if you want to talk about the issue, let me know. I can be all ears this afternoon." Such nudges let people know you're available to offer feedback; but if they don't take you up on your offer, keep quiet.

TIP 656: Identify What Kind of Advice the Other Person Wants.

If you can't tell what the other person wants by how he or she introduces a subject or asks a question, ask a few questions yourself. Does the person want to:

know how you did something?

know what you've observed others do well with good results?

hear key information and facts?

hear suggested options of which he or she is unaware?

know your opinion?

get help with brainstorming alternatives?

double-check his or her reasoning?

Asking specifically what the other person wants will save you both much time and produce better results.

TIP 657: Remember the Purpose of Advice/Feedback.

Your most important function may be to stimulate thinking and help formulate options. You provide a sounding board—listening for gaps in logic, missing information, tangent trails, or dangers lurking out of sight along paths a person has decided to take.

Being a good coach or adviser is often like being a good journalist—you listen for and investigate the what, who, when, where, why, how, and how much. If the advice seeker has provided all these answers, then your job will be to expand the answers, rethink the answers, or think of more suitable ones. Often, you as coach play the part of professor guiding graduate students in their doctoral research, asking questions that will lead the students down new paths of investigation rather than answering questions and closing doors in their faces. Be careful to keep the other person's motives and goals, not your own, in mind. Otherwise, the feedback will be useless.

TIP 658: Stifle the Urge to Give
Premature Feedback or Advice.

> If you fail to listen to all the information before you plunge into your advice, you're in danger of cutting off vital information—to you and the other person. When others reach into their psyches or souls to access and pass on information, they reflect on what they're saying. That reflection itself can be helpful in leading them to their own answers. Don't stifle it by jumping straight to "the answer" to their dilemma.

TIP 659: Continue to Test the Water as You Go Along.

> If you first offer feedback that makes the other person defensive, wade no further. Let the other person give you more information about the situation. Then stick your toe in to test again: "Is what I'm saying helpful?" "Does any of this make sense to you?" "Is this line of questioning keeping us on target?" "Let me know if I'm off base in my reasoning here." You don't want to plunge into the rapids and leave your friend standing on the beach.

TIP 660: Ask for Clarification on Comments
You Don't Understand.

> You don't want to give the impression of judging the other person. However, before you stimulate his or her thinking, you have to understand the situation. If you don't see the cause, the logic, or the meaning of something, ask in a nonthreatening tone: "Explain to me again why you think that . . ." "I don't understand what X has to do with Y." "Help me understand the difference between option 1 and option 3." "I think I'm missing something here. Larry said X and then you said Y. That seems to be a contradiction."

TIP 661: Feel Free to Offer the Opposing View.

> If people want only agreement and affirmation of what they intend to do or what they believe, oblige them. If, on the other hand, you think they sincerely want advice, feel free to give an honest opinion—with tact, of course: "That alternative just doesn't seem to stand up." "It doesn't feel right to me." "I'm afraid I don't see it that way." "I think you ought to reconsider one more time."

TIP 662: Use the Appropriate Tone.

> Offer your feedback as suggestions, ideas, or opinions. Avoid stating opinions as facts, ultimatums, solutions, directives, or musts.

TIP 663: Play the Part of Coach.

> If the other person's goals and yours match, you can play the part of coach with the right language. Your most successful gambit will be leading the other person through insightful self-critique to self-motivation. My graduate professor used the approach in my student-teaching days. After each session she observed, she'd pose these three questions: "What did you like about how the session went?" "If you did it over, what would you do differently?" "What information, help, or direction do you need from me?" Try variations of these questions in other situations where you're responsible for another person's results:
>
> > "Do you see a problem or difficulty?"
> >
> > "Are you getting the results you want?"
> >
> > "Can you describe the problem, difficulty, and result as you see it?"
> >
> > "What makes the problem worse?"
> >
> > "What helps the situation?"
> >
> > "What needs to change, improve, or happen differently?"
> >
> > "What kind of help do you need from me?"
> >
> > "What action do you plan to take?"

TIP 664: Make War Stories Realistic.

> From those who are successful, war stories are usually welcome. If you're successful, rich, happy, and at the place others want to be, they often want "this-is-how-I-did-it" stories. But they want realistic, not simplistic, ones. Don't look back from your lofty perch and throw out tidbits of encouragement and how-to's—just enough to tempt the other person. They want hard facts, good approaches, usable information. If you want raving fans, be straightforward and honest, not glib and condescending.

TIP 665: Go Around the "Friend of Mine" Framing.

> Sometimes people hesitate to present their own quandaries and instead frame them something like, "I've got a friend over in accounting who just

can't seem to get her mind in her work. She's got a lot of family problems and she thinks her boss won't be flexible about her hours. What do you think . . ." If you go along with the ploy and try to give second-hand advice to the person in need, your advice will be distant and usually off base. Why? Because you have to make too many assumptions without the liberty to ask questions and probe.

If all indications say you're talking to the person in need of advice, blow the cover and get to the heart of the matter. "Sherree, are you still having difficulty at home? If so, you can be frank with me, and we'll come up with a way to approach Frank about the flexible hours." Such a probe lets others know it's okay to be straight—that you accept rather than judge them.

TIP 666: Share "I Once Did/Thought/Had" Stories with Those Who Need Feedback but Won't Ask for It.

For example, "You know, I once had the same difficulty with a client in the oil-and-gas industry. For some reason, they considered the delivery terms unacceptable. So I offered to do X if they would do Y. That arrangement seemed to address their concerns, so they went ahead with the deal. Now whenever any client brings that up, I make the X offer again." Such stories have a testimonial ring, show others explicitly how you accomplished the good result, and take the pressure off them to actually follow the advice. Such advice comes across as helpful, not pushy.

TIP 667: Remember That the Other Person Has Final Say About the Advice.

Watch pushy language and a pushy attitude. Not: "I think you should . . ." "You simply have to . . ." "That'll never work. What you ought to do is . . ." Try: "Here's an idea. . . ." "What do you think about trying to . . . ?" "Here's an approach that could work. . . ." "Well, here's what I think. . . ." Remember that it's the other person's decision, career, pain, joy, life.

TIP 668: Don't Offer a Money-Back Guarantee.

Not even the most qualified professional advisers guarantee results. Trainers never promise their athletes that if they train eight hours a day, they will win an Olympic medal. Nor do stockbrokers promise their investors that if they buy certain stocks they'll double their money. Can you afford to be more confident? Guard against letting a naive advice seeker take your advice as "gospel" and bank all he or she has emotionally, physically, or spiritually on your feedback.

14

Getting Advice or Feedback That's Helpful

Many receive advice; few profit by it.
—PUBLILIUS SYRUS

Advice is what we ask for when we already know the answer but wish we didn't.
—ERICA JONG

No one wants advice—only corroboration.
—JOHN STEINBECK

Advice is like mushrooms. The wrong kind can prove fatal.   —no attribution

Always listen to the advice of others—it won't do you any harm, and it will make them feel better.   —no attribution

Three cases where supply exceeds demand are: taxes, trouble, and advice.   —no attribution

Listen to advice and accept instruction, that you may gain wisdom for the future.
—OLD TESTAMENT, PROVERBS 19:20

We don't have difficulty finding people who want to offer advice; the problem comes in finding the right people with advice that's profitable. When you're on the receiving end, the trick is to guide advisers down the paths you want to travel with the appropriate questions, the right details, and a correct analysis. These guidelines should help you decide how to profit from—or reject—the advice you receive.

TIP 669: Be Firm When You Don't Want Advice or Feedback; Don't Give Mixed Signals.

If you don't want advice, say so firmly, but gently. "Thank you for sharing that experience with me. I'll keep that in mind as I investigate my options." "Thanks for letting me know how you feel. I do think that I'm going to have to follow my own gut on this one, however." Don't ask for "advice" when you really want affirmation. When you state a position in a wistful, hesitant tone or express reservations about a course of action, people often interpret that wavering or hesitancy as indecision. They then offer "help."

If you're giving ambiguous messages and do resent interference, be firm: "I have already made my decision. I'd rather not discuss it any longer." Or: "I have the information I need, and I'll be making my decision next week." Others fear you've made the wrong choice; assure them that you'll handle the consequences.

TIP 670: Don't Telegraph the Answer You Want.

Most people will do their best to tell you what they think you want to hear. That's why it's important to give the other person "permission" to disagree with you, to give you "upsetting" facts, to offer "contradictory" opinions. If you do want unbiased feedback, ask your question or pose your position objectively. "I've just quit my job to set up my own consulting practice. Do you think I can make a go of computer troubleshooting as a consultant in this area?" If the listener has a heart at all, she'll offer encouragement and reaffirm the decision. If you, as advice seeker, want a real opinion, try: "In this area of the city, how much need do you think there is for a consultant doing computer troubleshooting?"

TIP 671: Ask Specifically for the Kind of Advice or Feedback You Need.

Do you want ideas? Insights? Data? Instruction? Reactions? Affirmations? Personal experience? If you include that information when you ask for feedback, you'll save yourself and the other person much time and often hurt feelings—yours and theirs. If you want someone to ask probing questions and double-check your thinking, say so. If you just want moral support for a decision you've already made, say so.

TIP 672: Ask for Comparisons Based on Criteria You Understand.

Someone's "excellent" may be the next person's "good." When you ask the hotel concierge for a recommendation on a "good" restaurant, do you mean good food, nice atmosphere, reasonable price, or quiet enough for business discussions? If you've ever been that vague, then you know the results can be disastrous.

Ask the adviser to make comparisons on specific terms.

Not: "Do you think Cary Martin would work well with the other people on this project?"

But: "Do you think Cary Martin or Cheryl Glass would work better with the others on this team?"

Not: "I'm in charge of refreshments and I was wondering if you expect a good attendance at this conference."

But: "I'm in charge of the refreshments, and I was wondering how many you expect to attend the conference. We had about 200 last year. Do you expect more or fewer than that?"

TIP 673: Avoid So Much Information That You "Freeze" Your Adviser.

If you give people too much "background" information, you may discourage them from even trying to understand enough to attempt to advise you. A greater danger in overloading the other person is passing on so many biased statements, invalid assumptions, and unsupported claims that they can't get a new perspective on the issue—they see the same things you do. If you push the same raw vegetables through the blender, you'll likely get the same kind of vegetable juice when you finish.

TIP 674: Don't State Your Opinion or Position and Then Argue if the Other Person Disagrees.

Arguing with the answer or position offered doesn't mean you want to win; it doesn't even mean you disagree. Unfortunately, however, people often think so. Sometimes any hint of disagreement translates to displeasure and often shuts the adviser down. To counter this tendency, you have to tread lightly at the beginning. Let the other person get the position stated, and then carefully point out—or simply ask about—gaps in logic.

TIP 675: Stifle Objections and Use Accepting Phrases.

> Even though you may not have asked for conclusions, you'll likely get
> them. If you begin to raise too many objections at the beginning, you'll
> stall your adviser. You can't be choosy about advice after it starts to flow.
> Use accepting phrases and let it come: "That's a new approach." "I don't
> think that option had occurred to me." "That's a different way to look at
> it." "I'm not sure I understand your point, but keep going." "Can you be
> more specific about why you think my approach was illogical?"

TIP 676: Lead Your Adviser to Argue Both Sides.

> On the other hand, you do want to hear and consider both sides of an
> issue. Rather than arguing against an adviser's perspective, simply ask for
> opposing views and let him or her argue both sides: "Would anybody with
> your same expertise disagree with what you've said?" "Would everybody
> agree with that position?" "Do you yourself have any concerns at all that
> this approach won't work?" "Do you think I should look out for anything
> along the way?" "Do you have any cautions for me if I do exactly as you
> say?" "Are there any extenuating circumstances that might alter your
> opinion?" Let the adviser play devil's advocate so you hear both sides with-
> out seeming rude or ungrateful for their best opinion.

TIP 677: Don't Overlook Good Advice
Because of Its Packaging.

> Some people ignore advice simply because they've heard it before (a big
> clue that it might be on target!), find it "to be expected," consider it too
> complex, or think it too simple. But . . . the repetitious can be true. The
> "expected" may be reality staring you in the face. The complex can be
> worth the effort. The simple may be profound.

TIP 678: Ask the Right Person or Group.

> That sounds obvious, but actually few people are so methodical in their
> quest for feedback that they choose work and play advisers with much
> forethought. Many of us ask advice from whoever happens to be around
> at the time or whoever has time to listen to us. If the situation has grave
> consequences, choose career advisers as carefully as you choose doctors.
> The pain can turn out to be similar and the result as grave.

TIP 679: Consider Several Sources Rather Than One "Perfect" Adviser.

Rarely does one person have the full scoop on anything. And even if he or she did, finding that perfect adviser could be extremely difficult and time-consuming. You need someone who is interested but not necessarily biased in the situation. You need someone who shows concern but does not become emotionally involved. You need someone who is knowledgeable but not overbearing. Therefore, if you can't find one person who suits the situation on all counts, ask for advice or feedback from several sources. Then pay particular attention to points where they agree and disagree. See if you can account for their disagreement—what are their biases, involvement, and levels of expertise?

TIP 680: Evaluate the Credibility of Each Source.

Some people get sidetracked by personality instead of credibility. They tend to value and accept feedback from those they like and discard feedback from those they don't like. You may want to accept a *date* based on personality, but where your career or future is concerned, evaluate ideas based on credibility. A particular client organization of mine has a staff psychologist who from time to time spends a few weeks shadowing key executives to observe their management styles. So when Ed speaks, they listen. He has academic credentials, he shares management's objectives, and he has supporting observations for his conclusions. In short, he's credible. He's the only person they meet and ask, "Hi, Ed, how am I doing?"

Is your coach or adviser in a position to know? Is she successful at doing what you want to learn? Does he have access to facts you think are relevant?

TIP 681: Remember That Advice Comes from Philosophy and Values.

Very little advice—outside facts or observations of a situation—can be separated from one's values and perspectives on life in general. For example, which weighs more on the decision of a job change: Possibility for increasing responsibilities? Better salary? Job security? Or a spouse's reluctance to move across the country? Don't expect the adviser to be able to give you the final tally on all the issues involved. He or she can only help you view the items, not score them.

TIP 682: Tell People You're Shopping Around.

> If—and only if—your adviser will ultimately know that you did or did not take his or her advice, state that subtly up front. Some people think advice given should be advice taken. When they discover that you discarded their feedback, they feel rejected and upset. If you think that may be the case, when you solicit feedback, say something like: "I'm shopping for personal experience about how supervising at-home employees has worked for various managers. What's your opinion on that arrangement?" Or: "I'm undecided about how to approach a client. I've asked several of our field reps how they handled the problem of X. I'm also interested in your expertise. If you were I, how do you think you'd handle the situation?"
>
> Then later if you don't follow their advice, they assume someone else was more persuasive, that the details somehow changed, that theirs was a minority opinion, or that you weren't particularly committed to following anyone's advice.

TIP 683: Thank People for Their Solicited
Feedback and Advice.

> Be specific when thanking others; tell them exactly what facts or insights will be most helpful to you. Specific thanks sounds more sincere than global praise. Even if you didn't find the feedback particularly helpful or insightful, thank people for the time and effort involved. After all, they could have been eating, sleeping, working, or playing.

15

Negotiating So Everyone Feels Like a Winner

Let us never negotiate out of fear. But let us never fear to negotiate. —JOHN F. KENNEDY

Compromise may be man's best friend.
—GEORGE WILL

Nothing astonishes men so much as common sense and plain dealing.
—RALPH WALDO EMERSON

When you are with someone you like, check your assumptions more often, because you will tend to do it less. —KARE ANDERSON

It is better to give away the wool than the sheep.
—Italian proverb

Know how to ask. There is nothing more difficult for some people. Nor for others, easier.
—BALTASAR GRACIAN

Nothing gives one person so much advantage over another as to remain cool and unruffled under all circumstances. —THOMAS JEFFERSON

Negotiations play a big part in our everyday work experience. We negotiate with coworkers, colleagues, and customers in accepting ideas and proposals, in winning jobs, in buying and selling products or services, and in solving conflicts. Yet repetition of the task hasn't made it any easier. For centuries, negotiating in a formal setting inflicted fear in the hearts of people: the fear of intimidation and the fear of losing. Only recently have negotiators embraced the idea that all parties can walk away from a discussion as winners.

Former President George Bush and his Secretary of State James Baker probably did more to shape our way of thinking about successful negotiations than any other pair of negotiators in modern history. Bush reasserted our security role in Panama, built the best relationship with Mexico in U.S. history, negotiated and signed the North American Free Trade Agreement, stood close to center stage in unifying Germany, remained resolute with regard to reshaping policies in South Africa, and held a careful balance on the sidelines during the collapse of the USSR. His finest hour was Desert Storm, when he assembled the largest coalition of nations in the history of the world to stand firm against Iraq's invasion of Kuwait.

How did this pair triumph on so many negotiating fronts involving so many cultures and economies? The following tips will shed some light on this formidable process.

TIP 684: Avoid the Term *Negotiate* When Possible.

The word *negotiate* connotes a winner and a loser, or at best a compromise between two dissatisfied people. Instead of "negotiating" use phrasing such as "come to an agreement," "work out a plan," or "arrive at a workable solution." Wording goes a long way in establishing a friendly atmosphere where everybody feels like a winner.

TIP 685: Consider Several Kinds of Goals Before You Begin Discussions.

To make sure you don't get sidetracked in talking, identify several different kinds of goals: your primary goal, your immediate goals, your long-term goals, your "nice to haves," and your safeguards. Within each of these frameworks, set ranges. What is the "best" you can expect and what is the "worst" position you can accept? Keep all in mind as you work toward agreement.

TIP 686: Research Your Position and the Situation.

Take the time and make the effort to support your position or requests. Read. Gather statistics. Talk to experts. Survey others for majority opinions. When you get ready to talk, you'll have adequate facts and opinions to support what you want done. And the more you know, the better your position to negotiate a win for everybody involved.

TIP 687: Refuse to Negotiate with a Missing Person.

This technique has been perfected in car dealerships around the world. The rep who shows you the car always has to trot to the back room to see if the head honcho "will okay the deal you've cut." A more familiar version: An employee walks into your office and asks you to consider "sharing" an administrative assistant, proposing that the assistant work 40 percent of the time in your department and 60 percent in his or her department. You discuss the division of labor and percentages back and forth and finally state "your best deal" for sharing salary and benefits. Then the employee announces that everything you've negotiated is subject to approval by the boss.

In effect, that means your "best deal" now becomes the starting point for the next round of discussions after you learn "what the boss said." To avoid putting yourself in this one-down situation, don't begin to negotiate until you are talking to the person who has authority to make a final decision.

TIP 688: Use Tact in Finding the Real Decision Maker.

When you're unsure whether you're talking with the individual who has final authority, check the situation out with comments and questions such as these: "If you and I come to some understanding here, can we move ahead with the first step?" "If you and I can agree on the X issue, will anyone else have to okay the terms?" "Will you be making the decision alone, or is there someone else we should get input from?" "Do you deal with a committee or team on matters like this?" "How exactly do things work in your organization—do individuals such as yourself make these decisions or must they all go through a project team?" "Who else do we need to consult about the specifications on this project before we can come to final terms?" "I'm sure you'll be advising other people about your plans here—do you mind if I sit in on those talks?" "I'd be happy to provide backup information by sitting in on other meetings that may be necessary in your coming to a final decision." Just be careful not to force the other person to admit powerlessness.

TIP 689: Set Up a Cooperative Atmosphere.

When the other person feels like a loser in your discussions, you'll worsen your own position. Yes, work to get what you need, but work also to get the other person what he or she needs. Body language, tone, and word choice go a long way in establishing cooperation rather than competition.

TIP 690: Give Something at the Very Beginning.

When you start a discussion, be gracious enough to offer something for the good of the others involved: give them a small gift, buy them dinner, spend extra time with them, give attention to their hobby or family, or concede a point. Thoughtfulness in any of these ways returns dividends. Giving something makes the other person feel as though he or she should reciprocate.

TIP 691: Ask Questions to Set the Tone for Mutual Advantage.

Some people fear a negotiating situation because they fear confrontation. So it's important to set the tone of a mutually rewarding discussion. Try questions like these: "What would you like to have as an outcome today?" "What things do you need from me?" "How can we help you in this situation?" "What are your goals?" "What things do you think we already have in common?" "What more can I tell you about my situation?" "What else can you tell me about your situation that would help me understand your perspective and needs?" "What ideas do you have for generating a more workable solution?"

How do you know if you've come to a good, cooperative agreement? Everybody involved will think the agreement is the best possible one. No one will feel "worse off" than before the agreement. Both people continue to have respect for the other and may even feel better about the other person. And finally, this agreement may result in even greater benefits than either of you thought possible.

TIP 692: Know How to Phrase Your Probing Questions.

Consider the difference in each of these pairs of questions:

1. "Do you mind if I come in an hour early every day next month so that I can leave early enough to take my son to soccer practice in the afternoons?" *versus* "Do you mind if I come in an hour early every day next month so that I can work without interruptions? I'd hate to leave things unfinished when I take off early to take my son to soccer practice."

2. "Can I wait to deliver his contract until I'm out for lunch?" *versus* "Would you like me to deliver this contract while I'm out for lunch?"

3. "Are you the only one who can make these kinds of decisions on bulk orders?" *versus* "Do all the decisions on bulk orders fall on your desk?"

Phrasing determines emphasis, and emphasis determines response.

TIP 693: Postpone Any Discussions When You're Surprised by a "Bomb Scare."

Here's the situation: You're trying to sell uniforms for servers at a large restaurant chain, as well as your laundry service for the uniforms. Just as you've gathered around the conference table to discuss your prices, product, and service, the buyer-manager walks in and drops a memo on the table saying that headquarters has just announced that uniforms are no longer mandatory at each restaurant, and that individual managers of each restaurant can make that decision for themselves.

In such a situation, what's the typical response to this sudden bombshell? The seller begins to make all kinds of offers to entice the other person and "save the deal." Beware. When you are suddenly surprised before negotiations are to begin, consider postponing your discussion until you rethink your position and plans. Take time to investigate the truth of the bombshell and its implications. A new situation warrants a new set of plans.

TIP 694: Send Up Trial Balloons Before "Getting Serious."

If you have something that those on the other side may consider bizarre, you can always pose that idea or solution as an offhanded suggestion and get their reaction. Try: "Well, you know we could always just . . . ," or "Frankly, the best way around all these issues would be to . . ." If the other person chokes, you'll be glad you didn't pose the solution as a "real" consideration. If the other person picks up the idea and plays with it, you can treat it seriously.

TIP 695: State Your Needs Up Front and Ask the Other Person to Do the Same.

You can both investigate invalid assumptions and find common areas of agreement before you tackle more difficult issues. Often people are surprised—pleasantly—that people's wants and needs are easier to satisfy than they first assumed.

TIP 696: Mention *Everything* You Want Sooner, Not Later.

If you delay in mentioning a key issue until later in the discussion, chances are the other person will consider your attempt to be deceptive. To avoid casting doubt on your intentions, start with all the issues on the table.

TIP 697: Focus on the Other Person's Needs First.

As you begin the discussion, ask what the other person wants and needs before you state your own goals. By demonstrating that you don't intend to run "slipshod" over them to get what you want, you'll build trust. Listen to what they say, ask questions about their needs and goals, show respect. Once you've figured out how to get what they want, they'll often be more helpful in getting what you want.

TIP 698: Appreciate the Value of What You Have to Bargain.

Sometimes people undervalue what they have to trade. Don't forget the intangibles. Attach value to everything before you begin your discussions. For example, as an employee you may own your own transportation to work and so can work early or late hours on special projects when asked without undue hardship. If that flexibility happens to be important to an employer, consider it a bargaining chip. Other assets of value include dependability, ethical behavior, responsiveness, contacts and networking opportunities, emotional ownership—not to mention any number of other skills or attitudes. Take a fresh look at what you have to offer in any situation.

TIP 699: Dilute Your Weaknesses by Listing Them.

This principle works like an apology. If you apologize profusely for an error, chances are a customer will accept your apology graciously. At the least, that customer will stop ranting and raving about how you goofed up and move on to the solution. The same often happens in negotiations. You lay your vulnerabilities on the line so the other person doesn't have to recount them to you. Then the discussion can move on to focus on what you do bring to the table. For example in interviewing for a job, the conversation might go like this: "I know I don't have the five years' sales experience you wanted, but I do speak three languages and think that fluency necessary to building rapport will more than compensate for . . . What I have gained in lieu of sales experience is years of . . ."

TIP 700: Watch Others' Body Language When They Toss Out "Unimportant" Comments.

When people seem to throw "by the way" comments into the conversation ("Oh, I almost forgot . . . ," "I forgot to tell you that . . . ," "By the way, does it matter that . . ."), watch for hidden meanings. They will usually become stiff, nervous, and apprehensive about your response. Those subtle body changes should cue you that the comment may not be so insignificant after all. Investigate the big-picture meaning.

TIP 701: Bring Success Stories to the Table.

As you begin discussions about conflicts or needs, suggest that both of you relate ways you've seen other people solve the same problem or conflict you're facing. Tossing out these stories as alternatives offers a starting point for your own situation in a "safe" way—sharing them reminds both people that success is possible.

TIP 702: Draw a Definite Distinction Between Wanting to Agree and Having to Agree.

Make it clear to the other person—and then remind yourself frequently—that you *want* to come to agreement, but never that you *must* come to agreement. Any time you feel (or signal the other person) that you absolutely must make a deal, you'll obviously be at a disadvantage. In fact, you may start a rock slide.

TIP 703: Be the Caller When Negotiating by Phone.

As the initiator of a discussion, you have the edge—notes in front of you, forethought, control of timing. The person called has to play catch-up, and if they're not good "on their feet," they'll often fumble when caught off guard by a phone call.

TIP 704: Negotiate as a Team, Not Individuals Working on a Team.

Another negotiating team may try to divide yours by addressing remarks to individuals separately—usually the ones who seem less knowledgeable and capable. In other words, they'll make eye contact with one individual and ask for a concession; that person will respond by agreeing with what they want. Then they'll select another individual and ask for a concession to which that person also agrees. In other words, they begin to negotiate with people as individuals rather than with the spokesperson, usually the most articulate, knowledgeable, and skilled of the group.

Don't let this divide-and-conquer routine work against you. If your team is negotiating on any matter, appoint a spokesperson to do the talking. When other team members want to contribute to the discussion, they can write that spokesperson notes or take breaks to discuss the issues among the group.

TIP 705: Take Notes.

If you think you may not be able to recall key information, don't hesitate to make notes as you go along. Don't worry that the note-taking may slow you down in your discussions, because it has several advantages. It ensures accuracy, it gives you time to think about and react to what has just been said, and it forces the other person to notice that you have recorded certain information should that person decide to "forget" what was promised or planned.

TIP 706: Make Good Eye Contact as You Negotiate.

If you avoid eye contact or look at the other person only briefly as you talk, that person may interpret your lack of contact as evasiveness, dishonesty, incompetence, or lack of conviction. To show your honesty and openness, look at people directly.

TIP 707: Start on the Less Important Issues and Work Toward the More Difficult.

You'll gain momentum toward agreement, and you'll have more time invested in finding a resolution. The more "success" you have in turning each minor point to mutual advantage, the more emotional strength you'll gain to work on the more complex issues.

TIP 708: Get Others to Invest in Agreement.

The more time, money, or effort people have spent in negotiating, the more likely they will continue trying to come to agreement. They hate to think all that work, money, frustration, or delay has amounted to nothing. The more time they spend working with you to hammer out an agreement, the more committed they will be to working out any problems that crop up along the way.

TIP 709: Be Willing to Jump Ship.

If you find yourself on the opposite side of the situation mentioned in the last tip, learn when enough is enough. I've seen a realtor friend of mine spend days showing property to buyers who couldn't make up their minds about which house to buy or whether they wanted to buy a new house at all. Why did the realtor keep spending Sunday afternoons showing them property? Because she'd already spent so much time showing them property!

Don't keep pouring more time, money, brainpower, and effort into a worsening situation just because you've already committed so much. The temptation to do so is great. Why? It's the same phenomenon that causes people to keep their money in sinking stocks, hoping the price will recover and their investment will recoup its value.

The reasoning goes like this: "I've already invested so much time and energy that I should stay with it and see if I can rescue that investment from being a total loss." That reasoning has kept the United States in third-world countries and in ill-conceived social programs. It also keeps individuals in damaging relationships and poor business deals.

TIP 710: Start with Goals, Then Move to Solutions.

If you start with solutions to a problem and one or both of you can't accept the stated solutions, you may remain at odds forever. If, on the other hand, you state only your goals or motivations, then you can either accept or reject solutions as necessary and still come to an agreement that allows both of you to meet your goals.

TIP 711: Adopt a Brainstorming Technique to Generate Solutions.

Once you have stated goals or motivations, then generate possible solutions together as a team rather than as adversaries. After you have a list of possible solutions, select the best two or three solutions and focus on those. Finally, work out the details of each of those solutions and select the best.

TIP 712: Present Fewer, Not More, Choices When Things Stall.

Having too many choices paralyzes people in decision making. Analysis paralysis sets in with even the smallest decisions. You walk into the local convenience store that has only Snickers and Milk Duds and you can make a choice in two seconds or less. But drift into a candy store that has 28 different candy bars and the decision will likely take you two minutes. The same happens in setting appointments. Invite a colleague to lunch "sometime this month" and you'll have a devil of a time getting together; invite the colleague to lunch either Tuesday or Friday and you'll get a quicker commitment.

When people seem puzzled and indecisive, don't take that as impetus to brainstorm more options. Instead, narrow the choices. Lead them to focus on the two or three best contenders and forget the rest.

TIP 713: Remember That Others' Perceptions
Govern What's "Fair."

Have you noticed how the young woman just graduated from college thinks "all the good jobs" go to the people who've been around longer? Then as that young woman ages into her forties, she thinks that "all the good jobs" go to the young people because management can hire them more cheaply? Have you noticed how the poor couple thinks the tax burden should fall on the middle class? Then when that couple works and earns their way into the middle class, they think the social programs for the poor are mismanaged, ineffective, and unnecessary? Everybody's overworked and underpaid. If you don't think so, ask them.

What's "fair" will always be determined by each person's own situation, viewpoint, and values. One administrative assistant leaving a job where she had a private office complained about the job where she had to work in a small cubicle. Another newly hired administrative assistant "inherited" the same work station with, "Great—my own cubicle and work station! In my former job, there were two of us sharing a space this same size. I had only one drawer that was totally mine."

The matter of perspective knows no organizational bounds. The president of a client organization related a similar incident with seven senior managers during a layoff, when he downsized from three floors to two in the building to reduce his overhead. When the managers began to complain about having to "double up" in their offices, he reminded them that they had another alternative to help him reduce costs. . . .

Perspective determines the meaning of "fairness" on any issue. Bottom line: If you have occasion for a committee to vote on your salary, make sure everybody on that committee earns more than the salary you want.

TIP 714: Substitute "We" for "You and I."

Let language imply your intention to work out an agreement to everyone's advantage. Examples: "What would we have to do to get X to happen?" "What if we changed our criteria for hiring to include only five years' experience?" "How can we design this schedule so your people don't have to work overtime and so our people can meet the customer's deadline?"

TIP 715: Reset Expectations.

Let people know when they're being outrageous without telling them so. As parents or sweethearts, you may want your loved ones to think you "hung the moon," but as negotiators, not so. When expectations about what you can offer, pay, do, approve, or provide are too high, the other person will always walk away feeling disappointed after you come to terms—as if getting a bad deal.

Before you get too far into discussions, reset expectations: "I hope you're not going to be disappointed that this year's order can't match the unusual one we placed last year." "I wish I controlled all the purse strings on this deal, but I don't." "With so many people who have to be pleased on these services, you're going to have to spend more time with us than you probably planned." "My budget isn't anywhere near what you're asking." "I don't think the price you quoted is competitive in this area." "The services you seem to be wanting us to provide are just not offered by companies like ours—at least not at the low fees we charge." "The changes you need may be way beyond the scope of what we plan in this remodeling project." The idea is to make the other person's starting point realistic.

TIP 716: Take the Other Person into Your Confidence About Your Own Restraints.

If you have special considerations or restraints, say so. You may have legitimate issues that bind you with regard to pricing, scheduling, shipping, staffing, deciding, or any number of things.

Then reverse the situation; ask the other person to level with you: "Do you have an especially tough time line you're working on?" "Will it be difficult to get your team to agree?" "What is the mood around your organization just now?" "Are you used to having to sell your ideas to the MIS department?" "Is there any other special need or consideration that I should know about here?" By sharing those restraints, you create trust, reset expectations, and genuinely help the other person see how to meet your needs.

TIP 717: Don't State Your Position Unilaterally.

Be careful that neither your words nor your tone sounds like "take it or leave it." Once you've stated your position as unchangeable, the discussion may go downhill fast. Why? You'll back yourself into a corner. Unless losing face is of no consequence to you, you'll resist changing your mind. If one side has to "give in," the other will feel embarrassed, defeated, or resentful. If nobody "gives in," you're at a stalemate. The best approach is for both people to start walking toward their goal and gradually fall in step.

TIP 718: Tag the Other Person's Unalterable Positions.

> As you brainstorm solutions and test the details, tag unalterable positions the other person mentions or implies. Determine the difference between "won'ts" and "can'ts." Once you tag the unalterables, you'll know how much leeway you really have in coming to agreement.

TIP 719: "Test the Details" Before Making or Asking for Full Commitment.

> Make it clear that you're not agreeing or committing to anything yet. Then sort out details to see which are acceptable and unacceptable in meeting the other person's needs. Try comments such as: "If we were able to get delivery in 30 days, would that work for you?" "If Sharon could come in an hour earlier for a month, would she be able to finish the task within your time frame?" If the idea is unacceptable, discard it immediately. If the idea is a "possibility," keep it in mind but remember that it is not a commitment yet until all details are worked out.

TIP 720: Listen for Loopholes.

> Nowhere is listening more crucial than when coming to an agreement in which everyone wins. Listen for needs and wants of the other person. Which are must-haves and which are nice-to-haves? Does the other person have to win on a certain point—or simply have to not lose? Does the other person have to have X or simply want a guarantee that Y won't happen? Listen for words that indicate which of the other person's points are negotiable. Listen for inconsistencies in "facts," wants, and values. Listening your way into agreements often pays bigger dividends than talking.

TIP 721: Make Your "No" Authoritative.

> If an issue is nonnegotiable, say so. And be specific about what parts of the issue are unacceptable. "No, I definitely can't agree to the up-front payment, but I might be able to give you some room on the delivery date." If the other person refuses to accept your "no," repeat it. Then repeat it. Then repeat it. If the broken-record technique doesn't seem to make the point, check your own body language and voice quality for inconsistency. Are your words saying "no" while your tone is saying "maybe"? Make both body language and behavior match your words.

TIP 722: Get the Other Side to Go First.

As far as possible, try to get the other person to state what he or she has in mind first. With this information, you can alter what you have in mind before committing to it. Try these comments: "What did you have in mind when you requested 'changes' for your office?" "You mentioned discounts earlier—what percentage are you accustomed to receiving?" "Can you give me some ideas about your budget?" When you must go first, state a range that allows you to ad lib as details become clearer about the possibilities and specifics.

TIP 723: Find Out Both Ends of the Range.

Try to discover the limits of other people's positions. What's the lowest price they'll accept and what's the best price they expect? What's the most time they'll donate and what are the fewest hours they expect to donate? On each issue, what's their range of responses? No information is more important to you. On the other hand, when someone is trying to find out the limits of your position and you want to signal that you're reaching your upward limit, increase your resistance to the ideas they're presenting and reduce the concessions you're granting.

TIP 724: Ask for More Than You Expect.

First, you might be surprised and get everything you want. Additionally, you allow yourself room to move—trading coupons for other issues you want to buy during the discussion. Finally, you have some spare coupons to give to the other person to make him or her feel like a winner also.

TIP 725: Circle the Target.

When haggling over price, this principle often comes down to "let's split the difference." You ask $12,000 for the car; the buyer offers $11,000; and you settle on $11,500. Salespeople circle the target when they present product lines to their customers by showing them "top-of-the-line" refrigerators, "good" refrigerators, and "value-priced" refrigerators. Having set the upper and lower boundaries, they're expecting you to shoot for the middle.

Expand this principle into issues other than money. "I've asked you for four weeks' vacation and you've said two weeks is standard. How about if we settle for three weeks?" Another example: "I need a full-time assistant for this project. You've offered no budget at all for an assistant. What about authorizing 20 hours a week for a temporary employee?"

TIP 726: Be Prepared to Add or Subtract.

Before you go into a meeting to make some agreement, list your must-haves and nice-to-haves. As your discussions move along, be prepared to offer concessions to "sweeten the deal" for the other person by adding on things you can do. If the other person demands that you give in on certain things, know what items you can remove from the gift bag and take back home with you. All the add-ons and subtractions protect the heart of your agreement so that when you walk away both sides feel as though they've shaped the final agreement.

TIP 727: Don't Counter an Outrageous Demand or Offer.

The term "lowballing" means that someone makes a preposterously low first offer and then edges up only by small steps. If you let this extremely low offer, on price for example, become the bottom range of your negotiations, then the logical and fair price you had in mind before you begin the negotiations becomes the "high" figure. To respond in such a situation, simply refuse to start serious talk until the beginning offer becomes reasonable.

Likewise with a demand. If you take someone's demands seriously enough to respond, they'll consider that outrageous demand their starting point. Simply keep silent or respond with humor to let the other person know you do not consider him or her seriously interested in coming to agreement.

TIP 728: Be Prepared to Add or Subtract Only upon Request.

Particularly pay attention to this principle when it comes to price. If you've ever traded used cars, you've probably run into the individual who stated his price this way: "I want $4000 for the car. Or, somewhere close. It's in good shape. Of course, it could use new tires—I could knock off $300 for that. $3700 would be a good price." People start stuttering and stair-stepping like this when they feel insecure or worried about the outcome—that the other person will walk away from the deal without even a salute. Never start making concessions until the other person asks you to do so. State your position on an issue and wait. Both of you may be in total agreement from the first step.

TIP 729: Add or Subtract in Small Increments.

You don't want to offer $400 for an item and then make your next offer $800, or ask for a new company car and then immediately concede that you'll settle for being authorized to use a company credit card for gas. If you make such sudden, drastic movements away from your first position, you'll lose credibility about what you want or need and sound uncommitted or unknowledgeable about the whole issue.

TIP 730: Ask for the Other Person's Reasons Behind a Particular Offer or Demand.

Rather than simply challenging a demand or refusing a request, ask the other person to explain his reasoning. And even if the other person unexpectedly makes a concession or offer, ask the reasoning behind it. This information can give you valuable insights into the other person's values and goals. Your asking for the basis of the offer or demand also identifies you as a reasonable person who wants to understand and arrive at the best possible outcome.

TIP 731: Reverse the Other Person's Logic.

People tend to use logic in presenting their side of an issue—but their logic is apparent from only one point of view. Your goal is to help them see the reasoning from both angles.

An example: An employee approaches you for a raise, saying that because the company plans to move headquarters farther out into the suburbs, he will have to travel farther to work. Reverse his logic: Would he be willing to accept a pay cut if you decide to move headquarters closer to his house?

Another example: The employee wants a raise because the company has had a profitable year. Would she be willing to sign an agreement for a decrease in pay if the company does poorly the next year?

TIP 732: Forget the Matching Exercise.

Don't feel as though you have to give something up every time the other person makes a concession. For example, on price, if the other person raises her offer by $200 to come closer to your asking price, don't feel as though you must lower the asking price by $200 as a move in good faith. Or, consider a discussion with your boss about new flextime hours:

YOU: I'd like to come in later in the mornings to allow more time to take care of my elderly mother living with me. I'd prefer to work 10 to 6, with no lunch hour.

YOUR BOSS: Well, I could give you some leeway from the set 8 to 5 schedule. How about coming in at 8:30?

YOU: Well, that's still a rush—I have to prepare my mother's meals for the day. I really need to have a 10 o'clock start time.

Don't feel obligated to give something or change something just because the other person has done so. Your request or position may have been closer than the other person's to an equitable arrangement at the beginning of the discussion.

TIP 733: Leave the Other Person Room to Back Down and Save Face.

Many a discussion has been lost when both parties wanted the same thing. Manager Karen states that she has given careful consideration to restructuring the business and has decided to transfer Matthew to Chicago. Matthew responds angrily, saying that under no conditions will he transfer to Chicago and threatens to leave the company if forced to do so. He may then follow up his emotional outburst with logical reasons about why it would be in the interest of the company not to force him to transfer. Karen may agree with his reasoning and wish she could change her mind.

But she won't. Why? She'll be embarrassed that her earlier decision seems now to have been a poor one. Or a worse loss of face, she'll fear a flip-flop on the decision would lead Matthew to believe none of her decisions is final. Both may want to forget about the transfer, but Matthew's attempt to push her in the corner and make her feel that he is one up by threatening a resignation will keep him from getting what he wants. If you want people to concede a point, you've got to give them room to change their minds without embarrassment.

TIP 734: Avoid an Adversarial Tone of Voice and Word Choice.

Which of the following two people would you prefer to work with?

Person A	*Person B*
I want $30,000 up front.	I need $30,000 up front.
You'll need to come up with . . .	Could you come up with . . . ?
This is what we want. . . .	What could you say to . . . ?
That shouldn't be a problem.	Will X be a problem?
The logical solution is . . .	Does that make sense to you?
You'll have to . . .	We'd appreciate it if you'd . . .
Take it or leave it. . . .	I'm afraid that's as high as I can go.
Your position is ridiculous.	I know my position may sound extreme, but here's my situation. . . .
That offer is an insult.	That's not what I had in mind.
You're crazy.	Possibly I have been unclear about why . . .
You should know better than something like that.	I don't think I agree.

Attitude may be the wedge that drives people apart.

TIP 735: Don't Lose Your Composure.

> When you get emotionally upset, you lose respect, trust, logic, and momentum. That's costly.

TIP 736: When Someone Makes a Threat,
Don't Respond at All.

> In the typical situation, threats elicit counterthreats. Then both parties lose because they begin moving into extreme positions and change the dynamics to "every person out to crush the competitor." To avoid this danger, don't respond to emotional outbursts or threats at all. Simply hear them, pause, or call for the other person to continue to elaborate. The point is to let that person spend his emotion and come back to a more reasonable position. When you counter the threat, solutions begin to disintegrate and the compromise position fades. The danger: You will either win big—or lose all.

TIP 737: Treat Silence as Golden—
Or Yellow or Amber.

> As an accessory to negotiations, silence changes colors as you need it. Silence is golden when you use it for reflection to avoid popping off without forethought. On other occasions, it may be yellow or amber; it may be taken as agreement or disagreement. When you don't want to commit yourself, simply listen and think about what the other person is saying.

TIP 738: Don't Let Silence Intimidate You.

> Because many people grow uncomfortable with silence, they talk . . . and talk . . . and talk. The more the other people remain silent in a discussion, the more uncomfortable they feel. As they feel more uncomfortable, they fear something has gone wrong in the discussion so they begin to offer concessions. "Well, you know, I guess I really could afford to let you . . ." or "Frankly, I'm willing to . . ."
>
> If others simply sit silently rather than react to what you say, sit silently with them. Don't begin promising the moon just because they seem to have lost interest in discussing a matter.

TIP 739: If You're at Wit's End, Ask the Other Person
How to Overcome His or Her Own Objection.

> If the other person has refused to accept any of your concessions or alternatives, put the monkey on his back. "Okay, I've run out of ideas. How do *you*

think we can work out this issue/overcome this objection/diffuse this concern?" The other person often has a suggestion in mind that is workable. And on other occasions, he or she may concede that the issue is unsolvable and, as a result, drop it as a criterion for coming to agreement.

TIP 740: Reduce Resistance to "Precedent Setting."

Sometimes people fear giving you what you want simply because they don't want to set a precedent for other people or for later dealings with you. You hear comments like these: "But if I do this for you, everybody will expect me to . . . ," "If I sell this one to you for X dollars, then you're going to want to buy all of them at X dollars," "But if I don't require *you* to do X, *nobody* will want to do X." To reduce this pressure on other people, you'll need to find a way to help them justify in their own minds how the current situation differs from others that may arise later. That difference becomes the crucial difference.

TIP 741: Borrow Someone's Library, One Book at a Time.

If you ask the other person for everything you want and that everything is a lot, your requests will be taken seriously. If, however, you're asking to borrow only one book at a time, the person may not even take the trouble to padlock the library. In negotiating for added job responsibilities, the principle might work like this: Instead of asking to move into a new job when someone resigns from the company, you might ask to add one of those job responsibilities to your current job. Six months later, you may ask for another responsibility from that original job. Before you know it, you may have borrowed someone's entire job, one task at a time.

TIP 742: Apply the Rule of Supply and Demand.

Have you ever shopped in a department store and expressed interest in a chair only to have the salesperson respond with, "Those may be all gone—let me check the stock on that." Then he or she returns with, "You're in luck—we have only two left." The tactic: If you want it, we'd better write up the order quickly before someone else beats you to it. The principle doesn't have to be used as trickery, however. If what you offer has a limitation, say so. Let the other person know that by waiting, the choices may be limited, the quality may decrease, the offer may be withdrawn, the process may get more complex, or the price may change.

TIP 743: Win Instant Credibility by Association.

When presenting a new idea, process, or approach, introduce your point by relating it to a more renowned or credible source. Example: "Last week I read in *Fortune* magazine that more than half of the top 50 companies encourage X, so I was thinking that we too might consider . . ." or: "Our legal department has always encouraged us to X, so I thought you would have no problem if I added this clause into the contract I intend to offer" or: "My approach parallels one used by our CEO in the strategic planning meeting he facilitated. It calls for . . ."

TIP 744: Do It and Then Tell Them You've Done It.

This principle is second-cousin to the "it's better to ask forgiveness than permission" rule. On occasion, you'll do better to take an action and then tell others what action you've taken and see if they let that action stand or counter it. For example, a vendor sends you a contract for signature containing a clause promising delivery in 90 days. Rather than phone the vendor to express your reservations and work out the complete deal before signature, you delete the 90-day clause, ink in 60-day delivery, and sign and return the contract. The vendor may decide to let the deletion stand to avoid reopening the negotiation and unraveling the whole deal.

Even in simple situations, this principle works well: Your spouse moves all the furniture in the house and then asks you how you like it.

TIP 745: Don't Accept the Printed Word as Holy Writ.

A store sign saying WE DO NOT GIVE REFUNDS carries a lot more weight with customers than a clerk at the register making the same pronouncement. To most people, printed policies, proposals, prices, and plans sound more persuasive and authoritative than oral ones. Though they may be "official," they may not be unalterable. Written words can be rewritten.

TIP 746: Set Deadlines with Care.

If you say to a vendor, "We'll give you until Friday noon to make up your mind about whether you can give us the volume discounts," what happens if the vendor isn't ready to make a decision by Friday noon? What if the company is still waiting for bids from its own suppliers? If you really want to work with this company and you have the leeway to wait longer for a decision about the volume discounts, you've put yourself in a bad position. Either you lose face by admitting you really didn't have such a deadline after all or you back yourself into the corner of having to go to your second-choice vendor. Deadlines can cut both ways. Set them carefully.

TIP 747: Don't Let Your Calendar or Clock Tick So Loudly.

You may have deadlines: Subscriptions run out. Contracts expire. People resign. Prices go up. But avoid making your deadline sound like an ultimatum to the other person. Pay particular attention to tactful, factual wording:

Not: "You'll need to give me an answer by tomorrow; otherwise, I'll go ahead and list the property on the open market."

But: "I'm going to be forced to list the property with a realtor by the first of the month. If you want to make an offer, I hope you can make a decision before that time."

Not: "If you don't have an answer for me by tomorrow at noon about whether you can customize the seats, I'm going to give the order to your competitor."

But: "I hope you can have an answer about the customizing right away. I've promised myself to make a decision by noon tomorrow."

Word choice conveys attitude, and the proper attitude solicits a favorable response.

TIP 748: Don't Let Others' Calendars or Clocks Wear You Down.

The attitude of "let's get it done" often wreaks havoc. Give yourself time to generate the best option and agreement. When the other person offers a concession or asks for a concession, wait, consider, ponder. The devil is in the details. This simple concept may be your saving virtue.

Yes, deadlines represent reality. But think back about decisions made up to now in your life and decide how pleased you are with the ones made "because you had to do something." When someone states to you, "I want an answer by five today," before rushing into a decision, ask yourself if you would decide to do X even if there were no deadline involved. If not, wait.

TIP 749: Don't Agree Too Quickly.

Even when you like a deal, be careful not to grab it and run. The other person will invariably think he or she made a bad deal after all and "left something on the table." When you fall into a favorable situation, walk away with it—don't run.

TIP 750: Keep Quiet Until Things Are Final.

As you make progress in coming to agreement, you'll be tempted to talk about it to others. Don't. Having outsiders know about what's going on can add unnecessary pressure—either positive or negative—on the other person involved. For example, let's say you're negotiating with manager Victor about allowing your staff to use his department's equipment one day a week. He promises to think it over. Then in the meantime, you mention to a mutual friend, Evan, what you've asked of Victor. Evan may decide that you're on to a good idea, that he would like that same treatment. So Evan goes to Victor with the same request about using the equipment for his own people. Victor may decide to turn you down because he doesn't want to give such special treatment to Evan's group. Had you kept the situation quiet, you'd have had a sweet deal instead of no deal.

TIP 751: Practice Your Response to the Nibbler.

After you come to a complete agreement, this individual wanders back into your office with "just one more little thing" or "by the way, I forgot to make sure it would be all right if . . ." This person wants to get every last crumb on the table. Be prepared with your response if this should happen to you: "I feel good about what we agreed to yesterday. I'd rather just stay with that arrangement" or "Actually, where we left things last week would be my preference. I really don't want to get into those issues again."

TIP 752: Be Persistent.

Few things of value have been gained on the first try. Research says most salespeople give up somewhere between the third and fifth attempt, and yet most buyers don't even remember your name until after the sixth impression. Persistence pays off in getting a customer's attention, it pays off in getting peers to cooperate, and it pays off in getting a boss to approve an idea.

TIP 753: Develop Trust.

To resolve a conflict, both people have to want to resolve it. When both people in a negotiating situation trust each other, they have a natural inclination to want to come to consensus and resolve any differences. When they distrust each other, one person may decide he or she doesn't care if they ever come to agreement. And typically, they won't.

TIP 754: Negotiate by "The Golden Rule."

Treat others with the same respect for their best interests as you would like to have shown for your own best interest. This rule should set the stage and raise and lower the curtain on any successful discussion.

16

Resolving Your Conflicts Without Punching Someone Out

*Only the weak are cruel. Gentleness can only be
expected from the strong.*   —LEO BUSCAGLIA

*We judge others on their actions and results and
want them to judge us on our intentions.*
                                    —no attribution

A soft answer turns away wrath.
                    —OLD TESTAMENT, PROVERBS 15:1

*Never, for the sake of peace and quiet, deny your
own experience or convictions.*
                    —DAG HAMMARSKJÖLD

*My idea of an agreeable person is one who
agrees with me.*   —SAMUEL JOHNSON

The person with no conflict on the job or at home should be mounted and
sold by Neiman Marcus in its one-of-a-kind gift catalog. Conflict can result
from excellent work or poor work, from good intentions or evil intentions,
from appropriate behavior or inappropriate behavior, from praise or insult.
When the inevitable conflict surfaces, you need to know how to identify and
deal with it so that it doesn't drain your energy, infect your whole life, and
sabotage your effectiveness.

TIP 755: Pull the Plug on "Little Discussions" Before They Mushroom.

What starts out as a minor issue can become a major issue fast. A glance. A smirk. A mutter. A shrug. An "Is that all you found wrong with it?" can take on an ominous appearance as quickly as rolling thunderclouds. When others seem on edge, back off. Give them maneuvering room.

TIP 756: Deal with Conflict Promptly.

Like hot coals, angry words or bad situations tend to grow hotter when they're allowed to smolder. Friends of mine, a married couple, have a long-time rule in their household of five (two mothers-in-law and a father-in-law, plus the husband and wife): They must deal with any conflict within an hour. If they decide they're too emotional to discuss something immediately when it happens, they call the one-hour cool-down rule, and then resume their conversation about the problem. Things unattended fester. Hearsay happens. Intentions become suspect. Hurt humiliates. The faster you broach the subject, the less infected the wounds.

TIP 757: Determine the Nature of the Conflict.

For the most part, conflicts can be divided into five categories: conflicts over personalities, conflicts over goals, conflicts over circumstances, conflicts over facts, and conflicts over values.

1. *Conflicts over personalities* can be solved by pinpointing traits that annoy or work patterns that irritate and by accommodating the other person's trait or style. Because personalities are difficult to change, the best coping strategy may be to limit contact with this person or overlook the habit or trait.

2. *Conflicts over goals* can be best handled by compromise. Creative alternatives allow both people to get their needs met. If both people can't reach their goals, the goals can be modified.

3. *Conflicts over circumstances* are easier than most to handle. Creative thinking will usually generate new limits, new details, or new choices to alter the bad situation.

4. *Conflicts over facts* fade easily. Facts can be verified or refuted. When both people become clear on the facts, their conflict goes away.

5. *Conflicts over values* cannot be resolved. The difference between attitudes and values is generally time. Attitudes change; values have taken

root in a person's life over a long period of time. Values form the basis for how people look at other people, at work, at ideas, and at life in general. If you consider a situation or action immoral or offensive, that judgment is based on values and you will not likely be satisfied with a compromise.

Once you have categorized the kind of conflict staring you in the face, you'll have a clear understanding about the effort involved in resolving it and the potential for a successful resolution. Some will be quick; some will be never-ending. Plan your future actions and reactions accordingly.

TIP 758: Surface Masked Hostility.

Recognize passive-aggressive behavior when you see it and develop a strategy to deal with it. The term passive-aggressive originated with Army psychiatrist Colonel William Menninger during World War II. Now it's tossed around in the workplace as frequently as faxes.

The label refers to hostility in disguise. The passive-aggressive person promises to represent you at a board meeting and shows up unprepared with the wrong slides. The passive-aggressive person tosses out little barbs meant "as a joke." The passive-aggressive person agrees to work late one evening to get out the last-minute orders but then has a headache and has to go home. The passive-aggressive person "misunderstands" your directions about the proposal he didn't think the client needed anyway.

All of these are attempts to buck authority when the person doesn't have the courage to do so openly. Only when you identify the recurring behavior can you deal with it effectively. Once you understand that the attitude—not the "reasons" and excuses given in various situations—is the problem, then you can cope with it as with any other confrontation about attitude. Unfortunate "mishaps" surrounding the events are only symptoms, not the problem.

TIP 759: Examine the Payoffs in Continuing Conflict.

Psychologists have counseled parents for years that sometimes children misbehave because negative attention is better than no attention. The same can be said of adult conflict. Ask yourself what you or the other person has to gain for refusing to end a running conflict. Does a continual uproar in the department create excitement for the group? Does the conflict feed someone's ego? Does the conflict serve as someone's excuse for not getting a task done or done well? Once you know what the payoff is, you can decide if you can meet the need—ego gratification, excitement, entertainment, or success—in a less emotionally draining or disruptive way.

TIP 760: Assume a Resolution.

To a large extent, life is a self-fulfilling prophecy. We get what we expect. Expect that the problem or issue is solvable. Attack it with that mindset.

TIP 761: Determine the Most Productive Behavior: Either Swallow or Spit Out Conflict.

When conflict and the associated emotional upset surface, you have two choices. You can either suppress your frustration or initiate a feedback session to bring the issues out in the open. Some people can swallow their pride, their feelings, and their goals to work together successfully. If the situation is temporary, of little importance in the big scheme of life, or risky to their future, they may decide to avoid the conflict—to swallow it. Other people may choke on such an option.

Determine which option is most productive for you at the very beginning. Don't wait until you're ready to explode before moving to the second option of feedback and resolution. Know yourself. Act accordingly.

TIP 762: If You Decide to Resolve a Conflict, Make a Conscious Choice Whether You Will Accommodate, Compromise, Overpower, or Collaborate.

Accommodate others in the following situations:

- When the issue is important to them and relatively unimportant to you
- When you cannot win or are wrong
- When you want to bank a favor for later recall
- When you want to shift responsibility for the outcome to the other person
- When harmony is more important than the issue

Compromise with the other person's wants and plans:

- When the issue is important to both of you but not worth "fighting" to the bitter end
- When the situation is temporary and will lead to a quick fix for the immediate problem
- When you don't have time to haggle but you need to meet some of your goals

Overpower to get your way when:

- When the situation is an emergency and you have to act quickly
- When you have to play the part of "statesman" and enforce unpopular principles or take unpopular actions

Collaborate to resolve issues:

- When the relationship is long-term and the situation will be recurring
- When both goals are too important to compromise
- When you need buy-in from both people on the outcome

Don't let conflict set you out to sea without knowing the kind of boat you need to get back to shore. Make a conscious choice about how to come to terms with the conflict. Even if you decide to accommodate, you'll do so with a better frame of mind if you realize you have a choice and understand the trade-offs.

TIP 763: Don't Forgive Prematurely.

To err is human; to forgive, divine. Just don't confuse forgiveness with forced suppression. Some people dread open conflict so strongly that they'll do anything to avoid it—including trying to convince themselves that the matter is "no big deal." They smile, accept another's apology, or even tell themselves that no apology is necessary.

But the problem keeps gnawing at them. They can't forget it. Their hurt or anger continues to show up in different ways: by sabotaging the success of the other person's project, by talking behind that person's back, by withdrawing their approval from that person, by isolating that person. If you can't forget, don't forgive. Be willing to talk the problem through and get to a real resolution.

TIP 764: Set Clear Expectations.

Many conflicts are simply a result of unclear expectations. Managers set standards for employees but don't tell them about those standards. Employees draw up a wish list for their bosses, but don't tell their bosses what would make them happy. Customers take their business elsewhere without giving the seller a chance to change or improve service.

When you discover that unstated expectations are at the heart of a conflict, you can empathize with the other's viewpoint: "I know I never explicitly told you to do X, so I know you must feel taken by surprise." "I know we never had a formal agreement for you to do Y." "I clearly understand your confusion now, because the policy was never circulated to your department." Once you acknowledge those unstated expectations, the other person can save face and so can you.

Outline the expectations relating to any relationship—formal or social. It's difficult to live up to expectations you don't know about and easy to be disappointed when others fail to meet yours.

TIP 765: Establish the Relationship Rule.

Manager Melissa says to her counterpart in the next department, "Would you make sure these printouts get stapled together properly before they come to our department for processing?" Manager Kevin snaps, "No, I don't see that that's necessary. Our people don't have any more time than yours to collate and staple."

This is not a conflict over stapling printouts; it's a conflict over relationships.

Does Melissa have the authority to demand that Kevin do things to suit her? That's the real issue. If she can tell him to staple the printouts, she can tell him how to run other areas of his department that affect her. His impulsive comeback is a reaction to a rule of the relationship he doesn't agree to. Melissa would have done better to remember up front that she had no right to impose or to assume about the relationship. Until both people agree on the rules of their relationship—what can be expected, what is an imposition, what should be a request, and what can be demanded—they will continue to clash on various issues.

TIP 766: Confront Privately on Private Issues.

Discussing someone's shortcomings has no place in a staff meeting, in the hallway, or in front of a colleague or customer at any location. When there's an audience, people begin to play to the galleries. Ego takes over. Pride rears its head. What would have normally elicited a simple, "Oh, I'm sorry; my fault; I should have caught that" will turn into a battle of pride and put-downs when mentioned in public.

TIP 767: Move from "Study" to "Act."

When you don't know all the facts affecting a specific conflict, you may need to dwell on the problem: When does the problem occur? What is causing the problem? Why is A or B a problem at all? How is the problem affecting others? How much is the problem costing in time, effort, and money? But once all the information comes to the forefront, move to a solution-centered discussion. Devise alternatives. Identify methods. Make comparisons and contrasts. Evaluate the efforts or costs. Propose solutions. Avoid analysis paralysis. In short, move from "study" to "act."

TIP 768: Focus on the Goal Rather Than the Obstacle.

When conflict creeps in, both sides tend to lose sight of what they have in common—to maintain a relationship, the profitability of the business, the success of a project, the cohesiveness of the team, the winning of an award, the welfare of their family or friends. Take time out to focus on the goal rather than the obstacle to that goal.

TIP 769: Put the Issue of "Winning" or "Losing" Aside.

The concept of winning and losing comes from sports. Conflict is not a sport. Dismiss the idea from your mind and focus on meaningful decisions. Do I want to compromise my needs to get some of them met? Do I want to help all involved get our needs met? The only competition should be within yourself—to control your words and actions in such a way that you get what you need. The other person does not have to lose for you to win.

TIP 770: Create Alternatives.

Define together what success will look like to all the people involved. Then work backward. Can we change the deadline? Can we get more help? Can we expand or cut the budget? Can we change the specifications? Can we alter the process? Can we break things into more "doable" chunks? Can we get more people involved? Can we get fewer people involved? Can we reverse the steps required? Can we redefine the problem altogether? Can we use different criteria to judge the resolution?

Try brainstorming. Put everybody involved into a big room and withhold food until you come up with a resolution. Generate ideas as fast as possible. Piggyback each other's ideas. No evaluation. No questioning the ideas for clarification. No holds barred. Just think and record what's said. After you've generated all the ideas time will allow, go back and evaluate them one by one. Cross off the ones that don't meet your criteria and prioritize those left. Start with the alternative that looks the most promising and work your way down the list. The secret of conflict resolution is creativity. If you don't think creatively, consider turning the problem over to someone who does.

TIP 771: Determine What Happened, What You Have Concluded About What Happened, and What You Feel About What Happened.

If people start giving you facts, ask them to interpret those facts. What conclusions have they come to from those facts? If people start giving you opinions, ask what facts they are basing those opinions on. If people have difficulty articulating the facts and opinions, ask them for feelings. How do they *feel* about what has happened or about the situation. When people express strong feelings, paraphrase those feelings back to them to verify that you have understood and that those are their true feelings. Then ask them for the events or facts underlying those feelings.

The idea is to help yourself and others distinguish between what actually happened, what they have concluded about what happened, or what they feel about what happened. In the process, you'll often uncover hidden, invalid assumptions, wrong interpretations, and inaccurate information. You'll get closer and closer to seeing what needs to be changed or corrected.

TIP 772: Challenge a Power Play with Inattention.

Inattention is the least expensive, easiest to use, and fastest weapon used to control a power play. If you don't believe it, watch a waitress at the local restaurant or a flight attendant on your next airplane trip handle an obnoxious customer that way. Simply ignore a person's requests, threats, or demands.

TIP 773: Work with People's "Want tos" Along with Their "Do Its."

Bad attitudes. We recognize them when we see them, but they're hard to define. That's why a problem resolved does not always *feel* like a problem resolved. Only the action has changed, not the person's attitude. A little girl tottered and weaved as she tiptoed along a ledge high above a canyon ravine. Her father asked her to get down, but she continued her effort to walk the narrow ledge. Finally, her father reached up and physically pulled her off the dangerous ledge and set her back on the picnic bench beside him. She screwed her face into a pout, "In my heart, I'm still standing up there."

On the job, it goes like this: Vonda misses several staff meetings, and Barry, her boss, tells her how important it is that she be there regularly and participate in decisions. Vonda starts coming to the meetings, but she arrives late, leaves early, and sits in silence. Barry would do well to express disappointment in both the "do it" and the "want to."

An elderly patient in the dentist's office wisely pinpointed the same problem with the receptionist. The patient paused briefly at the receptionist's window and handed her the charge slip. "Would you please file this on my insurance as usual," she said and started to walk away.

"We don't normally file insurance," the receptionist answered rather haughtily.

"Yes, ma'am, you've always filed on my insurance."

"We don't normally do it. It's just a courtesy if we do it. We're not set up to do it."

"Well, I'd like you to do it again, please."

"I don't have your policy number."

"It surely is in my file because no one has asked me for it before. You must have a record somewhere."

"Do you know how much your deductible is?"

"No, I don't. But that's probably in my file also."

"I can't file your insurance unless you bring in proof of having met your deductible and your policy number. We don't normally file. It's not our policy to do so."

"Yes, but I'd like you to do it, as always."

"That's not normally our policy."

After another two or three rounds of this repetition, the elderly patient finally cut to the heart of the matter. "Let me understand this. You said you'd file it, but it wasn't your policy to do so. I'm getting the message that you don't *want* to but that if I *push* you really hard and insist, you will." The receptionist blushed and took the charge slip.

The problem was the "want to," not the "do it." When you understand that, you can choose an appropriate coping technique. Such problems will not be resolved until the attitude behind the action or inaction changes. Plan to deal with both in any conflict.

TIP 774: Stand on the Sidelines of Territorial Conflict.

If you're having difficulties with people because they feel territorial, respect their boundaries. If they own the turf, get off it immediately. Take your cue from lines like these: "We don't report to Mr. Big." "That's my decision, and I'll make it." "Those requests have to come through me." "You're talking about *my* budget." "Those are our accounts to maintain." Yes, territorial people are petty and they generate a lot of laughs from those watching, but they do have the final say. Grant their wishes and meet their ego needs. Stand aside and ask "permission."

TIP 775: Identify Who Is Playing Defense.

Tone and inflection in the English language can be subtle, yet pack a walloping difference. Take these examples: "What proof do you have?" can be a straightforward request for more explanation or a challenge, meaning you're making unfounded allegations. "I don't know what you're talking about" can mean "That's nonsense" or "I'm puzzled." "Earlier you said X . . .; now you're saying Y" can mean "I think you're lying" or can mean "I'm confused; please sort out the seeming contradiction so I can follow."

Such lines can escalate a conversation into arguments that go like this:

"Why did you get so upset? All I said was blah, blah, blah."

"Yes, but what you meant was really blah, blah, blah."

"No, I didn't. All I said was blah, blah, blah."

Somebody is hiding behind the words as if the tone didn't matter. Tone, mood, and attitude all convey meaning.

The difficulty is deciding who is being defensive. Who is "reading into" the conversation. If you're the one on the defensive, you're likely to hear double meanings in straightforward requests and statements. If the other person is on the defensive, he or she will let the defensive tone creep in and then deny it when challenged.

Instead of sorting out the problem by starting with the words, start with the attitude. Decide who has the defensive attitude, and then determine the meaning of the words. It's a remarkably reliable system.

TIP 776: Avoid Others' Vulnerabilities.

We all have sore spots. Ask yourself where you feel the most insecure, where you see a weakness in yourself, what track record you want to keep hidden from the world. Those are the bruises that you want others to stay away from. Others have them too, and punching those sore spots unleashes emotions that can prevent resolution altogether. Examples: "George, I think this is just another example of where that college degree you didn't finish would have helped you out." "Karen, you're reacting like a JAP again. You may be your daddy's Jewish American Princess, but in the office you've got to stand in line just like everybody else." With one of those comments, you'll be dealing with explosives from the past as well as those from the future.

TIP 777: Discard the Old Chant,
"Sticks and Stones . . ."

Since children, we've heard the axiom, "Sticks and stones may break my bones but names will never hurt me." Our parents taught us the chant as a defense mechanism for use when some neighborhood bully overpowered us with words. It might have worked as children, but not as adults. Words do damage relationships forever. The most painful memories many of us have involve what someone said to us. "I lost control" is no excuse. The tongue as a weapon can destroy a reputation, a career, or a person.

TIP 778: Prefer Statements to Questions During Conflict.

By the time you decide to discuss a conflict openly, trust has usually fallen and tensions have risen. Questions will be suspect from either side. Why? Because most will contain accusations. "Why did you not tell me you wanted these by Friday?" "How did you think we could spend that kind of money on this engineering project?" Granted, they may be informational questions—but they won't sound like it when there's tension and resentment in the air.

Prefer to make statements about what you feel or think. "I would have appreciated advance notice that these items were needed by Friday." Or: "I think we can get this project done on a lot smaller budget." Ask questions only when you really are trying to gather information: "Is the deadline Thursday or Friday?" "Do you know if we have budget to use outside help?"

A statement usually generates a response—either agreement or disagreement. An accusing question usually generates an argument.

TIP 779: Use the Three Ds to Structure Your Resolution.

Describe. Discuss. Decide. Describe what's happening. Discuss the feelings or other ramifications of what's happening. Decide what to do about it.

Describe: "Letters are going out of this department with typos and grammatical errors."

Discuss: "As a result, our communication is creating a poor impression with our clients. If we're careless with our writing, clients may think we're careless with our analysis of their needs. Some of the grammatical errors even lead to clarity problems. It's embarrassing to me when a customer calls to point out careless errors like our misspelling a name."

Decide: "I think we need to make it a rule that at least two people proofread everything that goes outside the company. Do you have other or better suggestions?"

Describe. Discuss. Decide. That format focuses on the issues and a resolution without allowing room for sidetracking.

TIP 780: Use Thomas Gordon's Formula: "When You . . . , I Feel . . . , Because . . ."

Thomas Gordon, writing back in the late 1970s, introduced the concept of sending "I" messages. Example: "I feel angry when you forget to call when you're going to be late because I worry and can't get to sleep." He set up this formula:

"When you X, I feel Y, because Z."

This pattern includes all the variables—real and verifiable. X has to be an observable behavior. Y has to be a feeling, not an opinion. Z has to be an observable consequence.

Here's an improperly phrased statement that will bring argument: "When you act like some prima donna, I feel you don't care whether this company turns a profit or not because you get your commission no matter what the profit margin on what you told the customer we'd do." Such a comment won't work. "Acting like a prima donna" is a subjective statement. "I feel you don't care . . ." is an opinion, not a real feeling.

Here's the same sentiment expressed in a way that both parties can deal with: "When you fail to ask me about special discounts you want to offer your customers, I feel angry because we lose money on anything sold more than 20 percent below the retail price." That's a specific behavior, a true feeling, and verifiable consequence.

Example: "When you bring up my mistakes during a staff meeting, other people begin to blame me for things I have no control over. I feel helpless to defend myself or explain. As a result, they disregard my authority on the shop floor."

Example: "When you miss your deadline with the numbers on Friday, I can't close out my books and forward the final reports to Denver. And when they don't get the report by Monday morning, they can't issue checks to our suppliers, who add an interest charge on late payments. I feel really angry that I get grief from the Denver people for a delay caused by you."

Such a structure (1) describes the action, not labels it, (2) lets the other person know the consequences of the action, and (3) brings the related emotion out in the open. The resulting discussion will most likely, then, focus on the issue rather than personalities.

TIP 781: Describe; Don't Label.

People can respond to statements like "Your status reports are missing key information." They can't respond to "You're evasive." Descriptive: "You have taken off three Mondays in a row during a crucial project." Labeling: "You are lazy and inconsiderate of your coworkers." Specific information can be verified or refuted; labels and value judgments cannot.

TIP 782: Don't Use the Phrases "You'll Have to . . . ," "You Must . . . ," "You Should . . . ," or "You Ought to . . ."

People don't like to be told they *must* do anything. Think how perturbed you become when you hear one of these: "You'll have to check out at the next register." "You'll have to complete the XYZ form." "You'll have to get approval from Joe." "You'll have to move that." Try instead, "Would you please. . . ."

The same is true of *must, ought to, should.* Delete them from your conflict discussions.

TIP 783: Offer the Other Person Face-Saving Comments.

Examples: "Your mistake is understandable. The map is confusing. Several people have gotten lost at that point." "The details are complex. Most people don't realize how overwhelming so much information can be to sort through. I think you've made excellent progress so far." "Well, I can understand how you'd be upset. It's irritating when people don't let you know what's going on." If you expect the other person to take your side and come to agreement, make it easy on his or her pride.

TIP 784: Let the Other Person Exercise Options.

People must maintain some sense of power. That power may come from a strong self-esteem, from the freedom of choice about how and when a job gets done, from control over the success or failure of a project, from freedom to interact or not interact with others. Be cautious of taking away all the other person's choices. Otherwise, people will figure out a way to sabotage your project or will end the relationship altogether. Provide others opportunities to choose and control.

TIP 785: Shun Sarcasm.

Sarcasm humiliates people. "Thanks a lot. That was a big help—to have these figures two days after the report has been turned in." "Next time I'm having a problem, I'll be sure to call—if I want to be chewed out." "I appreciate your ordering lunch for me while I was in the meeting. My wife makes all the decisions at home; why shouldn't you take over the responsibility here?" Nasty no-nos.

TIP 786: Leave Exaggerations for TV Sitcoms.

When you exaggerate, the other person will always ignore the bigger issue and prove your exaggeration incorrect. You'll wind up arguing about the misstatement rather than the issue. Examples: "They never let us know when they're going to take the computers down." "These overnight-express shipping charges are putting us in the poorhouse." "You always find fault with every suggestion." These statements will generate responses like: "Yes, they do notify us. They sent out a memo last Tuesday that we'd be down two hours." "I don't think 68 dollars a month for shipping is putting us in the poorhouse." "Wrong. I don't find fault. I liked your suggestion about the flextime." With statements like these, you'll find yourself off the subject and onto defending the exaggeration.

TIP 787: Don't Act Incredulous.

The incredulous person greets the other person with a quizzical look of disbelief and shock at the "stupidity" of what has happened. Examples: "And you thought a phone call would solve the problem?" "So you left the car in the middle of the driveway so everybody would have to pull around it or hit it?" "Why in the world would you believe that?" "What makes you think that would work?"

Most people can tolerate disagreement when they have to, but most snap when it comes to humiliation. The amused grin, the mocking raised eyebrows, the outright laughter cut a person to the quick—even those who have right on their side.

TIP 788: Don't "Dismiss" People.

This "mood" pervades the atmosphere of conflict when one person makes it clear that talk will no longer help—that the details "no longer matter" and "won't change things," that the "mess" has gone too far for you to bother correcting, that what you're asking is totally out of the question and should not even be entertained with a discussion. Such a "dismissal" can be conveyed through words, gestures, or body language. We all know it when we see it.

TIP 789: Don't Question Someone's Integrity.

People can handle a comment like, "You should have submitted the report last week with the information available to you at the time." They can't handle:

"You were trying to put one over on us, weren't you? That's why you withheld the accident report. Did you think you could get away with that indefinitely?" A stab at their integrity brings a denial and a torrent of anger.

TIP 790: Avoid Reruns.

TV reruns can make a rainy Saturday afternoon's entertainment, but stay with current issues during bouts of conflict. Yes, what has happened in the past colors what happens in the future, but to discuss all the details from past run-ins gets you nowhere. Memories are fallible. The context of earlier problems also becomes muddled. Stay current.

TIP 791: Keep to One Issue.

Don't dump a decade's gripes into one discussion or you'll never get to the bottom of the current issue. Past details and experiences, while possibly relevant to why one or the other person feels or believes a certain way, will only confuse the issue. Response is next to impossible. You simply can't remember and process all that's being said. One discussion, one issue.

TIP 792: Forget Verbal Ultimatums.

Communicating to understand differs from communicating to control. Ultimatums hinge on manipulation and control. "If I do not hear from you by two o'clock this afternoon, I will cancel the extension on the contract." When someone communicates with an intention to control, threaten, hurt, or produce guilt in the other person, that person has missed the purpose of communication. The person may succeed in controlling but will fail in building understanding and repairing the relationship. Resentment will root out any good that may come from the resolution.

TIP 793: Ask for What You Want from the People Who Can Give It.

People complain to coworkers "I wish my boss would let us have an occasional party around here." "I wish my husband would get this car fixed." "I wish that receptionist would get my name right." "I wish the people who use this refrigerator to store their lunches would clean it out occasionally." But they never get around to telling the person who can do something about the situation.

Years ago when I worked on a military base in Okinawa, I reported to a GS-16 civilian boss who enjoyed having his comrades drop by to visit. During these social chats, he would frequently leave the door open between our offices while he and the friend swapped stories and escapades. Embarrassed at overhearing the conversations, I continued to complain—at home, not to the boss. Finally, my husband called the boss and calmly explained that such conversations embarrassed me and asked the boss to close the door during these visits. Expecting rather cool treatment the next morning and angry at my husband for taking such "confrontational" action without telling me, I had a surprise waiting. The boss stepped into my office, apologized for the offensive language and stories, and began to close the door during such visits. No grudges. No repercussions. No problem. And all just for the asking.

People complain, but they seldom state what they want to the person involved. They talk behind their backs, pout, threaten, hint, and hope. But they don't ask. Try stating exactly how you feel about a situation directly to the person or people involved and ask them to make a change. You might be surprised how easy it is to get what you want.

TIP 794: Don't Assume the Other Person Understands Your Point of View.

No matter if you think the issues and repercussions of someone's action are obvious, state them. Don't assume. What is obvious to you is not necessarily obvious to the other person.

TIP 795: Listen Until You Experience the Other Side of an Issue.

At a Boulder, Colorado, church one of the women had the most irritable dispositions I'd ever encountered. In addition to having a long face and sad eyes, she complained about the kids "making noise" in the nursery, about the money "wasted on the teenagers' programs," about the time spent on marital counseling that could be "better spent on the needy." Then one day she mentioned a past tragedy in her life. When she was born, her mother died. As a result, she had projected onto other parents and children all of her bitterness about not having a mother.

Her complaining became understandable to me.

Recently, we called a technician to take a look at an air-conditioner at home. When I came in from work that evening, I saw his mess. Rusty-looking splatters of water covered the kitchen cabinets, appliances, and floor. Obviously, he hadn't cleaned up after himself, I decided. I was perturbed as I scrubbed up the rusty mess. But when he returned the next day to finish the repair job on the air-conditioner, he explained. "Sorry, I left such a mess yesterday. Just as I was about to leave I noticed that you had a leak from some busted plumbing. The spillovers in the attic were just about to overflow and come down through your kitchen ceiling. So I rummaged around and found a bucket and tried to empty as much water off as I could. Saved your ceiling at least." My anger melted.

Listen to understand and experience the other side of an issue.

TIP 796: State the Real Reasons or Effects, Not Just Logical Ones.

People sometimes find themselves off base in their discussion because they give a less-than-honest reason and consequence of a problem.

Such was the case with an acquaintance of mine, Tom, who assumed a new position as training director for a large organization. He immediately found himself embroiled in a conflict with the vice president of operations, who had asked for a time-management course for his staff. The VP kept asking Tom when he intended to contact the outside vendor used for such classes and get a commitment on the date. Tom explained that he had been hesitant to set the date because the vendor had increased prices and was now "too expensive." The VP again insisted that he'd been pleased with other classes conducted by that vendor and wanted to move ahead. Tom countered that he didn't want to spend more money in his budget than was necessary for a quality course. The VP reluctantly agreed to wait a little longer while Tom solicited bids.

But when the bids came in, the VP and Tom could not agree on their criteria for decision. Tom's real reason for the foot dragging finally surfaced; he felt competitive toward the earlier successful vendor and wanted to develop the class himself. When he instead cited reasons such as "increased prices," "wasted budget," and "equal quality," they found their discussions off track. In desperation, they compromised on a new outside vendor. And in the process, they created extra work for themselves and neither felt their decision was the best—all because Tom substituted a "good" reason for the real reason. Had he simply told the VP up front that he, himself, wanted to develop and teach the course, the VP may have agreed to give him a shot. In either case, they both could have saved a lot of unnecessary time with the real reason on the table.

TIP 797: Let the Other Person Vent Emotions Before You Try to Come to Resolution.

Suggestions or concessions offered when someone is yelling sound less attractive than when the person becomes quiet and rational again. People cannot resolve anything when one or both are crying, cursing, or yelling.

Give the other person time to get the emotions out. Total silence will help. Whether you're on the phone or standing face to face, keep your face neutral and be silent. Eventually, the other person will run down and say something like "Are you still there?" (if you're on the phone) or "Do you understand what I'm saying?" (if you're face to face). When they stop their tirade, you can begin the discussion again.

TIP 798: Own Your Own Feelings.

Accusations frequently begin with "You make me feel _____." Fill in the blank with angry, inadequate, dumb, useless, ridiculous. Think about the meaning of such a line: One individual is saying the other person has control over his or her emotions. The other person will then usually counter with, "It's not my fault that you feel _____." The conversation then degenerates into whose fault it is.

Prefer to make statements that show you have control and choice in the matter and at least center on the problem rather than who's to blame. Example: "I feel stupid when you remind me over and over of a deadline. I'd prefer that you state the deadline once and then drop it." Only you can decide how you feel. Choose differently. Better yet: "I don't like you to remind me over and over of deadlines. Once is sufficient."

TIP 799: Make Sure Your Own Emotions Are Genuine and Appropriate.

Some people have learned to manipulate others by crying, yelling, or cursing. When they explode, people jump. It's a learned behavior that can be unlearned. Use this opportunity to take your own emotional temperature with the following checklist:

- How often do you "blow up"?
- When you get upset, can you pinpoint the cause, or do you just feel irritated at the world?
- Do you react in proportion to the problem?
- Who receives the brunt of your emotion—the person causing the problem, a scapegoat, or the nearest person to you at the time of impact?
- Do you let it "blow over" quickly, or do you pout or hold a grudge?
- Do you rant privately or publicly?
- Do you humiliate other people and generate animosity for yourself?
- Do you think before you react, or react and then think?

The answers to these questions should give you a good handle on whether you control your emotions or whether your emotions control you. More important, the answers may pinpoint the root of ongoing conflicts.

TIP 800: Define the Areas of Agreement or Disagreement.

Good negotiators understand success: They start on the easy issues and move to the more difficult points. Likewise, when discussing a conflict, begin by confirming the areas of agreement. That might mean confirming undisputed facts or shared goals for the outcome. Finding that you do agree on some issues gives momentum to take you through the harder issues.

Example: "Mandy, as I see it, we both think the employee survey is a good idea. And we agree that the wording of each question is important and will drastically affect the way our people will answer the questions. And we're together in wanting the results tabulated by December 1, correct? Okay, then our main differences involve whether we should pay a psychologist to help construct the survey and how long the survey should be." The sum total is three down, two to go. Encouraging.

TIP 801: Don't Interrupt the Other Person, and Don't Let the Other Person Interrupt You.

Some people think they're saving time by interrupting you in a recitation of the details when they already know them. Don't permit such interruptions: "Margie, I want to finish explaining what I consider to be the problem." Say it in a matter-of-fact tone and keep talking. This assertiveness establishes you as a person with a right to be heard. And remember if you're the person doing the interrupting, the issue is not time, nor even "your version." The goal is to hear both versions of an event or situation, to piece the truth together, and to sort out the feelings.

TIP 802: Take Turns for Airtime.

For all the griping and complaining from drivers ensnarled in traffic or those people taking mass transit, most would agree that the time involved is their own—at least mentally. It is uninterrupted time for listening to radio, reading, talking, or thinking.

When involved in a conflict, try the same principle. Give each other uninterrupted time to talk, say five or ten minutes, and then take turns. You'll have the best results if one person agrees to paraphrase what the other says to show that he or she listened. Only after the first person "signs off" that the other person has heard correctly does the second person get a turn to talk.

The process has these four benefits: (1) It stops arguments because the other person loses immediacy—he or she can't interrupt impulsively with a counterattack or denial. (2) The other person has to listen. (3) The plan builds in cool-off periods for emotions. (4) It helps people summarize and focus on the most important comments and issues because they can't remember the entire five-minute talk verbatim.

TIP 803: Discuss a Problem Sitting Down.

When both people are seated, they'll be less likely to use intimidating body language. They can't "tower" over the other, invade another's space, stomp across the room flailing their arms, or make a dramatic exit.

TIP 804: Eliminate Argumentative Words and Phrases.

Examples: "That's not true." "You're wrong." "You're confused." "You don't know what you're talking about." Commands are equally abrasive: "Stop interrupting me." "Hold on a minute." "Leave it alone."

Any of these sentiments can be expressed in a more acceptable, less abrasive way: "My facts don't agree with those." "I disagree." "There's some confusion here." "There are some issues you may not be aware of." "Please let me finish what I started to say." "Let's wait a moment." "I'd rather handle this myself." Avoid "fighting" words unless you want to fight.

TIP 805: Do Something Physical to Break the Spell.

If your discussions grow too tense, stand up, walk around, shuffle through your notes, get a drink of water, or glance out the window. Just don't use the movement to rant and rave. Instead, do something to break emotional contact and give yourself and the other person time to identify better coping techniques.

TIP 806: Don't Use Silence to Provoke.

Think of silence as a stabilizer, not a weapon. Don't use it as a provocative "action." If the other person begins to comment on your silence, it's time to speak. Lead into a meaningful discussion with something like, "I was trying to make sure I caught everything you were saying." If the other person has not been yelling or abusive and if you have simply withdrawn into silence to think, say so: "Yes, I have been quiet the last couple of days. I'm trying to figure out how to solve our differences." If you have used silence appropriately, it will calm people, not punish or provoke.

TIP 807: Remember That Only the Dead Keep Confidences.

Keep in mind that whatever happens during your conflict resolution, others will eventually know. People talk, and what they say will be their version of the truth. If they have a character weakness, they will control the way others interpret "the facts" by what details they choose to tell and which they omit. Face the frustration that two versions of "what happened" will circulate.

TIP 808: Realize That Two Sides Can Be Right.

People bring different backgrounds, values, roles, experiences, and goals to the workplace. All differences cannot be reconciled. Policy A may be bad for Joe and good for Manuel. Alton may define success as plenty of time off the job while Katherine may define success as a fat paycheck. Neither opinion—or goal—is necessarily wrong. Both may be very right. It's a fact of life difficult to accept but necessary to one's sanity.

TIP 809: Pick Your Fights.

You can't take on the world. Decide which conflicts are worth the effort to resolve. You are known by the opponents you have and friends you win.

17

Mediating Others' Conflicts Without Getting Caught in the Line of Fire

Ego, not content, causes the most communication standoffs. Contrary to what is commonly believed, most disagreements are caused not by conflict over what people need but how they actually talk and act about those needs.
—CARMINE DE LA ROSA

Hear the other side. —Latin proverb

In a heated argument we are apt to lose sight of the truth. —Latin proverb

The difference between discussing and arguing is whether the participants are using facts or opinions. —PHILIP B. CROSBY

Nothing makes an argument so one-sided as telling about it. —no attribution

Effective cooperation between the parties is all but impossible if each plays to the gallery. —ROGER FISHER and WILLIAM URY

You cannot sit on the fence and overlook the battleground without getting mud splashed on you from time to time. Those around you will have a conflict of goals, needs, values, or personalities. Having some connection or responsibility to both, you'll feel the need to intervene and do your part to mend relationships between coworkers or friends. If you handle the chore with skill, you can contain the conflict. If you handle it poorly, the situation may escalate to such an extent that you yourself become the enemy of both. The following guidelines will help keep you from falling off the fence.

TIP 810: Intervene Only When Asked; Proceed with Caution.

And even then, think twice. Most conflicts are best handled by the two people involved unless their difficulty affects the atmosphere or productivity of others. When you intervene needlessly, you may find yourself in the thankless position of giving it your best shot and ending up with both people angry at you.

TIP 811: Avoid "Taking Sides" and Talking the Opposition Over to the Other Viewpoint.

Work with both individuals from the very beginning. You may decide to meet with both people together or separately. If you decide to meet with each separately, be sure that both understand that what they share with you may *not* necessarily be withheld from the other person. You will have to use information from one person to verify and clarify with the other. If you don't warn them up front, they may lose confidence in your impartiality and think you are breaking their confidences.

TIP 812: Play the Role of Reporter; Go for the Five Ws.

Try to discover all the facts in a situation. Ask: who, what, where, why, when, how, how much? You can only begin to make sense of someone else's conflict when armed with the unbiased versions of events and circumstances. An even better approach than asking the two people involved is to unobtrusively ask "innocent bystanders" about the issues. Be careful, of course, that you don't just collect the data that was passed on to them from the other people directly involved. Probe for what they know or have observed firsthand. Identify facts, assumptions, assertions, and feelings. They all count.

TIP 813: Listen to Each Person's Criticism of the Other.

Why? Because each pile of criticism contains at least a grain of truth. Even if the whole of it misses the mark, you'll gain insights to follow up and examine more closely. When listening to the complaints of each, however, make sure that you remain neutral and do not let your body language convey that you agree with these criticisms. With only a nod, you may be surprised later to discover that one or the other of the two people "claims" you as their ally for having "agreed" with their recounting and charges.

TIP 814: Pass Along Complimentary Things Each Person Has Said or Believed About the Other in the Past and Express Your Confidence in Their Willingness to Come to a Resolution.

If you can pass on complimentary remarks from the current discussions with each person, do so. If not, you may have to dig into the past to find these gems. "Jill, Martin does respect your work. If you recall, last summer he asked to be assigned to your team on the soft drink campaign for the radio ads." Or: "Gloria agrees that you've always been fair in dealings with her, that you've never tried to force her to travel on projects that she felt another staff member could handle. She appreciates your sensitivity on that issue."

The purpose of passing on such comments is to help people recall their past good relationship, if there has been one. Sharing positive remarks adds credence to other things the person says. If someone is honest and willing to admit or confirm the good, chances are they're honest—as they see it—about the problem.

TIP 815: Restate Common Goals—Again and Again.

Focus on their common goals. Examples: "Joel, Marie, both of you want to see this client go to the proposal stage. You both have creative ideas to contribute about how we might analyze the client's financial systems. Both of you want to protect the client's privacy and both of you want to make the sale." Or: "Doug, you are concerned with cutting costs this quarter. Jerry, you have the same interest." They need constant reminders of where they're going—the finish line.

TIP 816: Point Out Where You Believe Both Have Miscommunicated in the Past.

You may decide to call both people together at this point, if you've not already done so. After all your searching and probing into the problem, share your conclusions. Be straightforward and honest. Point out invalid assumptions, conversations with double meanings, and perceived intentions, along with your judgments and labels on those intentions. This will be the toughest part of your task as mediator.

TIP 817: Ask Both People to Reverse Roles.

If you're not sure both people fully understand and appreciate the viewpoints and feelings of the other, lead them to reverse roles. Paint the picture for them from the other person's point of view and ask them to explain how they would feel in a similar situation. If they "don't get it," you may actually ask them to role-play the events with you. Repeat earlier conversations of the conflict and ask the other person to respond in the opposition's shoes. At the least, ask each person to paraphrase to you how he or she thinks the other views things and how he or she feels about those events or circumstances.

TIP 818: Advocate "No-Fault" Resolution.

When a third party is involved, such as yourself, the people in conflict have an added investment in maintaining their self-esteem. It's bad enough to admit error or fault to one person; it's doubly difficult to admit it to two people. Therefore, take every precaution to downplay any effort to affix blame.

Say it loudly, clearly, and frequently: "Conflict is inevitable. No one has to be at fault. Conflict just is. Let's focus on working things out." And then make sure your phrasing supports that premise. Avoid questions like "Then what caused/made you think that . . ." "So you were only responding to her comment about . . ." "So if John hadn't done X, then Mary wouldn't have done Y." Forget cause and effect for purposes of mediation.

TIP 819: Summarize the Needs and Goals of Both.

This step is particularly important if the mediation has taken several days or even weeks. Make sure both people know without a doubt what both of them want out of the situation or relationship.

TIP 820: Ask Those Involved to Suggest Resolutions.

If you suggest the resolution, it will be perceived as "yours," not "theirs." After clarifying the facts, identifying the misunderstandings, summarizing each person's needs, and reminding both of their goals, ask them for suggestions to resolve their differences. If necessary, reiterate their mutual criteria for coming to a resolution. As suggestions meet the criteria, accept them, record them, and ask for reaction from the other person. Accept. Check for agreement. Accept. Check for agreement.

TIP 821: Lead Them to Select the Solution That Best Meets the Needs of Both.

Your presence ensures that one person does not overpower the other. Your job as an impartial mediator who cares about both individuals is to see that the solution is acceptable to both, not a "win" for one and a "withdrawal" for the other.

TIP 822: Help Both to Keep the Lines of Communication Open.

Look over their shoulders occasionally to make sure they are still talking and interacting from day to day. Create conversations with them. Pass on "good news" from one to the other. If you've been successful in helping them through the crisis, they'll rely on you again and again. And you'll have the satisfaction of knowing you've deactivated a productivity problem and kept one more relationship intact.

18

Responding to Insults, Boasting, Insensitivity, Gossip, and Other Goofs Hurled at You

The real art of conversation is not only to say the right thing in the right place but to leave unsaid the wrong thing at the tempting moment. —DOROTHY NEVILL

The only graceful way to accept an insult is to ignore it; if you can't ignore it, top it; if you can't top it, laugh at it; if you can't laugh at it, it's probably deserved. —RUSSELL LYNES

There are times when silence has the loudest voice. —LEROY BROWNLOW

Wit should be used as a shield for defense rather than as a sword to wound others. —THOMAS FULLER

A closed mouth gathers no feet. —Kansas State *Collegian*

No matter how limited your vocabulary is, it's big enough to let you say something you'll later regret. —no attribution

Words can make a deeper scar than silence can ever heal. —no attribution

Some people habitually let anything that flows through their mind roll out their mouth. Others insult and offend with more forethought. Whichever the case, having an appropriate deflecting wit can shield us from some of the pain. But what happens when wit won't turn off the flow with those in the workplace? Try some of the following techniques for insulating yourself from the hurt or humiliation.

TIP 823: Avoid People Who Exhibit a "Put-Down" Demeanor and Manner.

A former professor acquaintance of mine has an air about him that causes people to slink away from him at cocktail parties as though they'd been slapped. Joe wears an amused grin, a slightly raised eyebrow, and a bored expression. Correspondingly, he uses a put-down tone when he speaks, offers silence when a response is expected, and gets sarcastic when straightforwardness would be appropriate. He sits on a condescending perch when equality would more accurately describe his relationship to those around him. In short, Joe's not a warm guy. If at all possible, minimize your contact with those people who put others down by both their demeanor and manner.

TIP 824: Pinpoint Others' Motivations for a Put-Down.

Some people have grown up in such a hostile environment that they don't recognize their irritable, hostile disposition. Their background was chock-full of daily fights: "Get out of the bathroom, will you?" "Turn down that TV, you idiot!" "Even someone as dim-witted as you should be able to add." This hostility and the resulting self-protective thinking follow them into adulthood.

Others put people down because they're miserable and want everybody else to join them in their sad state. We even have a saying about them: misery loves company.

Some people pounce on traits or weaknesses in those around them because they're aware of the same weaknesses in their own performance or life. For example, they hate disorganization in themselves, so they notice and gripe when they see it in other people. Still others put people down in an effort to build up their own egos.

If you can make a game of guessing the motivation behind those who habitually insult you, you may be able to take their barbs with less difficulty.

TIP 825: Identify Put-Downs Meant as a Test of Ego-Strength.

Some people make disparaging remarks in the workplace as a test of their coworker's ability to "take it." If the other person can top the put-down, or at least laugh at the one hurled at him, he passes the test. The coworker's ability to laugh at his own expense conveys a healthy self-esteem. So others respect him also.

With these people, you lose if you play the part of victim. If others observe that verbal barbs offered in "good-natured" fun ruffle your feathers, they smell blood. They begin to see you as a victim. And victims soon fall prey to others' attacks. At best, the victim just gets dropped out of the game. People ignore victims. If you're new to the group, identify yourself with players rather than with victims. If you want to pass the newcomer test and be admitted to the club, demonstrate that you're able to laugh at your own foibles.

TIP 826: Buy Thinking Time When Insulted.

For lessons, watch old TV westerns: The insulted cowboy slowly glances up from the card table, plays his ace, then slowly pushes away from his comrades and strolls up to the bar where the bad guy who insulted him sits. The move could take a good thirty seconds.

You can take a big breath and a long glance to buy a few seconds. Playing with props is always good for another five seconds—taking off or putting on your glasses, finishing your drink, turning off or on the computer, restacking your paperwork and pushing it aside. Just a few seconds is all you need to double-check the words, the tone, and the intention, and choose how you want to respond.

TIP 827: Ignore "Baiting" Comments.

Recognize them for what they are and refuse to play the game. With a look or a matter-of-fact tone, state that you are aware of the baiting game: "I won't stoop to responding in kind." "I don't get involved in shouting matches." "Your outbursts will not change my decision." "That's your opinion." "You're entitled to your feelings." "That may be your perception." "We certainly don't agree. But then that's not a must, thank goodness." "That was a barb for sure." "Don't you ever tire of that?" "I really don't have time to get into it with you." "I have my view, and you have yours." "Those are the facts as you see them, I guess." "You must be having a bad day." "Hmmm." Whatever you do, don't bite. You are "letting them get away with it" only when you succumb to letting other people make you lose control. When you don't bite, they *don't* "get away with it."

TIP 828: Tell the Other Person the "Insult Tactic" Doesn't Work with You.

When you think someone is yelling, cursing, or otherwise abusing you simply to get you to change your mind about something, say so. "Jeff, yelling and exploding at me won't work. I understand you're angry that you have to wait another couple of days, but those tactics don't work with me."

TIP 829: Use Body Language to End the Insulting Conversation.

Look bored. Yawn. Wave the person away with a flip of your hand. Continue your work or make an exit. Break eye contact. Your body should say, "I don't have time for such nonsense. Stop it."

TIP 830: Change the Subject.

When the conversation grows uncomfortable, simply change the subject. No explanation or transition is necessary.

TIP 831: Clarify Rather Than Counterattack When the Other Person Jumps the Gun.

A friendly competitor phoned me one day to say that she felt the need to write and publish a book to establish her authority as a consultant. She wanted to ask my advice about taking the steps involved. After I'd spent several minutes with her on the phone giving her the requested information, she asked me about literary agents.

"You really need agents," I said. "They can save you a lot of time in selling your manuscript. I work with two different agents, in fact, because they specialize."

"Would you mind sharing the name and phone number of one with me?" she asked.

I gave her the name of the agent who places my business books, and then said, "The other agency may not be interested in your book idea because they primarily handle TV and movie stars and other celebrity types, so—"

"So which are you?" she cut me off.

Taken aback at the sarcastic insult, I finally continued my interrupted sentence, ". . . so if you're a business-book author, as I am, you don't get as much attention as the movie stars."

I could tell she regretted her insult immediately; obviously, she was no longer in a position to ask for additional information from me—nor was I in the mood to give it.

But I had clarified rather than counterattacked. As a result of her quick-witted insulting retort, she left the encounter looking rather foolish. In fact, embarrassed; she still ducks her head when we meet.

TIP 832: Wear the Remark.

Try going along with the other person's comment. Such a response drains all the fun.

INSULTER: You took about twice as long as most people to do this report. Were you aware of that?

YOU: It's really closer to three times as long.

INSULTER: So did you realize we were all waiting on the information?

YOU: Yes, I knew it.

INSULTER: So what are you going to do to speed up the process next month?

YOU: I don't think I'll change a thing. It worked out just fine for me this way. I think I'll just try to see if I can set a new record for delivery time since I'm already so close.

TIP 833: Create Inside Humor.

A shared joke or amusement builds intimacy. Try to find something both of you have in common and develop a running joke about it—your lengthy staff meetings, the cafeteria pizza, customer Brown's absentmindedness. Try anything to give you a shared laugh. It's the same phenomenon of "our song" between lovers.

TIP 834: Use Self-Disparaging Humor.

A telemarketer at a major credit card company recently took an insult when she called to verify a prospect's receipt of his card: The prospect responded, "I do *not* want the card. What do I have to do to make that clear—tattoo it on your butt?"

The telemarketer started to laugh.

The prospect yelled, "What's so funny?"

She said, "Sir, if you only knew how big my butt is . . . it'd take all day."

The guy burst out laughing with her.

Various studies show that those who are credible and competent actually enhance their images with others when they use self-deprecating comments. Often, the most successful comedians are those who poke fun at themselves: the bald-headed man who tells "hairless" jokes, the obese lady who relates her tendencies to eat the whole pie, the Jewish mother who talks about forcing the mail carrier to eat her chicken soup. To others around them, these coworkers appear to be witty, generous, and likable. If you have a strong ego and are generally competent in your job, laugh at yourself and invite others to join you.

TIP 835: Write Down the Insult or Hostile Remark.

> Borrow the idea from your customer-service hassles. When hotel employees are discourteous or make poor judgment calls, you can always ask their names. They'll know you intend to write a letter to their supervisor. You can use the same idea with colleagues. When they make derogatory remarks, make a point to write them down in their presence—even asking them to repeat the remarks so you can record them correctly. If they ask why, make some flippant comment like: "They're a new chapter in my book." "I keep score." "I'm going to send them off for a contest." Whatever the remark, they'll immediately begin to see visions of HR people swarming around their desk. People think hard before "going on record" with insults.

TIP 836: Respond Only to the Surface Meaning and Words.

> Pretend you didn't even "get it." Ignore the tone and respond only to the words.
>
> *Insult:* "You're such an innocent. How do you think we win these contracts—by saying 'pretty please'?"
>
> *Response:* "I don't know for sure what customers would attribute our winning to—low price or quality products, I'd guess."
>
> *Insult:* "You act like this is your second month at work—where was your head during the last staff meeting when this was discussed?"
>
> *Response:* "That was probably brought up when I had to take that extended phone call."
>
> *Insult:* "My gosh—did you call every restaurant in the yellow pages to find a place this dumpy for Sam's retirement luncheon?"
>
> *Response:* "Actually, I called only three."
>
> *Insult:* "You're not the only person in this office who uses this lunchroom, you know."
>
> *Response:* "Oh, I thought I was."

TIP 837: Twist the Assumptions.

> That is, when the insult implies an assumption for its point, exchange the assumption for one of your own.
>
> *Insult:* "At this rate, the project is going to take all day."
>
> *Response:* "Did you intend to work even slower?"

Insult: "I can't read these confusing reports."

Response: "Should I help you with the terminology—which acronyms don't you understand?"

Insult: "Do you think we can go back to management and get more money just 'cuz Simon says?"

Response: "I never thought of that. Do you really want to try to play games with them?"

TIP 838: Prepare a Comeback.

The comeback can be serious, humorous, or insulting in return. The choice is yours, depending on what you want as an outcome. If you want to keep the relationship intact and want the barbs to end, be serious in your response. If you want to prove that you can take it and ruffle some feathers yourself, try light humor. If you want to kill the adversary and embroil yourself in an ongoing battle, go for the brutal barb.

Timing and tone may make the difference in each case. Examples: "Do you treat everybody like this, or am I just a favorite?" "I know what's bothering you—but your secret is safe with me." "You go for the kill, don't you?" "You're charming." "Everybody can't afford to go to finishing school." "Bad hair day, huh?" "I bet you go home and kick your dog, too."

TIP 839: Prepare Gossip Stoppers.

If the shared gossip insults someone else and you don't want to play a role in it, stop the conversation with one of these lines; vary your tone with your purpose: "I'm surprised to hear you say that—Janice always has such nice things to say about you." "Frankly, I'm puzzled. I've never known you to pass on rumors that haven't been checked out." "I really don't pay much attention to the grapevine—things get so twisted. Don't you agree?" "That story has probably gone through so many tellings that I bet half the details are missing." "Really? I think I'll mention that to Cindy so she'll know to set the record straight."

TIP 840: Level About How the Insult Makes You Feel.

Tell the other person that the constant sarcasm, jokes, or grumbling has gotten out of hand. Be as direct as you can: "That remark is insulting." "Why do you enjoy hurting my feelings?" "Remarks like that embarrass me in front of customers; it sounds as though you think I'm incompetent at my job." "I feel very angry when you make jokes about X." "Did you mean to insult me? Are you aware that you did?"

TIP 841: Blow the Other Person's Cover and Ask for Serious Feedback Point-Blank.

Some people bury their barbs in humor, in double-meanings, in sarcasm, or in innuendo. When you recognize an intent to hurt, identify it and confront the person directly.

Examples: "Bob, although you laughed when you said X, I sensed an underlying message. Do you think my work is off target?" "I note a repeated theme in your comments about the X project. Do you have real objections to my plans?" "Your words are teasing, but I detect something more in your tone. Are you angry for some reason?" "Do you have a complaint about my work? Your comments seem to have double meanings." "I want to make sure I understood what you just said. I took the comment as a negative statement about my organizational abilities. Is that what you meant?"

If you ask such a direct question, be prepared for a denial. Never mind, that's not the point. Your purpose is to call the other person's hand. Such comments force the hostility and/or work problem into the open so you can deal with it.

TIP 842: Minimize the Contact.

If you cannot get your message across because the other person refuses to hear, do whatever it takes to minimize contact with that person. Ask that he or she be transferred to another job. Resign from the committee. Time your errands so you do not pass that person. Write, rather than speak, any messages. Use go-betweens for any necessary interaction.

TIP 843: Create a Sense of Obligation.

Feed other people's beliefs that they must depend on you—either because of your job function, because of expertise you have and they need, or because of someone you know who can help or hurt their careers. People who realize they are dependent on you learn to cooperate with a much-improved attitude.

TIP 844: Don't Collect Injustices.

After once being hurt, some people keep a defensive mindset forever. For example, you walk into the office on Monday morning and someone asks, "How was your weekend?" You answer "Lousy. I planned to go skiing and it rained." He responds, "Well, don't blame me!" After a conflict has finally erupted and has been settled temporarily, be willing to let the tension unravel.

19

Praising (and Accepting Praise) So Your Comments Carry Weight

The deepest principle in human nature is the craving to be appreciated. —WILLIAM JAMES

Kind words do not cost much . . . Yet they accomplish much. —BLAISE PASCAL

The greatest efforts of the human race have been directly traceable to the love of praise.
—JOHN RUSKIN

I can live for two months on a good compliment.
—MARK TWAIN

As the Greek said, many men know how to flatter; few know how to praise.
—WENDELL PHILLIPS

Some pay a compliment as if they expected a receipt. —FRANK MCKINNEY HUBBARD

It is the greatest possible praise to be praised by a man who is himself deserving of praise.
—Latin proverb

Giving praise is much like giving love. The giver is usually the most benefited. He casts bread upon the waters and often gets back cake.
—IRVING FELDMAN

Just because praising others comes easily, don't be lulled into thinking all commendations and congratulations are equally effective and welcomed. Praise, just like constructive criticism, takes skillful delivery. And there's a big difference between flattery and praise.

For some people, accepting praise can be as difficult as accepting a gift. If you wouldn't consider insulting people who have given you a gift, you wouldn't want to insult them by not accepting their praise. These tips will provide perspective on both the giving and receiving end.

TIP 845: Distinguish Between Praise and Flattery.

Flattering comments focus on what someone has no control over and did nothing to earn. Praise, on the other hand, focuses on commendable character, performance, or behavior.

Flattery: "You're so tall. You strike an imposing figure as a leader."

Praise: "You have analyzed our situation well and come up with a unique strategy to build market share. Your plan is highly creative."

Phyllis McGinley puts it this way: "Praise is warming and desirable. But it is an earned thing. It has to be deserved, like an honorary degree or a hug from a child." Flattery, on the other hand, can leave people feeling as though they've been patted on the head like children.

TIP 846: Notice Opportunities to Praise.

There are many reasons people don't give praise: Others never come up to their standard of performance. Some managers hold the philosophy that punishment works better than praise. Some people are naturally impersonal and distant around others. Still others think they're too busy to notice or comment on "little things." And finally, some people's lack of praise can be attributed to the fact that they're too hard on themselves. They see even stellar performance as routine for themselves. They work, they get a paycheck; they also expect themselves to do good work without verbal pats on the back. Therefore, they take it for granted that others operate under that same principle.

You've probably heard the story about the husband married for forty years who had never told his wife he loved her. When she complained, he replied, "I told you I loved you the day we got married; if I change my mind, I'll let you know." Some bosses and coworkers operate under the same philosophy: "You're still working here, aren't you? If you make a mistake, I'll let you know."

For better relationships, take notice of praiseworthy effort, performance, or results. Something's bound to surface that deserves a compliment. If not, remind yourself to look harder.

TIP 847: Consider Emotional "Behavior" as Worthy of Praise.

For a customer service rep to keep her cool under pressure with an irate customer can take as much presence of mind as designing an ad campaign. And it can be as important, as well. When it comes to praise, don't limit your thinking to action or performance. Examples: "I appreciate your admitting the error. Many people would have pretended they didn't know what had happened to the machine." "Thank you for being honest about the situation and your misjudgment." "Your reaction to the criticism in the staff meeting this morning was commendable. You zeroed in on the issues and discarded the guff without defensiveness." "I admire the way you stood firm in your position yesterday, but did not become aggressive with the customer. That takes finesse and patience that many people don't have."

TIP 848: Follow the Army's Lead in Giving Medals.

Soldiers earn medals for everything from grooming themselves well to doing an assigned task well to saving a life. The benefits soldiers receive from medals include recognition of personal effort, security about the job, approval by others, a sense of belonging and camaraderie, the desire to continue to develop to the highest level of personal achievement. The list closely resembles Maslow's list of basic human needs, doesn't it? In the civilian world, praise can be as meaningful as medals.

TIP 849: Award Your Superiors with Praise.

Bosses usually dish out the praise to their staff, but that doesn't mean they would not benefit from and appreciate kind, sincere words from others. Recently, a two-star general in the U.S. Army arrived at the post to conduct the promotion ceremony for several lower-ranking officers. Afterward, with most people awed at the general's presence, few people moved in his direction. Finally one colonel who was most impressed with the ceremony approached the general and commented, "Sir, may I give you a little feedback?"

The general cleared his throat and nodded. The colonel continued, "As you can imagine, I've seen hundreds of these ceremonies and most are routine. But this one was not. You personalized your comments to each of the officers and you remarked about what they had done to deserve the promotion. That took time and preparation. I could tell it was a meaningful ceremony for the officers involved and their families."

The general smiled broadly. "Thanks for saying that. That'll make my day." He paused. "In fact, that's good enough to make my year."

Superiors seldom hear praise. If you mean it, say it.

TIP 850: Watch One-Up Praise.

A person who offers praise may appear to be placing himself or herself in a one-up position. For example, this comment delivered to a speaker after a presentation: "I enjoyed your presentation. You did a nice job in comparing one investment to another. I think you mentioned all the relevant tax laws most people need to concern themselves with." By its implication, that compliment says that the giver is in a position to judge the thoroughness or accuracy of what the speaker said. In a similar situation, take care not to word your compliment so that you are elevating your own expertise. A better phrasing of the previous compliment might have been: "I enjoyed your presentation. Your comparison of investments was intriguing, and your insights on the tax laws were some I've never heard shared before today."

TIP 851: Establish Your Credibility As a Praise Giver.

All praise is not equal. You can destroy the value of the praise you give if the receiver doesn't respect you, if he or she doesn't consider you in a position to judge. Other ways to damage your ability to praise include giving it lavishly, in the wrong place, at the wrong time, for the wrong purpose, with the wrong wording. Praise in and of itself is not "automatically" a motivator.

TIP 852: Be Aware That the Absence of Praise Can Mean Criticism.

If the boss customarily reinforces jobs well done with compliments and suddenly has nothing specifically positive to say, a staffer may fill in the blanks. "She didn't say anything about the brochure design. She must not have liked it."

TIP 853: Praise People When You Don't Want Anything.

Offering praise should not be a prelude to more work. "I really like the way this report is laid out. Do you have a few minutes to show me how to put the same kinds of graphics in mine?" is likely to bring a frown rather than a smile. Make praise an "end" in and of itself, not a transitional thought.

TIP 854: Praise Individuals Rather Than Groups.

Group praise leaves individuals feeling anonymous. Groups don't do work; individuals do. People feel better about their contribution when you recognize them individually by calling their names. Not: "I want to thank your group for its contribution on the project that turned out so well." But: "The project was finished ahead of time in a very tight window and within a skimpy budget—to the client's total satisfaction. Thanks to the creative thinking of Harriet, Andrea, Harvey, and Misong. I appreciate the contributions each of you make."

TIP 855: Be Specific in Your Praise.

Specific praise sounds more sincere than vague generalizations. Let other people know you understand what they had to do to get the good rating. Not: "Joe, you handle irate customers with finesse." But: "Joe, I observed how you handled that last customer. When he started yelling, that took a bit of restraint on your part to keep your cool. Sheryl said you even offered to deliver the customer's merchandise yourself on the way home. That's going to eat into your personal time. I appreciate that extra effort."

TIP 856: Comment on the Deed Rather Than the Person When the Issue Is Performance.

When you compliment people by labeling them, they don't necessarily know what they did to get the good rating. Therefore, they may feel the praise is insincere. And if they enjoyed the praise, they will lack direction in what they did well and how to get a repeat performance.

Not: "Connie, you're so thoughtful."

But: "Connie, stopping by to pick up lunch for us was thoughtful. That'll save a great deal of time I desperately need to spend at the computer. I'm glad you thought of that while you were out."

Not: "Leonard, you do good work!"

But: "Leonard, the proposal you submitted to Frank Hathaway was excellent. The benefit statements were well written and unique to that customer situation. Looks like you put a lot of effort into customizing it."

In the long run, Connie and Leonard will feel deserving of the sincere, specific compliments on their actions.

TIP 857: Credit the Person Rather Than the Deed When the Issue Is Character or Personality.

At times, you want to compliment people on their good judgment, on their ethics, on their supportive attitude, or on their disposition: "Max, you're a real solid employee." "Denise, I wish all our supervisors had your good judgment." If your observations are based on several situations over a long period of time, the comments will not come across as insincere flattery. Just be sure to mention a few of the specific situations that have led you to the praising conclusion.

TIP 858: Personalize Your Comments with "You."

Just as big corporations use the "you" approach in referring to individual customers by name ("Thank you, Ms. Harris, for shopping with us"), individuals should offer their praise that way. "You do a good job in maintaining this equipment" sounds more personal than "Good job on the maintenance." "Great idea" isn't as meaningful as "You came up with a great idea—thanks." "You put in a lot of extra time over the weekend" sounds more personal than "This took a lot of weekend time, I'm sure." Praise with the "you" approach.

TIP 859: Point Out the Positive Effects of the Behavior or Performance.

When you're at a loss for words about how to be specific with a compliment, simply comment on the positive results from a person's work or behavior. "Sidney, your survey at the customer's site certainly gave us a good starting point for proposing the new equipment and training. They had been sitting on the fence about whether to fund the project, and your survey pushed them over the edge. It was a smart idea that paid off."

TIP 860: Ignore Any Negative Outcomes.

Even a slight mention of a negative result will taint your compliment about the positive effort. If you're praising Joanne for doing an excellent job in drafting a contract, leave unsaid that the customer negotiated a better price in the final go-around. If you're complimenting the audio-visual manager about lavish stage decorations and lights, don't lament the fact that attendance at the convention was disappointingly low. Even though the low attendance was no reflection on the meeting planner, that negative thought puts a damper on the praise and the overall feeling of accomplishment.

TIP 861: Toss Out a Few Criticisms Occasionally.

Few people have the distinction of being upbeat and positive about everything that happens around them. If you're so lucky to have that kind of disposition and the wisdom to keep your mouth shut when you don't have good things to say, you'll have to alter your style slightly when praising. If you're always positive, people may not give much credence to your praising comments. Consider occasionally saying what you don't like so people believe you when you tell them what you do like about their work, their behavior, or their actions.

TIP 862: Avoid Praising One Person to Criticize Another.

A subtle way to criticize someone is to praise another person in his or her presence. Bert returns from vacation to hear: "Sharon certainly did a thorough job of tying up loose ends on all her projects before she left for vacation. It would have been nice if everyone had taken the time to do so." Parents make similar remarks about the obedient child to the "delinquent" child. The results? Resentment.

TIP 863: Follow Awkwardly Accepted Praise with a Question.

To lessen the awkward moment when your compliments might make other people stammer and stutter, simply follow your compliment with a question. The other person can focus on answering your question without having to handle a response to the praise. Examples: "Nice job in handling that customer. Has he been in here before?" "I like your menu selections for all the convention meals—most people just take whatever they offer and don't put in the time you invested in making sure we had such a variety. Do you plan all of the sales meetings?"

TIP 864: Consider Third-Person Praise.

In a staff meeting, the manager stands in the doorway and comments, "Where's Sylvia? That woman has the stamina of five people. She made thirty-two appointments last week. Will somebody find out what her secret is and let the rest of us in on it?" Somebody will be sure to pass on to Sylvia what the manager said about her performance. Third-party pass-ons build morale because they are even more believable delivered as "fact" to someone else.

TIP 865: Deliver "Eavesdropped" Praise.

Deliver your praise to a second person within earshot of the one being praised. You'll eliminate the person's need to respond and increase the value of the compliment because it was shared. Example: One colleague talks "around" a friend seated at the table with others. "Somebody should tell Carlos the campaign is over. He's still beating the bushes for new customers. Would you believe he reeled in three new accounts last week?" Carlos doesn't have to respond; he can smile modestly and bask in the glow.

TIP 866: Don't Overpraise.

In the workplace, few people veer even close to this situation, but there is danger in lavishing praise at the expense of helpful criticism. Much has been said about building or maintaining others' self-esteem, so much so that some people who are responsible for the career development of those they supervise feel uncomfortable in passing on any critique of poor performance at all. Giving only praise in an attempt to help people progress is like driving your car without a reverse gear. Sometimes you need to back up. Praise does generally accomplish more than criticism— but not to the total exclusion of criticism.

TIP 867: When Receiving a Compliment, Don't Match It.

You will sound insincere if you return the exact compliment someone paid you: "I like your new hairstyle." Response: "Well, yours looks nice also." The attempt to acknowledge the remark gracefully is appreciated, but the matching compliment will diminish the other person's gift of words to you. If you sincerely feel a matching compliment is in order, say something like, "You beat me to the punch; I was going to tell you how much I liked . . ."

TIP 868: When Receiving Praise, Avoid Put-Downs of Yourself or the Other Person.

Eliminate these as appropriate responses: "I did the best I could." "Tom had a big part in it also. I can't take all the credit." "It was really nothing." "Win some; lose some." "I was lucky, that's all." "Oh, I'm not so sure it was of any consequence." "I try." "It was no big deal." "Oh, that? I do that all the time." "Well, I see you finally noticed."

When you brush a compliment aside, you're implying the other person has made a mistake in offering it. You're insinuating that the person misjudged the accomplishment or effort and gave the praise to the wrong person, at the wrong time, in the wrong situation. At best, when you give such a response, you make the one who offered the praise feel he or she has done something to embarrass you rather than honor you. At worst, you'll make the other person angry at your refusing the gift of praise.

TIP 869: When Receiving Praise, Accept It Graciously.

Never simply shrug and let a compliment "roll off" as if unnoticed, expected, or unappreciated. If praise embarrasses you and you feel at a loss for words, a simple acknowledgment is enough: "Thank you." "I appreciate your noticing." "I like to hear that." "That makes me feel really good." "How nice of you to say that." "Thanks for mentioning that. It makes me feel good that you noticed." "Thank you. I'm glad you're pleased with the results." "Yes, I did have to double-step to get the project finished. Thanks for the acknowledgment of the extra effort." "Thank you. I'm pleased it turned out so well."

Gifts of praise arrive too infrequently. Enjoy them.

20

Giving Instructions So Nobody Feels Like a Fool

*People learn what you teach them; not what you
intend to teach them.*   —B.F. SKINNER

*Men must be taught as if you taught them not,
and things unknown proposed as things forgot.*
    —ALEXANDER POPE

*Everybody gets so much information all day
long that they lose their common sense.*
    —GERTRUDE STEIN

*Facts mean nothing unless they are rightly
understood, rightly related, and rightly
interpreted.*   —no attribution

*Getting the facts is only half the job; the other
half is to use them intelligently.*
    —no attribution

*The wise are instructed by reason; ordinary
minds by experience; the stupid by necessity;
and brutes by instinct.*   —Balance Sheet

*If at first you don't succeed, destroy all evidence
that you tried.*
    —Fahnestock's Rule for Failure

As coworkers, colleagues, and customers, we instruct people on how to use software, how to get to the cafeteria, how to calculate lease payments, how to strategize marketing efforts, and how to merge conglomerates without chaos. Granted, some tasks are easier than others, but they all involve certain principles of explaining the unknown to a novice or newcomer. The following tips cover everything from media and message to mastery.

TIP 870: Identify and Pay Attention to the Signs of Poor Instructions.

Listen to conversations around you in staff meetings, at the grocery store, or in the workroom. Here are the tidbits that provide telltale signs of trouble spots in instruction-giving. "Does anybody have any questions about what I just explained?" (You get only blank stares.) "Does anybody have any questions about what I just explained?" (Answer: "Would you say it again?") "Nobody told me that." "Why didn't you mention that before we started the project?" "If there's any way to screw it up, these people will." "What do you mean 'delegate'—I can do it better and faster myself." Repetitions of the following: "Would you tell me *again* how to set the timer (run this machine, make these copies, assemble these reports, adjust these buttons, draft this proposal, calculate these figures)?" If these sound familiar, you have a problem with instructions.

TIP 871: Understand the Magnitude of a Screw-Up.

Until people understand what a low-tech blunder can mean in a high-tech office, they won't be motivated to give instructions the attention they deserve. After we have to clean up our messes globally and culturally, we all eventually learn.

TIP 872: Motivate People to "Listen Up."

It's generally more difficult to do things you hate to do or don't consider relevant to your personal success than to do something that you enjoy or that will make you a billion dollars. Even when giving instructions, you have to motivate people to try. Make the project understandable, relevant, and important to their personal success. Dwell on personal benefits of the acquired knowledge or skill.

TIP 873: Decide Whether to Delegate Projects by Goals or Tasks.

A goal: "See what you can do to improve traffic flow around this office." A task: "Order some shelving that takes less floor space." Neither approach works all the time with all the people. To determine the best approach, consider both the delegatee and the project.

Goals such as "Develop a strategy to increase our market share by 3 percent this year" can excite the new marketing director eager to please, or can frustrate the new sales rep with no knowledge of your budget or customer base outside his region.

Tasks, on the other hand, may be equally worrisome or welcome: "Call Joan Frazier to ask how many people she expects to attend the luncheon, and then order engraved invitations. Get them in the mail by October 15. Then reserve a ballroom at the Hyatt, and select a salad menu, something under 10 dollars per person." To your new administrative assistant, such detailed instructions may be reassuring, but to the corporate meeting planner, they would be insulting or frustrating.

TIP 874: Organize Well.

Your choices are limited: you can organize by topic, location, chronology, importance, or frequency of the task. Organization of your instructions is the beginning of clarity.

TIP 875: Include Six Snippets of Information in Every Set of Instructions.

1. *Goal.* State your overall intention. If all else fails, the person can always follow the spirit of your instructions, if not the letter of the law. A mission might be "Make our star salespeople feel they're special to our executives."

2. *Results.* State the measurable results. How will the follower know he or she has been successful? What is the tangible, touchable final product? A conference in a resort location to which the star salespeople can bring their spouses?

3. *Procedure.* Give the steps, actions, and explanations. Should they select the star performers by the numbers, or will someone else determine the guest list? Do they handle all the arrangements or use a local meeting planner in the Caribbean? Should they make a personal site visit to several places before deciding on a location or go with a local referral?

4. *Timing.* State the deadline—either for the project as a whole or for various interim steps. When do you expect all the meeting details to be complete? When do you expect the star performers to receive an announcement about the event? When is the meeting to be held?

5. *Budget.* Mention the money available—upper and lower limits. You don't want to have in mind budget for a sit-down dinner and discover

that the meeting planner took your "watch-the-meal expenses" to mean a box lunch on the beach.

6. *Worry factors.*   Mention things the follower may encounter during the task that may create confusion and worry. With your advance warning, you'll lessen their apprehension when obstacles surface, when some steps take longer than anticipated, when negotiations or changes in plans may be appropriate. End your recital of the worry factors with a clear definition of failure. What is inappropriate for the sales meeting? At what points/decisions/problems should the person report back to you for help?

TIP 876: Give Followers a Context.

"Make yourself comfortable when you plan to give visitors a tour of the building." Does this mean jeans, t-shirt, halter top—or walking shoes rather than high heels, and lightweight fabrics rather than wools?

A manager asked his secretary to find out the middle initial of the former chairman of the board. He intended for her to check an old annual report on the shelf in the file room and supply the missing initial so he could use it on a gag birthday card. Not knowing the low priority of finding the correct initial when she discovered the annual report missing from the shelf, she spent two hours going to the downtown library looking for the information. Whenever you're giving employees instructions to do a task, also give them the goal and context of the task so they can make intelligent decisions along the way for things you can't anticipate.

TIP 877: Use Both Words and Pictures for Best Results.

If your instructions need to be repeated often, consider whether they should be in words (better for precision) or in pictures (better for speed). For best results, use both.

TIP 878: Give All the Pieces to the Puzzle.

I just returned from a 10-minute trip to a client's office that took 35 minutes. Why? Here were the directions: "As you exit the rental car parking lot, you'll be on I272. At the second signal light, turn left onto Magrauder Avenue. Then take the first left from Magrauder onto Bennet Street. Drive until the street dead-ends into the dock. Our plant is the building adjacent to the dock."

The problem? The client forgot to tell me that Bennet Street was called Division Street at the Magrauder intersection. It's difficult to remember how confusing something used to be before you learned it. To put it another way: It's difficult to give instructions for something you understand intimately and have known for a long time. One omitted detail can mean the difference between success and failure. "I thought you'd surely know that . . ." is a lame excuse for such omissions.

TIP 879: Avoid an Excess of Detail.

Too much is too much. "You'll be on Foster Street and you'll come to a flashing light, then a stop sign. There's a Texaco station on your left, a Shell station on your right. I think there's a Burger King just past that—you've gone too far if you see the Burger King "drive-thru." There's a driveway marked with a sign FOR DELIVERIES ONLY that angles off to the left, so don't be confused by that. Just keep going. . . ." Directions like that confuse, not clarify.

TIP 880: Prefer Clarity to Brevity.

Brevity is good; clarity is better. Never sacrifice a few words or sentences to be brief. Paper and air are cheap. Errors are expensive.

TIP 881: Remember Your Objective Is Not Necessarily to Simplify, but to Clarify.

Your instructions do not need to be given in six-word sentences composed of one-syllable words—although there's nothing wrong with simple words and simple sentences. When people question instructions, the problem is vagueness more often than complexity.

TIP 882: Limit "Use Your Own Judgment" Statements for the Exceptions.

A manager tells her employees, "Use your own judgment in responding to the customer by phone or mail." Does that mean they should use overnight mail for a 98-cent rush order? Does that mean they should place a person-to-person call to Kenya to make hotel reservations for a conference six months in the future? Such vague instructions beg for confusion. Instead, give precise guidelines for the most common situations and then use the catchall "use your own judgment" for the exceptions that no one can anticipate.

TIP 883: Clarify Whether Something Is a Must or a Preference.

"Wear protective lenses when entering the warehouse." Is this a guideline or an enforced safety regulation? Will employees feel less glare if they wear protective lenses, or will their eyesight be endangered if they don't wear them?

"Take a taxi to the hotel." Does this mean that employees should not ride the free shuttle if it happens to be passing as they exit the airport terminal? Or, is taking a taxi a must because time is of the essence and the shuttle makes three interim stops?

TIP 884: Mention the "Don'ts"; They Don't Necessarily Dictate the "Dos."

A sign on the mall doorway reads: "Do not enter through this door." So does that mean you enter the doorway adjacent to the one with the sign or you should go to the other side of the store? "Do not force this lever when paper becomes jammed." So how do you remove the jammed paper? Can you jiggle the lever? Should you lift the lever? Should you find another lever or button to manipulate? "Don't offer to prepare a time-consuming proposal for our clients unless they specifically ask for one." Is it okay to prepare a proposal if I can use an old boilerplate and prepare one quickly?

TIP 885: Don't Make False Claims or Promises.

"After you apply two or three coats, the shine will become hard and durable." If followers apply three coats and don't see a hard shine, they'll think they've done something wrong and often redo or undo the previous steps. "You'll have a newly wallpapered room in an hour" numbs the imagination of the worker who has been at the task all day.

TIP 886: Don't Insult Your Follower.

Watch phrases such as "You should be finished in ten minutes." "Everybody says it's as easy as falling off a log." "These instructions are idiot-proof; we've finally worked all the bugs out and you should have no trouble." Do you think the follower will admit to having any questions or doing it wrong?

TIP 887: Use Correct Grammar; the Meaning Often Depends on It.

At the Dallas–Fort Worth airport a sign at one of the restaurants reads NO SMOKING AREAS AVAILABLE. Does this mean they have no areas where patrons can smoke? Or, does this mean they have areas designated for nonsmokers? To solve this case of the missing hyphen, insert one appropriately: "No-smoking areas available."

"Turn the lever and depress the cylinder which opens the air chamber." Is this one action or two? Do you turn the lever and depress the cylinder simultaneously or take one action after the other? Or, is depression of the cylinder the result of turning the lever? Grammar is of paramount importance in instructions on technical procedures.

TIP 888: Avoid Hostile Repetition of the Same Words.

If someone does not understand your instructions, don't assume a patronizing or irritated tone and repeat the same words: "As I told you earlier, the equipment needs to be cleaned thoroughly." If you "told them earlier," don't tell them again in the same words. Assume the question is a good indication that the follower doesn't understand what "cleaned thoroughly" means. Use different words to express what you mean by "cleaned thoroughly": wiped with a damp cloth, sprayed with a water hose, or scrubbed with a disinfectant?

TIP 889: Curb a Superior Tone.

The person giving the instructions in any situation sits in the superior, smarter position. Often a subservient attitude (or, worse, a rebellious one) overcomes the learner—a holdover from classroom days: "Now, listen carefully as I call out the correct answers to this quiz." "Now, line up against the wall, and wait until I tell you to go." "Wait until I give you permission to leave." Keep that feeling in mind as you word your instructions to colleagues.

TIP 890: Be Approachable for Reruns.

Let others know it's okay to ask you additional questions as they move through the task—or even before they begin. Comments like "As you get into this, be sure to let me know if you discover I've left out something" or "If something I said was unclear, be sure to ask again rather than waste your time or become frustrated" lets followers know you're accepting some of the responsibility for clarity and success.

TIP 891: Take into Account the Frequency of the Task.

If you're telling someone how to complete a series of tax forms, expect that you'll have to tell them again each year for several years. Why? They don't do the task often enough to remember. When you know there'll be a time lapse between repetitions of the task you're teaching, plan for forgetting. Leave an example, model, or written instruction for a refresher. One time around won't do it.

TIP 892: Choose the Appropriate Medium Through Which to Give Your Instructions.

If the instructions are simple and concise, you may give them orally. If they're complex and will need to be referenced over and over, write them down. Or consider an audio or video recording, a class, or a live demonstration. Should instructions be light or serious? Be entertaining or matter-of-fact? Sometimes the delivery medium motivates people to understand the message.

TIP 893: Build Instructions into the Product or Process.

Either make information accessible or forget it. Manuals are not the answer. The number of manuals on average-knowledge workers' shelves grows proportionately to their own or the company's pocketbook—with each purchase of a new clock, electric blanket, spreadsheet package, printer, or insurance policy. Who reads manuals? Nobody. The needed information lies buried somewhere, but who has the time to search for it?

Through the years, my husband and I have used this "build-in" principle to create fun for our children's Easter egg hunts. We hide the candy-filled basket and plant clues on cards hidden around the house and yard. The children tackle the whole treasure hunt, instruction card by instruction card. When the first card leads them to where the second-clue instruction card is hidden, they retrieve that new card of instruction and begin searching for the third clue. Even in serious work situations, build-ins help.

If your information is complex enough to record for later use, then record it so people can find it. Build instructions into the item or process.

TIP 894: Categorize the Follower's Personality
and Attitude and Then Adapt Your Style.

Instruction takers fall into various categories:

- "Don't go so fast" types
- "I got it; I got it" types
- "I don't need instructions" types
- "I just don't get it" types
- "I'm all thumbs" types
- "While I'm thinking about it—I've got a question about Barcelona" types
- "I'll never need to know that" types
- "Who are you to tell me?" types
- "Where will you be if I need help?" types

Plan your pep talk, your order, your offer, and your phrasing accordingly.

TIP 895: Pinpoint Your Own Style and Modify What
Doesn't Work for You or the Other Person.

Instruction givers fall into several general categories. Do you see yourself in any of the following?

- "I don't have time to explain" types
- "Just let me put out this fire and I'll be back" types
- "Just believe me—it works; do it" types
- "Then you . . . Oh, I forgot to mention . . . Back to the . . . and while I'm thinking of it . . . Second, you try . . ." types
- "Now don't do anything until I tell you" types
- "Just do as I do" types
- "Forget how I do it—just listen to what I'm telling you" types
- "You're really going to love this" types
- "Even you can learn this" types
- "You don't need instructions, do you?" types

Identify your habitual instruction-giving mode and then reread this chapter. If you want a complete do-it-yourself course on the subject, read Richard Wurman's book, *Follow the Yellow Brick Road*. It's a masterpiece on "how to get there from here."

21
Minimizing Cross Talk Between Men and Women

Let us work without disputing; it is the only way to render life tolerable.
—FRANÇOIS MARIE VOLTAIRE

If a house be divided against itself, that house cannot stand. —New Testament, Mark 3:25

My first wife divorced me on grounds of incompatibility, and besides, I think she hated me. —OSCAR LEVANT

As soon as you cannot keep anything from a woman, you love her. —PAUL GERALDY

There are three things most men love but never understand: females, girls, and women.
—no attribution

Much research in the last 30 years has been done on gender communication issues. The result? Men and women communicate differently. You knew that. Some researchers previously theorized that all differences could be explained by differences in power and status in our culture. For example, they argued, when women have more power and status in the workplace, their language will change. To some extent, that has been true. Powerful people of either gender speak more confidently than lower-status people with no power. Stands to reason.

Nevertheless, differences remain in the conversational styles of men and women. In addition to my own research, these differences have also been investigated and reported by Drs. Robin Lakoff, Lillian Glass, John Gray, and Deborah Tannen, to name the most noteworthy researchers. As you read the following tips, keep in mind that all differences in conversation are a matter of degree and that all differences may not exist in all men or all women. We are first individuals, of course, with our own idiosyncrasies and ways of conversing. This chapter presents tendencies, not taboos or universal truths.

QUESTION OR OBJECTION?

As females grow up in our culture, they are taught not to be confrontational—not to make a scene or be aggressive or pushy. So how do they express opposition to an idea? Often they use indirect channels such as questions. They, of course, also use questions in the traditional way—to solicit information to make people rethink their positions, plans, or ideas.

Men, on the other hand, do not always recognize indirect messages or pick up on nuances in words or body language. In short, they don't always accurately "read between the lines" to understand a woman's meaning or question. The results: (1) Women ask questions meant as indirect objections, and men seem to ignore their objections and feelings. (2) Women ask questions meant only to solicit information to which men react defensively.

TIP 896 (for women): State Objections Directly.

Not: "Do you really think we should leave early?"

But: "I don't think we should leave early."

Not: "How much higher did you say Vendor A's bid is?"

But: "I think Vendor A's bid is too high."

TIP 897 (for men): Verify Whether Questions Are Solicitations for Information or Objections; Then Respond Appropriately.

If you're not sure how to take a question, probe before answering. Here's an example:

WOMAN: Have you already signed the contract for the computers?

MAN: Not yet. I'll get to it later in the week.

WOMAN: Didn't John have some concerns about the terms?

MAN: He cleared those up in the last meeting.

WOMAN: Do you think we should just forget about the staffing priorities since this new computer purchase will eat up all our cash this quarter?

MAN: I'm sensing maybe you're not sure the computers are a good decision. Do you still have some reservations there?

WOMAN: Well, yes, . . . I do. I think that . . .

With any objections in the open, you can deal with them more effectively.

DETAILS OR BIG PICTURE?

Women push for details generally for three reasons: to show concern about a person or situation, to vicariously participate in an experience or conversation, and to verify assumptions and check for accuracy. Men tend to gather details just long enough to get the big-picture message and then dump them as trivial, not worth remembering.

The results: (1) When men don't ask about or share details of a situation, women sometimes think they don't care about the people involved. (2) Women sometimes think that men intend to be secretive and distant. (3) Women sometimes doubt men's conclusions because they fear men have missed some of the important details. (4) Men sometimes think women "waste time" on the details rather than get to the main point. (5) Men think some details are irrelevant to their conclusions.

TIP 898 (for women): Get to the Point in Meetings.

If a discussion of the details is not germane to the point in a team meeting, be wary of men's impatience about that issue. State your big-picture assessment and offer the details as an option. If no one solicits the details for your conclusions, omit them and save yourself the trouble.

TIP 899 (for women): Ask for Details to
Verify Meaning.

In "sticky" situations, continue to probe for details to verify meanings and determine accurate conclusions. For example, when you're trying to verify the state of mind of an unhappy customer, dig out the details about the conversation you missed in order to double-check your sales plans. To echo Ross Perot: The devil is in the details.

TIP 900 (for women): Discuss Details
to Show Concern.

> Continue to ask questions and discuss situations that friends and colleagues
> toss out as means of showing support and interest. Whether or not men
> reciprocate when the situation is reversed should not inhibit your own car-
> ing attitude.

TIP 901 (for women): Don't Jump to the Conclusion
That Men Don't Care About a Situation Simply Because
They Don't Ask for or Give Details.

> Realize that men may not discuss details simply because they are not in the
> habit of doing so.

TIP 902 (for men): Use Women's Inclination
to Discuss Details to Verify Your Understanding
of a Problem or Situation.

> Realize that big-picture messages may be invalid if the detail selection and
> sifting process is hurried. Take advantage of a woman's penchant for such
> detailed analysis of a problem to make sure solutions you generate are
> solutions to the right problem.

TIP 903 (for men): Pay Attention to
Details to Show Concern.

> For example, a discussion of the colors of the new lobby decor may mean
> to a female engineer that you understand and care that the success of the
> renovation project will be important to her career.

SMALL TALK OR BIG TALK?

> Women talk to build rapport with others, and to explore their own feelings
> and opinions. Consequently, they consider most subjects worthy of conversa-
> tion. And they often talk about personal topics such as relationships, family,
> experiences, and activities. To women, an important aspect of conversation is
> simply "connecting" emotionally with another person. The information
> exchanged is secondary to that connection.
>
> Men, on the other hand, tend to view conversation for exchanging infor-
> mation or solving problems. They discuss events, facts, happenings in the

news, sports—generally topics not directly related to themselves. Other subjects about "routine" matters may, in men's estimation, not warrant conversational effort.

Results: (1) Women toss out conversational topics and men respond only minimally or not at all. As a result, women sometimes think men do not care about them personally. (2) Some men may think women "talk too much" about "trivial" subjects.

TIP 904 (for women): Continue to Signal Men About What's Important Enough for Conversation.

Let men know you expect a response when you pose a question or make a comment by the phrasing you choose.

TIP 905 (for women): State Outright That You Are Interested in Conversation Just for the Sake of Conversation and Connection.

Make a direct statement that you want conversation in the same way you might state that you want an opinion on a staff problem. Example: "Have you got a minute for a cup of coffee? I need to talk to somebody besides my computer for a change. Tell me about the project you're working on."

TIP 906 (for men): Expand Your Repertoire of Conversational Topics to Include "the Routine."

If conversation is good just for the sake of the camaraderie it generates, then any topic is as good as another. Don't pressure yourself into thinking every topic you introduce or every response you make has to be profound. Routine will do. The act of talking may be most important to your colleague or customer.

TIP 907 (for men): Explain Your Desire to "Connect" Despite Lack of Conversation.

If you simply can't think of information to share or appropriate responses to a woman's comments, say so directly but offer encouragement in the process: "I'm enjoying listening to your account of the meeting. Tell me more" or "I'm talked out, but don't let that stop you. If you've got time, I'd really like to hear how your project turned out." Then listen.

FACTS OR FEELINGS?

Women talk more about people than things. In our culture, females grow up with permission to express frustration, disappointment, or pain. They express their feelings, get them out, and move on to other things.

Males have been taught to suppress such feelings; unlike women, they hold on to those feelings longer under the surface. Yes, even after two decades of discussions about "the sensitive male," men's conversations still lean toward the factual rather than the personal. "Personal" does not necessarily mean "intimate," but rather simply off-the-record comments about personal activities, likes, dislikes, fears, hopes, or plans. Men talk more about things than about people.

Neither type of conversation—facts or feelings, people or things—is best; the issue involves sharing conversation for whatever relationship you want to create.

Result: (1) Women share feelings to create intimacy. When men don't reciprocate, women think men are intentionally creating distance. (2) Women do not often consider colleagues or customers close friends if they have never discussed personal topics and issues.

TIP 908 (for women): Share Both Facts and Feelings.

Model the sharing you want. Continue to share both facts and feelings in conversation so men will be encouraged to reciprocate.

TIP 909 (for women): Don't Assume That When Men Do Not Share Feelings They Are Trying to Create Distance.

Attribute a man's reluctance to share personal information—for example, his regret that he missed his son's ball game because of work-related travel—to discomfort with rather than disinterest in building camaraderie.

TIP 910 (for women): Talk More About Things with Men.

You can always start with the day's newspaper headlines and trade facts or opinions.

TIP 911 (for men): Share Feelings to Create Camaraderie or Intimacy in Personal Relationships.

Examples of personal information include things like plans for an upcoming family activity, enjoyment of a hobby, disappointment about how the economy is affecting your family, frustration over difficulties in working on a project, opinions on ethical situations, or plans for career and family.

TIP 912 (for men): Reveal Feelings to Build Loyalty in Customer or Colleague Relationships.

If you've ever lost a customer contract that you considered "safe," reevaluate the relationship. You may have considered a female customer a loyal friend simply because the two of you talked. She, on the other hand, may have considered the relationship tenuous because you only discussed "official" business during your calls and visits.

TIP 913 (for men): Talk More About People and Feelings with Women.

Women are interested in relationships and the well-being of others around them. Ask how others they know or work with are progressing on various projects, plans, or pursuits.

EMPATHY OR SOLUTION?

When a woman dumps a problem, she wants empathy along with a solution. In fact, being resourceful and creative herself, she may not want a solution at all. She wants to know that someone understands her frustration, disappointment, pain, or predicament. Again, one of woman's basic drives is emotional connection with other people.

But when a man hears a problem, he goes about trying to solve it: Try this. Try that. Try the other. Why? Because men win admiration by solving problems.

The reverse is true. When a man has a problem, he wants a specific suggestion for solving it. What does a woman give? What she'd want in return—empathy.

Results: (1) Women grow frustrated when they want empathy and get lectures or solutions. (2) Men grow frustrated when they want solutions and get lectures or empathy.

TIP 914 (for women): When Mentioning a Problem,
Be Specific About Whether
You're Soliciting Support or a Solution.

> Examples: "Got a minute? I need to blow off a little steam. That inventory system is archaic. It cost me two hours of overtime yesterday." "I'm so angry I could bite nails and not even taste the iron. Listen to what Jason said about . . ." Make it clear you're just passing on information, not asking for answers: "Yeah, yeah, I know how to handle him. I just didn't want to have to terminate him. I'm just complaining to a 'safe' person, you know what I mean?"

TIP 915 (for women): Interpret Solution-Giving
As Supportive.

> Consider a man's attempt at solving a problem itself a sign of empathetic support. After all, solutions take as much time as expressions of "ain't it awful?".

TIP 916 (for women): When a Man Mentions
a Problem, Offer Options, Not Just Empathy.

> Examples: "Well, as I see it, you've got two choices. . . ." "Have you thought about talking to Joe in HR about hiring some help?"

TIP 917 (for women): When a Man Mentions
a Problem, Do Not Editorialize with "Shoulds"
and "Oughts" About Past Actions and Future Actions.

> When your assessment of the predicament indicates that the whole problem could have been avoided, the temptation is to tell a man "helpful" things for next time. Example: "Rather than just signing a blank authorization next time, you should call to ask if you can examine the written documentation before you purchase the software." Such a comment makes the other person feel stupid and inadequate for the current problem.

TIP 918 (for women): Make Sure Men Know
You Are Not Necessarily Blaming Them
When You State a Problem.

> You may consider the following comment simply a statement of fact to which you expect a commensurate empathetic statement: "I ran out of gas this afternoon in the company car." Because men see themselves as prob-

lem solvers, a likely response might be: "Well, it's not my job to check it before we sign you out. We expect the user to do that." To lessen the defensiveness, add a lead-in to such comments: "I didn't check the gas gauge before I left in the company car you signed out for me. I ran out of gas." The pressure is off.

TIP 919 (for men): When Mentioning a Problem, Be Specific About What Kind of Response You Want.

Examples: "I forgot to find out the name of the furniture broker Harry says he prefers. Do you know anyone else who would know?" "I've had to work overtime four nights in a row because I couldn't figure out a way to schedule all the dinner breaks for my people in the shorter days. What do you use in your department—a manual system or a computer scheduling package?" The idea is to end the problem statement with a request for a solution.

TIP 920 (for men): Interpret Empathy-Giving As Supportive.

Empathy takes as much time as suggestions. Accept it, and then ask for suggestions specifically.

TIP 921 (for men): When a Woman Mentions a Problem, Offer Empathy, Not Just Solutions.

Examples: "Well, I gather you think he treated you unfairly under the circumstances. You must be concerned Bryan won't come through with the raise you needed." End of thought. End of discussion—unless she specifically asks for more help.

TIP 922 (for men): When a Woman Mentions a Problem, Don't Editorialize About How to Solve All Future Problems.

Squelch the temptation to add: "You know, you should have never let Bryan gloss over that morale problem in his department a year ago. And if it comes up again, you should . . ."

TIP 923 (for men): Understand When
a Woman States a Problem Involving You,
She Is Not Necessarily Blaming You.

> A statement of a problem is a statement of a problem, not an accusation.
> Don't feel as though you're being cited as the source.

QUESTIONS: RAPPORT-BUILDING OR INTRUSIVE?

> Women use questions to stimulate conversation. They ask questions some-
> times just to express interest in others and to get to know them. They hope
> men will reciprocate with questions of their own in return; thus, they can
> build camaraderie, making their working relationship more enjoyable.
> Men, on the other hand, don't feel such a driving need to connect emo-
> tionally. If they don't see a reason for the conversation, they may choose
> not to respond or to respond only minimally. Men initiate fewer questions
> just to encourage others to talk.
>   Results: (1) Women think some men remain aloof and are noncommu-
> nicative. (2) Men think some women invade their privacy.

TIP 924 (for women): Offer Information
About Yourself and Make a Man's Reciprocal
Response Optional.

> If you want to strike up a conversation with a brief acquaintance or a
> stranger, use statements rather than questions at the beginning.

TIP 925 (for women): If You Choose to Ask
a Series of Questions, Make Them Broad
and General Rather than Narrow and Personal.

> Try to add a lead-in that explains why you're asking questions that may
> seem unusual.

TIP 926 (for men): Interpret Questions
As a Show of Interest.

> The information shared is less important than the overture of conversation.

TIP 927 (for men): Learn to Self-Disclose
Nonthreatening, Nonconfidential Information
or Toss the Question Back to the Woman
and Show Interest in Her Response.

If you prefer not to share what you think or feel personally about an issue, offer a broad, general response: "Most people I've talked with do support the policy changes. What do you yourself think about the plans announced yesterday?"

HELP OR HUMILIATION?

Men tend to hold the person who has the information, skill, or know-how in a superior position. Information or skill equates to power or authority. As boys grow up, they use one-up statements to gain status: "Well, my big brother knows how to tie that kind of knot." "My dad knows how to get free tickets to the game." "My uncle knows all the senators by their first names." To a man's way of thinking, having "inside" access or information puts someone in a position of power and respect.

Not necessarily so with women. As children, girls grow up gaining approval by being helpful, by getting pats on the head for knowing the answers. Therefore, women like to give information to be helpful, and they assume everyone else does also. Women do not necessarily equate having information or a key skill with power or status. When others offer help to a woman she feels valued or loved—not necessarily insulted or inferior.

Results: (1) Men often resist having to ask for help or information. (2) Women become impatient and resentful when men cause delays or problems by resisting help.

TIP 928 (for women): Respect Men's Needs
to Solve Their Problems Independently of Others.

They need to feel self-sufficient.

TIP 929 (for women): Offer Help
in a Casual, Offhanded Way.

If the man refuses to ask for directions when you're driving somewhere, toss out your own experience: "Last year when our group drove up to this conference, we got lost because Highway 244 has so many detours. What we eventually had to do was . . ." Pass on information as "personal experience" and hope men use it.

TIP 930 (for men): Don't Equate Help or Information with Status.

Will Rogers was the first to admit: "Everybody is ignorant, only on different subjects."

TIP 931 (for men): Weigh Speed, Accuracy, and Results Against Delays and Status.

Remind yourself of your ultimate goal and consider asking for help or information a necessary step in accomplishing it.

SYMPATHY: SUPPORT OR PUT-DOWN?

Women love company with their misery. They share misfortunes, great and small, to elicit support and build camaraderie. When others, in turn, respond with similar stories of their own misfortunes, women feel encouraged and "not alone" in their predicaments. Misfortune makes best friends.

Men have a different view. Unless the relationship with the other person is already a close one, most men do not feel comfortable sharing troubles. Because they seek to gain admiration, misfortunes—particularly those they can't control, such as poor health or loss of a job—remind them they are *not* in total control of their lives. Misfortunes and related comments may be blows to a man's self-esteem.

Results: (1) Women offer sympathy freely to men, thinking their sympathy is supportive. (2) Men sometimes feel humiliated by a sympathetic comment, as if someone were "rubbing salt in the wound."

TIP 932 (for women): Test for Receptivity and Sensitivity Before Offering Sympathy.

If you don't know someone particularly well, broach the subject generally. If a man doesn't mention the problem you're aware of, don't bring it up yourself. Or, prefer to offer sympathy in general to "anonymous others." Example: "With layoffs so common these days, people are really in a tight spot. It's always more difficult to look for a job when you don't have one."

TIP 933 (for men): Interpret Sympathy
As a Sign of Caring Rather Than Humiliation.

> Consider it salve, not salt, in the wounds.

TO BE LIKED OR RESPECTED?

Given a choice between being liked or respected, most women would prefer to be liked. It's not that they don't enjoy admiration; it's just that being thought open, caring, and lovable score higher. Women also find it easier to work with people they like personally. On teams and with other projects, they work to build consensus. Their conversations sound like the following: "So what do *you* think, Miriam?" "Well, we certainly agree on that point." "You're certainly right about that." "Let's see where we can get together here."

Men like to be liked too. But being liked has little to do with gaining respect for their ideas and competing for the dollar or door prize. Men can argue and shout at one another over terms of a proposal, and then relax together on the golf course a half hour later. They are comfortable with competition. They vie for respect by outproducing, outperforming, and outthinking others. Their conversations sound like the following: "Well, I don't see it that way." "You're dead wrong on that point." "We'll never agree on that issue." "I disagree wholeheartedly." "Okay, so you do it your way, and I'll do it mine."

Results: (1) Women hate not being liked. (2) Men hate not being respected.

TIP 934 (for women): Learn to Swim
in a Competitive Environment.

> Men often equate your willingness to compete for your idea, project, or budget as commitment to it. If you don't fight for your work or ideas, you weaken them.

TIP 935 (for women): Learn to Work
with People You Don't Necessarily Like.

> Separate personality from performance. If necessary, keep reminding yourself how much you're making per hour to work with the other person.

TIP 936 (for men): Value Cooperation.

> Diversity contributes great value in the workplace. Prefer to gain through cooperation what might disappear in a competitive atmosphere.

TIP 937 (for men): Don't Equate a Woman's
Commitment or Passion for an Idea to Her Willingness
to Compete to Gain Acceptance of That Idea.

> Evaluate ideas on their own merit, not someone's delivery of them or willingness to parade them repetitively throughout a discussion.

OPINIONS: TAKE 'EM OR LEAVE 'EM

> Women ask for men's opinions in their attempt to explore their own feelings and come to conclusions. They may or may not make their decisions based on the opinions offered by others. When persuading their colleagues to come to a decision, women generally prefer building consensus rather than pulling rank.
>
> Men ask for opinions less often. And when they give requested opinions they often state their opinions as fact and consider the effort wasted when women do not act or make a decision based on those offered opinions. When persuading their colleagues to come to a decision, men generally prefer dictating a solution rather than "wasting time" to build consensus.
>
> Results: (1) Men think women waste their own and others' time "shopping" for opinions they don't use. (2) Women sometimes think male bosses "run over" them with decisions. (3) Men get frustrated when they can't tell if their female bosses are stating an opinion or a command. (4) Women get frustrated when male subordinates don't comply with what they themselves think are clear directives.

TIP 938 (for women): Make It Clear in Requesting
an Opinion That You Intend Only to Evaluate
the Opinion and Come to Your Own Conclusions.

TIP 939 (for women): Determine Whether
to Build Consensus or Dictate a Decision
on a Case-by-Case Basis.

TIP 940 (for women): Make Sure Subordinates
Know When You're Giving an Opinion or Making
a Request Versus Stating a Decision or a Directive.

TIP 941 (for men): Offer Your Opinions
Without Expectation or Obligation That
a Woman Will Act or Decide Based on Them.

TIP 942 (for men): Work to Build Consensus
When You Want Buy-in from Others on a Decision
and Want Others to Feel Valued for Their Input.

TIP 943 (for men): Make Sure Subordinates Know
They Have a Choice in a Situation if You Mean Your
Opinion As a Preference Rather Than a Directive.

DIRECTNESS OR INDIRECTNESS?

Women's language tends to be indirect, discreet, tactful, and at times manipulative. Women tend to give fewer directives and use more courtesy words with those directives. (Examples: "The approach is not exactly foreign to our designers" meaning "They are familiar with it." "Mary may not be available to handle the project" meaning "Mary doesn't want to handle the project." "Jerry, I have complete confidence in the way you deal with such customers—I trust you completely to make these kinds of decisions" meaning "I hope you'll keep taking care of these headaches without bothering me about them.")

Men's language tends to be direct, powerful, blunt, and even offensive. Men generally give more directives, with fewer courtesy words. (Examples: "Tom blew the deal with that client because of his stubborn refusal to negotiate on the delivery." "I will not approve that expense—it's unnecessary in my estimation." "That's a half-baked idea if I ever heard one. You're dead wrong.")

TIP 944 (for women): Use Straightforward Language
if You Want to Make Sure Your Message Gets Heard.

TIP 945 (for women): Be Objective and
To-the-Point so As Not to Dilute Performance
Feedback to a Colleague or Subordinate.

TIP 946 (for men): Use Tact and Show Respect for the Individual Even When You're Emotionally Upset and Even When You Have Someone Else's Best Interest at Heart.

TIP 947 (for men): In Social Settings, Use Less Directive Language When Expressing a Preference.

TO OVERLAP OR INTERRUPT?

Women overlap each other's speech as a show of encouragement to and identification with the other person speaking. In fact, two women can sometimes talk at the same time they're hearing the other person. This often expressive, passionate overlapping says, "I know exactly what you mean! That's so true!" Women allow more interruptions or overlapping.

Men focus, even when they talk. Either they talk or they listen—but not both at the same time. When men overlap, that overlapping is most often an attempt to interrupt.

Results: (1) When a woman overlaps conversation, she is showing support. (2) When a man's conversation is overlapped, he considers it rude and irritating.

TIP 948 (for women): Continue to Overlap Another Woman's Speech to Show Support and Identification with What's Being Said.

Talking at the same time to agree with the other person says, "I'm right with you."

TIP 949 (for women): Don't Overlap a Man's Speech Unless You Intend to Interrupt Him.

Allow a man to finish his statement before you jump in and add your opinion or information.

TIP 950 (for men): Don't Interrupt a Woman's Speech As a Power Play.

You interrupt rather than support when your volume is louder, when your body language intimidates, or when your tone shows either hostility or superiority.

NAGGING

Women tend to nag more than men. Because of their nurturing instinct with children, they often feel compelled to train, to improve, to help. If others don't follow their "nurturing," their tone often becomes whiny, petulant, or angry.

Men nag less because their attention focuses more on their own behavior and performance than on that of others. Men don't mind women nagging them if they interpret such remarks to be affectionate. ("Honey, don't forget your overcoat—I don't want you to get another cough and be sick for the weekend.") They resent nagging that they interpret to be disapproving or "telling them what to do." ("Would you clean up the mess you made with the newspapers and mail on the dining table?")

TIP 951 (for women): Nag Less;
Show Caring in Other Ways.

TIP 952 (for women): Offer Appreciation
for Behavior You Want to Encourage Rather
Than Disapproval for Behavior You Dislike.

TIP 953 (for men): Appreciate the Reason
Behind Affectionate Nagging.

SHOWING AFFECTION

Women generally show affection openly. They compliment people and express pleasure directly. They laugh and cry more often than men. When arguing, women bring up past wrongs because they see the relationship as fluid and evolving; they accuse more and hold grudges longer. They apologize more readily and easily. They do not see arguments as a contest and can bear the burden of being wrong. Women are motivated when they feel liked or loved.

Men tend to show affection less directly, through action. They compliment people less and instead use sarcasm and teasing to show liking. They laugh or cry less often than women. When arguing, men stick to the problem at hand, accuse less, hold fewer grudges, and forgive sooner. They apologize less and with difficulty. Men often see disagreements as a contest and insist on being

right, on winning. Men are motivated when they feel needed, admired,
or appreciated.

TIP 954 (for women): Stick to the Issues at Hand
When Arguing to Solve a Current Problem.

TIP 955 (for women): Forgive More,
and Forgive More Often.

TIP 956 (for women): Don't Try to Nag or Shame
a Man into Showing Affection More Openly.

TIP 957 (for women): Express Appreciation Frequently
to Men for Their Work and Results.

TIP 958 (for men): Consider Past Issues
and Events When Trying to Understand
Current Difficulties in a Relationship.

TIP 959 (for men): Apologize More,
and Apologize More Directly.

TIP 960 (for men): Show Affection More
Openly Through Direct Compliments
and More Emotional Intonation.

JOKE-TELLING AND HUMOR

Women tell fewer jokes and stories. When they use humor, they more often
tell self-deprecating anecdotes. Put-downs directed toward them or others,

even in jest, make women feel uncomfortable. They feel more compelled to be serious and "to quit kidding around" in the workplace.

Men tell more jokes and stories, and often their jokes and stories involve sexually or racially offensive comments. Rather than self-effacing humor, men usually direct their humor toward others. They use put-down humor and teasing with those they like and respect as well as with those they don't like and don't respect. They often "clown around" to break tension and lessen embarrassment.

TIP 961 (for women): Recognize the Value in Humor Even in Serious Discussions.

TIP 962 (for women): Practice Telling More Amusing Stories and Jokes in Safe Environments Until You Gain Confidence to Tell Them More Often in Larger Groups.

TIP 963 (for men): Avoid Offensive Sexual or Racial Humor.

TIP 964 (for men): Verify That Your Humor at Others' Expense Does Not Make Them Feel Uncomfortable.

ACCOMPLISHMENTS

Women tend to downplay their achievements so as not to create jealousy among their peers and generate distance or difficulty in a relationship. Because they enjoy working through consensus, they often share the credit with team members. As a result, their skills are underestimated and their achievements go unnoticed.

Men tend to announce their achievements so as to gain respect among their colleagues. They send memos, pass on testimonials from customers and peers on their behalf, and generally present themselves well. As a result, their skills win recognition and reward.

TIP 965 (for women): Find Ways to Display Skills
and Achievements So As to Win Rewards in the Workplace.

TIP 966 (for men): Continue to Gain Respect
for Your Accomplishments.

TIP 967 (for men): Recognize and Reward
Women's Achievements.

SELLING AND PERSUADING

Female salespeople tend to relate to men in one of four ways: the coquette, the daughter-to-father appeal, the mother-to-son adviser, or an equal colleague. Women sometimes have difficulty selling to a man when men raise objections; they are uncomfortable challenging a man's opinion, supposition, or reservation in buying. When a woman sells to a man and a man listens passively with little facial expression, the woman may become concerned that he's disbelieving or uninterested in what she's saying or selling. Her sense of timing falters; she doesn't know whether to back up or speed up to change his mind.

Male salespeople tend to relate to women in one of four ways: the flirtatious flamboyant, the father-to-daughter adviser, the ambitious young man wanting to make good and to please, or an equal colleague. A man has difficulty selling to women when he challenges the customer's objections bluntly or directly; a female customer shows discomfort when the buying conversation takes on a competitive tone. A male salesperson sometimes loses his sense of pacing when a female customer nods and smiles throughout the presentation. He speeds up, thinking she's agreeing and giving buying signals; then, when asking for the order, he discovers she has objections he skipped over hurriedly.

TIP 968 (for women): Avoid a Flirtatious Manner
to Prevent Creating Obligations About Other Interests.

TIP 969 (for women): Don't Create an Obligatory Buyer
if You Don't Want to Be Perceived As Less Powerful and
Damage Your Chances for Negotiating Your Terms.

TIP 970 (for women): Respect a Man's Ego When Explaining Your Product or Service; Show Confidence in His Intelligence and Quick Understanding.

TIP 971 (for women): Handle Confrontational or Blunt Statements As Requests for Further Evidence of What You're Saying, Not As Personal Affronts.

TIP 972 (for women): Depend on Your Own Proven Sense of Timing in Presenting Your Product or Service; Don't Interpret Matter-of-Fact Language and a Nonexpressive Face As Boredom or Disagreement.

TIP 973 (for women): Avoid a Matronly Tone As if Scolding, Demanding, or Condescending.

TIP 974 (for men): Forgo a Flirtatious Manner to Prevent Creating Obligations About Other Interests.

TIP 975 (for men): Put Aside a Fatherly Tone to Avoid Inciting a Woman's Inclination to Plead or Pout, Thus Damaging Your Own Negotiating Power.

TIP 976 (for men): Don't Damage a Woman's Self-Esteem and Disregard Her Intelligence with a Condescending Tone in Explaining Products or Services.

TIP 977 (for men): Avoid a Pleading or Oversolicitous Tone so As Not to Damage the Buyer's Confidence in Your Product or Weaken Your Negotiating Strength.

TIP 978 (for men): Guard Against a Competitive, Challenging Tone When a Female Customer Voices Objections and Reservations.

TIP 979 (for men): Depend on Your Proven Sense of Timing in Presenting Your Product or Service; Don't Interpret Nods and Smiles As Premature Buying Signals.

AIRTIME

Women tend to talk more in private; men talk more in public situations. Women hold the floor for shorter periods of time; men's contributions last longer. Women tend to carry on conversations—an exchange or dialogue; men's talk tends to focus on reporting facts and stating opinions. Women tend to shun disagreement and confrontation; men do not seem bothered by disagreement and confrontation. Men interrupt more than women do; women allow more interruptions.

TIP 980 (for women): Insist on Finishing Your Comments When Interrupted.

TIP 981 (for women): Avoid "Cowering" When Someone Disagrees with Your Opinion.

TIP 982 (for men): Share More Airtime if You Want to Be Perceived As Less Authoritarian or Less Opinionated.

LISTENING

Women tend to listen to others to relate and build rapport, and they respond more willingly than men. They show more facial expression, smile more often, nod more often, use more eye contact, and generally acknowledge and accept conversational topics men introduce. They use more tentative language and often answer questions with questions.

Men generally enjoy talking more than listening. They tend to listen only to gather information or solve a problem. Their face shows little or no expression but a frown or squint, they often grunt or give no response at all when spoken to, they give less eye contact, and they often refuse to accept conversational topics introduced by women, responding with silence or changing the subject back to their interests. They use more forceful language and tend to answer questions with opinions stated as facts.

TIP 983 (for women): Speak Up
or Change the Subject When You've
Listened More Than "Your Fair Share."

TIP 984 (for women): Take Care That You
Don't Mislead with Your Smiling and Nodding;
Men Often Take Such Responses As Agreement
with and Interest in What They're Saying.

TIP 985 (for women): Use More Forceful Language;
Avoid Tag Questions. Answer Questions
with Facts or Directly Stated Opinions.

TIP 986 (for women): Realize That When
a Man States an Opinion He Is Not Necessarily
Closed to Opposing Opinions or Facts.

TIP 987 (for men): Respect the Fact That a Woman
Is Not Necessarily Talking to Make a Point, but Rather
to Explore Feelings or Relieve Stress.

TIP 988 (for men): Acknowledge a Comment
Directed to You.

TIP 989 (for men): Encourage Women
to Speak Up When They Disagree or Have
Their Own Agendas to Discuss.

TIP 990 (for men): Identify Your Opinions As Such
Rather Than Stating Them As Irrefutable Facts.

TIP 991 (for men): Don't Continually Change
Conversational Topics Offered by Women.

BODY LANGUAGE

Men take up more space than women, using big, angular, and forceful
gestures out and away from their body. They hold their fingers together and
often point. They extend arms and legs and make possessions (books, papers,
briefcases) an extension of themselves to protect their territory. They lean
back when they listen, tend to shift their positions occasionally, and appear to
be more in control of their environment.

Women tend to pull themselves in, hold their arms and legs close to their
bodies, and make small and easy gestures toward rather than away from their
bodies. They hold their fingers apart and use circular hand movements.
When listening, they lean forward. Generally they move more fluidly, with
trunks of their bodies turning as their head, arms, and feet do. They gather
their possessions closely around them so as not to infringe on others' territory and often sit more quietly and rigidly.

TIP 992 (for women): Take Up More Space.

People who take up more space seem more confident, relaxed, and powerful. "Withdrawing into yourself" may make you seem less competent and
knowledgeable.

TIP 993 (for men): Be Careful Not to
Intimidate People by Size and Bigger-Than-Life
Gestures and Motions.

Avoid taking up more than "your fair share" of space in a work station or
meeting environment so as not to appear arrogant or aggressive.

WORD CHOICE

Much research has been done on the language and word choice of both genders. Dr. Robin Lakoff, a pioneer in this area, has written most extensively on this subject. Others' research has confirmed many of her conclusions and has also raised questions about earlier hypotheses, relating some issues to power and position in the work force rather than simply gender differences. The following differences between the genders, however, still stand:

Women use more intensive adverbs (*so, just, very, much*), more expressive adjectives (*gorgeous, electrifying, devoted, awesome*), more emotional words (*furious, lovingly, thrilled*), and more diminutives (*tiny, cute, precious*). Their color vocabulary is more extensive (*teal blue, periwinkle blue, baby blue, aqua*). Women tend to use tentative language. In general, they use less slang, more precise diction, and better grammar than men.

Men use more game analogies, stronger profanity, and more expletives than women do. They tend to use more forceful, confident language. They generally use more slang and colloquialisms, less precise diction, and more improper grammar than women.

TIP 994 (for women): Use More Nouns and Verbs Than Adjectives and Adverbs When You Want Your Comments to Sound More Factual Than Subjective.

TIP 995 (for women): Use Direct, Forceful Language When You Want to Sound Authoritative, Competent, and Confident.

TIP 996 (for men): Use More Tentative Language (Questions, Qualifiers, Hedgers) When You Want to Sound Less Dictatorial and More Open and Approachable.

META-MESSAGES

Meta-messages surround words and give them their complete meaning: tone of voice, actions, body language, context.

Women are more intuitive than men. They take words and examine them for nuances of meanings. They talk about talk and contemplate the how and why of what was said or left unsaid; they are fascinated by human interactions and motivations. A woman pays great attention to tone of voice when spoken to. Her own tone tends to be excited, upbeat, emotional, friendly, light, and soft. Women use inflection to emphasize feelings and key points. When women sense a problem in a relationship, they're inclined to bring it up and discuss it, "to work things out." They deal with stress by talking about it. In other words, the complete message—words and meanings—register on a woman's mind.

Men tend to take words at face value. They do not concern themselves necessarily with how or why things are said and gloss over reasons behind actions if those reasons don't change "reality." Men are less attentive to tone when spoken to. Their own tone is more matter-of-fact or blunt, with little intensity. Men use volume to emphasize key points. If men sense a problem in a relationship, they're inclined to ignore it and hope it will disappear. Men deal with stress in a relationship by withdrawing. In other words, men tend to focus primarily on the words of a message.

TIP 997 (for women): Guard Against an Attempt
to Decipher Meaning and Motivation
That Degenerates into Gossip.

TIP 998 (for women): Prevent "Reading into"
Words More Than Is Intended.

TIP 999 (for men): Don't Miss Real Messages
by Concentrating Only on the Words.

TIP 1000 (for men): Welcome Discussions
to Improve Relationships.

22

Crossing the Cultural Gulf

Cultural differences create hotbeds of miscommunication between CEOs and their employees, between managers and their staff, between salespeople and their customers, between coworkers and teams. Even though "diversity" has been a frequent topic of corporate training seminars and speeches, graduate school curricula, and management symposiums, there's still a big gulf between *awareness* of differences and *appreciation* of differences. These tips will further awareness. Appreciating the differences—a result of attitude and motivation—comes more slowly and with greater reward than mere acknowledgment.

TIP 1001: Choose the Right Time and Place to Discuss Business.

In Asian cultures, people dine first and strengthen friendships before doing business. In Western cultures, people may begin business over cocktails. Americans discuss business most any place and interpret others' refusal to do so as lack of interest or lack of aggressiveness.

TIP 1002: Come to Agreement
About the Meaning of Time.

> What passes as punctuality and good manners in one culture may mean
> rigidity and disregard for human nature in another culture. Swedes
> demand a two o'clock meeting to begin at two o'clock. Mexicans and
> Greeks see no such urgency if "something comes up."

TIP 1003: Determine the Appropriate
Ceremony for Exchanging Business Cards.

> The business card ritual merits careful attention. Westerners tend to
> exchange business cards at the end of a meeting, and they may make notes
> on each other's cards as reminders. If the card simply provides a reminder
> of title, phone number, or address, the receiver may simply slip it into a
> briefcase without looking at it in the other person's presence. In Japan,
> business people present their cards to each other upon first meeting.
> Ceremonially, the person of highest rank in a group gathering presents his
> or her card first; then others follow. The Japanese extend their cards with
> both hands so that the printing is readable to the receiver and expect the
> receiver to read the card carefully and nod approvingly of the title and/or
> company before tucking it away. Both a failure to read the card and the act
> of writing on the other person's card show rudeness.

TIP 1004: Recognize That Respect
May Be Shown in Numerous Ways.

> Anglos stand up to show respect, Fiji Islanders sit down to show respect, and
> Japanese bow to show respect. Some people raise their faces and their eyes
> to show respect; others lower their faces and eyes for the same reason. Some
> people shake hands to show respect; others refrain from doing so to show
> deference and humility. In addition to the Western handshake, traditional
> greetings and a show of goodwill may be expressed by hugs, nose rubs,
> kisses, hands together in a praying position, or a nod. Americans show
> respect and cordiality by using first names; Germans seldom use first names
> in business dealings. All in the name of respect.

TIP 1005: Maintain or Avoid Eye Contact
Depending on Your Relationship and Status.

> In Middle Eastern and Latin American cultures, to show respect an employee
> may look down or away from his boss. In Anglo cultures, employees show
> respect by maintaining eye contact with a boss to show interest and atten-
> tion. Anglos may also use strong eye contact to show aggression or power.
> Avoidance of eye contact in Anglo cultures may indicate low self-esteem,

shyness, evasiveness, dishonesty, disrespect, disdain, or boredom. The rules of eye contact vary greatly.

TIP 1006: Determine if Questions About Personal Life Are Appropriate.

In the United States, business acquaintances may ask general questions about one's personal life: "Do you play much golf?" "Does your family live in this part of the country?" In some African cultures, even on first meeting, it is appropriate to ask specific, personal questions: "Do you have boys or girls?" "Is your father rich or poor?" In Arab countries, such family or personal matters are totally off limits to business acquaintances.

TIP 1007: Treat Silence As Both Golden and Guarded.

The Japanese feel comfortable with silence and discreetness, particularly with confidential information. They particularly admire someone who gives careful thought before answering questions or making a point. Americans cover silences as if unwelcomed and unwarranted. They admire fluent speakers who move quickly from idea to idea without pause in an organized manner. Americans talk to *resolve* differences; Japanese keep silent to *avoid* differences. Americans talk to share feelings; Japanese keep quiet to share feelings. For Americans, silence represents a breakdown in communication; for the Japanese, silence represents harmony in communication.

TIP 1008: Identify Politeness Either As a Mask or a Goodwill Gesture.

In some cultures, people bow, smile, nod, and agree so as not to offend. Courtesy may cover very different feelings of estrangement and formality. In other cultures, people are not overly concerned with offending; therefore, a show of courtesy generally indicates goodwill.

TIP 1009: Verify That Stories You Tell Illustrate Shared Values.

If you're trying to make either a serious point or a humorous one, verify that your illustration does in fact make your point. For example, if you tell a story describing an "absent-minded" professor, you may intend the professor to be the butt of the joke and your listener may revere the professor because of his age. In a meeting you may relate the length of time it took a customer to make a buying decision. Your telling may imply time wasted, while the listener infers valued time in a thorough analysis.

Other examples: You tell a story about the purchasing agent who always buys from his neighbors and friends, implying impropriety and possibly kickbacks; while in your colleague's culture, people always do business with friends and neighbors rather than strangers. Or, you may tell a story glorifying individual ruggedness and resourcefulness while the listener in another culture values group decisions and a team spirit.

The storyteller has to understand varying, even conflicting values to illustrate them appropriately rather than hold them up to mockery.

TIP 1010: Adapt Your Humor.

Punch lines don't always work from one scene to the other. The crowd may be baffled, bored, or buffaloed. The slightest difference in word choice, use of slang, or even timing may send your punch line straight over others' heads. Not only will they not laugh; they may be offended or consider you a "fuzzy" thinker.

TIP 1011: Remember That All Laughter May Not Be Fun and Games.

Laughter and giggles in most cultures indicate good humor, goodwill, joy, and amusement. But in some cultures, laughter and giggling may mask pain or embarrassment. My Okinawan cleaning lady met me one day after work with a bad case of the giggles; she was embarrassed over breaking a cherished vase.

TIP 1012: Use Appropriate Sports Analogies.

People everywhere either watch, participate in, or know about sports. But the popular sports change from country to country. Take the point you want to make and transport it to the appropriate field, court, pole, pool, stadium, floor, arena, or ring.

TIP 1013: Select the Right Pronoun for "You."

In modern English, the second person *you* means one or many, familiar or formal, friend or foe. In other languages, the selection of the pronoun connotes age, sex, occupation, and social and professional status.

TIP 1014: Avoid Acronyms and Initials.

Letters that have a meaning in one culture may confuse and may even spell something offensive in another culture.

TIP 1015: Use Technical Terms When Appropriate.

Technicians understand the technical terms associated with the equipment and processes they use. Don't, however, confuse technically accurate terms with jargon inappropriately used to laypersons—unfamiliar because they are nontechnical, not because they are from another culture.

TIP 1016: Avoid Idioms, Clichés, and Colloquialisms.

In the United States, we refer to "springs" of water; in Mexico, people refer to the "eye" of the water (*ojo de la agua*). You'll have great difficulty explaining these tidbits to those from other cultures: "Put the shoe on the other foot." "He's robbing Peter to pay Paul." "It's raining cats and dogs." "Why don't you put your own house in order?" "Don't give me so much lip." "You'd better make hay while the sun shines."

Some people may not even realize they've been insulted with these comments: "Well, everybody knows that!" "Even you should be able to run this machine." "I'll explain it again—for all the good it'll do." "Look who's talking."

TIP 1017: Whistle, Hiss, or Applaud Appropriately to Show Approval or Disapproval.

Americans boo or hiss at a performer to show displeasure and whistle to show approval. Europeans hiss when they want silence and whistle when they're displeased. Americans, Europeans, and Asians applaud to show approval. Americans lift a fist to show contempt or anger; Russians lift a fist to show determination to try harder or improve.

TIP 1018: Be a Student of Expressiveness.

People in some cultures show expressiveness over the slightest pain or joy— wild gesturing and body movement, varying intonation, dramatic facial expressions. Those living in other cultures may experience the deepest pain or joy with no outward expressions at all—no gesturing, stoic faces, monotone voices, stillness. Can you imagine the difficulty physicians have in diagnosing and treating pain from an expressive hypochondriac or a stoic victim?

TIP 1019: Touch or Refrain from Touching, As Appropriate.

People stand close in some cultures and feel offended when those of other cultures pull away; other talkers keep a comfortable distance and feel invaded when colleagues come too close. Touching is taboo in some cultures (British, German, Japanese, Asian, Indonesian, Indian, Pakistani) and welcomed in others (Spanish, Latin American, Italian, Jewish, Arabian). The touchers hug, embrace, and pat each other to show goodwill, affection, concern, or trust. The nontouchers refrain for the same reasons.

TIP 1020: Gesture and Move with Care.

The United States "OK" sign conveys zero or worthlessness in France, money in Japan, and an obscenity in Russia and some South American cultures. A pointed finger, perfectly normal to Anglos, shows rudeness to Asians, Africans, Belgians. As a seminar leader in Malaysia, I had difficulty remembering to point with my closed palm and thumb. Waving is an insult in Greece or Nigeria, and a welcome in most western cultures. Snapping your fingers is considered vulgar in Belgium and France; it's a pasttime in the United States. Pointing the soles of your feet in the direction of a Thai will offend, but propping your feet up on the desk of a Canadian may show camaraderie and relaxation.

Be alert to watching gestures of others and aware when those of other cultures seem offended at your own gestures. Better, if you plan to visit a particular country, study a travel guide for appropriate or inappropriate gestures.

TIP 1021: Translate "Yes" and "No" with Care.

In various cultures, all the following gestures can mean yes: a raised head and chin, a nod forward, rocking the head from shoulder to shoulder four times, wagging the head from side to side, a backward nod with raised eyebrows, a smile.

Nos may be communicated by a finger wagging from side to side, a palm-down hand shaking side to side, a backward tilt of the head, a hand waved in front of the face, a clicking tongue. When traveling, these yes and no gestures are the first to master; otherwise, you may be buying more than you can pay for or selling more than you own.

23
Putting Your Best Body Forward

*When the eyes say one thing, and the tongue
another, a practiced man relies on the language
of the first.* —RALPH WALDO EMERSON

*The trouble with a fellow who talks too fast
is that he is liable to say something he hasn't
thought of yet.* —CALVIN COOLIDGE

*The shortest distance between two people is
a smile.* —VICTOR BORGE

*Watch out for the man whose stomach doesn't
move when he laughs.* —Cantonese proverb

*There's so much to say, but your eyes keep
interrupting me.* —CHRISTOPHER MORLEY

*She learned to say things with her eyes that
others waste time putting into words.*
—COREY FORD

What you see is what you get—on most computers and with most colleagues.
Body language is so much a part of the communication that the picture would
be out of focus without some attention to voice, visual presence, and verve.

TIP 1022: Avoid Typing Your Personality with Your Voice.

If you were participating in a corporate skit, how would you play the part of a complainer? (Whiny, nasal voice?) How would you play the part of a crook? (Raspy, harsh tone?) How would you play the role of an incompetent nerd? (High-pitched, rapid, quivering voice?) How about the role of a sexy coquette? (Breathy, lilting, slow speech?) An impatient teen? (High-pitched, fast speech, full of emotion?)

All other things being equal, movie producers accept or reject actors based on how their appearance and voice match the characters they're to impersonate. You may be typed for life by the impression your voice creates.

TIP 1023: Lower Your Pitch to Sound More Authoritative and Credible.

We generally use musical terms to categorize people's voices: soprano, alto, tenor, baritone, and bass. People with a high-pitched voice give the impression of being nervous, immature, lacking in confidence, or even slightly emotional and hysterical. People with low pitches sound confident and competent.

You can modify your own voice once you become aware of your pitch; voice coaches and self-help tapes and books tell you exactly how to effect and practice this change. If you want to make it to the board room, adopt the lower, hushed tones most often heard there.

TIP 1024: Speak at a Slower Rate to Convey Seriousness, Authority, and Thoughtful Deliberation.

A slow rate of speech implies well-chosen words and underscores the import of the message. The pace gives a listener time to contemplate what's being said and attach the appropriate significance.

TIP 1025: Speak at a Faster Rate to Convey Excitement, Enthusiasm, and Energy.

A faster rate creates interest and demands attention. The pace makes listeners work hard at hearing and translating what's being said, but prevents opportunity for their minds to wander. They have to "listen up" to stay up.

TIP 1026: Use the Appropriate Volume.

Loudness has become synonymous with vulgarity and unruliness; a soft volume has come to mean shyness, nervousness, and even incompetence. Stay away from these two extremes.

TIP 1027: Avoid Mannerisms and Toys When You Talk.

Watch trying to talk with a pen, pencil, paper clip, toothpick, or gum in your mouth. Other annoying habits include scratching your head, jerking a knot in your tie or scarf, jingling money or keys, strumming your fingers, twirling your pen or stapler or letter opener, clearing your throat, or snapping your fingers. Besides making it more difficult to understand you, these trinkets and mannerisms detract from an image of authority.

TIP 1028: Laugh on Purpose.

People generally smile to show amusement, excitement, happiness, or even relief. They also, unfortunately, communicate nervousness or embarrassment with a laugh. Smiles, smirks, or giggles may say you're more uncomfortable than amused. In some situations, inappropriate smiling may convey innocence or even dim-wittedness. Those who study politicians for a living insist that inappropriate smiling contributed to former Vice President Dan Quayle's reputation as being an inexperienced "lightweight."

When you laugh, laugh on purpose. Let it be a sign of interest and genuine amusement or happiness. People who are in control of their emotions and the situation control their laughter also.

TIP 1029: Smile with Your Mind, if Not Your Mouth.

For years, novelists have tried with mere words to convey false from true smiles. In some of my own novels, I've used statements such as: "Her smile rose and faded like the window shade" Or "Her smile was in her eyes." When you feel a smile, it shows in the rest of your face—the lines around the eyes, the pupils, the forehead, the cheeks. Likewise, when you're faking a smile, it shows: the timing isn't right, and the wrinkles don't follow. Use a smile genuinely.

Second, be wary of the fake smile of others. Take your cue from inappropriate timing (genuine emotions and expressions are brief; false ones last longer) and mismatches of words to expressions (they don't seem synchronized).

TIP 1030: Establish a Baseline Before You
Attach Deep Meanings to Body Language.

We've all read books and heard talks about what various gestures mean: that
arms folded across the chest indicate a closed, defensive attitude, that lean-
ing forward means interest, that shrugged shoulders mean indifference,
that narrow eyes and a set jaw mean defiance, that a smile and nodding
mean agreement. But few gestures convey meaning in and of themselves;
they have to be interpreted in clusters. The gestures and attached meanings
mentioned here do generally hold true, but the real meaning of a gesture
comes only with *context* and as exhibited by a *particular* individual, just as
in spoken messages, one boss's "excellent" on a performance appraisal is
another boss's "satisfactory." Interpreting nonverbal language accurately
involves paying attention to the variations and the habits for that particular
individual. Mitch may *always* sit with his arms folded across his chest—
when he's bored and when he's elated.

Before you decide to risk much on reading a customer's, committee's, or
team's body language, establish what's normal for that person or group.
Chat with them on a neutral subject to get a reading about what's normal
before you try to interpret how they react to something controversial you
may want to communicate.

One man's smile may be another man's belly laugh.

TIP 1031: Remind Yourself That People
May Give False, Nonverbal Cues.

People who smile and laugh at your jokes may be bored to tears; people
who look at you with a blank stare may be very interested in what you have
to say. I recall one seminar I conducted several years ago when one female
engineer rested her head in her hands and kept her eyes downcast while
doodling on a piece of paper the entire time. No amount of eye contact on
my part, gesturing, or raising and lowering my voice could stir her to look
up. After the first six hours, I gave up in trying to pique her interest and
turned my attention back to the rest of the group. Dreading what her final
evaluation of the seminar would say, I was surprised to read her comment:
"Best seminar I've ever attended in my fourteen years with the company.
This should be a required course for all employees."

So much for reading body language. Some people just never let their
emotions get to their face.

TIP 1032: Walk, Stand, and Sit with Good Posture.

You may have noticed these various postures among people in the workplace:
the shufflers, who shift weight from one foot to the other back and forth,
back and forth, but never move any place; the pacers, who walk and talk like

courtroom lawyers addressing the jury; the sprawlers, who tend to take up more than their fair share of space; the tired, who stand or sit as if they hardly have energy to hold themselves upright.

Good posture, on the other hand, conveys self-confidence and competence. Your control of a group or a situation can be won or lost by the image you present as you stand, walk, or sit.

TIP 1033: Keep Appropriate Distance.

Edward T. Hall has done extensive research on proper distances in our culture. Patting someone on the back, letting a friend cry on your shoulder, and reading a report over someone's shoulder represent *intimate* distances—touching range. *Personal* distance, from 1 to 4 feet, is appropriate for conversations you don't want to have overheard—like a problem shared in confidence. *Social* distance, about 4 to 12 feet, is comfortable when conversing with others when you don't mind if people overhear—at a cocktail party or in a sales presentation to a customer. *Public* distance, farther than 12 feet, is when we tell our children, "Don't shout; he'll see us and come over in a minute." We use public distance to establish formality and control when speaking before a group.

Conversing from the correct distance makes the difference in your control, authority, and rapport. That's why speakers who want to maintain authority step up on a podium away from individuals and in front of the larger group. When they want to build trust with an audience and establish an easy, open, informal dialogue, they move down among the audience.

Space is no less important for you when you're communicating one on one—especially when communicating with those of another culture, gender, or age. For example, women tend to sit next to people they like; men tend to sit facing people they like. Have you noticed that if women want more space, they tend to put things (coats, briefcase, papers) in the seat beside them to prevent others from joining them? When men have the same intentions, they block the seat in front of or behind them. Children and older people prefer to sit and stand closer to others than people of middle age. Extroverts stand and sit closer to others; introverts stand and sit farther away.

Awareness of these differences prevents you from making others feel as if they're being either "invaded" or ignored. People tend to trespass in our territory in one of three ways: (1) They "clutter" our space with their things, (2) they use and seem to take over what's ours, or (3) they step inside our personal bubble of space. For example, a salesperson who "towers" too close to a customer may intimidate her. Generally, the closer the relationship and the more comfortable people are with each other, the less personal space they need between them. The more discomfort or stress in the relationship, the more space they need. Be aware of all these trespasses in others' territories and the discomfort and anger they create.

TIP 1034: Place Your Office Furniture So
That People Respect Your Personal Space.

> If people seem to "lean over" and around you as they work, consider your own work space and equipment or desk items. Are they functionally placed so people who interact with you can reach what they need without invading your sense of space? Either use the "obstacles" to reinforce the personal space you need or remove them to create an open, inviting space for others to enter.

TIP 1035: Show Interest by Moving
Closer to the Other Person or Standing Up.

> Notice that in a conversation when people get interested in an idea they tend to lean forward, talk faster, gesture more, and even stand and move toward the other person. If the other person backs up, the pursuer sometimes doesn't even notice. Instead, he or she keeps leaning or walking forward. If your intention is to generate enthusiasm, go with your natural inclination to move forward, but be aware of any negative reaction.

TIP 1036: Use Touch When Appropriate.

> Pats, squeezes, brushes, strokes, and hugs all happen every day in the workplace. Some become the basis of sexual harassment charges; others convey sorrow and comfort at the death of a colleague. Touching underscores much of what we intend to communicate to colleagues. We touch to show friendliness, empathy, consolation, excitement, commitment, sincerity, goodwill, and hostility. Sorting out which is which presents a difficulty to some. If you think people recoil at your touch or if you feel hesitant to touch others when the occasion calls for it, ask a trusted friend to help you sort through the confusion.

TIP 1037: Respect Status with Your Eye Contact.

> The person with more authority has the privilege or responsibility of making or breaking eye contact. If you continue to stare belligerently after someone has broken eye contact and "dismissed" you, your behavior may be considered defiant and rude.

TIP 1038: Use Eye Contact to Build Rapport with Others.

Locking eyes with another individual can say to the other person that you're interested in them, that you think they're important, that you believe in what you're saying, or that you believe it's important they hear what you're saying. On the other hand, withholding eye contact can say to others that you don't think they're worth getting to know, that you're not interested in them, that you're lying, or that what you have to say is of little consequence.

Eye contact is so powerful in our culture that we summon waitresses or taxi drivers by "catching their eye." We reprimand a child with a glance. We show love by gazing into the lover's eyes.

Your eye contact can be the most powerful tool you have for building rapport—or your most dangerous weapon in destroying relationships.

TIP 1039: Adopt a Handshake That Matches Your Personality and Intention.

A limp handshake conveys shyness or aloofness; a macho handshake shows aggressiveness and a sense of competition. A "quickie" handshake tells others you don't want to get involved; a longer handshake shows interest. A prolonged handshake signals more than a business interest. So, for middle-of-the-road business occasions, offer a middle-of-the-road handshake: not too firm, not too limp, not too long, not too brief. Just right.

TIP 1040: Nod Your Head to Show "You're Home."

If you've ever heard people complain that they felt they were talking to a "brick wall," they were probably reacting to a lack of nodding from the listener. In our culture, a nodding head is very important. In various situations, it says, "I understand." "I like you." "I agree with you." "I identify with you." If you have the feeling that people seem aloof when you're present, be aware of the absence of head-nodding on your part. If you want to, you could literally nod your way to friendship.

TIP 1041: Don't Point Your Finger.

People often associate this gesture with an authoritarian in their life—a scolding parent or teacher or boss. Most people are turned off by a wagging finger in their face.

TIP 1042: Tell Your Body What Mood You're *Supposed* to Be In.

When a person feels sexy or romantic, the voice takes on a different pitch, the breathing rate changes, the eyes flirt, and the gestures and movement become more fluid. Or when an individual feels laid-back and informal, the voice seems to yawn with little or no energy, the eyes dim, the movements become more haphazard. All that coordination between mood and body is fine—unless the mood is inappropriate for the time, place, or relationship.

List of Tips

Tip 1. Find commonalities.

Tip 2. Show concern and compassion.

Tip 3. Demonstrate cooperation with good intentions.

Tip 4. Be consistent.

Tip 5. Demonstrate competence.

Tip 6. Be correct.

Tip 7. Admit what you don't know.

Tip 8. Be complete.

Tip 9. Be current.

Tip 10. Be clear.

Tip 11. Avoid doublespeak.

Tip 12. Avoid exaggeration.

Tip 13. Evaluate criticisms and objections.

Tip 14. Accept responsibility for decisions, actions, and results where you have/had some control.

Tip 15. Keep confidences.

Tip 16. Avoid lying "offstage."

Tip 17. Be sincere and genuine.

Tip 18. Be vulnerable.

Tip 19. Make your appearance work for you.

Tip 20. Recognize that those in less powerful positions want to win your goodwill; interpret their words and behavior accordingly.

Tip 21. If as a powerful person you want to build rapport with others, remove the status symbols and power barriers.

Tip 22. Assess others' knowledge and experiences exactly.

Tip 23. Set a level playing field.

Tip 24. Avoid coming across as a one-directional communicator.

Tip 25. Avoid a reputation as a manipulator.

Tip 26. Be interested, not just interesting.

Tip 27. To express interest in someone, soften whatever it is you're doing.

Tip 28. Use radical language to be a leader.

Tip 29. Have a sense of the dramatic when you talk.

Tip 30. Learn to self-disclose.

Tip 70. Don't switch from "you" to "me" back to "they" when you want a response about your own situation.

Tip 71. Don't tell other people how to think or feel.

Tip 72. Encourage others to vent emotions so they can clear their minds to hear you.

Tip 73. Seek out the causes of behavior; they'll be more worthwhile and revealing than the behavior itself.

Tip 74. Express an opposing viewpoint to build credibility, to entertain, or to do someone a favor.

Tip 75. Be tactful, not offensive or insensitive.

Tip 76. Don't ask others to cover for your insensitivity.

Tip 77. Consider the price of "nice."

Tip 78. Verify assumptions—your own and those of others.

Tip 79. Check out inferences.

Tip 80. Read others' cues and clues to determine the "so what?"

Tip 81. Check out hunches when someone denies intentions.

Tip 82. Challenge generalizations.

Tip 83. Test old axioms.

Tip 84. When you're listening, have a penchant for details; when speaking, take your cue from the listener and your purpose.

Tip 85. Differentiate between showing deference and being patronizing.

Tip 86. Avoid false courtesy.

Tip 87. Get people's attention first if you really want them to hear you.

Tip 88. When constantly interrupted, stop talking immediately and abruptly to make the interrupter aware of what he or she is doing.

Tip 89. Don't step on others' sentences.

Tip 90. Signal the other person when you receive a message.

Tip 91. Avoid playing tour guide through your own conversation.

Tip 92. Give glib reassurance sparingly.

Tip 93. Develop your memory. Those who forget what others tell them make people angry.

Tip 94. Don't tell others what they already know.

Tip 95. Don't overload yourself with information to the point of distortion.

Tip 96. Don't overload your listener with data that has to be processed before being usable.

Tip 97. Relate the unknown to the known.

Tip 98. Make information easy to access.

Tip 99. Reduce the number of interpreters.

Tip 100. Interpret facts and statistics rather than serving them raw.

Tip 101. Get acronyms and abbreviations right.

Tip 102. Don't use jargon as snobbery.

Tip 103. Avoid "as you are aware" statements intended as put-downs.

Tip 104. Use the simple word when the simple word will do.

Tip 105. Substitute new words permanently for those you can't pronounce.

Tip 106. Select powerful verbs.

Tip 107. Cut adjective and adverb clutter.

Tip 108. Avoid "et cetera" and other substitutes for lazy thinking.

Tip 109. Rid yourself of junk words.

Tip 110. Be specific.

Tip 111. Push other people to be specific.

Tip 112. Choose precise words.

Tip 113. Use concrete words rather than abstract ones.

Tip 114. Beware of misleading with connotation and denotation.

Tip 115. Make semantics a big concern.

Tip 116. Remember that personal experience affects interpretation.

Tip 117. Remember that meaning comes from context.

Tip 118. Don't attach too much significance to a less than well-chosen word used carelessly.

Tip 119. Use honest words.

Tip 120. Never say *never, none, all, everything, totally, constantly.*

Tip 121. Minimize times when you have to use *should, must, will, ought* statements.

Tip 122. Recognize weasel words as escape hatches.

Tip 123. Don't destroy your position with disclaimers.

Tip 124. Avoid ending every statement with a question.

Tip 125. Recognize the royal "we" as an epithet.

Tip 126. Pay attention to the stress on words.

Tip 127. Eliminate redundancies.

Tip 128. Grapple with grammar.

Tip 129. Use poor grammar only for an intended effect.

Tip 130. Use up-to-date slang.

Tip 131. Overcome sloppy diction.

Tip 132. Avoid being so overly precise that you sound like a stuffed shirt.

Tip 133. Use your speaking voice, not your writing voice.

Tip 134. Speak with the appropriate formality or informality.

Tip 135. Take cues about first-name/last-name preference from how the other person answers the telephone.

Tip 136. Recognize name-dropping as an attempt to gain status.

Tip 137. Avoid sexist language.

Tip 138. Know the value of understatement.

Tip 139. Don't exaggerate.

Tip 140. Fight the urge to top off the tank.

Tip 141. Avoid overqualifying.

Tip 142. Cut long prefaces to your points.

Tip 180. Tell people how much you need them.

Tip 181. Give people all the glory they're due when they know the inside scoop.

Tip 182. Show pleasure in the success of others.

Tip 183. Let another person know he or she is superior to you in some skill.

Tip 184. Let others impress you if you want to make a good impression yourself.

Tip 185. Think about the imposition and the options before you ask for a favor.

Tip 186. Don't presume on a friend; ask for permission.

Tip 187. Use the Ben Franklin technique to win a friend.

Tip 188. Take the pressure off others when they make an unintended gaffe.

Tip 189. Select the setting that suits your purpose.

Tip 190. Change your physical environment to promote the interaction you want.

Tip 191. Measure your relationship with others by the kind of conversation they share with you.

Tip 192. Recognize that intimacy breeds distance.

Tip 193. Select the implicit or explicit channel with care.

Tip 194. Work at building rapport.

Tip 195. Know when small talk is appropriate.

Tip 196. Accept the fact that some people don't want to make contact at all.

Tip 197. Think twice about using small talk on the telephone.

Tip 198. Risk being the first to say hello.

Tip 199. Introduce yourself in a way that allows people to respond or connect.

Tip 200. Help people remember your name.

Tip 201. Remember others' names.

Tip 202. Personalize greetings.

Tip 203. Gain partial credit by recalling the meeting if not the other person's name.

Tip 204. Recall to the person your topic of conversation the last time you were together.

Tip 205. Position yourself in the flow of traffic.

Tip 206. To relax yourself, strike up a conversation with someone who looks shy and uncomfortable.

Tip 207. Play host rather than guest.

Tip 208. Bring along your own PR person.

Tip 209. Don't intrude.

Tip 210. Choose a topic appropriate to the group, the atmosphere, the relationship, and your purpose.

Tip 211. Use opening lines that lead someplace.

Tip 212. To stir quiet people to expression, select a topic about which they can feel passionate.

Tip 213. Know which topics to avoid.

Tip 214. Play the part of the "stranger in town" with class.

Tip 215. Develop your timing instinct before bringing up an appropriate subject.

Tip 216. Read the other person's mindset by examining his or her opening comment.

Tip 217. Relax your body language if you want a relaxed conversation.

Tip 218. Recognize that the response you get will often reflect your own tone and delivery.

Tip 219. Ask easy questions first to relax people.

Tip 220. Ask for opinions rather than information.

Tip 221. Don't ask questions too broad to answer.

Tip 222. Tickle people's creative fancies.

Tip 223. Pique others' curiosities with an incomplete comment.

Tip 224. Avoid questions that lead people on when you have no interest in their answers.

Tip 225. Don't state the obvious.

Tip 226. Jump over the ho-hum screen.

Tip 227. Add fresh information or observations rather than echoing what has been said.

Tip 228. Ask to be enlightened when the conversation is over your head.

Tip 229. Keep your mouth shut if the conversation is *way* over your head.

Tip 230. Take no more and no less time than a subject is worth.

Tip 231. To share the topic, change the pace.

Tip 232. Add description as elaboration.

Tip 233. Make your aim to entertain.

Tip 234. Work on witty remarks.

Tip 235. Tell good stories.

Tip 236. Try to relate your stories to the subject at hand.

Tip 237. Make other people the hero or heroine of your anecdotes.

Tip 238. Respond with a "saver" if your remarks breed silence.

Tip 239. Do a reality check frequently to see if people are really interested in what you have to say.

Tip 240. Give your listener a chance to leave if bored.

Tip 241. When you're caught not listening, give a keep-talking nudge.

Tip 242. Avoid current stock fillers.

Tip 243. Unwind a nonstop speaker with a popquiz.

Tip 244. Encourage people to continue what they were saying before being interrupted.

Tip 245. When someone "pulls your leg," release it.

Tip 246. Cover your own and others' faux pas with past ones.

Tip 247. Tactfully reject questions that are too personal.

Tip 248. Signal before you're offended.

Tip 249. Consider your options when listening to a person with "fixed" ideas.

Tip 250. Be noncommittal if you want to avoid debate.

Tip 251. Avoid editorializing.

Tip 252. Accept specific compliments with sincerity.

Tip 253. Prepare self-effacing comebacks for frequent vague, or insincere compliments.

Tip 254. Gossip at your own great risk.

Tip 255. Stop gossip without offending the spreader.

Tip 256. Squelch complaints.

Tip 257. Don't hard-sell when the purpose is chitchat.

Tip 258. When you meet two VIPs at once, don't focus on one and ignore the other.

Tip 259. Make a graceful exit.

Tip 260. Recognize the importance of small talk.

Tip 261. Establish credibility.

Tip 262. Understand the three dynamics of persuasion: logic, character, emotion.

Tip 263. Identify the appropriate emotion of the moment.

Tip 264. Talk about rewards and incentives to those people who think in terms of payoffs.

Tip 265. Talk about facts and statistics to those who think analytically.

Tip 266. Talk about the "bandwagon" to those who like to jump on it.

Tip 267. Talk about obstacles to be overcome to those who welcome challenge and change.

Tip 268. Sell what people want to buy.

Tip 269. Appeal to self-interest.

Tip 270. Create immediacy.

Tip 271. Use associations from the past.

Tip 272. Ride with the flow as far as you can go.

Tip 273. Use the lesser-of-two-evils approach.

Tip 274. Provide a better and best option.

Tip 275. Use the jelly principle.

Tip 276. Try the Tom Sawyer approach.

Tip 277. Let the decision maker hear from the converted.

Tip 278. Play on the power of your expertise.

Tip 279. Roll with realities rather than hope for martyrs.

Tip 280. Choose your timing.

Tip 281. Create a favorable atmosphere.

Tip 282. Stand up for people to take you seriously.

Tip 283. Present your idea to several small groups rather than one large group.

Tip 284. When there's a parade, take the last spot.

Tip 285. Know the criteria before pushing the solution.

Tip 286. Limit your objectives.

Tip 287. Make a conscious decision about whether to present all sides of an issue or only yours.

Tip 288. Organize your ideas for greatest impact.

Tip 289. Use the bad-news-first approach.

Tip 290. Calculate the minimum gain you would need to justify investing time or money in your idea.

Tip 291. Point out what you know for a fact and "what seems to make sense."

Tip 292. Credit other people for their sound reasoning.

Tip 293. Recognize that people support what they help create.

Tip 294. Encourage others to state their own needs or problems to be solved.

Tip 295. Invite others to try on your idea.

Tip 296. Be careful about opening with a broad question.

Tip 297. Ask a question that showcases a benefit.

Tip 298. State quantifiable facts rather than opinions.

Tip 299. Cite your sources and ask for those of others.

Tip 300. Turn information, facts, and features into benefits.

Tip 301. Vary your intensity.

Tip 302. Increase your pace to increase comprehension—up to a point.

Tip 303. Personify abstract concepts or inanimate objects.

Tip 304. Speak metaphorically.

Tip 305. Use anecdotes and stories to make your points.

Tip 306. Use humor to raise receptivity.

Tip 307. Package ideas like products.

Tip 308. Create slogans.

Tip 309. Triple things—use triads and alliteration.

Tip 310. Don't be too cute.

Tip 311. Select selling words.

Tip 312. Prefer powerful phrasing.

Tip 313. Use both rounded and exact numbers.

Tip 314. Make statistics experiential.

Tip 315. Never let facts speak for themselves.

Tip 316. Consider the legitimacy of the printed word.

Tip 317. Provide memory aids.

Tip 318. Use visuals as aids, but don't let them dominate.

Tip 319. Don't ever read your key points.

Tip 320. Match the visual, auditory, and kinesthetic patterns.

Tip 321. Repeat, repeat, repeat.

Tip 322. Prefer understatement to overstatement.

Tip 323. Get past clichés, platitudes, and truisms.

Tip 324. Don't beg the question.

Tip 325. Anticipate questions.

Tip 326. Use others' questions to make your own points.

Tip 327. Notice whether people listen to your answers.

Tip 328. Prepare for the standard objections.

Tip 329. Recognize the body language of resistance.

Tip 330. Dig for unspoken reservations.

Tip 331. Investigate the standard causes of resistance.

Tip 332. Brace yourself through the negatives.

Tip 333. Guard against your own resistance to others' comments.

Tip 334. Don't censor emotional comments out-of-hand as irrelevant.

Tip 335. Agree before you disagree.

Tip 336. Use the every-cloud-has-a-silver-lining principle.

Tip 337. Ask for the reasoning behind someone's counterclaim.

Tip 338. Check for reasoning errors.

Tip 339. Unravel the thread of "why."

Tip 340. Paraphrase trivial objections.

Tip 341. Change yes-no issues to multiple-choice.

Tip 342. Propose the let's-write-it-into-the-contract alternative.

Tip 343. Develop a list of picturesque "saver" lines for recurring snags.

Tip 344. Don't aim to "outargue" them.

Tip 345. When someone pushes, don't push back.

Tip 346. Don't make the other person wrong for you to be right.

Tip 347. Minimize stress for the other person.

Tip 348. Hold the sarcasm; avoid detractors.

Tip 349. Avoid frames as power plays.

Tip 350. Lower others' guard with graciousness.

Tip 351. Dodge zaps and zingers to get to your goal.

Tip 352. Provide opportunity for a trial run.

Tip 353. Note the difference between selling an idea and motivating people to act.

Tip 354. Persuade people to do something specific.

Tip 355. Show passion.

Tip 356. To meet or not to meet—study the question.

Tip 357. Call a meeting only for the right reasons.

Tip 358. Set an agenda.

Tip 359. Start with the most important idea or issue and work backward.

Tip 360. Select attendees carefully.

Tip 361. Own the setting.

Tip 362. Stay out in front if you intend to lead.

Tip 363. Take your seat with forethought.

Tip 364. Take your body with you.

Tip 365. Encourage participation from others—if you want it.

Tip 521. Assume the "dumb" question has a connection you don't yet understand.

Tip 522. Unload "loaded" questions.

Tip 523. Turn a negative question into a benefit statement.

Tip 524. Challenge questions based on misinformation or invalid assumptions.

Tip 525. Define terms and agree on criteria before you give "value-based" answers.

Tip 526. Help questioners meet their objectives with their showcase questions.

Tip 527. Diffuse hostile questions.

Tip 528. Bridge from the questioner's agenda to yours.

Tip 529. Bridge from the abstract to the specific or from the specific to the abstract.

Tip 530. Use cliché answers with care.

Tip 531. Know when flippant answers are out of line.

Tip 532. Don't bomb when a BB gun will do.

Tip 533. Don't ignore questions to avoid confrontation.

Tip 534. Give multiple answers without claiming any as your own.

Tip 535. Fog the issue with an irrelevant point.

Tip 536. If you intend to be clear, ask for explicit confirmation and feedback.

Tip 537. Forget feedback if you want to show confidence in your answer.

Tip 538. When piggybacking someone else's answer, frame your comments tactfully.

Tip 539. Set boundaries for which questions you will and won't answer—and stick to them.

Tip 540. Before giving any answer, consider the costs and opportunities.

Tip 541. Use verbal stalls with care.

Tip 542. Remind yourself that you don't have to answer every question.

Tip 543. Remember that the whole performance counts.

Tip 544. Be clear about your own priorities.

Tip 545. Recall the three ways to say "no" and make a conscious choice.

Tip 546. Ask for time to think.

Tip 547. Forewarn people when you have devastating news.

Tip 548. When writing, be positive or neutral in introducing the bad news.

Tip 549. State the reasons or your criteria for making the "no" decision if you are in a more powerful position than the other person.

Tip 550. Remember that you generally do not have to give a reason for your "no."

Tip 551. Be firm, fair, and nonjudgmental in your response.

Tip 552. Phrase your "no" as positively as possible.

Tip 553. Learn to say "Yes, and" rather than "No, but."

Tip 554. Be dramatic with your "no."

Tip 555. Use the broken-record technique.

Tip 556. Use the sandwich technique.

Tip 557. Give the raincheck "no."

Tip 558. Offer alternatives.

Tip 559. Mention any conditions under which you might change your mind.

Tip 560. Let the facts speak for themselves; show rather than tell.

Tip 561. Find one kernel of good in the bad.

Tip 562. Sit on the other side of the table.

Tip 563. Deliver the worst news in person.

Tip 564. Decide what apologizing means in any given situation.

Tip 565. Apologize specifically.

Tip 566. State any corrective action you plan to take or have taken rather than reminding someone of the problem or issue.

Tip 567. Explain the reasoning behind corrective actions.

Tip 568. Avoid making excuses if the mistake was due to your carelessness or insensitivity.

Tip 569. Express regret for the results an inadvertent mistake caused.

Tip 570. Be sincere.

Tip 571. Reestablish rapport on a neutral subject.

Tip 572. Avoid apologizing to gain sympathy.

Tip 573. Consider apologies as an important way to build rapport.

Tip 574. Accept apologies graciously.

Tip 575. Identify your motive for criticizing.

Tip 576. Check for criticism preferences.

Tip 577. Realize the stress of hearing, "I'd like a word with you."

Tip 578. Watch the red-pencil mentality.

Tip 579. Separate fact from opinion as you gather your thoughts and information.

Tip 580. Make sure you know what you're talking about.

Tip 581. Screen yourself before being "frank" and "telling the truth."

Tip 582. Consider the positive results of the exchange: improved mental outlook, improved relationship, new insight, possibility of effecting a change.

Tip 583. Consider the negative results of the exchange: mental and emotional outlook, time involved to help with the change, probability of effecting a change, a severed relationship.

Tip 584. Consider whether you could foster the same change with praise rather than criticism.

Tip 585. Make sure you're not doing the same things you're criticizing.

Tip 586. Rehearse your criticism.

Tip 587. Select the appropriate emotional timing.

Tip 588. Select the proper "real time."

Tip 589. Criticize in private.

Tip 590. Avoid beginning with a trapping question.

Tip 591. Remove threats from the criticism.

Tip 592. Avoid an I-told-you-so tone.

Tip 593. Criticize specifically, not generally.

Tip 594. Criticize the viewpoint or the behavior, not the person.

Tip 595. Focus on observable behavior, not on conclusions about that behavior.

Tip 596. Don't turn comments about work problems into major character flaws.

Tip 597. Bring the criticism "forward."

Tip 598. Don't ask why.

Tip 599. Use "I need/want/expect" phrasing when possible.

Tip 600. Don't compare people.

Tip 601. Include credits with your criticisms.

Tip 602. Lead the person to do a self-critique.

Tip 603. Assume some of the blame yourself.

Tip 604. Substitute problem-solving for criticism when possible.

Tip 605. Couch your criticism as a request for help.

Tip 606. Criticize only one thing at a time.

Tip 607. Relate your criticism to some goal of theirs.

Tip 608. Criticize to some end.

Tip 609. Describe the behavior change or action you want others to take as a result of your criticism.

Tip 610. Monitor the pace of the conversation.

Tip 611. Check your response to the receiver's comments.

Tip 612. Summarize key points and actions for correction.

Tip 613. Don't ask if the person "understands" what you've said.

Tip 614. Recognize when enough is enough.

Tip 615. Decide who should and shouldn't know what.

Tip 616. End criticism with encouragement for the future.

Tip 617. Consider the value of criticism.

Tip 618. Remember that even the best get criticized.

Tip 619. Think twice before you invite criticism by habit or attitude.

Tip 620. Determine if the criticism is intended to be constructive or destructive.

Tip 621. Give people an invitation to criticize only if you mean it.

Tip 622. Consider the setting before you decide how to respond.

Tip 623. Arrange to have criticism leveled on your own turf.

Tip 624. Stifle an immediate denial.

Tip 625. Squelch the urge to counterattack.

Tip 626. Stifle the urge to rationalize.

Tip 627. Don't project the blame onto someone or something else.

Tip 628. Avoid superficial acceptance.

Tip 629. Don't pretend it's "no big deal."

Tip 630. Don't go home and yell at the dog.

Tip 631. Guard against overreaction on your sore spots.

Tip 632. Maintain your emotional equilibrium.

Tip 633. Be willing to accept responsibility without accepting blame.

Tip 634. Avoid taking all as "absolute truth."

Tip 635. Separate opinions from descriptions.

Tip 636. Listen to someone's criticism without interruption.

Tip 637. Consider the source.

Tip 638. Consider the emotional climate.

Tip 639. Ask yourself if others have made the same observations.

Tip 640. Agree with the criticism.

Tip 641. Ask for thinking time.

Tip 642. Express regret about the results of a situation.

Tip 643. Limit the application of the criticism to your goals while discarding the unusable.

Tip 644. Thank the criticizer for helpful comments.

Tip 645. Ask how the other person would have handled the situation.

Tip 646. Change the mistakes you alone control.

Tip 647. Rechannel your emotions to concentrate on your mission.

Tip 648. Agree on a plan for change and set timelines.

Tip 649. If you can't change, cancel bitterness as an alternative.

Tip 650. Keep yourself physically and spiritually strong.

Tip 651. Recall your list of strengths.

Tip 652. Don't take yourself too seriously.

Tip 653. Know your own motives for offering advice or feedback.

Tip 654. Don't sneak advice into informational statements.

Tip 655. Nudge people to ask for advice, but be willing to wait.

Tip 656. Identify what kind of advice the other person wants.

Tip 657. Remember the purpose of advice/feedback.

Tip 658. Stifle the urge to give premature feedback or advice.

Tip 659. Continue to test the water as you go along.

Tip 660. Ask for clarification on comments you don't understand.

Tip 661. Feel free to offer the opposing view.

Tip 662. Use the appropriate tone.

Tip 663. Play the part of coach.

Tip 664. Make war stories realistic.

Tip 665. Go around the "friend of mine" framing.

Tip 666. Share "I once did/thought/had" stories with those who need feedback but won't ask for it.

Tip 667. Remember that the other person has final say about the advice.

Tip 668. Don't offer a money-back guarantee.

Tip 669. Be firm when you don't want advice or feedback; don't give mixed signals.

Tip 670. Don't telegraph the answer you want.

Tip 671. Ask specifically for the kind of advice or feedback you need.

Tip 672. Ask for comparisons based on criteria you understand.

Tip 673. Avoid so much information that you "freeze" your adviser.

Tip 674. Don't state your opinion or position and then argue if the other person disagrees.

Tip 675. Stifle objections and use accepting phrases.

Tip 676. Lead your adviser to argue both sides.

Tip 677. Don't overlook good advice because of its packaging.

Tip 678. Ask the right person or group.

Tip 679. Consider several sources rather than one "perfect" adviser.

Tip 680. Evaluate the credibility of each source.

Tip 681. Remember that advice comes from philosophy and values.

Tip 682. Tell people you're shopping around.

Tip 683. Thank people for their solicited feedback and advice.

Tip 684. Avoid the term *negotiate* when possible.

Tip 685. Consider several kinds of goals before your begin discussions.

Tip 686. Research your position and the situation.

Tip 687. Refuse to negotiate with a missing person.

Tip 688. Use tact in finding the real decision maker.

Tip 689. Set up a cooperative atmosphere.

Tip 690. Give something at the very beginning.

Tip 691. Ask questions to set the tone for mutual advantage.

Tip 692. Know how to phrase your probing questions.

Tip 693. Postpone any discussions when you're surprised by a "bomb scare."

Tip 694. Send up trial balloons before "getting serious."

Tip 695. State your needs up front and ask the other person to do the same.

Tip 696. Mention *everything* you want sooner, not later.

Tip 697. Focus on the other person's needs first.

Tip 698. Appreciate the value of what you have to bargain.

Tip 699. Dilute your weaknesses by listing them.

Tip 700. Watch others' body language when they toss out "unimportant" comments.

Tip 701. Bring success stories to the table.

Tip 702. Draw a definite distinction between wanting to agree and having to agree.

Tip 703. Be the caller when negotiating by phone.

Tip 704. Negotiate as a team, not individuals working on a team.

Tip 705. Take notes.

Tip 706. Make good eye contact as you negotiate.

Tip 707. Start on the less important issues and work toward the more difficult.

Tip 708. Get others to invest in agreement.

Tip 709. Be willing to jump ship.

Tip 710. Start with goals, then move to solutions.

Tip 711. Adopt a brainstorming technique to generate solutions.

Tip 712. Present fewer, not more, choices when things stall.

Tip 713. Remember that others' perceptions govern what's "fair."

Tip 714. Substitute "we" for "you and I."

Tip 715. Reset expectations.

Tip 716. Take the other person into your confidence about your own restraints.

Tip 717. Don't state your position unilaterally.

Tip 718. Tag the other person's unalterable positions.

Tip 719. "Test the details" before making or asking for full commitment.

Tip 720. Listen for loopholes.

Tip 721. Make your "no" authoritative.

Tip 722. Get the other side to go first.

Tip 723. Find out both ends of the range.

Tip 724. Ask for more than you expect.

Tip 725. Circle the target.

Tip 726. Be prepared to add or substract.

Tip 727. Don't counter an outrageous demand or offer.

Tip 728. Be prepared to add or substract only upon request.

Tip 729. Add or subtract in small increments.

Tip 730. Ask for the other person's reasons behind a particular offer or demand.

Tip 731. Reverse the other person's logic.

Tip 732. Forget the matching exercise.

Tip 733. Leave the other person room to back down and save face.

Tip 734. Avoid an adversarial tone of voice and word choice.

Tip 735. Don't lose your composure.

Tip 736. When someone makes a threat, don't respond at all.

Tip 737. Treat silence as golden—or yellow or amber.

Tip 738. Don't let silence intimidate you.

Tip 739. If you're at wit's end, ask the other person how to overcome his or her own objection.

Tip 740. Reduce resistance to "precedent setting."

Tip 741. Borrow someone's library, one book at a time.

Tip 742. Apply the rule of supply and demand.

Tip 743. Win instant credibility by association.

Tip 744. Do it and then tell them you've done it.

Tip 745. Don't accept the printed word as holy writ.

Tip 746. Set deadlines with care.

Tip 747. Don't let your calendar or clock tick so loudly.

Tip 748. Don't let others' calendars or clocks wear you down.

Tip 749. Don't agree too quickly.

Tip 750. Keep quiet until things are final.

Tip 751. Practice your response to the nibbler.

Tip 752. Be persistent.

Tip 753. Develop trust.

Tip 754. Negotiate by "The Golden Rule."

Tip 755. Pull the plug on "little discussions" before they mushroom.

Tip 756. Deal with conflict promptly.

Tip 757. Determine the nature of the conflict.

Tip 758. Surface masked hostility.

Tip 759. Examine the payoffs in continuing conflict.

Tip 760. Assume a resolution.

Tip 761. Determine the most productive behavior: either swallow or spit out conflict.

Tip 762. If you decide to resolve a conflict, make a conscious choice whether you will accommodate, compromise, overpower, or collaborate.

Tip 763. Don't forgive prematurely.

Tip 764. Set clear expectations.

Tip 765. Establish the relationship rule.

Tip 766. Confront privately on private issues.

Tip 767. Move from "study" to "act."

Tip 768. Focus on the goal rather than the obstacle.

Tip 769. Put the issue of "winning" or "losing" aside.

Tip 770. Create alternatives.

Tip 771. Determine what happened, what you have concluded about what happened, and what you feel about what happened.

Tip 772. Challenge a power play with inattention.

Tip 773. Work with people's "want tos" along with their "do its."

Tip 774. Stand on the sidelines of territorial conflict.

Tip 775. Identify who is playing defense.

Tip 776. Avoid others' vulnerabilities.

Tip 777. Discard the old chant, "sticks and stones . . ."

Tip 778. Prefer statements to questions during conflict.

Tip 779. Use the three Ds to structure your resolution.

Tip 780. Use Thomas Gordon's formula: "When you . . . , I feel . . . , because . . ."

Tip 781. Describe; don't label.

Tip 782. Don't use the phrases "You'll have to . . . ," "You must . . . ," "You should . . . ," or "You ought to . . ."

Tip 783. Offer the other person face-saving comments.

Tip 784. Let the other person exercise options.

Tip 785. Shun sarcasm.

Tip 786. Leave exaggerations for TV sitcoms.

Tip 787. Don't act incredulous.

Tip 788. Don't "dismiss" people.

Tip 789. Don't question someone's integrity.

Tip 790. Avoid reruns.

Tip 791. Keep to one issue.

Tip 792. Forget verbal ultimatums.

Tip 793. Ask for what you want from the people who can give it.

Tip 794. Don't assume the other person understands your point of view.

Tip 795. Listen until you experience the other side of an issue.

Tip 796. State the real reasons or effects, not just logical ones.

Tip 797. Let the other person vent emotions before you try to come to resolution.

Tip 798. Own your own feelings.

Tip 799. Make sure your own emotions are genuine and appropriate.

Tip 800. Define the areas of agreement or disagreement.

Tip 801. Don't interrupt the other person, and don't let the other person interrupt you.

Tip 802. Take turns for airtime.

Tip 803. Discuss a problem sitting down.

Tip 804. Eliminate argumentative words and phrases.

Tip 805. Do something physical to break the spell.

Tip 806. Don't use silence to provoke.

Tip 807. Remember that only the dead keep confidences.

Tip 808. Realize that two sides can be right.

Tip 809. Pick your fights.

Tip 810. Intervene only when asked; proceed with caution.

Tip 811. Avoid "taking sides" and talking the opposition over to the other viewpoint.

Tip 812. Play the role of reporter; go for the five Ws.

Tip 813. Listen to each person's criticism of the other.

Tip 814. Pass along complimentary things each person has said or believed about the other in the past and express your confidence in their willingness to come to a resolution.

Tip 815. Restate common goals—again and again.

Tip 816. Point out where you believe both have miscommunicated in the past.

Tip 817. Ask both people to reverse roles.

Tip 818. Advocate "no-fault" resolution.

Tip 819. Summarize the needs and goals of both.

Tip 820. Ask those involved to suggest resolutions.

Tip 821. Lead them to select the solution that best meets the needs of both.

Tip 822. Help both to keep the lines of communication open.

Tip 823. Avoid people who exhibit a "putdown" demeanor and manner.

Tip 824. Pinpoint others' motivations for a put-down.

Tip 825. Identify put-downs meant as a test of ego-strength.

Tip 826. Buy thinking time when insulted.

Tip 827. Ignore "baiting" comments.

Tip 828. Tell the other person the "insult tactic" doesn't work with you.

Tip 829. Use body language to end the insulting conversation.

Tip 830. Change the subject.

Tip 831. Clarify rather than counterattack when the other person jumps the gun.

Tip 832. Wear the remark.

Tip 833. Create inside humor.

Tip 834. Use self-disparaging humor.

Tip 835. Write down the insult or hostile remark.

Tip 836. Respond only to the surface meaning and words.

Tip 837. Twist the assumptions.

Tip 838. Prepare a comeback.

Tip 839. Prepare gossip stoppers.

Tip 840. Level about how the insult makes you feel.

Tip 841. Blow the other person's cover and ask for serious feedback point-blank.

Tip 842. Minimize the contact.

Tip 843. Create a sense of obligation.

Tip 844. Don't collect injustices.

Tip 845. Distinguish between praise and flattery.

Tip 846. Notice opportunities to praise.

Tip 847. Consider emotional "behavior" as worthy of praise.

Tip 848. Follow the Army's lead in giving medals.

Tip 849. Award your superiors with praise.

Tip 850. Watch one-up praise.

Tip 851. Establish your credibility as a praise giver.

Tip 852. Be aware that the absence of praise can mean criticism.

Tip 853. Praise people when you don't want anything.

Tip 854. Praise individuals rather than groups.

Tip 855. Be specific in your praise.

Tip 856. Comment on the dead rather than the person when the issue is performance.

Tip 857. Credit the person rather than the deed when the issue is character or personality.

Tip 858. Personalize your comments with "you."

Tip 859. Point out the positive effects of the behavior or performance.

Tip 860. Ignore any negative outcomes.

Tip 861. Toss out a few criticisms occasionally.

Tip 862. Avoid praising one person to criticize another.

Tip 863. Follow awkwardly accepted praise with a question.

Tip 864. Consider third-person praise.

Tip 865. Deliver "eavesdropped" praise.

Tip 866. Don't overpraise.

Tip 867. When receiving a compliment, don't match it.

Tip 868. When receiving praise, avoid put-downs of yourself or the other person.

Tip 869. When receiving praise, accept it graciously.

Tip 870. Identify and pay attention to the signs of poor instructions.

Tip 871. Understand the magnitude of a screw-up.

Tip 872. Motivate people to "listen up."

Tip 873. Decide whether to delegate projects by goals or tasks.

Tip 874. Organize well.

Tip 875. Include six snippets of information in every set of instructions.

Tip 876. Give followers a context.

Tip 877. Use both words and pictures for best results.

Tip 878. Give all the pieces to the puzzle.

Tip 879. Avoid an excess of detail.

Tip 880. Prefer clarity to brevity.

Tip 881. Remember your objective is not necessarily to simplify, but to clarify.

Tip 882. Limit "use your own judgment" statements for the exceptions.

Tip 883. Clarify whether something is a must or a preference.

Tip 884. Mention the "don'ts"; they don't necessarily dictate the "dos."

Tip 885. Don't make false claims or promises.

Tip 886. Don't insult your follower.

Tip 887. Use correct grammar; the meaning often depends on it.

Tip 888. Avoid hostile repetition of the same words.

Tip 889. Curb a superior tone.

Tip 890. Be approachable for reruns.

Tip 891. Take into account the frequency of the task.

Tip 892. Choose the appropriate medium through which to give your instructions.

Tip 893. Build instructions into the product or process.

Tip 894. Categorize the follower's personality and attitude and then adapt your style.

Tip 895. Pinpoint your own style and modify what doesn't work for you or the other person.

Tip 896 (for women). State objections directly.

Tip 897 (for men). Verify whether questions are solicitations for information or objections; then respond appropriately.

Tip 898 (for women). Get to the point in meetings.

Tip 899 (for women). Ask for details to verify meaning.

Tip 900 (for women). Discuss details to show concern.

Tip 901 (for women). Don't jump to the conclusion that men don't care about a situation simply because they don't ask for or give details.

Tip 902 (for men). Use women's inclinations to discuss details to verify your understanding of a problem or situation.

Tip 903 (for men). Pay attention to details to show concern.

Tip 904 (for women). Continue to signal men about what's important enough for conversation.

Tip 905 (for women). State outright that you are interested in conversation just for the sake of conversation and connection.

Tip 906 (for men). Expand your repertoire of conversational topics to include "the routine."

Tip 907 (for men). Explain your desire to "connect" despite lack of conversation.

Tip 908 (for women). Share both facts and feelings.

Tip 909 (for women). Don't assume that when men do not share feelings they are trying to create distance.

Tip 910 (for women). Talk more about things with men.

Tip 911 (for men). Share feelings to create camaraderie or intimacy in personal relationships.

Tip 912 (for men). Reveal feelings to build loyalty in customer or colleague relationships.

Tip 913 (for men). Talk more about people with women.

Tip 914 (for women). When mentioning a problem, be specific about whether you're soliciting support or a solution.

Tip 915 (for women). Interpret solution-giving as supportive.

Tip 916 (for women). When a man mentions a problem, offer options, not just empathy.

Tip 917 (for women). When a man mentions a problem, do not editorialize with "shoulds" and "oughts" about past actions and future actions.

Tip 918 (for women). Make sure men know you are not necessarily blaming them when you state a problem.

Tip 919 (for men). When mentioning a problem, be specific about what kind of response you want.

Tip 920 (for men). Interpret empathy-giving as supportive.

Tip 921 (for men). When a woman mentions a problem, offer empathy, not just solutions.

Tip 922 (for men). When a woman mentions a problem, don't editorialize about how to solve all future problems.

Tip 923 (for men). Understand when a woman states a problem involving you, she is not necessarily blaming you.

Tip 924 (for women). Offer information about yourself and make a man's reciprocal response optional.

Tip 925 (for women). If you choose to ask a series of questions, make them broad and general rather than narrow and personal.

Tip 926 (for men). Interpret questions as a show of interest.

Tip 927 (for men). Learn to self-disclose nonthreatening, nonconfidential information or toss the question back to the woman and show interest in her response.

Tip 928 (for women). Respect men's needs to solve their problems independently of others.

Tip 929 (for women). Offer help in a casual, offhanded way.

Tip 930 (for men). Don't equate help or information with status.

Tip 931 (for men). Weigh speed, accuracy, and results against delays and status.

Tip 932 (for women). Test for receptivity and sensitivity before offering sympathy.

Tip 933 (for men). Interpret sympathy as a sign of caring rather than humiliation.

Tip 934 (for women). Learn to swim in a competitive environment.

Tip 935 (for women). Learn to work with people you don't necessarily like.

Tip 936 (for men). Value cooperation.

Tip 937 (for men). Don't equate a woman's commitment or passion for an idea to her willingness to compete to gain acceptance of that idea.

Tip 938 (for women). Make it clear in requesting an opinion that you intend only to evaluate the opinion and come to your own conclusions.

Tip 939 (for women). Determine whether to build consensus or dictate a decision on a case-by-case basis.

Tip 940 (for women). Make sure subordinates know when you're giving an opinion or making a request versus stating a decision or a directive.

Tip 941 (for men). Offer your opinions without expectation or obligation that a woman will act or decide based on them.

Tip 942 (for men). Work to build consensus when you want buy-in from others on a decision and want others to feel valued for their input.

Tip 943 (for men). Make sure subordinates know they have a choice in a situation if you mean your opinion as a preference rather than a directive.

Tip 944 (for women). Use straightforward language if you want to make sure your message gets heard.

Tip 945 (for women). Be objective and to the point so as not to dilute performance feedback to a colleague or subordinate.

Tip 946 (for men). Use tact and show respect for the individual even when you're emotionally upset and even when you have someone else's best interest at heart.

Tip 947 (for men). In social settings, use less directive language when expressing a preference.

Tip 948 (for women). Continue to overlap another woman's speech to show support and identification with what's being said.

Tip 949 (for women). Don't overlap a man's speech unless you intend to interrupt him.

Tip 950 (for men). Don't interrupt a woman's speech as a power play.

Tip 951 (for women). Nag less; show caring in other ways.

Tip 952 (for women). Offer appreciation for behavior you want to encourage rather than disapproval for behavior you dislike.

Tip 953 (for men). Appreciate the reason behind affectionate nagging.

Tip 954 (for women). Stick to the issues at hand when arguing to solve a current problem.

Tip 955 (for women). Forgive more, and forgive more often.

Tip 956 (for women). Don't try to nag or shame a man into showing affection more openly.

Tip 957 (for women). Express appreciation frequently to men for their work and results.

Tip 958 (for men). Consider past issues and events when trying to understand current difficulties in a relationship.

Tip 959 (for men). Apologize more, and apologize more directly.

Tip 960 (for men). Show affection more openly through direct compliments and more emotional intonation.

Tip 961 (for women). Recognize the value in humor even in serious discussions.

Tip 962 (for women). Practice telling more amusing stories and jokes in safe environments until you gain confidence to tell them more often in larger groups.

Tip 963 (for men). Avoid offensive sexual or racial humor.

Tip 964 (for men). Verify that your humor at others' expense does not make them uncomfortable.

Tip 965 (for women). Find ways to display skills and achievements so as to win rewards in the workplace.

Tip 966 (for men). Continue to gain respect for your accomplishments.

Tip 967 (for men). Recognize and reward women's achievements.

Tip 968 (for women). Avoid a flirtatious manner to prevent creating obligations about other interests.

Tip 969 (for women). Don't create an obligatory buyer if you don't want to be perceived as less powerful and damage your chances for negotiating your terms.

Tip 970 (for women). Respect a man's ego when explaining your product or service; show confidence in his intelligence and quick understanding.

Tip 971 (for women). Handle confrontational or blunt statements as requests for further evidence of what you're saying, not as personal affronts.

Tip 972 (for women). Depend on your own proven sense of timing in presenting your product or service; don't interpet matter-of-fact language and a nonexpressive face as boredom or disagreement.

Tip 973 (for women). Avoid a matronly tone as if scolding, demanding, or condescending.

Tip 974 (for men). Forgo a flirtatious manner to prevent creating obligations about other interests.

Tip 975 (for men). Put aside a fatherly tone to avoid inciting a woman's inclination to plead or pout, thus damaging your own negotiating power.

Tip 976 (for men). Don't damage a woman's self-esteem and disregard her intelligence with a condescending tone in explaining products or services.

Tip 977 (for men). Avoid a pleading or oversolicitous tone so as not to damage the buyer's confidence in your product or weaken your negotiating strength.

Tip 978 (for men). Guard against a competitive, challenging tone when a female customer voices objections and reservations.

Tip 979 (for men). Depend on your proven sense of timing in presenting your product or service; don't interpret nods and smiles as premature buying signals.

Tip 980 (for women). Insist on finishing your comments when interrupted.

Tip 981 (for women). Avoid "cowering" when someone disagrees with your opinion.

Tip 982 (for men). Share more airtime if you want to be perceived as less authoritarian or less opinionated.

Tip 983 (for women). Speak up or change the subject when you've listened more than "your fair share."

Tip 984 (for women). Take care that you don't mislead with your smiling and nodding; men often take such responses as agreement with and interest in what they're saying.

Tip 985 (for women). Use more forceful language; avoid tag questions. Answer questions with facts or directly stated opinions.

Tip 986 (for women). Realize that when a man states an opinion he is not necessarily closed to opposing opinions or facts.

Tip 987 (for men). Respect the fact that a woman is not necessarily talking to make a point, but rather to explore feelings or relieve stress.

Tip 988 (for men). Acknowledge a comment directed to you.

Tip 989 (for men). Encourage women to speak up when they disagree or have their own agendas to discuss.

Tip 990 (for men). Identify your opinions as such rather than stating them as irrefutable facts.

Tip 991 (for men). Don't continually change conversational topics offered by women.

Tip 992 (for women). Take up more space.

Tip 993 (for men). Be careful not to intimidate people by size and bigger-than-life gestures and motions.

Tip 994 (for women). Use more nouns and verbs than adjectives and adverbs when you want your comments to sound more factual than subjective.

Tip 995 (for women). Use direct, forceful language when you want to sound authoritative, competent, and confident.

Tip 996 (for men). Use more tentative language (questions, qualifiers, hedgers) when you want to sound less dictatorial and more open and approachable.

Tip 997 (for women). Guard against an attempt to decipher meaning and motivation that degenerates into gossip.

Tip 998 (for women). Prevent "reading into" words more than is intended.

Tip 999 (for men). Don't miss real messages by concentrating only on the words.

Tip 1000 (for men). Welcome discussions to improve relationships.

Tip 1001. Choose the right time and place to discuss business.

Tip 1002. Come to agreement about the meaning of time.

Tip 1003. Determine the appropriate ceremony for exchanging business cards.

Tip 1004. Recognize that respect may be shown in numerous ways.

Tip 1005. Maintain or avoid eye contact depending on your relationship and status.

Tip 1006. Determine if questions about personal life are appropriate.

Tip 1007. Treat silence as both golden and guarded.

Tip 1008. Identify politeness either as a mask or a goodwill gesture.

Tip 1009. Verify that stories you tell illustrate shared values.

Tip 1010. Adapt your humor.

Tip 1011. Remember that all laughter may not be fun and games.

Tip 1012. Use appropriate sports analogies.

Tip 1013. Select the right pronoun for "you."

Tip 1014. Avoid acronyms and initials.

Tip 1015. Use technical terms when appropriate.

Tip 1016. Avoid idioms, clichés, and colloquialisms.

Tip 1017. Whistle, hiss, or applaud appropriately to show approval or disapproval.

Tip 1018. Be a student of expressiveness.

Tip 1019. Touch or refrain from touching, as appropriate.

Tip 1020. Gesture and move with care.

Tip 1021. Translate "yes" and "no" with care.

Tip 1022. Avoid typing your personality with your voice.

Tip 1023. Lower your pitch to sound more authoritative and credible.

Tip 1024. Speak at a slower rate to convey seriousness, authority, and thoughtful deliberation.

Tip 1025. Speak at a faster rate to convey excitement, enthusiasm, and energy.

Tip 1026. Use the appropriate volume.

Tip 1027. Avoid mannerisms and toys when you talk.

Tip 1028. Laugh on purpose.

Tip 1029. Smile with your mind, if not your mouth.

Tip 1030. Establish a baseline before you attach deep meanings to body language.

Tip 1031. Remind yourself that people may give false, nonverbal cues.

Tip 1032. Walk, stand, and sit with good posture.

Tip 1033. Keep appropriate distance.

Tip 1034. Place your office furniture so that people respect your personal space.

Tip 1035. Show interest by moving closer to the other person or standing up.

Tip 1036. Use touch when appropriate.

Tip 1037. Respect status with your eye contact.

Tip 1038. Use eye contact to build rapport with others.

Tip 1039. Adopt a handshake that matches your personality and intention.

Tip 1040. Nod your head to show "you're home."

Tip 1041. Don't point your finger.

Tip 1042. Tell your body what mood you're *supposed* to be in.

Bibliography

Abrams, Kathleen S., *Communication at Work: Listening, Speaking, Writing, and Reading,* Prentice-Hall, Englewood Cliffs, N.J., 1986.

Adler, Ronald B., *Communicating at Work: Principles and Practices for Business and the Professions,* McGraw-Hill, New York, 1992.

———, *Talking Straight,* Holt, Rinehart, and Winston, New York, 1977.

Alberti, Robert E., and Michael L. Emmons, *Your Perfect Right: A Guide to Assertive Living,* Impact Publishers, San Luis Obispo, Calif., 1986.

Alessandra, Tony, Michael J. O'Connor, and Janice Alessandra, *People Smart: Powerful Techniques for Turning Every Encounter Into a Mutual Win,* Keynote Publishing, La Jolla, Calif., 1990.

Allen, Donald E., and Rebecca F. Guy, *Conversation Analysis: The Sociology of Talk,* Mouton & Co., N.V., The Hague, Netherlands, 1974.

Anderson, Allen R., and Cara J. Abeyta, *Face-to-Face Interactions: Experiencing the Dyadic Communication Process,* Kendall/Hunt, Dubuque, Iowa, 1988.

Anderson, Kare, *Getting What You Want: How to Reach Agreement and Resolve Conflict Every Time,* Dutton/Penguin Books, New York, 1993.

Arliss, Laurie P., *Gender Communication,* Prentice-Hall, Englewood Cliffs, N.J., 1991.

Atwater, Eastwood, *"I Hear You": Listening Skills to Make You a Better Manager,* Prentice-Hall, Englewood Cliffs, N.J., 1981.

Auger, B. Y., *How to Run Better Business Meetings,* Minnesota Mining and Manufacturing, St. Paul, Minn., 1979.

Augsburger, David, *Caring Enough to Hear and Be Heard,* Regal Books, Ventura, Calif., 1982.

———, *Caring Enough to Confront,* Regal Books, Ventura, Calif., 1981.

Aviel, David, "The Manager's Response to Cultural Barriers," *Industrial Management,* vol. 32, May/June 1990, pp. 9–14.

Baker, Stephanie, *I Hate Meetings,* Macmillan, New York, 1983.

Bandler, Richard, and John Grinder, *Frogs Into Princes: Neurolinguistic Programming.* Real People Press, Moab, Utah, n.d.

Banville, Thomas G., *How to Listen—How to Be Heard,* Nelson-Hall, Chicago, 1978.

Barrack, Martin K., *How We Communicate: The Most Vital Skill,* Glenbridge Publishing Ltd., Macomb, Ill., 1988.

Barton, Michael., "Manage Words Effectively," *Personnel Journal,* vol. 69, Jan. 1990, pp. 32–37.

Baskin Otis W., and Craig E. Aronoff, *Interpersonal Communication in Organizations,* Goodyear Publishing Co., Santa Monica, Calif., 1980.

Bauby, Cathrina, *Understanding Each Other*, International Society for General Semantics, San Francisco, 1976.

Bender, Peter Urs, *Secrets of Power Presentations*, The Achievement Group, Toronto, 1991.

Berent, Irwin M., and Rod L. Evans, *The Right Words: The 350 Best Things to Say to Get Along with People*, Warner Books, New York, 1992.

Berg, Karen, and Andrew Gilman, *Get to the Point: How to Say What You Mean and Get What You Want*, Bantam Books, Toronto, 1989.

Bernstein, Albert J., and Sydney Craft Rozen, *Dinosaur Brains: Dealing with All Those Impossible People at Work*, John Wiley & Sons, New York, 1989.

———, "Preventing Turf Wars," *Executive Female*, vol. 13, Jan.–Feb. 1990, pp. 22–24.

Bhide, Amar, and Howard H. Stevenson, "Why Be Honest If Honesty Doesn't Pay?," *Harvard Business Review*, vol. 68, Sept.–Oct. 1990, pp. 121–130.

Birdwhistell, Ray L., *Introduction to Kinesics*, University of Louisville Press, Louisville, Ky., 1952.

———, *Kinesics and Context*, University of Pennsylvania Press, Philadelphia, 1970.

Bittner, John R., *Each Other*, Prentice-Hall, Englewood Cliffs, N.J., 1983.

Bixler, Susan, "Does Your Body Language Spell Success? How to Make Your Office Actions Speak Louder than Words," *Mademoiselle*, vol. 6, March 1990, p. 220.

Bohan, George P., "Build, Don't Battle," *Training & Development Journal*, vol. 44, Feb. 1990, pp. 15–19.

Bolton, Robert, *People Skills*, Prentice-Hall, Englewood Cliffs, N.J., 1979.

Booher, Dianna, *Clean Up Your Act!*, Warner Books, New York, N.Y., 1992.

———, *The Complete Letterwriter's Almanac*, Prentice Hall, Englewood Cliffs, N.J., 1991.

———, *Cutting Paperwork in the Corporate Culture*, Facts on File, New York, N.Y., 1986.

———, *Executive's Portfolio of Model Speeches for All Occasions*, Prentice Hall, Englewood Cliffs, N.J., 1991.

———, *Good Grief, Good Grammar*, Facts on File, New York, N.Y., 1988.

———, *The New Secretary: How to Handle People As Well As You Handle Paper*, Facts on File, New York, N.Y., 1985.

———, *Send Me A Memo*, Facts on File, New York, N.Y., 1984.

———, *To the Letter: A Handbook of Model Letters for the Busy Executive*, Macmillan, New York, N.Y., 1988.

———, *Winning Sales Letters*, Macmillan, New York, N.Y., 1990.

———, *Would You Put That in Writing?*, Facts on File, New York, N.Y., 1992.

———, *Writing for Technical Professionals*, John Wiley and Sons, New York, N.Y., 1989.

Bormann, Ernest G., and Nancy C. Borman, *Effective Small Group Communication*, Burgess Publishing, Edina, Minn., 1986.

Bostrom, Robert N., *Communicating in Public: Speaking and Listening*, Burgess Publishing, Edina, Minn., 1988.

Bramson, Robert M., *Coping with Difficult Bosses*, Carol Publishing Group, New York, 1992.

Braude, Jacob M., *Proverbs, Epigrams, Aphorisms, Sayings and Bon Mots, Complete Speaker's and Toastmaster's Library*, Prentice-Hall, Englewood Cliffs, N.J., 1965.

Bright, Deborah, *Criticism in Your Life,* Master Media Limited, New York, 1988.

Brownell, Judi, *Building Active Listening Skills,* Prentice-Hall, Englewood Cliffs, N.J., 1986.

Burley-Allen, Madelyn, *Listening: The Forgotten Skill,* John Wiley & Sons, New York, 1982.

Butler, Pamela E., *Self-Assertion for Women,* Harper & Row, San Francisco, 1981.

Campbell, Susan M., *Beyond the Power Struggle,* Impact Publishers, San Luis Obispo, Calif., 1984.

Carnes, William T., *Effective Meetings for Busy People: Let's Decide It and Go Home,* McGraw-Hill, New York, 1980.

Caroselli, Marlene, *The Language of Leadership,* Human Resource Development Press, Amherst, Mass., 1990.

Carter, Arnold, *Communicate Effectively,* Pelican Publishing, Gretna, La., 1978.

Carter, Jay, *Nasty People,* Unicorn Press, Monmouth Junction, N.J., 1983.

Carter, Kathryn, and Carole Spitzack (eds.), *Doing Research in Women's Communication,* Ablex Publishing, Norwood, N.J., 1989.

"A Certain Smile," *Psychology Today,* vol. 25, Jan.–Feb. 1992, p. 20.

Chapman, Elwood N., *Your Attitude Is Showing,* Macmillan, New York, 1993.

Coffin, Roy A., *The Negotiator,* AMACOM, New York, 1973.

Cohen, Allen R., *Influence Without Authority,* John Wiley & Sons, New York, 1990.

Cohen, Herb, *You Can Negotiate Anything,* Lyle Stuart, Secaucus, N.J., 1980.

Coleman, Paul, "Cease Fire! Ending No Win Arguments and Becoming a Happier Couple," *Redbook,* vol. 177, Aug. 1991, p. 92.

Comeau, John, and Gwen Diehn, *Communication on the Job: A Practical Approach,* Prentice-Hall, Englewood Cliffs, N.J., 1987.

Conklin, Robert, *How to Get People to Do Things,* Contemporary Books, Chicago, 1979.

Connelly, J. Campbell, *A Manager's Guide to Speaking and Listening,* American Managment Association, New York, 1967.

Cory, Lloyd (comp.), *Quotable Quotations,* Victor Books, Wheaton, Ill., 1985.

Cox, Taylor H., Sharon A. Lobel, and Poppy Lauretta McLeod, "Effects of Ethnic Group Cultural Differences on Cooperative and Competitive Behavior on a Group Task," *Academy of Management Journal,* vol. 34, Dec. 1991, pp. 827–847.

Crook, Thomas, and Christine Allison, *How to Remember Names,* HarperCollins, New York, 1992.

———, "The Art of Remembering Names," *Reader's Digest,* vol. 141, July 1992, pp. 71–74.

Crum, Thomas F., *The Magic of Conflict,* Simon & Schuster, New York, 1987.

Cunningham, Chet, *50 Secrets: How to Meet People and Make Friends,* United Research Publishers, Leucadia, Calif., 1992.

Cushman, Donald P., and Dudly D. Cahn Jr., *Communication in Interpersonal Relationships,* SUNY Press, Albany, N.Y., 1985.

Cyr, John E., *Psychology of Motivation and Persuasion in Real Estate Selling,* Prentice-Hall, Englewood Cliffs, N.J., 1975.

Danow, Sheila, and Caroline Bailey, *Developing Skills with People,* John Wiley & Sons, N.Y., 1988.

Davis, Wynn, comp., *The Best of Success,* Great Quotations Publishing Company, Lombard, Ill., 1988.

Dawson, Roger, *The Confident Decision Maker,* William Morrow and Company, New York, 1993.

———, *Secrets of Power Persuasion,* Prentice-Hall, Englewood Cliffs, N.J., 1992.

Decker, Bert, *The Art of Communicating: Achieving Interpersonal Impact in Business,* Crisp Publications, Los Altos, Calif., 1988.

Deep, Sam, and Lyle Sussman, *Smart Moves,* Addison-Wesley Publishing, 1990.

———, *What to Say to Get What You Want,* Addison-Wesley Publishing, 1992.

Derlega, Valerian J., ed., *Communication, Intimacy, and Close Relationships,* Academic Press, Orlando, Fla., 1984.

Diehm, William J., *Criticizing,* Augsburg Publishing House, Minneapolis, Minn., 1986.

Diekman, John R., *Human Connections: How to Make Communication Work,* Prentice-Hall, Englewood Cliffs, N.J., 1982.

Dilenschneider, Robert L., *Power and Influence: Mastering the Art of Persuasion,* Prentice-Hall Press, New York, 1990.

Dilley, Josiah S., *. . . and I thought I knew how to communicate!,* Educational Media Corporation, Minneapolis, Minn., 1985.

Dillon, J. T., *The Practice of Questioning,* Routledge, London, 1990.

Donaldson, Les, *Conversational Magic: The Key to Poise, Popularity and Success,* Parker Publishing Company, West Nyack, N.Y., 1981.

Doyle, Michael, and David Straus, *How to Make Meetings Work,* Wyden Books, New York, 1976.

Drakeford, John W., *The Awesome Power of Positive Attention,* Broadman Press, Nashville, Tenn., 1990.

Dunsing, Richard J., *You and I Have Simply Got to Stop Meeting This Way,* AMA-COM, New York, 1978.

Earley, Christopher P., "Perceived Importance of Praise and Criticism, and Work Performance: An Examination of Feedback in the United States and England," *The Journal of Management,* vol. 12, Winter 1986, pp. 457–473.

Edwards, Richard T., "You Cannot Communicate Unless You Are a Good Listener," *American Salesman,* vol. 35, Oct. 1990, p. 28.

Edwards, Tryon (comp.), *The New Dictionary of Thoughts,* Standard Book Company, New York, 1974.

Eigen, Lewis D., and Jonathan P. Siegel, *The Manager's Book of Quotations,* AMA-COM, New York, 1989.

Eisen, Jeffrey, with Pat Farley, *Powertalk!,* Simon & Schuster, New York, 1984.

Elgin, Suzette Haden, *Genderspeak: Men, Women, and the Gentle Art of Verbal Self-Defense,* John Wiley & Sons, New York, 1993.

———, *More on the Gentle Art of Verbal Self-Defense,* Prentice-Hall, Englewood Cliffs, N.J., 1983.

———, *The Gentle Art of Verbal Self-Defense,* Dorset Press, New York, 1980.

English, Gary, "Curing the Meeting Blues," *Management Review,* vol. 79, June 1990, p. 60.

Erickson, Kenneth A., *The Power of Communication,* Concordia Publishing House, St. Louis, Mo., 1986.

Evatt, Cris, *He & She: 60 Significant Differences Between Men and Women,* Conari Press, Berkeley, Calif., 1992.

Fast, Julius, *Subtext: Making Body Language Work in the Workplace,* Viking, New York, 1991.

————, and Barbara Fast, *Talking Between the Lines,* Viking, New York, 1979.

Finegan, Jay, "48 Hours with the King of Cold Calls," *Inc,* vol. 13, no. 6, June 1991, pp. 100–107.

Fisher, Dalmar, *Communication in Organizations,* West Publishing Company, St. Paul, Minn., 1981.

France, Kim, "Sleeping with the Enemy: How to Fight with the Man You Love," *Mademoiselle,* vol. 97, Oct. 1991, p. 146.

Frank, Milo O., *How to Run a Successful Meeting in Half the Time,* Simon & Schuster, New York, 1989.

Friedman, Paul G., *How to Deal with Difficult People,* SkillPath Publications, Mission, Kan., 1989.

Gabor, Don, *How to Talk to the People You Love,* Simon & Schuster, New York, 1989.

Garner, Alan, *Conversationally Speaking: Tested New Ways to Increase Your Personal and Social Effectiveness,* McGraw-Hill, New York, 1981.

Gates, Anita, "The Smartest Way to Give a Performance Review," *Working Woman,* vol. 16, May 1991, pp. 65–67.

Gerstenzang, Peter, "Look Who's Talking Too Much," *Cosmopolitan,* vol. 212, March 1992, p. 110.

Girard, Joe, *How to Sell Yourself,* Warner Books, New York, 1981.

Glaser, Susan R., and Anna Eblen, *Toward Communication Competency: Developing Interpersonal Skills,* Holt, Rinehart and Winston, New York, 1986.

Glass, Lillian, *He Says, She Says,* G.P. Putnam's Sons, New York, 1992.

————, *Say It Right: How to Talk in Any Social or Business Situation,* G.P. Putnam's Sons, New York, 1991.

Glatthorn, Allan A., and Herbert R. Adams, *Listening Your Way to Management Success,* Scott, Foresman and Company, Glenview, Ill., 1983.

"Go Along and Get Along," *The Economist,* vol. 317, Nov. 24, 1990, p. 76.

Golde, Roger A., *What You Say Is What You Get,* Hawthorn Books, New York, 1979.

Goodman, Gerald, and Glenn Esterly, *The Talk Book: The Intimate Science of Communicating in Close Relationships,* Rodale Press, Emmaus, Pa., 1988.

Goodson, Jane R., Gail W. McGee, and Anson Seers, "Giving Appropriate Performance Feedback to Managers: An Empirical Test of Content and Outcomes," *The Journal of Business Communication,* vol. 29, Fall 1992, pp. 329–341.

Gordon, Myron, *Making Meetings More Productive,* Sterling Publishing Company, New York, 1981.

Gorman, Ronald H., "Sell the Solution," *Personnel Journal,* vol. 69, Sept. 1990, p. 37.

Gray, John, *Men Are from Mars, Women Are from Venus,* HarperCollins, New York, 1992.

————, *Men, Women and Relationships: Making Peace with the Opposite Sex,* Beyond Words Publishing, Hillsboro, Ore., 1990.

Greenburger, Francis, with Thomas Kiernan, *How to Ask for More and Get It: The Art of Creative Negotiation,* Doubleday & Company, New York, 1978.

Guirdham, Maureen, *Interpersonal Skills at Work,* Prentice-Hall, Englewood Cliffs, N.J., 1990.

Hajdu, David, "Why Not Talk Like a Grown-Up?" *Cosmopolitan,* vol. 208, Feb. 1990, p. 128.

Hamilton, Beatrice, "Hearing, Analyzing, Empathizing, and Succeeding in Management," *Training & Development Journal,* vol. 44, Aug. 1990, p. 16.

Hamlin, Sonya, *How to Talk So People Listen,* Harper & Row, New York, 1988.

"Hands On (illustration)," *Inc,* vol. 12, Oct. 1990, p. 150.

Haney, William V., *Communication and Interpersonal Relations: Text and Cases,* Irwin, Homewood, Ill., 1992.

Hanks, Kurt, *Getting Your Message Across,* Crisp Publications, Los Altos, Calif., 1991.

————, *Motivating People,* Argus Communications, Allen, Tex., 1982.

Hanna, Sharon L., *Person to Person: Positive Relationships Don't Just Happen,* Prentice-Hall, Englewood Cliffs, N.J., 1991.

Harbaugh, Frederick W., "Accentuate the Positive," *Technical Communication,* vol. 38, Feb. 1991, p. 73.

Hegarty, Edward J., *Making What You Say Pay Off,* Parker Publishing Co., Inc., West Nyack, N.Y., 1968.

Henley, Nancy, and Barrie Thorne (comp.), *She Said/He Said: An Annotated Bibliography of Sex Differences in Language, Speech, and Nonverbal Communication,* Know, Inc., Pittsburgh, Pa., 1975.

Hensley, Carl Wayne, "What You Share Is What You Get: Tips for Effective Communication (speech)," *Vital Speeches,* vol. 59, Dec. 1, 1992, pp. 115–118.

Holden, Lorraine, "Teamwork: A Delicate Balance," *Managers Magazine,* vol. 65, Aug. 1990, pp. 29–33.

Howell, William Smiley, *The Empathetic Communicator,* Wadsworth Publishing Company, Belmont, Calif., 1982.

Hutchins, Robert M., ed., *Great Books of the Western World,* vol. 9: *The Works of Aristotle,* vol. II, William Benton, Chicago, 1952.

Hybels, Saundra, and Richard L. Weaver II, *Communicating Effectively,* McGraw-Hill, New York, 1992.

Impoco, James, and Betsy Streisand, "The Great Divide: U.S.-Japanese Business Deals Are Often Unable to Bridge a Vast Cultural Gap," *U.S. News and World Report,* vol. 113, July 6, 1992, p. 52.

James, Jennifer, *You Know I Wouldn't Say This If I Didn't Love You,* Newmarket Press, New York, 1990.

Jamieson, G. H., *Communication and Persuasion,* Croom Helm, London, 1985.

Jandt, Fred E., *Conflict Resolution through Communication,* Harper & Row, New York, 1973.

Johnson, David W., *Human Relations in Your Career,* Prentice-Hall, Englewood Cliffs, N.J., 1991.

Jones, Norman, *Keep in Touch: How to Communicate Better by Responding to the Feeling Instead of the Event,* Prentice-Hall, Englewood Cliffs, N.J., 1981.

Jones, G. Brian, *Men Have Feelings, Too!: A Book for Men (And the Women Who Love Them),* Victor Books, Wheaton, Ill., 1988.

Kane, Kimberly F., "MBAs: A Recruiter's-eye View," *Business Horizons,* vol. 36, Jan.–Feb. 1993, pp. 65–71.

Kaplan, Burton, *Strategic Communication,* HarperCollins, New York, 1991.

Kaplan, Michael, "The Secrets of Super Sales People," *Working Woman,* vol. 15, May 1992, pp. 92–96.

Karrass, Chester L., "There's Plenty of Give and Take in Making Concessions," *Purchasing,* vol. 109, Oct. 11, 1990, p. 55.

Katz, Sally N., "Power Skills for Executive Meetings," *Training & Development Journal*, vol. 45, July 1991, p. 53.

Kaufman, Joanne, "Hot Copy," *Ladies Home Journal*, vol. 108, July 1991, pp. 43–44.

Key, Mary Ritchie, *Male/Female Language*, The Scarecrow Press, Metuchen, N.J., 1975.

Kiefer, George David, *The Strategy of Meetings*, Simon & Schuster, New York, 1988.

Kirby, Tom, *Communicate with Confidence* (audiotape), Listen USA, Greenwich, Conn., 1984.

Kirkpatrick, Ronald L., *How to Plan and Conduct Productive Business Meetings*, AMACOM, New York, 1987.

Kizilos, Peter, "Fixing Fatal Flaws," *Training*, vol. 28, Sept. 1991, pp. 66, 68–70.

Kotker, Zane, "The 'Feminine' Behavior of Powerless People," *Savvy*, March 1980, pp. 36–42.

Krafft, Susan, "Killing the Messenger," *American Demographics*, vol. 13, July 1991, pp. 40–41.

———, "How to Break Bad News," *American Demographics*, vol. 13, July 1991, p. 43.

Kramer, Cheris, Barrie Thorne, and Nancy Henley, "Perspectives on Language and Communication," *Signs 3*, no. 31, Spring 1978.

Lakoff, Robin Tolmach, *Language and Woman's Place*, Harper Colophon Books, New York, 1975.

———, *Talking Power*, Basic Books, New York, 1990.

Langs, Robert, *Unconscious Communication in Everyday Life*, Jason Aronson, Inc., New York, 1983.

Lee, Irving J, *How to Talk with People*, Harper & Row, New York, 1952.

Leeds, Dorothy, *Smart Questions: A New Strategy for Successful Managers*, McGraw-Hill, New York, 1987.

Leritz, Len, *No-Fault Negotiating*, Warner Books, New York, 1987.

LeRoux, Paul, *Selling to a Group: Presentation Strategies*, Barnes & Noble Books, New York, 1984.

Lesly, Philip, *How We Discommunicate*, AMACOM, New York, 1979.

Letich, Larry, "Ins and Outs: Ignoring the Psychological Side of a Small Meeting Can Be Hazardous to Its Success," *Meetings & Conventions*, vol. 25, Aug. 1990, pp. 4–8.

Lindskold, Svenn, *You and Me: The Why and How of Interpersonal Behavior*, Nelson-Hall, Chicago, 1982.

Linkemer, Bobbi, *How to Run a Meeting*, American Management Association, New York, 1987.

Littauer, Florence, *How to Get Along with Difficult People*, Harvest House Publishers, Eugene, Ore., 1984.

Long, Lynette, Louis V. Paradise, and Thomas J. Long, *Questioning: Skills for the Helping Process*, Brooks/Cole Publishing Company, Monterrey, Calif., 1981.

Lukaszewski, James E., "Bridging the Communication Gap," *Sales & Marketing Management*, vol. 143, Aug. 1991, pp. 62–66.

Lusardi, Lee A., "When a Woman Speaks, Does Anybody Listen?" *Working Woman*, vol. 15, July 1990, pp. 92–95.

Madonik, Barbara Haber: "I Hear What You Say, But What Are You Telling Me?" *The Canadian Manager*, vol. 15, Spring 1990, pp. 18–21.

Margerison, Charles J., *If Only I Had Said*, Mercury Books, London, 1987.

Martel, Myles, *Mastering the Art of Q and A: A Survival Guide for Tough, Trick and Hostile Questions,* Dow Jones-Irwin, Homewood, Ill., 1989.

Martinet, Jeanne, "Who Says You Can't Be a Good Mixer?" *Cosmopolitan,* vol. 213, Nov. 1992.

———, *The Art of Mingling,* St. Martin's Press, New York, 1992.

Maude, Barry, *Communication at Work,* Business Books Limited, London, 1977.

Maxwell, John C., *Be a People Person,* SP Publications, Inc., Wheaton, Ill., 1989.

Mayo, Clara, and Nancy M. Henley (eds.), *Gender and Nonverbal Behavior,* Springer-Verlag, New York, 1981.

McCabe, Bernard P., Jr., and Coleman C. Bender, *Speaking Is a Practical Matter,* Holbrook Press, Boston, Mass., 1976.

McCallister, Linda, *I Wish I'd Said That!,* John Wiley & Sons, New York, 1992.

McCroskey, James C., Virginia P. Richmond, Robert A. Stewart, *One on One: The Foundation of Interpersonal Communication,* Prentice-Hall, Englewood Cliffs, N.J., 1986.

McGill, Michael E., *The McGill Report on Male Intimacy,* Holt, Rinehart and Winston, New York, 1985.

McKenzie, E.C., *14,000 Quips & Quotes,* Greenwich House, New York, 1984.

McLaughlin, Margaret L., *Conversation: How Talk Is Organized,* Sage Publications, Beverly Hills, Calif., 1984.

McLellan, Diana, "Who's Smiling Now?" *The Washingtonian,* vol. 25, Feb. 1990, pp. 108–111.

Mead, Richard, *Cross-Cultural Management Communication,* John Wiley & Sons, New York, 1990.

Mehrabian, Albert, *Silent Messages,* Wadsworth Publishing Group, Belmont, Calif., 1971.

———, "Communication Without Words," *Psychology Today 2,* Sept. 1968, pp. 53–55.

Meyer, Paul J., *The Art of Creative Listening,* Paul J. Meyer, Waco, Tex., 1980.

Molcho, Samy, *Body Speech,* St. Martin's Press, New York, 1985.

Moran, Robert, "Watch Your Body Language," *International Management,* vol. 45, May 1990.

Murnighan, J. Keith, *Bargaining Games,* William Morrow and Company, New York, 1992.

Myers, Pennie, and Don Nance, *The Upset Book,* Academic Publications, South Bend, Ind., 1986.

Nelson, Carol, "If It Isn't Direct, It Doesn't Follow," *Direct Marketing,* vol. 52, March 1990, p. 66.

Nelson, Sara, "Why Men Can't Take Criticism," *Glamour,* vol. 90, Aug. 1992, p. 152.

Nelton, Sharon, "The Womanly Art of the Deal," *Nation's Business,* vol. 81, Jan. 1993, p. 60.

Nierenberg, Gerard I., *Creative Business Negotiating,* Hawthorn Books, New York, 1971.

———, *How to Give & Receive Advice,* Simon & Schuster, New York, 1975.

———, *The Art of Negotiating,* Cornerstone Library, New York, 1977.

———, *The Complete Negotiator,* Nierenbery & Zeif Publishers, New York, 1986.

———, and Henry H. Calero, *How to Read a Person Like a Book,* Simon & Schuster, New York, 1971.

————, *Meta-Talk,* Pocket Books, New York, 1975.

Nierenberg, Juliet, and Irene S. Ross, *Women and the Art of Negotiating,* Simon & Schuster, New York, 1985.

Nirenberg, Jesse S., *Breaking Through to Each Other: Creative Persuasion on the Job and in the Home,* Harper & Row, New York, 1976.

————, *Getting Through to People,* Prentice-Hall, Englewood Cliffs, N.J., 1963.

————, *How to Sell Your Ideas,* McGraw-Hill, New York, 1984.

Osborn, Denise, "Managing Meeting Disrupters," *Manage,* vol. 42, May 1991, pp. 8–12.

Parkinson, J. Robert, *How to Get People To Do Things Your Way,* NTC Business Books, Lincolnwood, Ill., 1986.

Parlee, Mary Brown, "Conversational Politics," *Psychology Today,* vol. 12, May 1979, pp. 48–56.

Payne, Stanley L., *The Art of Asking Questions,* Princeton University Press, Princeton, N.J., 1951.

Penn, C. Ray, "A Choice of Words Is a Choice of Worlds (speech transcript)," *Vital Speeches,* vol. 57, Dec. 1, 1990, pp. 116–117.

Pettit, John D., "Interpersonal Skills Training: A Prerequisite for Success," *Business,* vol. 40, April–June 1990.

Phillips, Bob, *The Delicate Art of Dancing with Porcupines,* Regal Books, Ventura, Calif., 1989.

Phillips, Gerald M., *Help for Shy People,* Prentice-Hall, Englewood Cliffs, N.J., 1981.

Pietsch, William V., *Human Be-Ing: How to Have a Creative Relationship Instead of a Power Struggle,* Signet, New York, 1975.

Postman, Neil, *Crazy Talk, Stupid Talk,* Delacorte Press, New York, 1976.

Potash, Marlin S., *Hidden Agendas,* Delacorte Press, New York, 1990.

Pritchett, Price, and Ron Pound, *Team ReConstruction,* Pritchett Publishing Co., Dallas, Tex., 1992.

Prochnow, Herbert V., *Speaker's & Toastmaster's Handbook,* Prima Publishing & Communications, Rocklin, Calif., 1990.

Reck, Ross R., and Brian G. Long, *The Win-Win Negotiator: How to Negotiate Favorable Agreements That Last,* Pocket Books, New York, 1987.

Reeves, Elton T., *How to Get Along with Almost Everybody,* AMACOM, New York, 1973.

Richmond, Virginia P., James C. McCroskey, Steven K. Payne, *Nonverbal Behavior in Interpersonal Relations,* Prentice-Hall, Englewood Cliffs, N.J., 1987.

Ricks, David A., *Big Business Blunders: Mistakes in Multinational Marketing,* Dow Jones-Irwin, Homewood, Ill., 1983.

Roane, Susan, *How to Work a Room,* Warner Books, New York, 1989.

Rogers, Carl R., and Barry Stevens, *Person to Person: The Problem of Being Human,* Real People Press, Lafayette, Calif., 1967.

Rosenbaum, Bernard L., "Making Presentations: How to Persuade Others to Accept Your Ideas," *American Salesman,* vol. 37, Feb. 1992, pp. 16–19.

Russell, Anne M., and Lorraine Calvacca, "Should You Be Funny at Work?" *Working Woman,* vol. 16, March 1991, pp. 74–78.

Sandberg, Jared, "People Are Hugging a Lot More Now and Seem to Like It," *The Wall Street Journal,* March 15, 1993, p. A1, col. 4.

Sands, Ken, *The Peacemaker,* Baker Book House, Grand Rapids, Mich., 1991.

Sandstrom, Teena, *Working Better Together: A Human Relations Guidebook for Office Professionals,* Professional Training Associates, Round Rock, Tex., 1990.

Sanford, John A., *Between People: Communicating One-to-One,* Paulist Press, New York, 1982.

Sanzotta, Donald, *The Manager's Guide to Interpersonal Relations,* AMACOM, New York, 1979.

Satran, Pamela Redmond, "When Not to Talk About It," *Redbook,* vol. 178, March 1992.

Schabacker, Kirsten, "A Short, Snappy Guide to Meaningful Meetings," *Working Woman,* vol. 16, June 1991, pp. 70–74.

Schulte, Lucy, "How to Negotiate Your Way Into Almost Anything," *Mademoiselle,* vol. 98, May 1992, p. 198.

Scott, Bill, *The Skills of Negotiating,* John Wiley & Sons, New York, 1981.

Sedgwick, John, "Talking," *Boston Magazine,* vol. 84, Sept. 1992, p. 45.

Seltz, David D., and Alfred J. Modica, *Negotiate Your Way to Success,* Farnsworth Publishing Co., Rockville Centre, N.Y., 1980.

Sharif, Karim, "Customs Problems," *Los Angeles Business Journal,* vol. 14, Aug. 3, 1992, pp. S30–31.

Shields, Donald J., Lela K. Bullerdick, and Donald G. Shields, *Effective Communication for Professionals,* Kendall/Hunt Publishing Company, Dubuque, Iowa, 1989.

Simon, Sidney B., *Negative Criticism,* Argus Communications, Allen, Tex., 1978.

Simon, George F., and Deborah Weissman, *Men and Women: Partners at Work,* Crisp Publications, Palo Alto, Calif., 1990.

Smith, Gerald Walker, *Hidden Meanings: A Psychological Dictionary,* Peter H. Wyden Publisher, New York, 1975.

Smith, Wen, "Why 'Bye-Bye' Is a No-No," *Saturday Evening Post,* vol. 264, Sept.–Oct. 1992, p. 36.

Snell, Frank, *How to Hold a Better Meeting,* Harper and Brothers, New York, 1958.
———, *How to Win the Meeting,* Hawthorn Books, New York, 1979.

Sondak, Arthur, "What's Your Conflict Barometer," *Supervisory Management,* vol. 35, May 1990.

Sparks, Donald B., *The Dynamics of Effective Negotiation,* Gulf Publishing Company, Houston, 1982.

Stark, Amy, *Because I Said So,* Pharos Books, New York, 1992.

Stenzler-Centonze, Marjorie, "EE's Next Challenge: People Not Products," *EDN,* vol. 35, Aug. 23, 1990, p. 39.

Stewart, John (ed.), *Bridges Not Walls,* McGraw-Hill, New York, 1990.

Stewart, Nathaniel, *Winning Friends at Work,* Ballantine Books, New York, 1985.

Stewart, Susan, "The Truth About Lying," *Current Health 2,* Oct. 1992.

Stiebel, David, "What to Do When Talking Makes Things Worse," *Journal of Public Management,* vol. 72, Aug. 1990, pp. 20–21.

Strayhorn, Joseph M., Jr., *Talking It Out,* Research Press Company, 1977.

Stubbs, Lucy: "Speak for Yourself," *New Statesman and Society,* vol. 3, May 25, 1990, p. 24.

Swets, Paul W., *The Art of Talking So That People Will Listen,* Prentice-Hall, 1983.

Tannen, Deborah, "How Men and Women Use Language Differently in Their Lives and in the Classroom," *Education Digest,* vol. 57, Feb. 1992, pp. 3–6.

——, *That's Not What I Meant,* Ballantine Books, New York, 1986.

——, *You Just Don't Understand: Women and Men in Conversation,* William Morrow and Company, New York, 1990.

Thomsett, Michael C., *The Little Black Book of Business Speaking,* American Management Association, New York, 1989.

Thorne, Barrie, Cheris Kramarae, and Nancy Henley (eds.), *Language, Gender, and Society,* Newbury House, Rowley, Mass., 1983.

"Tips That Can Enhance Your Business Lunch," *Profit Building-Strategies for Business Owners,* vol. 20, Sept. 1990, p. 16.

Tropman, John, and Gersh Morningstar, *Meetings: How to Make Them Work for You,* Van Nostrand Reinhold, New York, 1985.

Truitt, John, *Phone Tactics for Instant Influence,* Dembner Books, New York, 1990.

Tucker, Raymond K., *Fighting It Out with Difficult—If Not Impossible—People,* Kendall/Hunt Publishing Company, Dubuque, Iowa, 1987.

Uris, Dorothy, *Everybody's Book of Better Speaking,* David McKay Company, New York, 1960.

Van Fleet, James K., *Lifetime Conversation Guide,* Prentice-Hall, Englewood Cliffs, N.J., 1984.

——, *Power with People,* Parker Publishing Company, West Nyack, N.Y., 1970.

——, *Twenty-five Steps to Power and Mastery Over People,* Parker Publishing Company, West Nyack, N.Y., 1983.

Vargas, Marjorie Fink, *Louder Than Words: An Introduction to Nonverbal Communication,* Iowa State University, Ames, Iowa, 1986.

Verderber, Rudolph F., *The Challenge of Effective Speaking,* Wadsworth Publishing Company, Belmont, Calif., 1988.

——, and Kathleen S. Verderber, *Inter-Act: Using Interpersonal Communication Skills,* Wadsworth Publishing Company, Belmont, Calif., 1980.

Voges, Ken, and Ron Braud, *Understanding How Others Misunderstand You,* Moody Press, Chicago, Ill., 1990.

Walters, Barbara, *How to Talk with Practically Anybody About Practically Anything,* Dell, New York, 1970.

Walther, George, *Phone Power: How to Make the Telephone Your Most Profitable Business Tool,* G.P. Putnam's Sons, New York, 1986.

Walton, Donald, *Are You Communicating? You Can't Manage Without It,* McGraw-Hill, New York, 1989.

Warschaw, Tessa Albert, *Winning by Negotiation,* McGraw-Hill, New York, 1980.

Wassmer, Arthur C., *Making Contact,* The Dial Press, New York, 1978.

Weaver, Richard L., II, *Understanding Interpersonal Communication,* Scott, Foresman and Company, Glenview, Ill., 1987.

Weeks, Dudley, *Conflict Partnership,* Trans World Productions, Orange, Calif., 1984.

Weiner-Davis, Michele, "The Strategy That's Guaranteed to Improve Your Marriage," *McCall's,* vol. 119, January 1992.

Weisinger, Hendrie, *The Critical Edge: How to Criticize Up and Down,* Little, Brown and Company, Boston, 1989.

——, and Norman M. Lobsenz, *Nobody's Perfect: How to Give Criticism and Get Results,* Stratford Press, Los Angeles, 1981.

Weiss, Donald H., *How to Deal with Difficult People,* AMACOM, New York, 1987.

Wells, Theodora, *Keeping Your Cool Under Fire,* McGraw-Hill, New York, 1980.

Wetzler, Scott, "Sugercoated Hostility," *Newsweek,* vol. 120, Oct. 12, 1992, p. 14.

Wiesendanger, Betsy, "A Conversation on Conversation with Deborah Tannen," *Sales & Marketing Management,* vol. 143, April 1991, pp. 38–43.

Wiksell, Wesley, *Do They Understand You?* Macmillan, New York, 1960.

Williams, Jonathan, *Quote, Unquote,* Ten Speed Press, Berkeley, Calif., 1983.

Wilson, Gerald L., Alan M. Hantz, and Michael S. Hanna, *Interpersonal Growth Through Communication,* Wm. C. Brown Publishers, Dubuque, Iowa, 1989.

Winawer, H.H., *Expression is 9/10 of the Flaw,* Double HH Publications, Holladay, Utah, 1983.

Wisniewiski, Jeanine G., "Wicked Words: Getting to the Roots of Words," *English Journal,* vol. 79, April 1990, pp. 78–79.

Wolk, Rober L., and Arthur Henley, *Yes Power,* Peter H. Wyden, New York, 1969.

Woodall, Marian K., *How to Talk So Men Will Listen,* Contemporary Books, Chicago, 1993.

Woolf, Bob, *Friendly Persuasion: My Life As a Negotiator,* G.P. Putnam's Sons, New York, 1990.

———, "Ways to Win," *Reader's Digest,* vol. 138, May 1991, pp. 23–28.

Wortman, Art (ed.), *Will Rogers: Wise and Witty Sayings of a Great American Humorist,* The Castle Press, n.p., 1969.

Wright, Milton, *The Art of Conversation and How to Apply Its Technique,* McGraw-Hill, New York, 1936.

Wurman, Richard Saul, and Loring Leifer, *Follow the Yellow Brick Road,* Bantam Books, New York, 1992.

Yamada, Haru, *American and Japanese Business Discourse: A Comparison of Interactional Styles,* Ablex Publishing, Norwood, N.J., 1992.

Yanow, Morton, "Mutual Agreement: Tactics for Negotiating," *Whole Earth Review,* Spring 1992.

Zander, Alvin, *Making Groups Effective,* Jossey-Bass Publishers, San Francisco, 1982.